YORUBA
HOMETOWNS

YORUBA HOMETOWNS

Community, Identity, and Development in Nigeria

LILLIAN TRAGER

LYNNE
RIENNER
PUBLISHERS

BOULDER
LONDON

Published in the United States of America in 2001 by
Lynne Rienner Publishers, Inc.
1800 30th Street, Boulder, Colorado 80301
www.rienner.com

and in the United Kingdom by
Lynne Rienner Publishers, Inc.
3 Henrietta Street, Covent Garden, London WC2E 8LU

Library of Congress Cataloging-in-Publication Data
Trager, Lillian, 1947–
    Yoruba hometowns : community, identity, and development in Nigeria / Lillian Trager.
      p. cm.
    Includes bibliographical references and index.
    ISBN 1-55587-949-7 (alk. paper)
    ISBN 1-55587-981-0 (pbk. : alk. paper)
    1. Yoruba (African people)—Kinship. 2. Yoruba (African people)—Ethnic identity.
  3. Philosophy, Yoruba—Nigeria—Ijesa Region. 4. Community life—Nigeria—
Ijesa Region. 5. Community development—Nigeria—Ijesa Region.
6. Rural development—Nigeria—Ijesa Region. 7. Ijesa Region
(Nigeria)—Social life and customs. I. Title.
DT515.45.Y67 T73 2001
305.896'3330669—dc21

                                                  00-066503

British Cataloguing in Publication Data
A Cataloguing in Publication record for this book
is available from the British Library.

Printed and bound in the United States of America

    5 4 3 2 1

Contents

List of Illustrations   vii
Acknowledgments   ix

1   Introduction   1

2   Community-Day Celebrations: A New Tradition at Home   15

3   Knowing Your Place: The Hometown and Identity   37

4   "We Are Just Sojourners Here": Ijesa Migration   59

5   "We Love Ourselves Abroad":
    Hometown Organizations and Their Members   89

6   Ceremonies and Celebrations:
    The Symbolism of Hometown Links   119

7   Local Development and the Economic Crisis   145

8   Self-Help and the Practice of Local Development in Ijesaland   165

9   The Elusive Goal of Unity: Politics, Conflict, and Morality   205

10 Conclusion: Communities and Development   235

References   279
Index   291
About the Book   299

Illustrations

Maps

3.1   Nigeria   39
3.2   The Ijesa Region   40
3.3   Ilesa   45

Tables

4.1   Locales to Which Migrants Moved   66

Photographs

Dignitaries at Iloko Day   24
The new Methodist church in Iloko   50
Ijesa *obas* and other guests at the coronation of
    Oba Oladele Olashore   136
Oba Oladele Olashore in his palace on the day
    of his coronation, April 1997   142
Farm and fishpond of a prominent Ijesa   170
Ijebu-Jesa Community Bank customer   176

Acknowledgments

Numerous people and institutions helped make possible the research on which this book is based. First, and most important, I want to thank the people of the Ijesa communities, whose insights and hospitality have led to a rich and enjoyable research experience that has continued over many years. Beginning with the Ijesa market women who welcomed me and introduced me to the complexities of their lives in the early 1970s, and continuing through many subsequent visits to Ilesa and surrounding towns and villages, I have been privileged to learn not only about Yoruba culture but also about communities in general. Several people have been especially important in this process: Dr. and Mrs. E. A. Ifaturoti, Justice and Mrs. Kayode Eso, Oba Oladele Olashore, and Professor Bolanle Awe. Others, including Chief A. O. Lamikanra, Dr. Tina Fatiregun, and Mr. and Mrs. Akin Akinola, have assisted me at crucial times in my research. Many others, some of whom are named in the text, helped me to understand aspects of their lives and activities; I am grateful to all.

Colleagues and friends in Ife, Oshogbo, Ibadan, and Lagos all encouraged and assisted me over the years. To Agbo Folarin, Richard Olaniyan, Nike Davies Okundaye, Judith Asuni, Nina Mba, and Nike Afolabi, I say *e se pupo* (thank you) for all you have done. I am grateful to Bodunde Motoni for his research assistance throughout most of the research period, and to others associated with the Nike Centre for Art and Culture for their help at key points.

The Department of Sociology and Anthropology at Obafemi Awolowo University provided me with formal affiliation as a visiting professor at the beginning of the research; that affiliation has continued informally in subsequent years. Colleagues in the department have been gracious hosts, and I thank them.

The research was supported by the National Science Foundation (grant BNS-9120584), which not only provided funds for fieldwork but also later provided funds for several undergraduate students at the University of Wisconsin–Parkside to work with me in data analysis, through Research Experience for Undergraduates grants. The University of Wisconsin–Parkside Committee on Research and Creative Activity also provided funding at several crucial times. During part of the research period I was codirector of a U.S. Information Agency University Affiliations grant for a faculty exchange between the University of Wisconsin–Parkside and Obafemi Awolowo University. That grant supported some of my travel to Nigeria.

I would like to thank the University of Wisconsin–Parkside undergraduates who worked with me at various stages, several of whom contributed important insights. They include Kim Boyajian, Jackie Handford, Mary Ritchie, Heather Spencer, and Joel Tishken. Staff of the university's Media Services Department have also been very helpful; Kate Pietri's and Don Lintner's assistance with maps, photographs, and preparation of the companion videotape is greatly appreciated. I would also like to thank my colleagues in the Department of Sociology and Anthropology at the University of Wisconsin–Parkside, who have understood the importance of my regular trips to Nigeria and who have supported me throughout.

Many colleagues both in Nigeria and the United States have commented on aspects of the research and have assisted me in a variety of ways. In particular, I want to thank Niyi Akinnaso, Paulina Makinwa-Adebusoye, Jacob Olupona, Tola Pearce, Josef Gugler, Deborah Winslow, Brooke Grundfest Schoepf, and Michael McNulty. The enthusiastic interest of Bridget Julian, editor at Lynne Rienner Publishers, helped bring the project to completion.

This book is dedicated to my parents, William and Ida Trager, who first introduced me to Nigeria, and to my husband, Dick Ammann, who has helped make possible my many recent journeys there.

1

Introduction

It was 8:30 in the morning on Saturday, May 22, 1993. I stood in the parking lot of the Diganga Hotel in Ife, Nigeria, waiting for my assistants who would drive with me to Iloko, a town about twenty miles to the east, where we planned to attend the Iloko Day festivities. I had arrived from the United States two days before, having changed the date of my trip to be here in time to attend the second annual Iloko Day. An hour later I was still waiting, then about ten cars with sirens sounding passed on the main road outside the hotel, and I guessed that this was the entourage of the state governor en route to Iloko. I had heard an announcement on Osun State television the night before that the governor, recently elected in the first gubernatorial election in many years, planned to attend Iloko Day. Although I had a car to use it had no gas, and there was a fuel shortage, so none of the gas stations in Ife had any gas available. I had visions of traveling 6,000 miles to end up twenty miles from my destination and being unable to get there on time. A few minutes later my assistants arrived (delayed by having to charge the battery on the video camera we were to use), and we set out for Iloko, arriving after the governor and a few other dignitaries but long before the day's events officially began at 11 A.M.

❧   ❧   ❧

The events of that morning symbolize the vagaries of my ethnographic research in the Ijesa area of Yorubaland—a combination of drama and routine, uncertainty and serendipity. In many ways, the events of that morning reflected on the broader situation in Nigeria during the research period, which ranged from the relative optimism of 1991–1992, when a transition to civilian rule was in progress, to the disappointment and depression many felt after the cancellation of the June 1993 presidential elections; this situation continued into 1998. At the same time that events in the larger polity have been traumatic, many Nigerians have sought in many ways to contin-

1

ue working to improve their own lives, and those of others in their communities. Even though they may be depressed and uncertain about the direction of political and economic events in their country, individuals and groups seek to effect change in the locales with which they have the closest ties and where they have the strongest identity—the communities to which they belong.

This book considers the ramifications and implications of such efforts in one region, the Ijesa Yoruba area of southwestern Nigeria. Focusing on five Ijesa communities, it shows how those who consider those locales to be their "hometown" engage in a range of activities, from fund-raising, to problem-solving, to ritual and celebration. It considers the results of such engagement, both positive and negative, for the communities and the region.

Central to this process are people who live in the large cities such as Lagos and Ibadan but who maintain ties with their "home" communities, usually the town to which they have kinship links through their father. Many are urban professionals, members of the national urban elite who have received their training in other parts of Nigeria and abroad and who live and work outside their home community; others are individuals who have retired to their hometown after working elsewhere.

When I describe this involvement to American students and colleagues, the most frequently asked question is Why? Why do people who no longer live in a place, who may never have lived there, continue to be involved, to spend their money and time there? What is the motivation for someone who may have an important job, who is well-known and involved in urban organizations, to come home to a small city or rural town or village? Students have been impressed, too, by the commitment to efforts at community development, to the belief that there is a continuing obligation to the hometown community and people in it. Especially at a time when the notion of *community* in the United States is being questioned, when many are concerned that Americans no longer show a concern for their communities, the notion that one's hometown is a continuing place of obligation and influence, regardless of where one resides, strikes many as both unusual and significant.

Themes and Comparative Issues:
Community, Identity, Civil Society, and Development

In exploring these issues and in seeking to understand the continuing importance of the hometown for the Ijesa Yoruba, this book raises several issues, especially questions of community, development, and identity. It also raises questions about the ways in which broad economic and political processes both shape and are shaped by local events and perceptions. These issues are important for understanding Yoruba society and culture. But they are not peculiar to the Yoruba, or to Nigeria. Important theoretical and comparative questions arise as a result of the consideration of Yoruba hometowns and the linkages people maintain with them.

The notion of *community* as a fixed locale comes into question. How can a community be a place to which people have ties but in which they are not residing on a regular basis? This leads in turn to a discussion of multilocality, the idea that people have ties to more than one place, and ties to other people in several places. Understanding the development of multilocality requires one to consider migration and the formation and maintenance of linkages among people in a variety of locales, a process taking place not only in Nigeria but in many other parts of the world. Community has been a much-discussed concept, yet one where considerable controversy still exists. What is a *community*? With increasing mobility of populations all over the world, how do people retain ties with their homes and why? This has become an issue not only in the study of internal migration but also in discussions of international migration. In Africa, urban-rural linkages have been shown to have a strength and importance that continues over more than one generation (Gugler 1991). Studies of international migration have likewise argued that "transnational" communities are forming that not only span space within a given country but also include people in different countries and continents. This book argues that the Ijesa Yoruba, in a context of high mobility, have communities with a spatial locus (the hometown) but where members are spread about in several locales. They identify with that place and take action in relation to it.

Issues of *identity* are also central to this discussion. Who exactly is involved in the maintenance of hometown ties, and why? The question of how and why people identify with a hometown—where they may never have actually lived—is central to understanding contemporary socioeconomic life among the Ijesa Yoruba. For them, the hometown *(ilu)* is the place where one has kinship connections, usually the place where one's father's lineage is from. More than a place of origin, it provides a source of social identity and a web of social connections. How do those not residing at home identify with the hometown, and in what ways do they influence decisionmaking in those communities? Conversely, how do those at home perceive those who are outside, or "abroad," as it is usually stated in Nigerian English? An Ilesa chief, A. O. Lamikanra, once stated in an interview that "we love ourselves abroad more than we do at home." What does he mean about the different points of view that may be found in a community—and how those differences affect the direction of developments there?

At the same time, the hometown is only one aspect of a set of influences that affect identity and interaction in a complex and changing situation. Many people can draw on ties to more than one community while also identifying on the basis of status, religion, education, and a variety of other characteristics. How do these varying sources of identity affect interaction within and across communities? This study demonstrates how members of the elite—many of whom are professionals living in large cities—play major roles in their hometown communities. These individuals identify not only with those in their hometown but also with others of similar status from other communities. The analysis in this book contributes to the understanding of how identity is shaped over time and in complex situations.

Issues of community and identity have broader implications for society. If it is true that the most significant source of identity is the hometown, and that as a result people are most involved in what happens in the places they identify as the hometown, then what does this mean for divisions within Nigerian society and for political and economic development more generally? In a recent book, Kayode Eso, a retired justice of the Supreme Court of Nigeria, refers to "the age of tribalistic formations of 'state unions' and 'the egbes' [clubs] which though [they] started their existence innocently, later bred tribalism and tribal hatred" (1996: 12). Although he was referring to an earlier period in Nigerian history, might the same be said of some of the current formations of hometown associations and community development organizations, which, in emphasizing the development of a particular community, work against the development and unity of the larger society? This is an issue widely discussed in the communities studied, with some, like Justice Eso, who is himself from Ilesa, having strong views about the potential for increased divisions within the larger society.

At the same time that the activities under study have implications for the larger society, it is also the case that those activities, and the perspectives that shape them, are themselves shaped by events in Nigeria as a whole. The research for this book took place over seven years during a period of considerable political and economic change, changes that most people have seen as worsening their situations. The political uncertainty, as well as the continuing economic crisis, have affected people's ability to be involved in local community activities as well as their perceptions about the need to be involved. Some in fact have argued that it is only because of the high level of uncertainty in the wider society that hometown connections are so crucial, that if Nigeria were like the United States, they say, and an individual could move anywhere and be "at home" there, then there would be no continuing need for the links with the hometown. But since that is not the case, and one can be "at home" only in the place that is truly one's home (i.e., the hometown), it is essential to maintain and build on those connections. As one of those central to this research,

Dr. E. A. Ifaturoti, put it in an interview, "At present in Nigeria the only place you have security, the only place you can be sure of, is your home-town. That is the place where you are known, and where people will protect you."

What are the broader implications of attachment to locale, especially when the underlying identity for such attachments is defined by ethnicity? What are the implications for civil society and for the idea of citizenship? Recent attention to civil society not only in Africa but around the world (e.g., Putnam 1993) has focused on the importance of civic participation and engagement. In Africa, political scientists have noted the rich associa-tional life that has countered the state. But when associations are formed on the basis of ethnic and local identities, as is the case with those formed as a result of hometown affiliation, the question arises as to whether those asso-ciations represent an "ethnicization" of politics, or whether they represent the basis on which democratic participation can develop. This study argues that hometown-based organizations and activities need to be viewed as key local institutions that are a major dimension of political and social activity, with great meaning for those involved. These are not "primordial" or "tra-ditional" institutions, but rather ones whose agendas and activities are con-stantly being shaped and reshaped by contemporary economic and political situations.

Another set of issues considered here involves the notion of *develop-ment*. What is it that Ijesa Yoruba seek to do when they "develop" their communities? To address this question, we must consider how people themselves define development, what it is that they are trying to do, and why. It is also useful to consider connections between indigenous concepts of development and those used by social scientists and development practi-tioners when they discuss local-level, grassroots, community-based devel-opment in the Third World. When a Yoruba academic states, "What else is development other than helping your hometown?"—as Niyi Akinnaso said to me some years ago—does he reflect a convergence of indigenous and scholarly views of development?

This book argues that local, indigenous understandings of develop-ment underlie the activities undertaken by local communities. In the com-munities studied, nearly everyone states that they want development. What do they mean by this? And how do they go about seeking to develop their communities? Ijesas pride themselves on their self-help efforts to bring social and economic improvement to their communities. In what ways are such efforts similar to broader concepts of indigenous and participatory development? And what are the limits of such approaches to development? Despite the shared commitment to development, complex local realities must be taken into account. Differences of power, wealth, and status among community members lead to consideration of whose agenda and what interests are being followed in local development efforts. A related question focuses on who benefits from the projects undertaken. There are differences not only within communities but also among communities. In the context of structural adjustment and economic crisis, communities are adopting survival strategies that draw on a variety of resources, looking not only to their own members but also to wider networks of influential people. Similar processes are occurring elsewhere in West Africa, with the communities that are most successful being better financed and having more "modern" facilities than others. In the long run, local communities are inevitably limited in the resources to which they have access. If development means improvement in people's lives across a region or country, then the local development efforts considered here suggests that the long-term implications may be the opposite, with greater unevenness in overall development.

Each of these issues is discussed throughout the book. Chapter 10 focuses on the comparative and theoretical implications of the evidence from the Ijesa communities studied.

Changing and Diverse Perspectives

The activities discussed in this book are dynamic and still changing. Nearly everyone who has been a part of my research continues today to be involved in their home communities, some in the same ways as they have been during the past several years, others in new ways. Organizations, likewise, do not remain static. Some had just formed at the start of the research, with much promise and ambitious goals. Some of those goals have since changed, and there is no doubt that there will be further change, as the members address new issues and seek to respond to new developments. This book, in other words, reflects an ongoing, unfinished process.

This book also seeks to reflect the diversity of perspectives within the communities studied. When I began the research, I selected four (later five) communities within a defined geographic region, in order to consider both similarities and differences among those places. Although it turned out that there is indeed considerable variation among communities, it also has become apparent that there is diversity within communities as well. Indeed, one of the major concerns expressed by people in Ijesa communities is the lack of "unity" in them. And though it is true that divisions within and among communities often cause problems and make it difficult to agree on a course of direction, it may also be that diverse points of view lead to greater dynamism in the long run, with different individuals and groups trying out varying approaches to the problems of their local communities.

Why This Research?

I am frequently asked how I became interested in research in Nigeria and why I undertook this particular research. The answers to both questions have both personal and academic roots. In the early 1970s, when I went to Nigeria to do research for my Ph.D., I selected the city of Ilesa as my central focus for a study of regional marketplaces and trade (Trager 1976), not only because it fit into the academic criteria I was looking for but also because I found the women in the marketplace welcoming and helpful; others I met from Ilesa provided me with important connections to key individuals in the community. Subsequently, I became interested in changes in the urban economy (1985a; 1985b) and in trade as one form of linkage between rural and urban areas (1988a). I continued to examine these processes in the Ijesa area. Later, I undertook research on migration, rural-urban linkages, and family ties in the Philippines (1988b) and, in the process, made the point that it seemed that in West Africa, unlike the Philippines and other places, individuals who migrated from their home communities maintained ties not only with family but also with the community itself. Others had, of course, begun to examine these issues in Nigeria and elsewhere in West Africa, and the work of Aronson (1978), Peel (1983), and Gugler (1971, 1991) has been especially important in demonstrating the ways in which individuals keep their connections with others from the home place, as well as the impact of those connections on developments at home.

A shift in my orientation took place in the mid-1980s, when I spent two years working in the Ford Foundation's West Africa office, heading the office in Lagos and developing programs on community development and women's issues. An important part of the job was an effort to work with nongovernmental organizations (NGOs) involved in development, of which there were very few in Nigeria at the time. It struck me that even though there were few formal NGOs, there were a great many local organizations in which people were involved—market women's organizations, craft associations, hometown organizations, church organizations, "old boys" associations of schoolmates, elite organizations such as Rotary—and that many people were involved in several of these. Furthermore, some of these organizations were tackling development issues, or at least seemed to be concerned about finding ways to improve their local communities. Yet most of these, except for the elite organizations, operated locally and were concerned primarily with the needs of their own members.

It seemed to me that those of us in the academic and practitioner communities who are concerned about development needed to consider how people in their own communities define *development* and how they go about undertaking what they consider to be development projects. In the long run this is the way in which change and development take place—by the involvement of people in their own communities. However, it was also clear that in the Yoruba case the involvement of people who are not residing in a community but consider themselves part of that community, and who can provide access to various resources, was key to the success of local efforts. Even now, despite an increasing interest in development circles in community-based, local, grassroots development, there has been little attention paid to the role of those from a community but not currently residing in it.

In addition, the comparative questions raised in my research in the Philippines seemed significant: Why is it that Yoruba, and some other West African societies as well, place such an emphasis on continuing ties with the home place, rather than simply on connections with family wherever they may be, as seems to be the case elsewhere?

The Research Area

In undertaking the research on which this book is based, I decided to return to the Ijesa area. Rather than study the entire region, I chose several specific communities: the major center of Ilesa; two medium-sized towns, Osu and Ijebu-Jesa; and one small community, Iwoye. Soon after the research began, I became aware of several activities in another small community, Iloko, and added that to the array. Although these places became the main focus of the study, people from other Ijesa communities were part of some of the activities and organizations examined, and toward the end of the research I spent some time in still another small town, Ido-Oko. Each of these communities is part of a region commonly referred to as Ijesaland (a map is provided in Chapter 3; see Map 3.2). Despite acknowledgment of a shared history and identity as Ijesa, each community also has its distinctive characteristics. Detailed descriptions of the region and of the communities studied are provided in Chapter 3.

The Implications of Long-term Field Research

Many of the connections on which I drew in this research go back to my first fieldwork in Ilesa in 1973–1974, and even as far back as my first visit to Nigeria as a child in 1958–1959. When I returned to Nigeria in October 1991, one of the first people I called on was Bolanle Awe, a professor at the University of Ibadan who had assisted me with connections for my dissertation research. She was not home, as she was preparing for the funeral of her aunt in Ilesa. I soon realized that the aunt, whose funeral was to take place that weekend, was the woman whom professor Awe had first sent me to in 1973; she was the cloth trader who had been instrumental in helping me to meet and talk with many of the market women in Ilesa. When I attended the funeral that weekend, with another academic colleague who is also from Ilesa, I felt the intertwining of my personal friendships with my academic interests in a way that had not previously occurred. Such interconnections became apparent on several subsequent occasions. Kunle and Tinu Ifaturoti had provided me with advice and friendship during my earlier stay in Nigeria; they had welcomed me and my husband to their home when we came for a visit in the late 1970s. My ties with them went back even further (in an indirect sense, at least), as they were close friends of my family's closest friends in Vom, outside Jos, where we lived while my father conducted biological research in 1958. On my return to Nigeria in 1991, it became apparent that Kunle Ifaturoti would be central to my new research project, as he was deeply involved in a new organization seeking to improve conditions in the Ijesa area. Whereas he had been helpful, but not personally interested, in my research on markets, he now became a key person for understanding events.

At times, the interconnections of personal friendships and academic interests had complicated dimensions. When an old friend, who had been my research assistant in 1973–1974, asked me to help her meet a new acquaintance from my research, to see if she might be able to get a job in his firm, I felt uncomfortable, feeling that I was being drawn into relationships where I wasn't quite sure what my role should be, or how I would be perceived. No longer simply a researcher from abroad coming to study people and their activities, I had become part of the complicated relationships I was studying—yet certainly not fully part of them. Many anthropologists have experienced this, even in research that takes place over short periods. But now, even though I leave Nigeria to return to my home in the United States, my multiple ties and many visits mean that it is always assumed that I will be back and that in some ways, like Ijesas themselves, I will continue to feel connected with those communities and the people in them. Telephone communications and travel by Nigerians have made this ever more possible. When I left Nigeria suddenly in June 1993 and missed an event I had been planning to attend the following weekend, I telephoned the hostess from Wisconsin the next week to explain my absence. Several of those who have participated in the research have visited me in the United States, and this has given us time not always available in their busy schedules at home in Nigeria.

The research itself has taken place over a considerable length of time, beginning in October 1991. Originally conceived as a sabbatical-year project (1991–1992), I was fortunate in being able to return to Nigeria for varying lengths of time in subsequent years, enabling me to observe activities and conduct interviews in the changing political and economic context of the 1990s. Data discussed in this book continued to be collected through June 1998.[1] An update of some information from late 1999 and early 2000 is provided in the Conclusion (Chapter 10).

Names and Places

The standard anthropological convention is to disguise the names of people and even places in order to maintain confidentiality and protect the privacy of those who provide information and insights in ethnographic research. Historians, of course, approach the issue differently and provide footnotes to every interview and written source. Researchers on the Yoruba, and on Nigeria more generally, have used both approaches. The identification of places is common practice; there is far too much variation among Yoruba communities for research reports to be meaningful if they simply refer to some disguised, unnamed Yoruba community. Some ethnographers such as Dan Aronson have provided pseudonyms for their key informants, whereas others such as J.D.Y. Peel have written social history and identified people by name.

My approach has been to discuss the issue with some of those who provided the information. Since they will be among those reading this book, and other readers will include their friends and acquaintances in Ijesaland and elsewhere in Nigeria, I wanted to know whether they preferred having their own names used or not. The response was overwhelmingly in favor of using real names. I have therefore identified people where they are central to the events described, or where an individual provided specific information on a specific issue or offered an opinion or perspective on some issue. However, since my data also contain information from meetings attended by people I did not otherwise talk with, as well as survey data where a larger set of people provided answers to a defined set of questions, I do not identify people who provided information in those contexts.

Yoruba Spelling

Contemporary Yoruba spelling utilizes specialized diacritical markings to indicate the sounds "sh" and specific pronounciations of "o" and "e." For example, Ilesa and Ijesa are pronounced "Ilesha" and "Ijesha." Typesetters were unable to provide the necessary fonts to show these diacritical markings, and therefore they have been omitted. Older forms of spelling, which used the "sh," appear in some quotations and references.

A Guide to the Organization of This Book

The study begins with description of specific events and processes and then moves to the consideration of more general issues. Several key events and activities recur throughout the book. These include a set of celebrations and rituals—community-day celebrations—which have become an important part of community identity and community development; the activities of a major new organization, the Ijesa Solidarity Group (ISG); and the community development efforts in one of the communities studied, Iloko.

Key themes and questions are considered throughout. These are introduced in Chapter 2, then discussed in greater detail in later chapters. Chapters 2–6 focus almost entirely on people, events, and activities within the Ijesa region; Chapters 7–9 connect local events to broader political and economic processes in Nigeria. Throughout the book, case studies of individuals, organizations, and events are used to provide the rich, detailed description that gives the foundation for ethnographic understanding.

In some respects, this book is not a conventional ethnography, in that it draws on data from several communities and from people whose lives span several different locales. In other respects, it represents what in my view is central to ethnography: detailed description as the basis for analysis and theoretical understanding.

Chapter 2 begins with a description and analysis of community-day celebrations, an important new "tradition" in Ijesa communities. Drawing on data from several of these celebrations, I consider variations both over time and among communities, analyzing them as rituals that draw on Yoruba tradition but that also reflect new dimensions of local communities. Four major themes and several counterthemes are introduced; these appear not only at community-day celebrations but in many other contexts as well. These include the importance of self-help, countered by the role of government; unity, countered by an emphasis on individualism; coming home to develop one's community while recognizing the high mobility of the population; and an elaboration of specific community problems and goals.

Chapter 3 begins with a description of the Ijesa region and the five communities where the research took place, noting similarities and differences among them. It then discusses the Yoruba concept of *ilu*, considering the importance of the hometown as a source of identity for Ijesa people and the ways in which contemporary social and economic processes have contributed to its continuing centrality in their lives.

An understanding of the importance of community and hometown requires consideration of the role of migration among the Ijesa Yoruba, which is the focus of Chapter 4. Highly mobile and long involved in trade and the professions, many Ijesas have lived and worked outside their home communities. Most retain some type of connection with those homes. But there is considerable variation in the extent of those ties, variation that reflects status and feelings of obligation, as well as the extent to which those at home are able to exert influence on those elsewhere. Both men and women maintain links to home, but there are differences in the importance and extent of involvement. Both survey and case-study data are used to examine migration and linkages among Ijesas.

One significant way in which many individuals maintain ties with home is in membership in hometown organizations, which are considered in Chapter 5. There I examine a variety of types of organizations, focusing on several that are currently active in promoting local development activities. Contained in the analysis are some of the historical antecedents to the contemporary organizations, including an extended case study of one new organization, the Ijesa Solidarity Group. Hometown organizations reflect many of the same themes discussed in Chapter 2—concerns with unity, development, and self-help.

Chapter 6 focuses on events in which people recognize and celebrate their hometown connections through rituals and ceremonial activities. These include events honoring individuals; efforts at organizing a regional "national day"; and a contemporary celebration of a traditional ritual—the installation and coronation of a new *oba* (king).

Chapters 7–9 move outward from the Ijesa region to consider the broader economic and political context of current efforts at local community development. The Nigerian economic crisis of recent years, and the structural adjustment program of the late 1980s and early 1990s, have shaped the ways in which people perceive the necessity of self-help and local development efforts. Chapter 7 considers this context while discussing the meaning of development to local people in Ijesaland. Chapter 8 examines specific local development efforts undertaken in the communities studied, with case studies of the establishment of community banks in two towns; efforts to establish industry undertaken by the Ijesa Solidarity Group; and a variety of community-wide efforts in Iloko. Some of the difficulties, as well as the successes, are considered.

Chapter 9 considers the political context of hometown activities. Nigerian political events in the 1990s have at times encouraged and at other times discouraged involvement in local organizations and community development efforts. At the same time, local political issues, including conflicts within and between Ijesa communities, have affected people's activities. Chapter 9 considers how the reality of local politics affects the ideal of unity.

Finally, Chapter 10 addresses broader theoretical issues of communities and development, within a comparative framework, and suggests that the comparative value of understanding these processes has relevance not only for understanding community development elsewhere in Africa and the Third World but also for contemporary community development efforts in the United States. I conclude with a reexamination of the Ijesa emphasis on development within the context of Yoruba culture, arguing that this emphasis is best understood from a perspective that sees Yoruba culture as both innovative and integrative—able to incorporate the new at the same time as it maintains cultural integrity as Yoruba.

Notes

1. In 1991–1992, I began the research on which this study is based while on sabbatical from the University of Wisconsin–Parkside. I spent eight months doing field research (October-December 1991; March–July 1992); I then returned for an additional period of research in May–June 1993. I was able to continue the research in December–January 1994–1995 and in May–June 1995. In March 1996 I again returned to Nigeria, this time as part of a faculty exchange with Obafemi Awolowo University, supported by the U.S. Information Agency, and was again able to spend much of my time from late March through the first part of June following up on my earlier research. Additional short research visits took place in April and June 1997 and in June 1998.

2

Community-Day Celebrations:
A New Tradition at Home

Iloko Day, 1993

The narrow, partially paved road led out of Ijebu-Jesa toward Iloko, past the large cement-block building housing the headquarters of the Oriade local government offices. On the outskirts of Iloko, a large banner was strung over the road, announcing "Welcome to Iloko Day." At the crossroads in the center of the town, next to the palace, Mercedes and Peugeot 504 cars were turning to enter the grounds of the primary school. Talking drummers welcomed the visiting officials and other guests as they left their cars, while the local Boys Brigade band played on their trumpets and other instruments, creating a cacophony of disparate sounds. At one end of the primary school grounds, viewing stands were set up, with two rows of large upholstered chairs for the most important guests. The governor of Osun State, Alhaji Isiaka Adeleke, arrived in his car with sirens sounding, and stepped out, resplendent in a flowing turquoise *agbada*. Several ministers of the federal government followed, as well as the deputy governor of the state and the wives of both the governor and deputy governor. They were joined by *obas* from surrounding communities, all in white or brightly colored *agbadas* and with long necklaces of coral-colored beads and beaded walking sticks signifying their status as traditional rulers. All were seated on the upholstered chairs, under the brightly colored canopy.

Moving among the crowd of arriving dignitaries was a leading son of the soil—Omo Oba (Prince) Oladele Olashore, the son of the late *oba* of the town and, at the time of this ceremony, minister of finance in the federal government of Nigeria. He exchanged words of greeting with all, chatting briefly, helping them find their seats. As the guests sat down and greeted one another, the two masters of ceremonies announced each new arrival, encouraging the growing crowd to welcome them with applause. Young girls mixed in the crowd, providing each guest willing to pay a few naira (the Nigerian currency) with a brightly colored ribbon announcing the Iloko Day celebrations and a printed program for the day's events.

At the same time, groups of townspeople began arriving at the school grounds, taking their seats in metal chairs set up under canopies along the two sides of the field. Local chiefs—elderly men in dark *agbadas*—sat on one side. Banners announcing some of the local organizations—the Federation of Iloko-Ijesa Students Union, the Iloko Women Progressive Elites, and others—identified the location of members of those groups along the other side. Other visitors were seated on plastic chairs behind the government officials and traditional rulers.

As more people arrived and took their seats, the master of ceremonies led a song in Yoruba: "I'm happy that I'm born in Iloko. Congratulations, my friends, shake my hand." Meanwhile, the Boys Brigade band and a group from the Girl Guides continued to play. To the right of the master of ceremonies was displayed a large model of the community hall to be built with the funds that were to be raised as part of the day's activities.

At 11:15 A.M., the national anthem was sung, signaling the official start of the festivities. Then the master of ceremonies announced that they would sing the Iloko anthem; following the words printed in Yoruba in the program, the crowd joined those few who were actually familiar with the song.[1]

> Chorus:
> *I-LO-KO*
> *Ilu Olokiki Ni*
> *N'o maa wa Igbegaa Re*
> *N'o maa wa iree Re.*
>
> 1. *Ilu ta t'edo si ese oke oru*
> *Waseye 'leni akoko o*
> *Obalogun, jagun-jagun fun aabo ilu*
> *Ajagbusi Ekun kinni l'oba to ko je.*
> Chorus: *I-LO-KO, etc.*
>
> 2. *Ejeka s'owo po*
> *Ka tun le yii se*
> *Ki 'se awon asaajuu wa*
> *Mase ja sasun.*
>
> Chorus: *I-LO-KO, etc.*
> [Iloko, a town with a great name.
> I will always look for its upbringing
> I will always look for its success.
> The town that was founded at the foot of a high hill

Waseye was the first person (founder) of the town
Obalogun, the warrior who protects the town,
Ajagbusi Ekun was the first *oba* of the town.
Let's bring our hands together
For the success of our land
So that the works of our leaders will not be in vain.]

A few minutes later, as most visitors settled into their seats, the speeches began. The first speaker was J. I. Omoniyi, chairman of the Iloko-Ijesa Development Committee and chairman of the day's events. He began by welcoming everyone:[2]

> On behalf of the regent of Iloko, the chiefs and the entire community, I wish to welcome you all to Iloko-Ijesa on the occasion of the second Iloko Day. We welcome to Iloko His Excellency, Alhaji Isiaka Adeleke, the governor of Osun State; we welcomed you once in the past through your deputy, Prince Adesuyi Haastrup. But today we are privileged to have you in person physically in our midst, for the first time, and the entire community has feelings of satisfaction at seeing for the first time their elected executive governor. We in Iloko are peace-loving people and are always ready to cooperate with government. We salute you, your excellency, for a laudable effort to give Osun State a good image.... I am sure very soon we will have to make you an honorary son of Iloko. We welcome to Iloko our royal fathers; we feel very much honored by your presence. We cherish the kind gesture you always show to us by attending to our invitation. We welcome to Iloko members of the Transitional Council [Ministers of the federal government of Nigeria] all the way from Abuja, who have come as a guest to one of them. We appreciate the kind gesture you have shown and the entire community is grateful to you. We salute all our friends from far and near who have done us proud as usual.... We volunteer to take any of you who is interested to go with all the Iloko citizens to climb the hill. The founder of the town, Waseye—that was the hill that he came down from before he founded Iloko. Come with us this afternoon to this popular place, which you are seeing right in front of me now, which forms one of the most beautiful sceneries in Ijesaland.

Then he began to describe the many problems facing the town, apologizing in the process for doing so, but saying "it is not often that one is blessed with the presence of such august visitors in our midst, so we have to take this opportunity to bare our minds. I am sure your excellencies will understand." He described one of the roads leading into town, the Iwaraja-Iloko-Ijebu-Jesa Road:

> We already commended the old Oyo State government for tarring this road, which is now full of potholes. We already request-

ed that the state government help us to widen and tar this road.
We are happy that the state government has accepted our
request. Our plea now is that one should start on the road before
the coming rainy season inflicts further damage to the road. We
pray your excellency to kindly force action to be taken urgently.

He described the situation at the school, saying "there are not sufficient teachers to teach essential subjects, such as mathematics,
English, the sciences and the humanities" and urging the state Ministry
of Education to assist them. He then went on to one of the major problems: the town's water supply:

Pipe-borne water. We are awaiting official government reaction
to our demand for a big overhead tank to distribute water from
existing boreholes in the town. We are hopeful that our prayers
will be heard. This town is connected with the water scheme at
Esa Odo. Yet unfortunately the water never flows here. We are
aware of the plan of Osun State government to improve the
working efficiency of the existing water scheme. We plead that
this town's plight, as far as the Esa Odo water scheme is con-
cerned, is given some due consideration in this scheme.

The chairman concluded his speech by referring to the first Iloko
Day held the previous year, and the launching of the town's N10 million development fund.[3] He thanked those who had contributed, saying
that the contributions had enabled them to begin building the community center, and adding that "we are still very far from achieving our
target for the fund. We look forward to our friends and well-wishers for
assistance, to enable us to reach our goal, and we trust you will show to
us your usual generosity."

A speech by the governor followed, in which he praised the community for its spirit of self-help and responded to some of the requests:

It gives me a great joy to be in your midst in this honorable
occasion, of the celebration of the second Iloko Day. I therefore
wish to congratulate the regent of Iloko and also felicitate with
the great prince of the town, Omo Oba Oladele Olashore, and
the entire people of Iloko.... This day will among other things
bring all the sons and daughters of the community together, to
plan for the development of their motherland. In fact, it will
afford our people who have for long been away from home the
opportunity to visit home again, see the progress and develop-
ment that had occurred, and make conscious effort toward con-
tributing their own quota to our development.

I wish to charge you that the task of community develop-
ment cannot be left to government alone. There is quite a lot you
can do individually and as corporate bodies to bring develop-
ment to our doorsteps. Indeed, I wish to commend the self-help
spirit of the people of Iloko, who have not waited for the govern-

*ment to provide everything for them, but decided to find avenues
of solving some of the problems themselves. During the first
Iloko Day, I learned you realized over 1 million naira, which
you have utilized to provide two boreholes for the community.
You have also commenced work on the construction of the community center which incorporates a multipurpose community
hall, library, and a police post. All these are commendable
efforts. I believe by the next Iloko Day, I will be here to commission the community center. The Nigerian economy, having been
deregulated, reduced the public-sector participation in business
and industrial ventures. It is the private sector that is being
encouraged to take up the task of setting up viable industries
and businesses.*

*The government is primarily concerned with the provision
of a conducive atmosphere for industrial and business activities.
I therefore use this medium to call on all our industrialists and
businessmen and women to come to Osun State to aid our industrial and business development by way of setting up viable ventures. The state has what it takes to set up industrial concerns. I
will also seize this opportunity to call on all wealthy sons and
daughters of not only Iloko but the entire Ijesaland to come
hooome [his emphasis], and invest to make their birthplace a
worthy and proud place to live in. Abuja or Lagos is not your
home. Come home and join hands in development of your motherland.*

The governor then went on to refer to the election scheduled to
take place a few weeks later (June 12) and to urge people to turn out to
"perform your civic duties on election day." He concluded by responding to the requests made by the chairman, announcing that work was to
begin on the rehabilitation of the road as part of a project funded by a
World Bank loan and that the water project is also "ongoing." He then
announced that he would make "a personal humble donation toward
the community center of N25,000."

Finally, the governor added a plea from the state to the federal
government: "I am glad your son is the secretary for finance and there
are other members of the Transitional Council here. I want to implore,
I want to beg of them when they get to Abuja, to please see to the
plight of states. Osun State today, after the payment of salaries, is left
with only N2 million. Out of which a whopping N400,000 is expended
on water treatment chemicals a month. How do you run a state with
N1.6 million? I don't know."

He then turned toward Prince Olashore, saying, "Secretary for
Finance, *odi owo yin o* [it's in your hands]."

Although the chairman and governor used microphones for their
speeches, not everyone in the stands could hear them over the continuing noise of new arrivals and conversations in the crowd. Since they

both gave their speeches in English, many of those listening did not understand all that they said; however, the two masters of ceremonies followed each speech with a short translation into Yoruba.

Toward the end of the governor's speech, sirens could be heard in the distance, heralding the arrival of more dignitaries. The *ooni* (king) of Ife had arrived, one of the most important *obas* in Yorubaland, surrounded by a large entourage, attendants holding huge, colored umbrellas to shield him, and drummers and trumpeters to welcome him. He took his seat next to the governor, and a few minutes later the leading *oba* in the Ijesa region, the *owa* (king) of Ilesa, also arrived and was seated on the other side of the governor. The masters of ceremonies took this opportunity to announce the presence of other distinguished guests, such as one of the directors of Mobil-Nigeria.

At this point, large donations were announced. First, the minister of agriculture spoke, announcing that he was there to represent President Ibrahim Babangida "in his personal capacity" and to make a personal donation of N150,000 for him. He also announced his own donation and that of two other ministers who were present, emphasizing that each was a "personal" donation. The donations from government officials totaled N325,000. Then the master of ceremonies announced a donation from the *ooni* of Ife of N250,000. This, like the other donations, was greeted with applause and songs of thanks led by the masters of ceremonies.

Several more donations were announced, and then Prince Olashore made a speech to thank the governor and ministers, saying that they had other engagements and had to leave but encouraging others to stay for the rest of the day's events. He stressed how honored he was by their attendance: "I feel really personally honored that they still were able to fix into their program that they were able to be here with us this afternoon. Honestly, I was not sure how many of my colleagues could make it. When I saw them coming one by one, I saw that, well, the day is really made." More sirens sounded as the Mercedes and Peugeot 504s departed with the distinguished guests.

The program then resumed with an interlude of cultural performances—dancing and drumming by a local hunters' group; a dance performance from the Delta Steel Company, a company located in Delta State but headed by a manager from Iloko; and a local dance troupe. As the performances took place, some of the dancers were "sprayed" with money by those attending (bills were pasted on their foreheads as they danced), and many more of the audience milled around, talking and visiting with one another.

The master of ceremonies held up the model of the community

hall and announced that trays would be circulated for further donations. More large donations, as well as some smaller ones, were
announced. Many of the donations were from visitors from outside
Iloko; others were from key people from Iloko; and still others were
from organizations of people from Iloko, such as the Inner Circle Club
of Iloko, the Women Progressive Society of Iloko, and the Iloko
Descendants Union–Ibadan branch.

Then the *owa* of Ilesa spoke, giving the only speech that was presented in Yoruba. He emphasized the fact that as the Owa Obokun of
Ijesaland (the traditional ruler of Ilesa and vicinity) he represents not
just himself but all the Ijesa people. Finally, Prince Olashore delivered
the final speech of the day, once again thanking everyone who had
attended, especially the *obas*. He concluded by focusing on the importance of unity: "My regent, my respected people of Iloko Ijesa, I think
you have seen what it is like to be united. I believe you will continue to
be united in all your endeavors. It is only then that you will be responsible within the community of Ijesas and be responsible within the
community of this country."

More sirens sounded as the remaining dignitaries left the site,
while townspeople also began to leave to return to their homes or the
homes of friends to continue to socialize with those who had come
from out of town.

Community-Day Celebrations in Ijesaland

The celebration of the second Iloko Day, described here, culminated in the
collection of a substantial amount of money and led, within a few weeks, to
the beginning of construction of the Ultra Modern Community Hall as
intended by the organizers of the event, the Iloko-Ijesa Development
Committee. This celebration had elements common to other community-
day celebrations that took place in Ijesaland in the early 1990s, yet it also
differed from others in significant ways. In this section I describe some of
the variations in the structure and organization of these celebrations. I then
consider the major themes that emerge in the speeches and in discussions of
these events, followed by a discussion of the goals and objectives of those
who organize them. Conscious efforts have been made by organizers to create new rituals and traditions, modeled in some respects on older ritual
activities. Finally, I suggest that there has been variable success in institut-
ing community-day celebrations as new types of ritual. The themes and

goals that are articulated in these celebrations recur in many other events and activities discussed in later chapters of this book.

Community-day celebrations began in the Ijesa area around 1990. In the communities that were studied, Iwoye was the first to hold such a celebration, in September 1990. Ijebu-Jesa had its first Ijebu-Jesa Day in November 1991, and Iloko its first in May 1992. Similar events were being organized around the same time, and even earlier, in many other Yoruba communities, as well as elsewhere in the country. It has become common to see a sign or banner announcing the first, second, or even fourth or fifth annual celebration in towns around southwestern Nigeria. Large cities, such as Ile-Ife,[4] have organized such events, as well as many small communities. As shall be discussed in Chapter 6, attempts to have either an Ilesa Day or an Ijesa National Day in the city of Ilesa have been less successful. Likewise, even in those communities where such events have been successfully organized, they have not always taken place on an annual basis, and there does not seem to be agreement among organizers whether they should be annual, or whether it will be possible to sustain the momentum that generated these celebrations to begin with.

Drawing on older traditions and rituals, as well as creating new ones, the community-day celebrations have been organized to bring community members home to celebrate their town while also raising money for community projects and encouraging people to participate in community events. The celebration in Iloko in May 1993 was both typical and atypical of such events. The underlying reasons for having such a celebration, and its general structure and organization, were like those in other places. At the same time, specific aspects of this event differed from those elsewhere and also from earlier and later celebrations in Iloko itself.

In all cases, the community-day celebrations are organized by a committee, either the town's development committee or a committee established for this purpose. For example, in Ijebu-Jesa, the Ijebu-Jesa Unions' Conference, consisting of seventy-six organizations in the town, took the decision to organize the first Ijebu-Jesa Day, after the suggestion was made by one of the member associations. A planning committee was established, chaired by Prince 'Tunde Olashore (the brother of Prince Oladele Olashore). In his welcome address at the event, Prince 'Tunde Olashore described one of the major reasons for the celebration:

> Every society or community not only in Yorubaland but indeed all over the world has a period set aside for itself to celebrate one festival or the other either in remembrance of its founder or in commemoration of one [of] its fetish gods or again in celebration of a season such as the yam festival. In Ijebu-Jesa the Ogun festival, the Agada festival, and the new yam festival were all occasions when the whole community was in festive mood when these festivals were celebrated with the pomp and pageantry

they deserved. With the growth of the Christian and Moslem beliefs in the community the apathy toward these festivals became pronounced as very few people are today interested in them. In fact some festivals of minor importance in the community have become extinct.

It is for this reason, that when Agboja Club of Ijebu-Jesa one of the associations that constitute the Unions' Conference first brought the idea of the Ijebu-Jesa Day event some four or five years ago, it received a wide support firstly because it is an event that has no connection with any religious belief be it Christian, Moslem or Traditional and secondly because the people see it as a forum where everybody will come together in the celebration in honour of AGIGIRI the founding father of this great town. (T. Olashore 1991)

In a later interview, Prince 'Tunde Olashore explained that it took four years of planning from the time the idea was first presented to the actual date of the event. During that time, a great deal of discussion focused on the question of whether the date should be at the time of a traditional religious festival or at some other time; it was decided to hold the celebration on a neutral date, so that they could "celebrate a day where everyone could be involved and it didn't involve religion." In contrast, in another town, Osu, a local festival was established to celebrate the importance of salt in the history of the town. But here, too, the celebration is not directly connected to traditional religious festivals. Elsewhere, such as Ilesa, there have been debates about this issue, with some strongly advocating the value of a "traditional" date with historical meaning to the community, and others arguing for establishing a new date not connected to any traditional rituals. This debate continues in some communities.

The basic structure of the event from town to town is similar, with speeches and fund-raising for the community as key features. In some towns, chieftaincy titles have also been given as part of the occasion. For example, in Ijebu-Jesa, the *oba* conferred honorary titles on several individuals, including people from the town as well as others who were not indigenes of the community. In some cases, the celebration has been stretched out over several days. The First Ijesa National Day, held in Ilesa in April 1993, had events spread over five days, including a secondary school competition, a lecture on Ijesa history, an agricultural/industrial show, and a symposium on the development of Ijesaland. But the major event was on a Saturday and included the launching of a N50 million industrial development fund for Ijesaland.

Despite the similarities in organization and structure, there are many differences among these celebrations, both in the way they are carried out and in their success at fulfilling the goals articulated by the organizers. The second Iloko Day was unusual in the number of very high status people from outside the town who attended and in the size of the donations that were announced.

Dignitaries at Iloko Day

Clearly, many of those who attended did so because of Prince Oladele Olashore; as minister of finance in the Transitional Council, he held one of the most influential cabinet positions in the federal government. Not surprisingly, therefore, other ministers attended and made donations not only in their own names but also in the names of other government officials, including the head of state, General Ibrahim Babangida. Likewise, key *obas* such as the Ooni of Ife attended and gave donations because of their ties to important individuals in the community. Nevertheless, both the first Iloko Day in 1992, when Prince Olashore was not yet in government, and Ijebu-Jesa Day in 1991, also drew distinguished guests from outside the community. They were not high government officials, perhaps, but they did included retired generals, businessmen and -women from Lagos, as well as individuals from other Ijesa communities who came to show their support for the town and its celebration. Nearly all those who attend such events who are not themselves members of the community expect to make donations. However, as shall be discussed below, the amounts donated vary considerably, and there is also great variation in the ways in which those donations are subsequently used. As a result, some of those who willingly attended such celebrations in 1992 and 1993 had become increasingly skeptical about their value by 1995 and 1996.

Conditions inside as well as outside the communities have affected the holding of community-day celebrations. For example, neither Iwoye nor Iloko had a celebration in 1994. As one person from Iwoye put it, they decided not to have one in 1994 because of the "ups and downs of the country." Similarly, the regent of Iloko stated in an interview in June 1995 that there was no Iloko Day in 1994 "because the economic situation was too bad, and people were disillusioned with the June 12 palaver; they felt that people wouldn't have come for it. People didn't have money, and they wouldn't have the push, or urge to come. Even the sons of the soil would have to spend a lot to come home, just for petrol and travel costs."[5]

At the same time, community leaders in Iloko felt that they should not ask for further contributions from non–community members, because they had not yet finished the town hall. They wanted to invite all those visitors back after the hall was completed. By June 1995 they had, however, decided that they "need to have an Iloko Day again, to use it for bringing people together." But they decided that they would celebrate the third Iloko Day "just with close friends and indigenes" of the town and that they would raise money internally. At that event, in October 1995, the regent made a point of stating in his speech that they had not invited "commissioners, the governor, or people from outside this town." He said that, instead, "it was good that people from the town are the only ones there, sitting down talking to each other. It is really an honor for people of the town, to discuss development among themselves."

Nearly all the speeches at the third Iloko Day were given in Yoruba rather than English, as at the earlier celebrations. For example, Prince Oladele Olashore's speech was primarily focused on encouraging contributions from townspeople, whereas his speeches at the earlier event were in English and focused on thanking those who came from outside the town. He said that "all the [previous] Iloko Days shouldn't be counted as the real Iloko Day; this is the real Iloko Day because it is the people of the town sitting down to talk about the development of the town." He went on: "If we invite people from outside we wouldn't have time to say everything we have said, and some things, such as about fighting in the town, we wouldn't want to say if there are visitors." He also suggested that there is a traditional celebration called *oba oologun* and suggested that in the future they should schedule Iloko Day on that day, and then "everyone would come home, there would be time to talk and solve all the problems in the village."[6]

According to J. I. Omoniyi, the chairman of the Iloko-Ijesa Development Committee, about 1,300 people attended the third Iloko Day. They were either residents of the town, or people who are from Iloko living elsewhere. They levied themselves, and funds were contributed—but far less than at the previous occasion. Still, Omoniyi felt that the point of the day was not only to raise money but also to bring members of the community together, and that they were successful in that effort. He said they spent about four hours talking among themselves, discussing the problems of the town, and this was something that had not been done previously.

Themes

Major themes of community-day celebrations emerge in the speeches and other activities at these events. These same themes reappear regularly in other contexts as well. Four major themes and several counterthemes are apparent.

An emphasis on self-help appears over and over in the speeches; the major countertheme focuses on the role, or nonrole, of government. In his speech at the first Ijebu-Jesa Day in November 1991, Prince 'Tunde Olashore stated:

> For a very long time, Ijebu-Jesa people have always believed in the old adage which says: "The Heavens help those who help themselves."[7] It is for this reason that apart from what the Government, State and Local alike, have been able to provide for us, we have always believed in self-development. This spirit handed down by our great ancestors has yielded fruits such as—the Maternity Centre, Ijebu-Jesa Grammar School, Urban Day Grammar School, the market, the Ultra Modern Town Hall, and the sixty-bed general hospital all completed entirely by the community as self-help projects. We are indeed not tired and we are still in our quest to provide more amenities for our people and our Kabiyesi *[oba]*. (T. Olashore 1991)

He then went on to enumerate the specific projects currently being undertaken by the town.

At all the events similar statements are made, commending the community for the projects undertaken in the past and encouraging them to contribute to new projects. The speech by the governor of Osun State, quoted above, carries this theme further, not simply noting the value of self-help but also emphasizing the countertheme that "the task of ... development cannot be left to government alone." In a statement published in the program for the Ijesa National Day celebration in 1993, the deregulation of markets and privatization of public companies were noted as setting the stage for investment in local industrial development ("Write Up on the First Ijesa National Day and Launching of a N50 million Industrial Development Fund," 1993).

However, the sharp distinction made in these speeches and statements between community self-help and government involvement in development is much less clear in reality. Many self-help projects, such as schools and hospitals, have in the past been turned over to government to run. The first Ijesa National Day was initiated by the deputy governor, and officials of the local government areas in Ijesaland were also involved in its organization and promotion. Furthermore, the actual meaning of "self-help" is open to question, as is clear from the range of people who contributed funds at the second Iloko Day.

The second major theme at community-day events is unity. Like the theme of self-help, the notion of *unity* has multiple meanings. In some contexts it refers to the unity of the specific town where the celebration is being held, as in the closing statements made by Prince Olashore at the second Iloko Day, when he said, "I think you have seen what it is like to be united. I believe you will continue to be united in all your endeavors." However, it can also refer to the unity of Ijesa communities in general, as well as to larger units—the state and even the nation. The focus on Ijesa unity appears with great regularity not only in speeches at celebrations but also in interviews and discussions about the problems of the region. An example of a blunt statement on this issue appears in the program for the first Ijesa National Day. The chairman of the Atakumosa local government (one of the local government areas [LGAs] that makes up the Ijesa region) begins his published statement in this brochure, "It is an indisputable fact that the Ijesa as a people are lacking in adequate unity, solidarity and a common purpose" (Amasa 1993).

Countering the theme of unity is individualism—that Ijesa are "too individualistic." Although this is less emphasized at the community-day celebrations, it is an important part of the perceptions that Ijesas have of themselves and of their problems. The multiple meanings of these ideas and their use in a variety of contexts will be considered at greater length in later chapters, especially Chapter 9.

Coming home to develop one's community is a third theme evident in community-day celebrations. Again, the speech by the Osun State governor is a good example:

"I will also seize this opportunity to call on all wealthy sons and daughters of not only Iloko but the entire Ijesaland to come home, and invest to make their birthplace a worthy and proud place to live in. Abuja or Lagos is not your *home*. Come home and join hands in development of your motherland." In his speech, he gave special emphasis to the word *home*, pronouncing it in an exaggerated way. Similar statements are heard over and over, not only at community celebrations but also at many other events and in other contexts. Frequently, those making these statements note that Ijesas are prominent all over the country, even beyond. In his contribution to the first Ijesa National Day brochure, the chairman, Chief A. O. Lamikanra, stated:

> There is no town of note, and there is hardly any village of any conse-
> quence in Nigeria, without a colony of Ijesas. We are an adventurous race
> who have no fear of distance and strange customs, we have exploited
> these characteristics to spread our influence far and wide.... The Ijesas in
> the diaspora, welded together by the powerful ties of a common language,
> customs and character are quite wonderfully united. It is now time to
> import this spirit of togetherness into Ijesaland so that the fatherland can
> enjoy the scale of development which Ijesas, by dint of hard work and
> perseverance in the face of long odds, have been able to bring to the
> places of their homes away from home. (Lamikanra 1993)

A listing or elaboration of specific problems to be solved or needs of
the community provides the fourth major theme of community-day events.
The speech given by the chairman of the second Iloko Day is clear in this
regard, when he enumerates the major difficulties facing the town—the
road, the school, the water supply. At the third Iloko Day, community leaders were pleased because they had come together to discuss their problems,
in a way that would not have been possible if there had been outsiders
there. Likewise, in Ijebu-Jesa, the speech given by Prince 'Tunde Olashore
listed the projects being undertaken in the community: "the completion of
the Oba's Palace estimated to cost N2 million, the provision of all facilities
in the town-hall, provision of more amenities in the two secondary
schools ..., provision of street lighting and finally the provision of potable
water for the hospital complex" (T. Olashore 1991). These lists go beyond
the specific projects for which funds are being raised on a given day. In
fact, the governor used the occasion of the second Iloko Day to list the
problems faced by Osun State, not for the benefit of those from the local
community but so those from the federal government who were present at
the ceremony would hear. This particular event was unusual in having so
many high-level federal officials in attendance, since the key host from the
community, Prince Olashore, was then minister of finance. The governor
made reference to this fact when he referred to the state's budget problems.

Goals and Objectives

These themes indicate the major goals and objectives of community-day
celebrations. The organizers of the celebrations have some clearly stated
instrumental and practical goals. Foremost among these is the raising of
money for the development of the town, and, more specifically, for whatever project or projects have been decided on by the organizing committee
and others in the community. At the first Iloko Day, money was raised for
the digging of boreholes (deep wells) for water as well as for starting the
community hall project. The second Iloko Day focused on raising funds for
the construction of the community hall, with an architect's model of the

building on display. At the time of the third Iloko Day, money was again raised for the hall, this time from community members only, in order to complete the construction. By that time, the structure itself had been built—a very large, cement-block building—and the celebration was held inside the building rather than on the primary school grounds, as before. But money was still needed to connect electricity and water, finish the floors and windows, and landscape around the building. In the towns of Iwoye and Ijebu-Jesa, the primary projects for which money was being raised were the renovation or rebuilding of the *oba*'s palace in each town. In both communities, construction had begun but had not been completed, and donations were directed toward that effort.

In other cases, the objective of fund-raising is more vague. Sometimes, the launching of a general community development fund takes place. In Ilesa, the Ijesa National Day celebration included the launching of an industrial development fund. However, participants and visitors to these events prefer donating money when it is being used for a specific project, especially one that has visible results, such as the construction of a building. Otherwise, they complain, people are likely to "chop" the money (use it for their own personal purposes), and it will disappear without benefiting the community.

However, community-day celebrations are not simply fund-raisers. In fact, the organizers and leaders emphasize a set of much less immediately practical goals: bringing community members home, getting people together to discuss and solve problems, celebrating the traditions of the community. For example, a man interviewed in Iwoye pointed out that when the community began to organize Iwoye Day, they "hoped to influence those outside through that." He said that they expected many educated people and traders to come, and that they weren't expected to contribute money but to use the occasion to "discuss things affecting the progress of the town." They also discussed the origins and history of the community. In Iloko, the wife of the chairman of the event believes that the celebration helps to bring people together who have been scattered by going away to work, and who have lost their identity. She also pointed out that it makes people appreciate what is being done in the town. And, she noted, the children who are being brought up in other parts of the country get to know one another through these events.

Old Traditions and New Rituals

Throughout the speeches and conversations about community-day celebrations there is frequent reference to traditions of the past—religious festivals that formerly brought people home once a year and that brought people of the town together in common celebration. As Prince 'Tunde Olashore noted in his speech at the first Ijebu-Jesa Day, there is no longer any common set of religious beliefs that unite community members. Although some have suggested that community-day celebrations should take place on a day that would coincide with a traditional festival, so far the celebrations in Ijesaland have taken place on neutral dates unconnected to any particular event of the past. They have also taken place on neutral territory—a school grounds or the recently constructed town hall in Iloko. When chieftaincy titles were conferred at the first Ijebu-Jesa Day, the organizers thanked the *oba* for allowing them to carry out the ceremony outside the palace.

Margaret Drewal has described a similar type of celebration, the Imewuro Annual Rally, organized in a small town in another part of Yorubaland—the Ijebu area. The overall goals of the events are similar: "to bring all our people abroad home to see each other once a year" (quoted in Drewal 1992: 164). But in that case, the organizers have brought together the various religious festivals traditionally celebrated in the town in a weeklong annual event, incorporating Egungun masquerades, sacrificial animals, and processions to shrines, along with Christian and Muslim prayers.

In contrast, the community-day celebrations in Ijesaland refer to past traditions and to the history of the town, without incorporating any of the key elements of major religious festivals. Beliefs are expressed indicating an assumption that religious festivals and rituals of the past were successful mechanisms for bringing people home and for uniting the community. People feel that a new mechanism needs to be found to do this, and they believe that community-day celebrations could be that mechanism. In the effort to incorporate everyone, neutral dates and neutral sites are being selected. The result is an invented tradition, a consciously created ritual that is modeled on ideas of past ritual practice and represents a contemporary cultural enactment of ideas about community solidarity (Hobsbawm and Ranger 1983; Ranger 1993). Like other activities to be discussed in this book, community-day celebrations represent the successful incorporation of new ideas and approaches into Yoruba cultural expressions that emphasize the significance and importance of the hometown (Trager 1993).

Successes and Failures

Any time a new tradition or ritual is invented, it raises the question of whether it will work—that is, will it accomplish the goals for which it was created, and will it become a meaningful set of practices for the people involved? (See, e.g., Hobsbawm and Ranger 1983.) In the case of community-day celebrations, there are really several different questions. In the first instance, have these events been successful in meeting the short-term and instrumental goals articulated by their organizers—do they indeed raise the expected funds? Second, have they met the more general objectives of bringing people home and creating or maintaining their connections at home? And third, will these celebrations become meaningful cultural practices for people in their communities over the long term?

It is clear that in some communities the immediate goals of fund-raising and bringing community members together have been met. The second Iloko Day in 1993 raised something on the order of N2 million, which was unusual, and due to the number of outsiders who attended and the size of their donations.[8] Other celebrations have raised much less yet are still viewed as successful by their organizers. And in those instances where the focus has been less on fund-raising and more on bringing people home to discuss community problems, organizers have again expressed satisfaction that they were able to accomplish their aims.

However, not everyone sees community-day celebrations as worthwhile events, and over the past several years there has been increasing skepticism as more and more communities seek to organize such celebrations and to raise money at them without necessarily identifying clear goals as to the use of that money. For example, some commented that such events are reasonable in a place like Iloko, where there is someone who can monitor the money that is contributed and make sure that it is put to good use.[9] In other communities, however, it is not clear what happens to the money. A man from Ilesa described going to a community-day celebration in another Ijesa town, where he contributed N5,000 and his friend, who chaired the occasion, contributed N25,000. But he asked, "What has happened to the money?" He said that they hadn't seen anything happen since that time in the town, and he assumes that the organizers themselves chopped the money to the detriment of the community. This is one of the reasons why there is such an emphasis on spending the funds on a specific project. When that is done, as in the case of the Iloko community hall, or the palaces in Ijebu-Jesa and Iwoye, then there is literally concrete evidence that the donated money has been put to good use.

With regard to the second question—whether these celebrations are bringing people home and helping to reinforce ties among community members—there is evidence that this is indeed occurring in some communities. Organizers of the community-day celebrations in Iwoye, Iloko, and Ijebu-Jesa all expressed satisfaction that these events have helped create a situation in which community members living outside have come home and participated, alongside those who live in the community. Several emphasized the importance of having discussions about the problems of the town, as we have seen above. However, the question must be asked of who actually attends and participates. In other words, which community members are involved in these events, and in what ways? In the first celebrations in Ijebu-Jesa and Iloko in 1991, 1992, and 1993, several distinct sets of people participated. Much of the attention was focused on those who came from outside, especially the high-status visitors who were not from the town and who were expected to make substantial donations (in the case of Iloko) or were given chieftaincy titles (Ijebu-Jesa). The second set consisted of community members who reside outside the community, primarily in Lagos and Ibadan. Elites and professionals who were able to travel home from Lagos and other cities are especially important in organizing and carrying out community-day celebrations. A third set included the *obas* and chiefs, both visiting *obas* from other towns and chiefs from the town itself. And finally, townspeople formed a fourth set, organized in their associations and clubs, who were seated together and who, at Ijebu-Jesa Day, paraded around the field to greet the *obas* and chiefs. The seating arrangement, similar at each of these events, made clear the status of these distinct sets of people, with the large, upholstered chairs reserved for visiting dignitaries, plastic chairs for other visitors, and metal chairs on the sides for local chiefs and town associations.

The language used at these events also suggests that they were oriented primarily to those who came from outside, including both elite community members and guests from elsewhere. Nearly all speeches were made in English, and although there were translations into Yoruba given by the masters of ceremonies, there was clearly an assumption that English was the appropriate language to use.

The situation was very different, however, at the third Iloko Day in 1995. There, all the speeches were in Yoruba, even though several were given by the same individuals who had participated in the previous Iloko Days. The participants were also different: no dignitaries from outside the town were invited. Instead, the focus was on community members, including those elites who were residing outside as well as those living in the town itself. The seating arrangement was different as well, with chairs arranged from front to back inside the community hall. This was a "home-grown affair," as one participant described it.

Discussions with town residents in the three towns of Iloko, Ijebu-Jesa, and Iwoye as well as with those residing outside suggest that many both inside and outside the towns have come to see community-day celebrations as important and worthy of participation. For example, market women in Iloko reported that they had attended Iloko Day in 1993 and had made contributions as members of social clubs to which they belong. As we shall see in Chapter 8, many people in each of the three towns state that they had contributed to or participated in community-day celebrations. An Ijebu-Jesa woman who resides in Ile-Ife said that she had attended the first Ijebu-Jesa Day as a member of her women's organization, the Egburo Ladies Social

Club, most of whose members live in Ibadan. The organization includes women who are from Ijebu-Jesa, as well as women married to men from the town. Each organization was asked to make a donation for Ijebu-Jesa Day, and each member of her club contributed N50. They also wore *aso ebi* (dresses made from the same cloth) for the occasion. For her, Ijebu-Jesa Day was just one event among many for which she returns home. She goes there regularly, about twice a month, both for special occasions like weddings and funerals, as well as for visits. Her mother's senior brother, as well as her own brother, live there, so she goes to visit them. But she says that even if they weren't there, she would still go, that she enjoys being there, and is "homesick" if she stays away too long. This woman emphasized the importance of continuing to be involved in Ijebu-Jesa. She said that "you know where you come from," and she added that her children also like to go there and do so even if she doesn't, indicating that in this case, at least, the younger generation is continuing to be involved in networks at home.

There are also individuals for whom community-day celebrations have created a tie that previously did not exist. The wife of the chairman of the Iloko Day celebrations described one woman whose parents were from Iloko, but she had been born in Lagos and had never been to Iloko. Her parents had died. She heard about Iloko Day and decided to come. No one there knew her. But when she came and introduced herself, others introduced themselves to her, including relatives that she had not previously known. According to the chairman's wife, the woman was very excited. In her view, someone like this had lost her identity, and Iloko Day had helped to re-create these connections and restore identities.

In contrast, not all such events have been effective in drawing community members. Several attempts to organize either an Ilesa Day or an Ijesa National Day in the city of Ilesa have been relatively unsuccessful. These efforts are discussed in greater detail in Chapter 6.

This leads to consideration of the third question raised above: Are community-day celebrations meaningful to those involved, and will they over time become incorporated into the cultural landscape of Ijesaland? To the extent that this question can be answered at all, a relatively short time after these events first began, it seems obvious that the evidence is mixed. In some communities, such as Iloko, several community-day celebrations have taken place, people have participated, money has been raised, and for some, at least, it has helped to renew and even create ties with the community. In other communities, such as Ilesa, there has not yet been a successful celebration, and it is unlikely that there will continue to be Ijesa National Days, or that such days have much meaning for those who do participate.

In innovating community-day celebrations, as in other invented traditions, there is an intention to both inculcate certain values and norms of behavior, as well as to imply continuity with the past (Hobsbawm 1983). Whether these celebrations will successfully become "tradition" remains to be seen. But there is no doubt that the organizers seek to establish such a new tradition. As the *oba* of Ijebu-Jesa said in his speech at the first Ijebu-Day celebration:

> To you my loving people, I say welcome to home to this occasion. I must express my appreciation to you for making this day, when we remember our dear homeland and its ancestors, a reality and I am confident that by the Grace of Almighty God, what we have started today will continue to be celebrated year in year out with equal vigor and enthusiasm as we see today. (Kabiyesi Ajayi Palmer Ajifolokun II, Oba of Ijebu-Jesa, 1991)

As part of the process of incorporating these events into "tradition," they also continue to change. For example, the time of year for the Iloko celebration has changed, and local leaders are considering having it coincide with one of the older traditional festivals.

By focusing on community-day celebrations, this chapter has introduced some of the issues involved as people in the Ijesa region seek to both maintain and reinforce identities while carrying out instrumental goals in assisting their home communities. In Chapter 3, the question of identity will be examined further, as we consider in greater detail the specific communities being studied, the importance of hometown linkages both historically and in the present time, and the ways in which multiple locales have become important for Ijesa identity and interaction.

Notes

1. The Iloko anthem was introduced for the first time at the first Iloko Day in 1992; the text here is taken from the program for the 1993 Iloko Day. The words and music are by Sayo Dada, assisted by Abiodun Omojola. The music is more similar to that of church hymns than to traditional Yoruba songs. The song was translated by my research assistants, Bodunde Motoni and Folorunso Kolade.

2. Long quotations from speeches are based on transcriptions from videotapes recorded at the event, and on notes; most of the speeches were in English.

3. During the period under discussion, the exchange rate changed frequently, with rapid devaluation of the Nigerian currency, the naira. For part of this period there were also both official and unofficial (black market) rates; later, the official exchange rate essentially became equal to the black market rate. It is therefore very difficult to provide dollar equivalents that will be accurate for specific dates.

By May–June 1992, the exchange rate was about N20 = U.S.$1; in other words, the development fund established for Iloko aimed at raising about U.S.$500,000. By December 1993, the black market rate was about N40 = U.S.$1. Later, in 1994–95, the rate went down further, to N100 = U.S.$1 and then stabilized at around N80 = U.S.$1. Donations of, for example, N100,000 at a community day in 1992 were worth about $5,000. The same donation in 1995 was worth about $1,250. See Chapter 7 for discussion of the economic context of changing exchange rates.

4. Ile-Ife is the official name for the city about twenty miles west of Ilesa, but it is most often referred to simply by the shortened version of the name, Ife.

5. The June 12 palaver refers to the aftermath of the June 12, 1993, annulment of the presidential elections in Nigeria (see Chapter 9). The comment about petrol refers to the fact that the prices of fuel had gone up considerably and to the fact that there were recurring shortages of fuel, making travel increasingly expensive and difficult. (However, there were also fuel shortages at the times of the celebrations in 1992 and 1993, and that didn't prevent them from taking place.)

6. These quotations are translated from the Yoruba speech, which was video-taped.

7. There is no evidence that he was referring to a Yoruba proverb here; he was speaking in English.

8. Although I noted donations as they were announced, it is not possible to determine the actual amount of all donations. Some people donated privately to the organizers, whereas others presented checks that later bounced. The totals given here are based on interviews with the organizers.

9. Prince Olashore was not only minister of finance for a time; he is a leading banker, the head of a merchant bank in Lagos, and seen as someone who will be sure that money is well handled and well spent.

3

Knowing Your Place:
The Hometown and Identity

Odo ki i san ko gbagbe isun
[A river does not flow so far that it forgets its source].

The proverb quoted here is one of many Yoruba proverbs that emphasize the importance of remembering one's origins. As Oyekan Owomoyela explains, the proverb means that "the flowing river always remains connected with its source, however far it might flow; otherwise it dies." According to him, the proverb is used "to remind people that wherever they might be, however distant from their homes, and however high they might rise above their origins, they must always remember where they came from" (Owomoyela 1988: 268). For the Yoruba, the home place, or hometown, is a significant and continuing source of a person's identity throughout life. Individuals act with that sense of identity in mind, and they are likewise reminded by others that there are expectations and obligations based on that identity. However, a sense of origins, of place, is not quite so simple as it might first appear. On the one hand, the hometown can be simply defined as the place where one's father's lineage is from. On the other hand, it turns out that there is considerable flexibility and choice involved in maintaining connections with one's place of origins; there is choice about which place (or places) is considered to be the hometown, and there is also contextual and situational flexibility, with various types of places providing identity in different contexts.

This chapter will explore the concepts of hometown and identity within the Ijesa context, considering their continuing importance as well as the ways in which they are changing. The first section describes the five Ijesa communities on which the research focused as well as the regional context in which those communities are located. Each of these communities is a "hometown" for a considerable number of people, including many of those

37

currently living there and others who live elsewhere. At the same time, there are also contexts in which people operate not in terms of a specific hometown but in terms of a regional identity. The second section discusses the various ways in which Ijesa people identify with a place, or places of origin, demonstrating the considerable complexity that exists with regard to the admonition that one must always remember one's origins.

The Ijesa Region

East of Ife and southeast of Oshogbo, the land becomes increasingly hilly and forested. The area known as Ijesaland begins a few miles east of Ife and south of Oshogbo; much of the southern part of the region, heading toward Ondo, was at one time mainly forest. It became an area for cocoa and kola-nut production, and much of the forest has disappeared in recent years. To the north, the vegetation is increasingly that of the savanna, and the major crops are yams, cassava, maize, and a variety of other locally consumed commodities. In eastern Ijesaland, rice has become an important crop in recent years. Major roads have long linked Ilesa, the major Ijesa city, with other major cities in the area, including Ife, Oshogbo, and Akure; no road goes directly from Ilesa to Ondo to the south. (See Maps 3.1 and 3.2.)

The area called Ijesaland is located in eastern Yorubaland, within southwestern Nigeria, in what is now Osun State. The people living in this region are called Ijesa; they are one of several Yoruba-speaking groups and are commonly recognized by both themselves and others as having a degree of cultural and linguistic unity and distinctiveness from other Yoruba. As we shall see below, the extent to which a person considers himself or herself Ijesa as opposed to Yoruba, Nigerian, or other identifiers is highly variable and contextual.

The Ijesa area can be considered a region in the sense that it is a recognized territory, which in the past had political and economic dimensions and today continues to have significant cultural and linguistic dimensions. The region extends in a radius of approximately twenty miles from the city of Ilesa, the political and economic center. The Owa Obokun of Ijesaland is the traditional ruler (*oba*, or "king") of the city of Ilesa as well as the surrounding area; the extent to which he is, or was, paramount over other Ijesa communities is the source of continuing disputes. Some Ijesa communities are considered to have been independent of Ilesa historically, whereas others were founded by people from Ilesa (Oni n.d.); today, many Ijesa communities have their own *obas* and prefer to view themselves as independent of Ilesa. This is especially the case with towns in the northern part of Ijesaland, many of which claim histories showing that they were founded

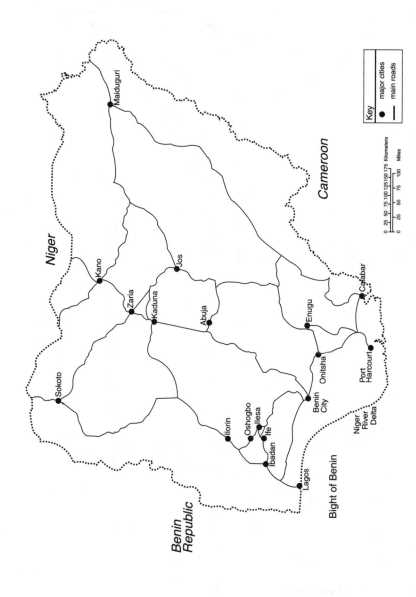

Map 3.1 Nigeria

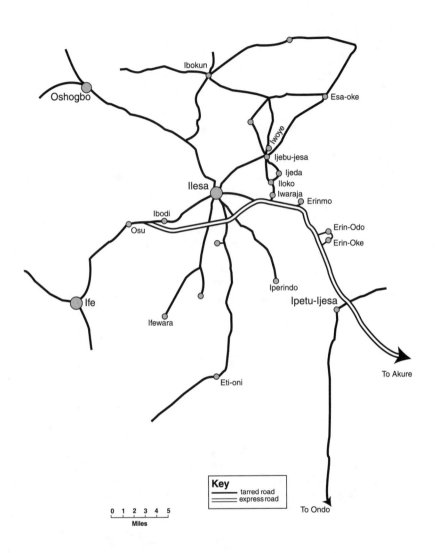

Map 3.2   The Ijesa Region

directly from Ile-Ife; southern Ijesa communities are more likely to recognize close ties with Ilesa. However, the Owa Obokun continues to play an important symbolic role in the region and is generally recognized as one of the major *obas* in Yorubaland.

Today, Ijesaland is located within Osun State, a political entity that was created by the Nigerian government in 1991; prior to that time, it was part of Oyo State. There are now six local government areas within Ijesaland; however, during the time of most of the research, there were four (Ilesa, Oriade, Ibokun, and Atakumosa).[1] The local government areas (LGAs) are the smallest official jurisdictions in Nigeria; in most cases, the LGA comprises several separate smaller communities, although cities usually make up a single LGA, and large cities may have several LGAs within them. There is continual pressure throughout Nigeria from local groups for the formation of new LGAs and states, as these are seen as key bases for resources. For example, in 1995 people in the Ijesa and Ife areas petitioned for a new state, and one hears public remarks that Ijesaland should have a state of its own.

Economically, the Ijesa area has also had a degree of unity, with a road network and system of marketplaces that enable distribution both within the region as well as to and from the region (see Trager 1976, 1976–1977, 1979, 1981). Predominantly agricultural, the northern part of the region supplied yams and other food crops, whereas the southern part became important in the production of cocoa and kola nuts. The city of Ilesa, as well as some of the other larger towns such as Ijebu-Jesa, had many people engaged in trade and commerce, and by the early twentieth century Ijesa people had become known throughout much of Nigeria for their commercial activities (see Peel 1983).

In the latter half of the twentieth century, many Ijesas migrated to other parts of the country for education and professional opportunities; economic ties now extend not only throughout the country but also abroad. Many of those who today are central to the maintenance of hometown ties in Ijesaland are those who have participated in such migration; and in many cases, their parents and other relatives were also migrants—traders and low-level civil servants during the colonial period. Chapter 4 discusses Ijesa migration at greater length.

The Ijesa region also has linguistic and cultural dimensions. The Ijesa dialect is a recognized variant of Yoruba, one that is not spoken or well understood by those who speak standard Yoruba or other dialectical variants. Ijesas themselves may choose to speak Ijesa or standard Yoruba (or English), depending on the context—who they are speaking to and where. Older people, and those without formal education, mainly speak Ijesa.

The extent to which people see themselves as culturally the same— Ijesa, rather than Yoruba—is also highly variable and contextual. Arguments are made to the effect that "we are all Ijesa" and therefore should act together, but it is also the case that many people see themselves not as Ijesa but as members of specific communities. At the same time, Ijesa do see themselves as having cultural characteristics that distinguish them from other Yoruba groups, such as the Ijebu, Egba, and Ibadan Yorubas. Disputes within the former Oyo State focused on the extent to which Ijesa dominated high positions within state government; now, in Osun State, Ijesa claim that they are being discriminated against by those from other (i.e., Yoruba) ethnic groups. In their personal lives, too, the extent to which Ijesa choose to emphasize their Ijesa identity also varies. Two distinguished Lagos-based lawyers once argued in a discussion with me about the merits of encouraging their children to marry other Ijesa. One, whose daughter was about to marry, said that he would prefer it if she had chosen a man who was Ijesa; because she had not, the wedding would take place in Lagos rather than Ilesa, "as a protest." The other argued that he is more "liberal" in such matters and that his children could select whomever they want to marry.

Whereas the official governing units—states and LGAs—have clearly specified boundaries, the boundaries of the Ijesa region are fuzzy, with claims and counterclaims over whether a community is Ijesa or not. This is particularly the case with some communities on the borders of Ijesaland and neighboring areas such as Ife, Oshogbo, and Ondo. In the past, there have been boundary disputes, especially in the southern Ijesa area. The symbolic value and meaning of being Ijesa, and of being from Ijesaland, is much greater than being from a specific LGA or from Osun State. The latter entities have changed frequently with the agendas of varying governments as new governing units are carved out. People have little sense of identity with these official units, although there are some circumstances in which state- and local-government identities have begun to form, as we shall discuss below. But even though an individual may choose whether or not to emphasize his or her Ijesa identity, there is never doubt as to the existence of that identity. As a woman explained in a discussion about her son, who has grown up in Ibadan, on the grounds of the school where his father teaches, he "would never call himself an Ibadan man"; according to her, he knows that he is Ijesa.

Five Ijesa Communities

The Ijesa area includes a large number of separate communities, ranging in size from the city of Ilesa to small villages and farm hamlets (see Map 3.2). Ilesa is the political, economic, and geographical center of the region and by far the largest settlement in terms of population and territory. Among the other settlements, several are considered to be historically important, such as Ibokun, Ijebu-Jesa, Ipetu-Ijesa, and Osu (Oni n.d.); these also tend to be the largest population centers outside Ilesa. Other communities began largely as farm hamlets, places where people spent part of their time while working on their farms before returning to their home compounds in Ilesa. However, such settlements have now become small towns and villages, with a full-time resident population of people who consider those settlements to be their hometowns. Each Ijesa settlement has its own history, some of which have been published (e.g., Oni n.d. provides brief accounts of the founding of twelve Ijesa towns; Ogunjulugbe 1993 is an account of the town of Ipetu-Ijesa). Others have been compiled in connection with local celebrations, and still other communities have not yet produced such documents. In all cases, there are disputes about the histories; as Peel (1983) has shown, much of the production of history in Ijesaland is in fact more about the present than the past.

Census data for Ijesa communities, as for the rest of Nigeria, are poor. The provisional results of the 1991 census that have been published provide data only at the level of local government areas and not for specific communities; furthermore, the results have been questioned by those residing in the area, as they are significantly below what was expected. The provisional results show Ilesa with a population of 138,321, Atakumosa with 99,263, Obokun with 61,099, and Oriade with 80,242, for a total population of 378,925 (Federal Republic of Nigeria 1992).

In carrying out the research for this study, I decided to focus on five communities. Initially, four communities were selected: the city of Ilesa; two medium-sized towns, Osu in the southern Ijesa area and Ijebu-Jesa in the north; and one small town, Iwoye. Soon after the research began, my attention was drawn to activities in another small town, Iloko, and I decided to include that as well. Both Iwoye and Iloko are near Ijebu-Jesa. Osu is located in Atakumosa local government area, while Ijebu-Jesa, Iloko, and Iwoye are in Oriade local government area. Although no community in Obokun local government area was selected for intense study, I did later spend some time in one village in that area.

Ilesa

Approaching Ilesa from Ile-Ife to the west, the old road into the city meanders through the village of Ibodi and past the Osun State College of Education, then enters the city in the area where there were formerly a few government offices during the colonial and the first part of the postindependence periods. The police station and prison are at this end of the city, as well as the area known as the Government Reservation Area (GRA), a residential area that has become home for many Ilesa people who mainly live and work in other parts of Nigeria. As the road gets closer to the center of the city, the number of commercial enterprises—mainly small shops—increases, as does the congestion, especially around the petrol stations and motor park. Just before the central roundabout, a road to the right leads to Wesley Guild Hospital, famous as a Methodist missionary hospital that pioneered work with children and now part of the Obafemi Awolowo University Teaching Hospital (see Map 3.3).

The roundabout provides the central point in the city, with roads leading from it to all major sections; it is adjacent to the *oba*'s palace, the large marketplace, and the mosque, as well as several banks and commercial enterprises. A large sign over one road announces the entrance to the palace grounds, beyond which are located the town hall, post office, and marketplace. The market, with stalls for more than 1,000 traders, is an urban retail and wholesale market, providing Ilesa residents with both food and other basic commodities, as well as functioning as a distribution point for goods such as kola nuts distributed to other parts of the country (Trager 1976, 1976–1977, 1985a, 1985b, 1987). Several of the oldest quarters of the city are located adjacent to the roundabout: Ijoka; Adeti, which was once the center for cloth trade in the city; and Ifofin, where the Catholic church is located. Continuing straight past the roundabout, the road goes past still more small shops, beyond the turnoff to the general hospital, and out to the quarters of Isokun and Ikoti, major residential areas. Old compounds and newer bungalows and two-story houses mix with small shops where women sell provisions, food, and other goods. Eventually, the road deteriorates as it gets to the petrol stations and what were formerly the headquarters of several trading companies, such as GB Ollivant, and then continues past large, two-story houses and beyond toward several villages and Oshogbo.[2]

To the right at the roundabout, the road leads to another old section of the city, Okesa, as well as to the junction that goes to Ijoka and Egbe Idi, quarters with many old compounds. The Methodist church is located in Ijoka, and beyond that quarter the road goes out to Ijebu-Jesa. The Okesa area is lined with shops, including bookstores selling stationery and schoolbooks, hardware, and other items not found in the marketplace. Past Okesa are located several key establishments: the Ilesa Grammar School, the oldest secondary school in the city; the headquarters for Lawrence Omole and Sons, one of the biggest cocoa distributors and transporters, as well as the grounds of the very large house and compound belonging to Lawrence Omole, an important local businessman; and a modern bank building. Beyond these are several more schools and an agricultural project. At one time, the city essentially ended at this point.

However, since the establishment of International Breweries Limited (IBL) in 1978 at the far end of the town, in the area known as Imo, there has been extensive development of the city in this direction. More houses, a

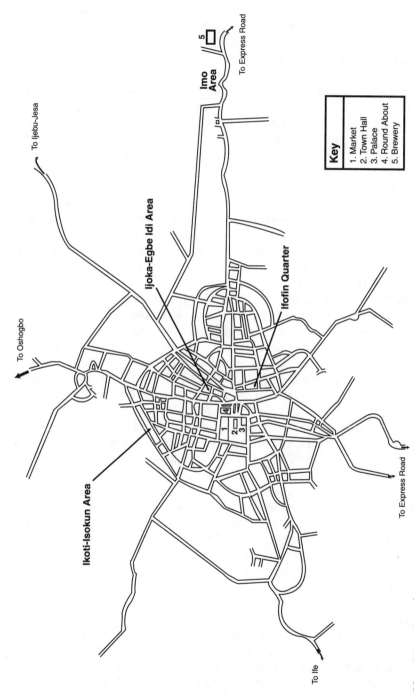

To Ijebu-Jesa

To Oshogbo

Ijoka-Egbe Idi Area

Ikoti-Isokun Area

Ifofin Quarter

Imo Area

5

To Express Road

To Express Road

To Ife

Key

1. Market
2. Town Hall
3. Palace
4. Round About
5. Brewery

Map 3.3   Ilesa (map not to scale)

marketplace, a private medical center, and several other small industries have made this into the area of Ilesa that has seen the greatest growth in recent years. Many houses have been built here as well as on a road running parallel to Okesa (Trager 1985a). The brewery affected commercial development in the city as well, with women who were formerly trading in the marketplace switching to the more lucrative trade of beer distribution (Trager 1985b), and is frequently cited as evidence of successful local development. And on Imo Hill, the dominant feature on the landscape behind the brewery, a commercial farm has been established. Just beyond the brewery, the road joins what is now the main road from Ife to Akure and beyond—the "Express," which bypasses Ilesa (see Maps 3.2 and 3.3; Y. Odeyemi 1999: 61–65).

Ilesa is the major urban center of the Ijesa region. Like other Yoruba cities, it has its own specific history and characteristics, as well as the more general characteristics common to Yoruba towns (Krapf-Askari 1969; Bascom 1955, 1959). Its origin myth relates the story of migration from Ile-Ife, through what are today several smaller Ijesa towns to what has become Ilesa (Oni n.d.). According to local histories, the sixth Owa Obokun of Ijesaland began a continuous line of succession at Ilesa (Oni n.d.: 30); there is a complex hierarchy of chiefs who were involved in the precolonial administration of the territory. Like residents of other Yoruba cities, the population of Ilesa was primarily involved in agricultural activities, going to farms outside the city on a daily or weekly basis. A system of periodic markets for farm produce developed, and by the late nineteenth century and early twentieth century commerce had become increasingly important.

By the 1930s, several key Ilesa individuals had developed significant commercial activities, both as *osomaalo* (traders located in other Nigerian communities) and in cocoa buying and selling, as well as in transport. Although it lost out when colonial authorities decided to locate the railroad in Oshogbo, the city became a dynamic commercial center, with many of its leading figures becoming wealthy in the cocoa and transport sectors.

Ilesa also became a regional educational center; the first secondary school, Ilesa Grammar School, was founded in 1934 by the Egbe Atunluse Ile Ijesa (Ijesa Improvement Society), an organization of educated Ijesa (Ifaturoti and Orolugbagbe 1992: 29–39; see also Chapter 5). Other schools, including those founded by missionary organizations, followed, and by the 1990s there were eighteen secondary schools in Ilesa (Orolugbagbe 1997: 37).

Ilesa today continues to be primarily a commercial and trading center, dominated by a wide range of small-scale, informal-sector occupations. Other than the brewery, there has been little successful industrial development. As described above, there has been visible growth in several residential sections of the city. This growth does not seem to be reflected in population figures: According to the 1963 census, the population was 165,822; the 1991 census gives the figure for the Ilesa LGA (essentially the city) as 138,321. Other attempts to estimate the population give much larger figures. One person who has studied the Ijesa area suggests that the current population is about 500,000 (O. Onabajo, personal communication). In effect, no one knows the actual population of Ilesa. Expansion in residential areas partly results from construction of houses outside the old compounds, in many cases by people whose primary residence is elsewhere. But most such houses do have at least some occupants (tenants, relatives, etc.); relatively few are completely closed up.

Osu and Ijebu-Jesa

Osu and Ijebu-Jesa can be considered medium-sized towns in the Yoruba context (Trager 1979). With population sizes ranging from 5,000 to 15,000,[3] they have long functioned as market centers for their surrounding regions and, in recent years, have become political centers as well, with their designation as LGA headquarters. The two towns have very different histories, however.

The road from Ife winds through several villages and around many hills before descending into Osu, located nearly equidistant between Ife and Ilesa. The town spreads along the road for about a mile, with several separate quarters, reflecting several different periods of settlement (Oni n.d.: 33–35). At the center of town, where these quarters meet, lie the marketplace, the palace, the post office, and a new town hall; on the outskirts are located the secondary school and the local-government offices. The town center is also the location for numerous roadside vendors selling *akara Osu* to travelers—fried bean cakes for which the town has become famous.

Osu is primarily agricultural; kola nuts and cocoa are among the commodities produced on its farms. Its periodic market, which meets every four days, is an important one in the region (Trager 1976, 1979) and is a source for kola nuts which are bought by traders from Ilesa and elsewhere.

According to local historians, Osu was founded by people from Ilesa. As J. O. Oni (n.d.: 35) puts it, "The Oshu people are mostly citizens of Ilesha and to them Oshu is like a country home. Many Oshu people have their homes in Ilesha and they simply come here to farm and little by little they start to settle down permanently."

Politically, Osu is considered to be closely tied to Ilesa, with its head chief using the title *loja* and considered to be "the son" of the Owa Obokun and eligible to become *owa*. In recent years, as in other Ijesa towns, this history has been debated by some, and some residents have begun to emphasize their ties to Osu rather than their connections to Ilesa. This has implications for our discussion below of identity and hometown connections.

Unlike Osu, Ijebu-Jesa's history emphasizes its relative independence from Ilesa, with an origin story that asserts that the founder of Ijebu-Jesa was the senior brother to the Owa Obokun. According to local history, "Ijebu-Jesha is closely linked with Ilesha and traditionally, Ijebu-Jesha is the next in rank to Ilesa" (Oni n.d.: 21). Oni also explains that there is a close relationship between the Owa Obokun and the *oba* of Ijebu-Jesa.

The center of Ijebu-Jesa is dominated by the mosque on one side and the marketplace on the other; before the road was widened in the early 1970s a large iroko tree stood at the junction next to the marketplace. The main road is crossed by a road that leads to Iwoye in one direction and Iloko and Ijeda in the other; another road goes to the hospital and then to the village of Ere. On the outskirts at one end of town is the large compound of the Ijebu-Jesa Grammar School, as well as several two-story houses and commercial establishments; at the other end, beyond the settled portion of the town, is the large, fenced-in farm belonging to a local resident who retired home in order to go into full-time agriculture.

The community bank (described in Chapter 8) is also visible along the main road into town, while the town hall, the *oba*'s palace (under construction during most of the research), and major churches are located on side roads.

Ijebu-Jesa is both a commercial and agricultural center. Its periodic market, meeting every other day, is important in the distribution of local agricultural products such as yams, and there are several small shops selling provisions and other basic goods on a daily basis (Trager 1979). In recent years, there has been increasing emphasis on the independence of Ijebu-Jesa from Ilesa, and with the installation of the present *oba* of the town in 1997 there have also been efforts to use a new title for the *oba*. There is also greater emphasis on local identity for those from Ijebu-Jesa; this has consequences for efforts at local development (see Chapters 8 and 9).

Iwoye-Ijesa and Iloko-Ijesa

The smallest of the communities considered in this book are Iwoye and Iloko, both located near Ijebu-Jesa. Ijebu-Jesa and Iwoye are just a few kilometers apart, and houses are stretched along the road joining the two communities. A sign announcing the entrance to Iwoye and a stream are the only visible markers of a boundary. Historically, too, the two communities are closely connected, with Iwoye having been founded from Ijebu-Jesa (Oni n.d.: 23).

Iwoye has just one main road. The center of the town is marked by a small periodic market where a few women sell farm products. To the right of the market is the old palace, which has disintegrated, and behind that, but not visible from the road, is the newly constructed palace. Past the palace, land has been cleared for construction of a community health center. In front of the old palace is the building where the Iwoye Community Bank was established in 1995; the bank and other recent development efforts are considered at greater length in Chapter 8.

Iloko can be approached either from Ijebu-Jesa or from the Express Road out of Ilesa, traveling first through Iwaraja, another small town. Just behind the town lies a large hill, the dominant feature of the landscape and visible from all parts of the village. Two roads cross at the junction in the center of town; in one direction is the palace, with its decorated walls and large gate. Across the street is the old periodic marketplace, where a few women sell some provisions and local produce, and a few shops. Farther down the road is the primary school and the Methodist church. In the other direction, the road leads past a community health center and a few houses, then goes to the nearby town of Ijeda.

The past few years have seen several major construction projects along the road leading from Iloko to Ijebu-Jesa: the establishment of Olashore International School, a private boarding school; the building of the private house of Oladele Olashore, the founder of the school; a community hall; and, most recently, clearing of land for a large new marketplace. All of these activities are described in more detail in subsequent chapters.

As part of the ceremonies celebrating the coronation of Oladele Olashore as *oba* of Iloko in 1997, a history of the community was published. This history emphasizes the independent origins of Iloko as well as giving the historical basis for the title of the *oba*, Ajagbusi Ekun, Aloko of Iloko. According to this history, Iloko was founded in A.D. 1113 "by Ajagbusi-Ekun a prince of Ile-Ife who was widely known for his great success in warfare" and who traveled from Ife to several other places before settling near the stream located just outside Iloko (Coronation Program, pp. 11–12). As is the case with the histories of Ijesa communities in general, this history is disputed by some, especially people from Ilesa, who argue for a closer connection of Iloko with Ilesa.

The Concept of the Hometown: Ideas and Practice

For Ijesa, as for Yoruba in general, a crucial concept that informs behavior and motivates action is the concept of *ilu*, translated in English as "hometown." The hometown is the place where one has kinship connections, usually the place where one's father's lineage is from. It is, however, more

The new Methodist church in Iloko

than the place of origin; it provides a source of social identity and a web of social connections, which influence actions regardless of where a person is residing. In general, Ijesa feel that people with origins there who live elsewhere "should associate themselves with the town, build houses and spend money there, and above all give it effective leadership in the competition of communities for the resources of the state" (Peel 1983: 260; Trager 1992, 1993).

Any settlement, of any size—city, town, village—may be considered an *ilu*. Although the phrase *ancestral city* has been used to refer to the places that Yoruba peoples consider to be their place of origin, the more commonly used term is *hometown* (see Laitin 1986; Barber 1991; Barkan, McNulty, and Ayeni 1991). Although some might argue that Ilesa is the ancestral city for all Ijesa, the reality is that most Ijesas point to a specific community where their kinship ties are strong. For many, this is indeed the city of Ilesa; but for many others, it is Ijebu-Jesa, or Osu, or one of the many other Ijesa settlements. Furthermore, each individual may have more than one hometown; some people have two, or even more, places to which they have hometown ties.

The hometown is *not* the same as birthplace, and there is no assumption that an individual has actually lived for all or most of his life in his hometown; some people have spent few or no years of their lives in their hometowns, yet they still consider themselves to have important connections there. At the same time, there are also people who have dropped the connections with one place while reinforcing ties with another; during the course of my research, I have been told of people who are "really" Ijesa (from Ilesa or another Ijesa town) but who have not been to Ilesa in years and no longer know anyone there. These individuals are said to now consider some other place, such as Ibadan or Abeokuta, to be their hometown.

Although some people may have dropped their affiliation with a particular hometown, the vast majority of people retain some sort of tie and do something to indicate their connection and affiliation with the hometown. However, as Dan Aronson (1978) demonstrated some years ago in his study of Ijebu Yoruba migrants in Ibadan, the extent and type of connection varies with individual circumstances. Age, gender, and economic success all play a role in the type of connection maintained. In general, men, older people, and those who are successful are considered to have the greatest obligation to their hometowns. But the maintenance of hometown connections is not by any means limited to men, to older people, or to the economically successful. Many women also retain some type of connection, often to both their own and their husband's communities, and successful women are likely to have multiple ties, involving regular visits, monetary contributions, and taking of chieftaincy titles (Trager 1995a, 1995b). At a minimum, nearly everyone retains enough of a tie so that they are acquainted with kin at home; most plan to be buried at home; and they want their children to be aware of their hometown.

There are two basic types of connections maintained with the hometown. On the one hand, there are family and kin connections. These involve visiting home on a regular basis and giving assistance to family members at home, through monetary remittances and in other ways. For those who are well-off economically, it also usually means building a house at home. The obligation to build a house is strong, and even those who state that they have no intention to ever live in the hometown again, and who have little interest in the community's affairs, still feel that they should build a house at home. If parents are alive, the pressure often comes from them to do so. Increasingly, however, the houses that are built are not located in the family compound but rather on the outskirts of the town, on land that is acquired specifically for that purpose. In Ilesa, for example, many houses have been built in areas on the outskirts that were formerly farms; in many cases, the owners are not living in those houses but visit on weekends or holidays. In some cases, the owners have retired to Ilesa and now live in the houses that they built when living and working in Lagos or other large cities. Family and kin connections are discussed at greater length in Chapter 4, as part of the discussion of migration in Ijesaland.

The second type of connection is with the hometown or community itself. Again, there are several ways in which this type of tie is expressed.

These include joining hometown organizations; contributing to community fund-raising activities; and becoming involved in solving community problems. These are the focus of Chapters 5 and 6.

The Hometown as a Source of Identity

For the vast majority of Ijesas, one's hometown is an important—perhaps the most important—aspect of one's identity. It is not simply a place to which a person maintains ties for instrumental reasons, to come to when there are problems elsewhere or to flaunt success. Neither, however, is it simply a primordial identity, fixed and unchanging. Rather, hometown identity is a complex construct that encompasses flexibility and choice and that, although based on ideas about one's "roots," responds to contemporary social, political, and economic contexts. Nor is it the only significant basis for an individual's identity and actions.

The hometown has long been a source of social and cultural identity among Yoruba. As Karin Barber has pointed out in her study of *oriki* (praise poems) in northern Yorubaland, social identity "through membership of a common town of origin" was probably particularly important in precolonial Yorubaland (1991: 149). However, her study also demonstrates the complexity of Yoruba notions of place of origin. According to her, "every present-day town, in the northern and central Yoruba areas, is made up of numerous *ile*—'lineages' or 'compounds'—which ... identify themselves in terms of an origin *outside* the town they live in.... When it comes to origin they disown the town they live in and appeal to a distant and often no longer existent place" (1994: 13). As she points out, there is evidence of considerable population movement in Yorubaland even prior to the nineteenth-century Yoruba wars. That movement has continued, although for different reasons, up to the present. Barber argues that although the attachment to the "actual" hometown (birthplace of father, grandfather, etc.) is no doubt very strong, the continuation of a sense of place linked to other places, through the *oriki orile* (praise poem of the lineage), emphasizes the importance of alternatives. She argues that "the determination to preserve alternatives—whether they are taken up or not—is the key to identity and to political and social action in general in western Nigeria" (1994: 13).

The notion of *choice*, of alternatives, is fundamental to understanding the importance of hometown for contemporary Yorubas. The mobility of Yorubas in both the past and present has meant that there is considerable flexibility in what place a person chooses as his or her place of origin. One can find among people with similar biographies variation in the place with which they identify. For example, two brothers with claims to several Ijesa towns each emphasize a different place as "home"; more dramatically, one man whose father was a successful businessman in Ibadan may now consider himself an "Ibadan man" while another has chosen to emphasize his Ijesa connections. A woman may be more involved in her husband's hometown than in her own, but in some specific situations she may renew her ties at home, building her own house there or in other ways participating in activities there. Despite this flexibility, having a hometown with which one identifies continues to be viewed as highly significant. In ordinary conversation, Yorubas can easily identify where they and others are "from" and assume a variety of implications of that identity.

At a minimum, most people believe that the maintenance of some sort of identity with their hometown is necessary, so that when they die, people at home will know who they are and they will be able to be buried there. In surveys, everyone questioned can state where their hometown is and will refer to only one hometown (see Chapter 4). However, in more informal conversations, many people will point out that they have connections in several places; a man may say that while his father is from Iloko his mother is from Ijebu-Jesa. The strength of identity and connections may change among these locales during a person's lifetime. For example, according to Oladele Olashore, his father had not lived in Iloko until he was brought home from northern Nigeria to become *oba*. Olashore himself built his house in Ijebu-Jesa, his mother's hometown, and only much later did he build a house in Iloko and become increasingly identified with that town, leading up to the time in 1997 when he became the *oba* (see Chapter 6).

Yet his brother has his house in Ijebu-Jesa and sees this as his hometown. According to his brother, Prince 'Tunde Olashore, a lawyer who works in Ibadan, his attitude toward his hometown has changed in recent years. Twenty years ago, he said, he would not have thought of building a good house in Ijebu-Jesa; he was living comfortably in Ibadan. But then he became aware that "he wanted to identify with where he belongs." He said that in 1974 the area where his house is located was "virtually bush." But now, "people are putting up houses here, and identify themselves with this place." He added that his house in Ibadan isn't as good or as big as the one in Ijebu-Jesa.

According to 'Tunde Olashore, the awareness that one belongs to a particular place became more important in the 1970s, although in Ijebu-Jesa there has always been some involvement in developing the town. Even young men are building their first house there, before they build a house in their place of residence. At the same time, he pointed out that there are contrary examples, people who are not involved at all in their hometowns. He gave an example of a businessman in Lagos, who is also from Ijebu-Jesa. His father never brought him home, and he will say that he doesn't know the place. "If you meet him in Lagos, and he finds out that you're from Ijebu-Jesa, he will ask about it, and say that he is from there, but that he doesn't know the place." So, in the view of Prince Olashore, "the urge is there to know the home place, but since there are no connections, they never come home."

Two questions arise from the current emphasis on hometown identity—whether people now in middle age think that they will eventually come home to live, and whether their children, growing up outside the hometown, are developing as strong an identity. Both questions are problematic, and individual perspectives on them are highly varied. In the case of Prince 'Tunde Olashore, when asked whether he thinks he will ever live in Ijebu-Jesa, he responded that perhaps he will, in his old age. He said that if he weren't practicing law and could carry out his work from there (e.g., if he had a phone and fax there), he could be in Ijebu-Jesa. "It's more peaceful here," he said. As will be discussed in subsequent chapters, some people have retired home, or even come home to live before retirement, but many do not.

Similarly, variation occurs with regard to children's involvement in the hometown. When I asked Prince 'Tunde Olashore whether his children will have connections with their hometown as he does, he responded that in the past there was "a tendency for some to forget their home place. But the new instinct is to identify more with home." He said that his children know that they are from Ijebu-Jesa, and he asks them to come home with him. He hopes that they will have some attachment at home even if they're not as involved as he. He said that they are aware of his activities, so they might want to follow his example. He pointed out that he had his education elsewhere, and lived elsewhere most of the time he was growing up, yet he's still involved at home. He said that it depends a lot on the individuals. Some don't bring their children home at all, and they lose touch. Those who come home only occasionally have to be reminded of where they are from.

At times, the example of one individual can influence the identity and actions of others. In the case of the *oba* of another small Ijesa town, Iwara, the man who became *oba* there wasn't born there, and his father had left the town as a young man. He was living in Lagos when people found out about him, and he got interested in the community and in becoming *oba*. He built a big mansion there. Then they asked him to become *oba*, and now he's rebuilding the palace. This has affected others from the town: they now want to identify as being from Iwara, rather than from Ilesa.

Another source of variability is whether an individual identifies with a specific town or more generally with being Ijesa. For most, the town is crucial; they will say they are from a specific town first, and only then that they are Ijesa. Others, however, argue that the emphasis on a small town serves only to divide Ijesa from one another and to emphasize "tribalism."

For example, Justice Kayode Eso stated in an interview that the local hometown associations and community-day celebrations foster local tribal prejudices. In his view, these little units break the Ijesa area apart in the same way that larger tribal associations break Nigeria apart rather than unify it. He was therefore working with an Ijesa-wide organization, the Ijesa Solidarity Group (see Chapter 5), which he hoped would strengthen Ijesa identity and unity. Others, too, argue that they are all Ijesa and that it does not matter which town you are from. They point to the fact that those from outside the region do not distinguish among the various Ijesa towns.

The extent to which one emphasizes one's own town as opposed to being Ijesa seems to depend in part on which town one is from, and which part of Ijesaland. Those from Ilesa itself, as the largest and most dominant place in the region, tend to simply identify themselves as Ijesa and to argue that that is the only significant identity. But those from towns in the northern part of Ijesaland such as Ijebu-Jesa, which have historical and political distinctions from Ilesa, tend to emphasize their specific town of origin. Those in the southern part of Ijesaland, with stronger historical ties to Ilesa and with less distinct political origins, are more likely to emphasize that they are Ijesa, or even that they are from Ilesa. However, this, too, is changing, and there is considerable individual variation, even within families, in whether one emphasizes that one is Ijesa or from a distinct Ijesa hometown. In fact, most people note multiple identities: They are from a particular hometown (or hometowns); they are Ijesa; they are Yoruba; and so on. And, of course, identities are not limited to those connected to place.

In recent years, there has also been some identification with the newer political units of the LGA and the state. In June 1993, for example, the Oriade Local Government Area Council had a ceremony to honor three successful men from the LGA, each from a different town.[4] In the speeches made at the event, links were made to their towns, the LGA, Ijesaland, and even Osun State and the entire country. In the speech honoring Oladele Olashore, one of the recipients and then–minister of finance of Nigeria, the speaker stated, "To you, Iloko is the biggest city in the world.... Life has full meaning to you when you are around your own people." He went on to describe the various things the recipient had done for the community and the area, saying "we thank God that you have used your position" to advance "the position of your own people, and of the people of Nigeria."

In his response, Olashore emphasized the local government area and Ijesaland. He said, "I believe we have quite a lot to do in Oriade local government, and we have a lot to do in Ijesaland." After discussing the formation of additional local governments, and noting that the only way to ensure that benefits get to one's own area is through this process, he focused again on Ijesaland as a whole, stating that it is important to "have a more vibrant Ijesaland to fight for." He continued:

> Because nobody realizes whether you are an Ijesa of Oriade local government origin or Ijesa of Obokun local government origin, or indeed of Ilesa, or of Atakumosa local government origin, or any other that may come up in the future, we are all referred to as "Ijesas." And I do believe that ... we must identify ourselves, and really fight vibrantly to uplift this entire society.

As this speech makes clear, the reasons for identifying with a hometown, a local government area, or other specific place-bound unit are not simply emotional or cultural; neither are they only because of social obligations and expectations. There are real benefits, as well as constraints, in the contemporary structure of Nigerian society that affect the maintenance of hometown identity and ties. For example, entrance into certain schools requires information on the hometown of the father, and children from certain areas get preference over others. Entrance into formal politics also requires a hometown base. As F. Niyi Akinnaso (1994) points out in his recent discussion of linguistic unification and language rights, "Nigerian local governments now function ... as the first point at which those who wish to succeed in politics must begin their careers—every politician aspiring to office at any level must begin his/her accreditation and nomination here."[5] The political and economic uncertainty of the past few years, particularly since the introduction of the Structural Adjustment Program in the mid-1980s and the political crises that began in June 1993, have likewise affected hometown connections. Although some, because of their personal economic situation, find it difficult or impossible to maintain ties to the extent they would like, others are making greater contributions than in the past. These political and economic impacts are considered at greater length in Chapters 7–9.

In fact, some argue that were it not for the political and economic uncertainty of the overall situation, hometowns would be becoming less, not more, important. They point to circumstances, such as events in the 1960s prior to and during the civil war in Nigeria, where the only recourse that some individuals had was to return home from other parts of the country. They point as well to the fact that even successful individuals in other parts of the country (e.g., Lagos) will be restricted from certain types of positions because they are not indigenes of that area. And they note that even within Osun State there has been discrimination against those in state government who are from Ijesaland.

However, there is little evidence that political and economic insecurity are the only reasons for the strength of hometown and other local identities. These identities continue to have strong emotional and symbolic value, even as they are flexible and changing. For example, many people who own cars make a special effort to register their car in their home LGA and state, so that anyone seeing their license plate will know where they are from.

At the same time, however, it would be wrong to overemphasize home-place identities to the neglect of other sources of identity. The same people who have strong place identities are also likely to identify themselves in several other ways that cut across those identities—through professional and occupational ties, religious affiliation, and schools. Each of these other sources of identity, like those for place, leads to action and participation, often through formal organizations. These dimensions of identity will be apparent in later chapters of the book.

Nevertheless, no matter how involved an individual is, no matter how well known within his or her profession, it is still important for that individual to retain his or her hometown identity and to be known at home. As one individual stated, "It's true that someone like me can have national, even international recognition. But if you're not recognized at home, you're nothing." As another explained, a Yoruba won't be satisfied unless he has recognition from others of his success, that he is put in prominent places, that he has people around him, that he has people calling him to participate in ceremonies, and so on. He "needs to have this recognition at home, to have a home place, home base."

❧   ❧   ❧

This need for a home base and obligation to that home base are emphasized in proverbs, which continue to be cited as the basis for appropriate behavior. Like the proverb quoted at the beginning of this chapter, these emphasize the importance of knowing one's hometown: *Omo a le loun fi owo osi je we ile baba e* [The bastard child that uses the left hand to describe his father's house]. In other words, it is only a child who doesn't know his father who would use his left hand (only to be used for dirty activities) to point out his father's house. Another proverb emphasizes the importance of being able to come home: *Ile l'abo isinmi oko* [After farming one returns home]. In other words, one's home is one's resting place. And a third, specific to the Ijesa region, emphasizes not only knowing one's father's place, but also one's mother's:

Oni mo bi an bi baba re
Ibanuje ti ba l'Uleesa
Oni mo bi an bi yeye re
Ori-buruku ti ba.

[One who doesn't know where his own father is born,
he's plagued with sorrow at Ilesa.
One who doesn't know where his own mother is born,
is plagued with bad fortune.][6]

As T. M. Ilesanmi explained with regard to this last proverb (stated in Ijesa dialect), it is important to know what one's father did and, by extension, one's forefathers and to know the implications of these past activities and relations for the present. "People are often told to remember whose son or daughter they are, that they should not forget their own background." In addition, people should prefer to help those from their own background, and they should "show gratitude to God and to the people who brought them up by helping others to get amenities."

Notes

1. In 1996 Atakumosa was divided into two local governments, as was the city of Ilesa (*Ijesa Year Book* 1997: 40).

2. This road, known as the Oshogbo Road, once provided easy access between Ilesa and Oshogbo, less than twenty miles away, but deteriorated to the point where it became difficult for vehicles to maneuver on it at all. It has been under repair for several years, but repairs have not yet been completed.

3. According to the 1963 census, Osu had a population of 6,169 and Ijebu-Jesa a population of 14,262 (Nigeria 1964).

4. This was an elected council; the ceremony took place just after the June 12, 1993, elections, the period when it was uncertain what was going to happen with regard to the elections. Later, these elected councils were disbanded by the military government.

5. This refers to the situation during the last years of the Babangida military administration, during which local councils and statewide offices were elected as part of the democratic transition. That transition was terminated in 1993, and in late 1993 the new military leader, Sani Abacha, disbanded elected local councils and other elected positions.

6. The first of these proverbs was given to me by my research assistants in a conversation in November 1993; the other two were stated by T. M. Ilesanmi in a discussion of Ijesa hometown connections on June 13, 1995.

4

"We Are Just Sojourners Here": Ijesa Migration

We are just sojourners here, whereas our place of abode is at home; attachment to home is always there.
  —statement by a Lagos-based woman who is a chief in Ilesa
  (June 18, 1992)

A most noticeable feature of their developing culture in the economic sphere is the ubiquitous "Osomalo...." They are to be found in every nook and corner of Nigeria and beyond, pioneering trade and bringing back home their profits to develop their home towns by putting up impressive buildings and contributing to their development efforts.
  —Bolanle Awe and B. Agbaje-Williams (1997: 12)

A lecturer at Obafemi Awolowo University once described to me how in the 1970s he would travel to Ijebu-Jesa simply to view a house that had recently been built there; at the time, he did not know who the owner was but was so impressed with the design and beauty of the structure that he would take visitors to see it. The house, owned by a prominent Ijesa man who lived in another part of Nigeria, is one of many that now dot the landscape of Ijesa towns. They are usually located on the edge of the built-up area of the town, but occasionally in the heart of the town; some of those constructed in recent years are mansions or estates with several buildings, in contemporary architectural designs, surrounded by walls and impressive gates. These houses contrast sharply with most of the other buildings in the community, mud-brick and cement structures that are often dilapidated. But they represent the current success of the most wealthy and prominent Ijesas residing outside their hometowns, just as the fathers (and sometimes the mothers) of these individuals earlier built houses in the Brazilian architectural style that dominated during the 1930s. Although some visitors are struck by what appears to be an ostentatious display of wealth, townspeople usually point to these edifices with pride, as they represent the success of their "sons of the soil," the most visible results of the mobility in which nearly all town residents have participated.

Ijesas have long been highly mobile. In some respects the patterns of mobility that one finds among Ijesas are similar to those of other Yoruba; evidence from other Yoruba areas shows that people move in and out of their hometowns, residing there for some period of time, moving to other places, including larger cities, and moving back to the hometown. For example, Sara Berry found that in one village over a period of seven years, the total population remained stable but 60 percent of the people counted the first time had left and been replaced by others seven years later (1985: 70). Aronson's study of the Ijebu in Ibadan likewise demonstrates the propensity of Yoruba groups to migrate and settle in other communities while retaining ties with their home areas (1978).

Such high mobility is not unusual in Nigeria; a national survey in 1986 found that 25.8 percent of urban residents interviewed, and 16.9 percent of rural residents, were life-time migrants (Federal Republic of Nigeria 1989: 6).[1] In Oyo State, including what is now Osun State, the rates were 29.9 percent in urban areas, 29.6 percent in rural areas (Federal Republic of Nigeria 1989: 14, table 1). This survey (1989: 17, table 3) also showed that a large percentage of those who were migrants had little or no education. A later survey showed that 51 percent of a nationwide sample were either migrants or return migrants; in Osun State 63 percent of males and 54 percent of females were migrants (Nigerian Institute of Social and Economic Research 1997: 45, tables 5.30 and 5.31).[2] As we shall see in the discussion below, migration is something that people of all educational and occupational categories participate in; people currently residing in small towns and villages, as well as in cities, are all involved in migration.

However, there are also specific Ijesa patterns of migration that have affected the dynamics of mobility and linkages in the Ijesa region. These include *osomaalo*—trade in areas outside Ijesaland—which has come to symbolize the Ijesa both for Ijesas themselves and for others, as well as the early responses to educational and employment opportunities that led to movement to large cities. This chapter considers both historical and contemporary migration patterns among the Ijesa, utilizing survey data from the five communities studied as well as case studies of individual migrants. The latter demonstrate the extent to which people move about among places while remaining connected to a variety of locales. Such multilocality—the attachment to and participation in social and economic activities in several places—is crucial for understanding residential and behavioral patterns among the Ijesa. The chapter also examines the linkages that migrants maintain with family and kin through visiting and remittances.

The History of Ijesa Mobility

As is the case for Yoruba-speaking people in general, the history of the Ijesa is one of migration and mobility right from the start. Origin stories for the Ijesa people as a whole, and for specific Ijesa towns, relate the movement of key individuals and their followers. According to Awe and Agbaje-Williams,

> An analysis of the Ijesa traditions of origin points to at least four waves of migration into Ijesaland: (1) a pre-Ife settlement, (2) a non-Obokun Ife settlement, (3) an Obokun (the Ife prince considered to be the ancestor of Ijesas) settlement, (4) later settlements. (1997: 4–5)

As they point out, many of the settlements considered to derive from the first two migrations continue to exist and "proudly keep alive the traditions of their independent migrations from Ife" (1997: 5). Later conflicts with other groups, such as the Nupe, also led to migrations both into and out of the Ijesa area. These, too, have influenced both the political culture of the region, especially the relationships among various communities symbolized by their chiefs, as well as traditional religious practices, with worship of Osun and Ogun helping to "bind together many Ijesa towns" (Awe and Agbaje-Williams 1997: 6). Continuing conflicts among chiefs of the various Ijesa towns, discussed in Chapter 9, are among the contemporary reverberations of the traditions of origin and migration.

In the nineteenth century, warfare with Ibadan and the capture of Ijesas led to further movement of Ijesas, both in and out of the region. Many Ijesa towns were destroyed during the fighting with Ibadan, and later in the century Ijesa and Ekiti forces united in the Ekitiparapo alliance against Ibadan forces, led by the Ijesa warrior Ogedengbe. Ijesas taken as slaves to Cuba, Brazil, and Trinidad continued to maintain their separate identity as Ijesas; later, when some of those who were freed were able to return to Nigeria, they settled in Lagos and Abeokuta but assisted Ijesas in their fight against Ibadan. Some assisted in the acquisition of weapons. Others came back to Ijesaland to settle, where they "established prosperous farms and introduced new cash crops to the kingdom" (Awe and Agbaje-Williams 1997: 10). Others remained in Lagos but maintained links to Ijesaland; descendants of some of these families continue to be involved in Ijesaland today.

By the middle of the nineteenth century, the Baptist missionary William H. Clarke described the physical development of Ilesa as impressive, noting the structure of the palace, the layout of the town, and the high wall surrounding the palace land (1972: 130–138). Even more important, he noted the extensive commercial life in the region, describing the market at Oke Bode, an Ijesa town:

At this place every fifth day are collected together several thousand people from all the surrounding country, with their various articles of
exchange, and trading is carried on to such an extent in goods—manufac-
tures and provisions—that quite astonish one not acquainted with the
commercial spirit of this ... country. (1972: 127)

Trade and commerce became key features of the Ijesa economy,
although agriculture was also important. The migration of individuals out
of Ijesaland in order to engage in trade began in the late nineteenth century,
with traders traveling to Ejinrin on the coast with farm produce and returning with commodities such as cloth and other manufactured goods. Trade
expanded in the early twentieth century and, by the 1920s, was a source of
wealth and prestige for many Ijesas. Some became large-scale traders and
transporters, and "transport linked with produce-buying [of cocoa] was ...
the route to the greatest local fortunes" (Peel 1983: 135). Many became
osomaalo traders, migrating out of Ijesaland to engage in cloth trade in
other parts of the country.[3] J.D.Y. Peel, in his 1974 survey data of household heads in Ilesa, shows that there was a very high proportion of males
who migrated out in the years before 1930 and that of those men a very
high proportion migrated to become *osomaalo* traders. Such patterns continued later on; Peel concludes that "a high proportion of Ilesha's male population, very steady at around three-quarters since early in the century, ...
moved outside Ijeshaland to find employment for a significant period of
their lives" (1983: 148). And even though in recent years there have been
many other types of employment opportunities, many of those interviewed
in my own survey had either been involved in *osomaalo* trade themselves
or had relatives who were; I will consider this data below.

People began to refer to Ijesas as *osomaalos* whether or not they were
engaged in trade; the term became a derogatory one when used by non-
Ijesas, and Ijesas themselves continue to use the term to refer to themselves, often to refer to what are perceived as negative characteristics. For
example, in one interview a Lagos-based Ijesa explained that Ijesas have
difficulty pooling resources, because they are too individualistic and focus
on their individual success:

An *osomaalo* is an individual who goes about trading and makes himself.
[My] family is famous because they have worked hard and made themselves. *Osomaalos* made money, built houses, but they can't pool
resources. If you ask an Ijesa for N50,000 [for a project], will he bring it?
He'll say he's not interested.

Despite the negative associations of the *osomaalo* tradition, the participation of Ijesas in trade throughout Nigeria had important consequences for
the development of the region. As Peel has shown, the involvement of

Ijesas in trade led to their early participation in politics and their incorporation into the wider polity of Nigeria. In addition, many Ijesas traveled outside the region to pursue education in Ibadan, Lagos, Sierra Leone, and
Britain. They then established themselves in Lagos or other large cities in
professions such as engineering, law, and business. Such individuals were
particularly influential in shaping the interests of Ijesas in educational and
economic opportunities outside the region. As will be discussed in Chapter
5, hometown organizations such as the Egbe Atunluse Ile Ijesa (Ijesa
Improvement Society) formed in the 1920s and helped to develop educational institutions in the area. Case studies of individual migrants later in
this chapter demonstrate the roles of educational and economic opportunities in encouraging Ijesa migration.

It should be emphasized that it was not just the highly educated and
professionals who participated in migration outside Ijesaland. Most of
those active as *osomaalos* had had little formal schooling. Today, as well,
many Ijesas, of all educational and social backgrounds, have experience as
migrants, experience that is both central to individual life histories and key
to shaping the communities from which they come.

Contemporary Patterns of Ijesa Mobility

The extent to which mobility plays a role in the lives of nearly all Ijesas can
hardly be overemphasized. There is hardly anyone who has not, at some
time in his or her life, lived outside the hometown. And even for those who
themselves have not moved, members of their families have; linkages and
remittances between family members away from the hometown and those
at home are important for all. This section of the chapter considers survey
data, providing an overview of migration and mobility among Ijesa today
and in the recent past. This is followed by a set of case studies of individuals, providing detailed life-history information that gives insights into the
decisions people have made about mobility as well as about their continuing links with home.

This section is based on data collected in May 1992, in which a sample
of 280 people in the five communities was interviewed.[4] In the sample as a
whole, 46 percent are male, 54 percent female; less than 1 percent are
under age 20, 31 percent are 20–35 years old, 22 percent are 36–50 years
old, 23 percent are 51–65, and another 23 percent are over 65. A large percentage—44 percent—have had no formal schooling, while 22 percent
have at least some primary education and 20 percent have at least some
secondary education. Five percent have received some type of education
beyond the secondary level, such as teacher training or technical college,
while another 6 percent have had university education, including several

who are currently university students. The remaining 1 percent of the sample had religious or other specialized training. In terms of occupation, 19 percent are farmers; 38 percent are traders; 21 percent are in informal service occupations, such as tailors, seamstresses, and mechanics; 7 percent are in clerical or professional occupations, such as teaching; 6 percent are students or apprentices, and 9 percent are unemployed, including those who are elderly and no longer working. The majority of the sample, 71 percent, are married, while 13 percent are single and 16 percent are widowed. The current residence of the sample reflects the size of the towns in which the survey was taken: 44 percent reside in Ilesa, 21 percent in Osu and another 21 percent in Ijebu-Jesa, 6 percent in Iloko, and 7 percent in Iwoye, with another 2 percent (five people) describing themselves as people who move back and forth between a residence in the town where they were interviewed and a residence somewhere else.[5]

Of particular interest for this discussion is information on the hometowns of respondents. Seventy-nine percent come from within Ijesaland, and 95 percent are from towns in southwestern Nigeria, including other towns in Osun State, as well as Oyo and Ondo States, all of which are predominantly Yoruba. The remaining 5 percent are from communities in Enugu, Delta, and Edo States to the east, and from Kwara, Kogi, and Benue States to the north. In other words, the overwhelming majority of respondents are from Yoruba-speaking areas, and a large percentage are either from the communities studied or from neighboring communities in Ijesaland. Of those interviewed, 191 (68 percent) were currently living in their hometown, while 89 (32 percent) were living outside their hometown.

The fact that the vast majority are from Ijesaland should not be taken as an indication of a lack of mobility. To the contrary: nearly everyone in this sample, male and female, old and young, educated and not, have been migrants at some time in their lives. For the whole sample, only 31 people (11 percent) have lived in one place for their entire lives; in other words, 89 percent of the sample have lived in two or more places. Of those who are currently living in their hometowns, 162 (85 percent) have at some time lived outside the hometown. The extent of mobility is demonstrated further by the fact that the mean number of places in which people have lived is 3.5, with 53 percent having lived in four or more different places, including one person who reported having lived in nine different locales.

There are few characteristics that distinguish those who have moved from those who have not. Mobility is greater among men than among women, and among younger people than older; those who have moved least are older women. Of the women in the survey, 16 percent have lived in only one place, compared to 5 percent of men. Men have moved more times than women: 33 percent have lived in five or more places, whereas only 14 percent of women have lived in that many places; 70 percent of women and 62 percent of men have lived in two to four different places.

Overall, there is not much variation in extent of mobility by age. Among those who have not moved at all, 10 percent are 20–35 years old, 8 percent are 36–50, 14 percent are 51–65, and 13 percent are over 65. However, among women there is a greater percentage of nonmigrants among those who are older. Twenty percent of females over fifty have lived in only one place, whereas among males over fifty, only three (5 percent) have lived in just one locale.

There is little relationship between the amount of education and the extent to which people have moved. Overall, 18 percent of those who have no formal schooling have lived in only one place; this contrasts with those who have postsecondary education, all of whom have lived in more than one place. There is some difference between males and females with regard to education. Twenty-four percent of the females with no education have never moved, compared with 7 percent of males. But it is important to emphasize that this means that 76 percent of women with no education have been migrants.

Contrary to what might be expected, nonmigrants do not come from smaller and more rural communities. In fact, the opposite is the case. The sample in the city of Ilesa has a higher percentage of nonmigrants (14 percent) than any other community, with one section, Ikoti, having 23 percent who have never moved. In contrast, in Iloko, the smallest of the communities studied, all those interviewed have been migrants at some time in their lives.

Locales and Reasons for Mobility

Once we know that migration to one or more places is a predominant pattern in the lives of the majority of people interviewed in the five Ijesa communities, many questions remain. Why did people move? Where did they go? How long did they stay? What did they do there? For those who moved to other places and later returned to their hometowns, we must also consider their reasons for returning home. In this discussion, we begin with information on birthplace, rather than hometown, since the two are not necessarily the same; it is not necessary to have been born in a place, or ever to have lived there, to consider it one's hometown.

As with hometown, the majority of respondents were born in Ijesa communities, with 196 (70 percent) born in one of the five communities studied, and 208 (76 percent) born in Ijesaland as a whole. The rest were born in other towns in Osun and Oyo States (36, or 13 percent), other Yoruba-speaking towns in the southwest (14, or 5 percent), and a scattering from states to the east and north, as well as one person born in Ghana.

Among the 174 respondents who indicated how long they spent in their place of birth before moving for the first time, 20 percent spent under ten years, and another 39 percent spent under twenty years. Thirty-four percent first moved after spending between twenty and thirty years in their birthplace, and a small percentage (6 percent) moved after they had spent forty or more years there. Many others simply responded that they had spent their "youth period" in their birthplace.

People have moved to, and lived in, a large number of different places. There is no single migration pattern in which respondents have participated. Overall, for the 226 people who reported the name of the area to which they first moved, a total of ninety different locales were given. However, most of these places were named by only one or two people. Although there is no single pattern of migration, many people have moved to major cities, primarily Ibadan and Lagos, as well as to smaller cities in the region such as Ilesa, Ife, and Oshogbo. They have also moved to cities in other parts of the country, especially in the north, such as Ilorin and Kano. Moves to eight major cities account for about 50 percent of all moves made. The other 50 percent includes a wide range of places: smaller communities in the region, such as other Ijesa towns as well as towns elsewhere in Osun and Oyo States; cities and towns in regions to the east, including large cities such as Benin, Warri, and Port Harcourt; both small and large towns in the north, including Jos, Kaduna, and Sokoto as well as more rural places; and a scattering of places elsewhere in Africa, including Ghana, the Republic of Benin, Niger, and Egypt. Table 4.1 summarizes these movement patterns for first, second, and third moves, as well as for the total number of moves.

Just as with the destinations of migrants, the reasons why people have moved are quite varied. Overall, about one-third of the moves are for work-related reasons, including moving for work, to look for work, or for a job transfer. If these are added to those who moved to trade, then nearly one-half of the moves are work-related. Very few people moved to engage in farming, but many moved in order to study or to learn a trade. The other

Table 4.1   Locales to Which Migrants Moved

	First Move		Second Move		Third Move		Total	
	No.	%	No.	%	No.	%	No.	%
8 major cities[a]	16	51	66	48	32	48	214	50
Other	110	49	71	52	35	52	216	50
Totals	226		13		67		430	

Source: Survey data, May 1992.

a. The eight major cities are Ibadan, Lagos, Ilesa, Ife, Oshogbo, Ilorin, Abeokuta, and Kano, in order of importance.

major set of reasons for moving is related to family decisions: to follow their parents somewhere, to go with a spouse, to stay with relatives, to stay with children. Between one-quarter and one-third of the moves are for family reasons, with family being slightly less important for later moves.

There are major differences between men and women in the reasons they give for moving. Among males, 38 percent give work as the reason for their first move; another 20 percent stated that trade was the reason; and still an additional 20 percent said they moved to study or learn a trade. Only 18 percent of males stated that their reason for their first move involved family; in contrast, 56 percent of females stated that the reason for their first move was family, including moving with parents or spouse. Eighteen percent of women gave work-related reasons; 11 percent said that the reason was to trade; and 15 percent said they first moved to study or learn a trade. Similar patterns appear in the reasons for those who moved a second and a third time; the vast majority of men stated that work, trade, or studying provided the impetus for moving, and only a few referred to family as the reason. Women, in contrast, referred mainly to family, although work and trade still play some role. The role of family seems to become even more pronounced in later moves; 60 percent of females who moved a third time gave family as the reason. For men, later moves continue to be primarily for work or trade; only 5 percent explained that they made their third move for family reasons.

Despite the number of moves that many people have made, the length of time respondents stayed in one locale is relatively long, with most staying at least two to five years in a place before moving on. Forty percent spent between two and five years in the first place they moved to, and another 26 percent spent six or more years in their first locale. This is true with later moves as well: 43 percent stayed between two and five years in the second locale, and another 16 percent stayed six or more years. With third moves, too, 55 percent reported staying two to five years, and another 14 percent stayed more than six.

The Osomaalo Influence

Even though most Ijesa migrants in the 1990s would not call themselves *osomaalos*, the tradition of working as traders outside the Ijesa region continues to influence migration patterns and the activities of migrants. Of those interviewed in the survey, 153 (55 percent) reported that someone in their family had been an *osomaalo;* 31 (20 percent) stated that they themselves had been an *osomaalo,* and others reported that their father and/or mother worked as *osomaalos* (56 and 36 percent); their husband (14, or 9 percent); a sibling or cousin (45, or 29 percent); or other relative (7, or 5 percent). As would be expected given the history of *osomaalo* trading among Ijesas, most stated that this activity was sometime in the past; most referred to periods between the 1930s and 1950s as the time when they or their relatives were active as *osomaalos*, although a few stated that the activity continued up to the present. The locales where people worked as *osomaalos* reflect the destinations to which Ijesas migrated in general; about 40 percent went to towns and villages in southwestern Nigeria, with Ibadan and Abeokuta predominating; another 23 percent worked in the northern part of the country, with Kano and vicinity predominating.

For example, one elderly man reported that when he was young, he was an *osomaalo*, selling cloth in Ilorin, a northern Yoruba city. He traveled from Ilesa to Ilorin and the villages around Ilorin. Later, he went to Ibadan to work, again selling cloth. He didn't have a shop, but he sold around Ibadan. Another explained that his father was an *osomaalo*, selling cloth, and that as a child he went around with his father while he traded. His father also did some farming and worked as a contractor while the railway line was being built. But, he said, "the traditional trade was called *osomaalo*, and we all had a part in it."

Some of those interviewed referred to the *osomaalo* tradition to explain the lack of development in their communities. In Iwoye, for example, one man stated that 90 percent of the people in the town are *osomaalos* who later return home to farm. He explained that the education level is low and that the local organizations are basically organizations of *osomaalos* and therefore not successful at helping the town. Another stated, referring not just to the past but also to the present, that "Ijesas are essentially traders. It was good for our grandfathers and for our fathers, but does that make it good for us?" He went on to say that because they are *osomaalos*, Ijesas are not concerned with the overall community. Yet as we shall see in later chapters, there is ample evidence that those who migrated for trade became active in hometown development efforts, just as others did.

The case studies below further demonstrate the ways in which migration as traders affected the lives not only of the *osomaalos* but also their children and other family members.

Return to Hometown

Of the 191 respondents currently living in their hometown, 92 percent of males and 78 percent of females have lived outside the hometown at some point. Most people return home in old age: of those interviewed who are over 65, 97 percent of both men and women are now living in their hometowns. In contrast, 61 percent of men between the ages of 51 and 65 and 71 percent of women 51–65 are living in their hometown. Ninety-four percent of males and 79 percent of females over 65 who are now at home have lived outside the hometown. In other words, although the vast majority of both men and women in Ijesa communities have lived outside their home-towns, by the time they are in their late sixties most have returned home to live.

For those who have moved back to their hometowns after living else-where, their reasons for doing so differ considerably from the reasons given for migration, discussed above. Of the 149 people who have moved home and who provided an explanation for their return, 48 (32 percent) gave fam-ily related reasons, and another 40 (27 percent) stated that they were old and that it was now time to settle at home. Others gave reasons relating to difficulties they experienced elsewhere, including financial problems, expulsion from farmland or from another country where they were residing, and local civil unrest in other regions of the country. Some of the family-related explanations also involved problems, such as the illness or death of a spouse or other relative. Very few returned home to work, although some did say that they came home to establish a business or to farm. This is not surprising, since most of those who return home do so when they are quite elderly. Again, the reasons given by males and females differ somewhat. Of the 72 men who have returned home, 31 percent stated that they came home to retire or settle at home. Similarly, of the 77 women who have returned, 26 percent came home to retire. But 44 percent of women and only 19 percent of men gave family as the reason for coming home; 24 per-cent of men stated they returned home to work, and another 8 percent to farm; only 12 percent of women returned home to work, 2 percent to farm.

People Living Outside Their Hometowns

Of the total sample of 280, 89 respondents are currently living outside their hometown. Of these, six (7 percent) have never lived in the hometown. Of the remainder, many were born in the hometown or spent their youth there; the majority spent less than twenty years in the hometown, while 18 per-cent spent more than twenty years there. The reasons for leaving the home-town are largely the same as the reasons of other migrants—work, study, family. Again, there are differences between males and females. Of the 38 men who reported the reason for leaving their hometown, 50 percent gave work-related reasons; 26 percent said it was to study; 18 percent said it was for family reasons. In contrast, of the 43 women who reported reasons, only 14 percent said that they moved for work; 16 percent to study; and 67 per-cent for family, including accompanying their parents or spouse.

Similar patterns emerge in the reasons for moving to their current resi-dence in one of the five communities studied. Of the 40 men who reported their reasons, 58 percent said they moved because of work and 20 percent for family reasons. Of the 48 women who are living outside their home-town, only 10 percent said that they moved to their current residence for work, and 77 percent gave family reasons, primarily to accompany their spouse.

Some of the specific reasons given by respondents are interesting: Three said that they moved because "business is better" here; four moved to establish a business; one said he moved "to make more money." Two others gave reasons related to the location: that Ilesa is the main town in the area, and that he moved because of the creation of the new Osun State.

It is also interesting that despite the importance of family as a motivation to move, many of those living outside the hometown moved by themselves; 38 (45 percent) said that no one accompanied them on the move to their current residence, and another 58 (71 percent) said that no one joined them later. This suggests two basic patterns of movement among those who are not living in their hometown: those who have moved alone, basically to work in the place, and those who moved there because another member of the family went there.

⚜   ⚜   ⚜

In sum, overall patterns of movement are reflected in this data: beyond the fact that nearly everyone has migrated at some time in their lives, it is clear that relatively few major cities function as destination points for many migrants and that men refer primarily to work and women to family reasons as the major motivations for movement. In old age, the vast majority return to their hometowns to live. However, within these broad patterns of movement, the specific moves and motivations vary greatly for individuals and families. The life-history and migration-history case studies below provide deeper insights into the complexities of migration for Ijesa people.

Family and Migration—Where Are Other Family Members?

The survey data provide information not only on individual respondents but also on other family and household members.[6] From this information, it is evident that not only have individuals migrated from one place to another with some frequency but also that within families and households at any given time, members tend to be spread out in several locales. As would be expected, most respondents lived in households that included other relatives; 87 percent reported that they had at least one close relative—a spouse, child, parent, sibling, or grandchild—living in the same household. Yet many people have close relatives living in other towns and cities. For example, 61 respondents (22 percent) reported that their husband or wife lives in a different household from them, and 49 (17 percent) stated that that household was in another town or city. The numbers are far higher for parents, siblings, and children: 113 respondents (40 percent) stated that their mother and/or father lives in another locale; 151 (53 percent) have at least one child living else-where (and one individual reported on seven children living in various other locales); and 186 (66 percent) have at least one sibling living elsewhere.[7]

Of course, one would expect people who are from some other town or region of the country to have parents, siblings, or children living in other places, including their own hometown. Therefore, the following discussion refers only to those 205 respondents who are from one of the five Ijesa communities studied.[8] It provides an indication of the extent of migration among Ijesa and the degree to which members of the same immediate kin group are likely to live in different locales.

Forty-three of the 205 respondents (21 percent) reported that their spouse lives in a different household from them. Of these, twelve live in the same town, and the remaining 31 (15 percent of the total) live in other places, including other towns in Ijesaland and Osun State, as well as Lagos, Ibadan, and northern cities such as Kano and Kaduna. Many more have children in other communities; of the 205 respondents, 120 (59 percent) reported having at least one child living in another town or city. Of these, 6 percent are in Ilesa, 20 percent in Ibadan, and 38 percent in Lagos; the rest are scattered around the country, especially in northern towns, and a few are in other countries. Forty-four percent reported having a second child living in another locale, 21 percent a third child. Again, these children are located primarily in Ibadan and Lagos, with smaller percentages in Ilesa and northern cities and a few outside the country.[9]

In contrast, only 22 respondents (11 percent) reported that their mother lives in another town, and 16 (8 percent) indicate that their father lives else-where. Of those with parents in another locale, most are living in Ilesa, and only a few live in Lagos, Ibadan, or northern Nigeria. These results are not surprising. First, many of those interviewed do not have parents still alive; second, parents in their old age are most likely to have returned to live in their hometowns.

A much larger number of respondents reported having siblings living in other locales. Of the 205 respondents, 119 (58 percent) reported having at least one sibling residing elsewhere. The residence patterns of these sib-lings are similar to those of children: 5 percent reside in Ilesa, 13 percent in Ibadan, and 32 percent in Lagos. Another 8 percent live in the other major cities of Osun State, Ife and Oshogbo, and the rest are scattered around Nigeria, in northern and eastern cities, while a few live outside the country. Forty percent reported having a second sibling in another locale, 15 percent a third sibling. Again, these siblings live in Lagos (33 percent), Ibadan (19 percent), Ilesa, Ife, and Oshogbo (about 15 percent), and in northern and eastern Nigerian cities.

The residence patterns of close family members reflect the types of movements followed by individuals—movement of young adults to large cities in the south, or to towns in northern Nigeria, primarily for work or schooling, and subsequent return to the hometown or region (Ijesa communities if not the hometown) in old age. The residence of spouses in separate locales reflects a somewhat different set of issues: separate movement by spouses, usually for work or family reasons, with some returning to the hometown while their spouse lives elsewhere.[10] The extent to which kin may be spread out at a given point in time will become even more clear in the discussion of individual cases below.

The fact of residence in different locales does not, however, mean that kin do not keep in touch or have regular contact with one another. On the contrary, the vast majority of people who are themselves migrants, or who have kin involved in migration, retain close ties with family members elsewhere. The final section below considers some of the ways in which family members keep their connections with one another, regardless of where they are living.

Individuals and Migration: Life Histories

Although the discussion so far gives us some idea of the patterns of migration in which people in Ijesaland participate, it does not give us a sense of the activities of specific individuals within these broader patterns. For that, it is helpful to turn to cases of specific individuals, where we can follow their life histories in greater detail and with more depth. Although each case is not necessarily typical, each does exemplify some aspect of the broader patterns already considered.

A Tailor in Bendel State

Janet Famurewa lives in a house nearly at the end of one of the roads leading into farmland in Osu. She returned to Osu about ten years previous to our 1992 interview, from Bendel State, where she had worked as a tailor. Now in her fifties, she was born in Osu and first went to live in Bendel State with her husband, living in two towns there for a total of about ten years. She returned to Osu with her children, and her husband followed later. When she returned to Osu, she became a cooked food seller; as she put it, she has many children, and "if you're selling food, the children can eat." According to her, she came back to Osu because "she just likes to come home."

Since returning, she has been active in an organization, the Egbe Cooperative Alajeseku, which has both men and women as members. It is a savings-and-credit organization *(esusu)*, in which members can contribute money and then borrow money; after one loan, a member has to wait six months to get another one. She also makes contributions in the town, paying for helping to support the town's nightwatchmen. Like other women, she pays N10 a year. In addition, if the chiefs want to do something in the town and ask for contributions, she will contribute her share. If she had money, she says, she would make larger contributions for the improvement of the town, such as assisting to improve the water supply.

There have been improvements in Osu in the time since she returned home. According to her, there was no electricity and no tarred road, and the area around her house had no other houses. Now there is electricity, a tarred road, and houses are being built. "It could have been even better," she says, but "there's no money."

Teachers in the North

The Falobis both worked as teachers in northern Nigeria before returning to Iwoye to live, later retiring to become farmers and traders, active in local politics. They live in a two-story house on the road between Ijebu-Jesa and Iwoye; he built the house in 1961 while working in the north. The calendars hanging on the walls of the sitting room include ones for political candidates, reflecting the political interests and involvement of the Falobis.

Born in Iwoye in 1927, S. O. Falobi worked in many parts of the country over the course of his life. He started out in Ilesa at the teachers' training college, then was the principal of a school in Ijebu-Jesa. In 1955 he went to Zaria to attend the Nigerian College of Art, Science, and Technology, having received a scholarship to study there. He then worked in eastern Nigeria before returning to the north, where he spent about fifteen years altogether.

In his last appointment in the north, he was in a place called Mubi, part of the former Northern Cameroons, in northeastern Nigeria. He was in charge of teacher training and inspection for that region. He traveled a lot, as he was responsible for training that would improve teachers' skills. While living in the north he would come home at least one month every year for his leave.

He returned home in 1974 because he received a circular saying that one would be able to receive one's pension only in the state where one retired. "I didn't want to travel 1,000 kilometers to get my pension," he said. So he transferred to the then–Western State, working for a while in Ijebu-Jesa and in Osu but living in Iwoye; he retired in 1984.

After retiring Falobi took up farming. He had a small farm around his quarters when he lived in the north, but now, he said, "I am engaged in real farming." He had a farm of about forty-five acres but had to reduce the size of it after his son, who was helping him, died. He now has a farm of only about six acres. He grows maize and cassava on it. He also has a rice mill and is involved in several other food-processing activities.

Falobi has also long been involved in politics, having been active early on when he still lived at home and, later, within the Yoruba community in the north. Since returning to Iwoye, however, he has been less active, but his wife continues to participate in political activities.

Falobi gives several explanations for his decision to return to Iwoye to live. First, he said, his wife is a native of the town and didn't want to settle anywhere else. Second, he thinks that it is important for educated people like himself to return to their homes; he has encouraged his brothers to do the same thing and is critical of others from Iwoye who have not done so. And third, he did not want his children to "take to the patterns [lifestyle] of the north." He wanted to have his children get their education in the south; his oldest daughter went to secondary school in the north, then to the University of Lagos. The other children received their primary and secondary educations in the south. Overall, "this may have been the strongest reason" for his decision to return to Iwoye.

Since returning, he has been involved in several organizations; he was the first secretary of the Iwoye-Ijesa Descendants Union but is now less active (he was also chairman of the Iwoye Progressive Union). But now he thinks that younger people should play a larger role than someone like himself: "When one is above sixty-five, you will soon die if you are involved in too many activities."

Janet Falobi was born and grew up in Iwoye, leaving in 1949 to study in Ikirun. Her parents were already there, working as traders. After finishing primary school in 1952, she taught primary school in Oshogbo for one year before doing a teachers' training course there. In the late 1950s she again taught primary school first in Ikirun and then in Ilesa. She got married in 1959, and went with her husband to his post in Benue State. She taught primary school there and later in Mubi, Keffi, and Gombe, all in different areas of northern Nigeria. By 1968–1969 she had received a promotion as a result of additional training that she had undertaken.

She joined her husband back in Iwoye in 1975 and was posted to a school in Ijebu-Jesa, then to one just outside Ijebu-Jesa. She went to the Federal Advanced Teachers College in Kontagora, in northern Nigeria, from 1978 to 1981, studying fine arts and receiving her national certificate of education, the highest level of teacher training other than university. She then was required to do her Youth Corps service, like all postsecondary graduates, serving in Ijebu-Jesa Grammar School, the local secondary school. She continued to work there until her retirement in 1989.

Since her retirement, she has become a "pensioner-cum-trader." She has a provisions and patent-medicine shop in Iwoye and had also been elected as an LGA councilor in 1993 and served until the council was disbanded by the federal government. This was her first involvement in politics, and as a ward councilor she represented not just Iwoye but seven other villages as well. She described the job as one that necessitates interacting with the community, going around to see people, listening to their complaints, and taking suggestions to the council. As the only woman elected in the whole region, she had a special concern with issues that would improve the conditions for women in Iwoye and surrounding communities.

According to Janet Falobi, there have been many changes in Iwoye between the time that she left there and when she returned. When she was young, there was no road, just a footpath, to the town. Now there is a road, as well as electricity and pipe-borne water. There are two primary schools as well as a secondary school. The town itself has expanded and "is a bit more civilized than before," with changes in the mode of living—dressing, eating, and living habits. But there is still need for improvement; the roads need repairs, and people in Iwoye would like to see two new roads linking them to other communities nearby. They also would like to rehabilitate the health center and the primary school. And even though there is pipe-borne water, not all areas receive water, so they want to dig wells.

The Falobis' children live all over Nigeria. The eldest and youngest are in Warri, where one works and the other goes to school; one is a lecturer at Kontagora teachers' college, in the north; two are in Lagos, working as journalists; another is in Ilesa, teaching; and another is doing Youth Corps service in Calabar, in the southeast. They come to visit their parents in Iwoye about every three to six months.

A Trader in the North

P. A. Olashore is a man in his eighties who spent the majority of his adult life living and working in northern Nigeria. He returned to Ijesaland in the early 1990s and lives in a cement bungalow near the palace in Iloko. Olashore was born in Iloko and stayed there until he was about twelve. Then he went to the north with his uncle, who many years later became the *oba* of Iloko (the father of the present *oba*, Oladele Olashore). He first lived in Zongo-Dawura with his uncle, where he did some work assisting as a United Africa Company (UAC) storekeeper. He also did his schooling in the area and speaks Hausa fluently. In 1944 the UAC transferred him to Kazaure, located in what is now Jigawa State, north of Kano, toward the Niger Republic. There he worked as a storekeeper and produce buyer. He ran a UAC store there, selling merchandise and buying produce. He bought groundnuts, Niger gum (which is used for chewing gum), and ghee butter (Fulani butter); these would then be sent to Kano, and from there they would be sent overseas.

He retired from the UAC in 1958 and continued to buy groundnuts and deliver them to others for resale. He also carried out other trade; he bought things in Kano and had people to sell them for him. He also had the postal agency at his shop. He lived in Kazaure and had a house and farm there, where he grew groundnuts, millet, and beans. He also stated that he worked as a building contractor. When he left the north he sold his farm, but he retained his house and compound there.

Although Olashore stayed in the north and got his own education there, his children only began their schooling in the north. He sent them home to complete their education; they stayed with his mother and other family members, because he felt that the schools were better in Ijesaland. When he was young, Olashore would come home to visit for a period of time and then go back to the north. Later, he came home for his yearly leave, staying in Ijebu-Jesa, where his father was a chief. It was only after his uncle became the *oba* of Iloko that he began to come to Iloko rather than Ijebu-Jesa.

His return to Iloko in February 1992 took place because the family said that he should come home to help, since he was the head of the family. "When I was told to come home and lead the family, I was compelled to come home and do so." Since returning to Iloko, he has assisted in local activities by contributing to Iloko Day, and he is pleased that the residents are "trying very hard to do things in the town." His older children work in Lagos, Ibadan, and Akure, while the younger ones are still in school. He visits his adult children about once a year, and they visit him somewhat more often; they give him money when such visits take place.[11]

A Clerk and Manager in Lagos

Chief Moses B. Ilesanmi was born in September 1923 in Ilesa. His father was a farmer, going out to his land in the Imo Hill area from his house in Ilesa every day. As a child, Chief Ilesanmi helped his father on the farm; his father did not send him to school until he was eleven years old. After six years in primary school, he attended Ilesa Grammar School, finishing there in 1945, when he was twenty-two. There were no employment opportunities in Ilesa at that time; most of those who finished secondary school had to go to Lagos or Ibadan to find jobs. Also, it was the end of World War II, and there was competition for jobs from returning soldiers. Chief Ilesanmi took the Cambridge School Certificate exam and passed; this entitled him to university admission in England, but he did not have the funds to travel abroad or to further his education. So he went to Lagos to look for a job.

He first lived in Lagos with his uncle, who was a plank (lumber) dealer; he helped him sell planks until he got a job as a clerk with the Post and Telegraph Department. He worked in the accounts department for four years, leaving in 1951 to begin working for the UAC. While at the Post and Telegraph Department, he also became active in trade union activities, as the secretary for the Clerical Staff Union.

At UAC he first worked as a clerk and again became active in issues concerning workers' welfare, first by helping to set up a consultative committee between UAC management and the workers and, later, as head of the UAC African Workers Union.

In 1955 the government of the Western Region of Nigeria offered him a scholarship to study in Britain. But the UAC didn't want him to leave, so they offered him a promotion to chief clerk and advised him not to accept the scholarship. Then they arranged for him to take courses and appointed him to the management staff in 1957. He became office manager and later administrative manager/sales manager in the motor vehicle division of the company. UAC also arranged for him to visit Britain for six months in 1961 to take a course on industrial relations.

In the meantime, Chief Ilesanmi also became involved in politics in Lagos. He contested the local government election as a member of one of the major political parties and won election to the Lagos town council, where he served from 1959 thru 1961. Then UAC transferred him to Kano and gave him a promotion; this led to his resignation from the town council in late 1961. He returned to Lagos in December 1962, by which time he had, he said, "lost interest in partisan politics."

In Kano, Chief Ilesanmi was branch manager of UAC Motors Division, and after he returned to Lagos he became the credit control manager for the motors division for the whole country. He continued in that position until 1967, when he decided to resign from the UAC to establish his own business. Since he had set up the UAC car-rental system, he decided to start a car-rental business of his own. He started out with three cars that he bought from the UAC, and by 1970 had nine cars, some of which he hired out to a single company on a contract basis; the rest were rented with drivers to individuals, such as foreign journalists who needed to get around during the Nigerian civil war. But by the early 1970s a dissatisfied employee damaged his cars, and he was forced to close the business and once again seek salaried employment. He became a manager in the motor division of another organization, owned by Chief Michael Ibru, a former UAC colleague. They sold cars and trucks. He continued with Ibru, receiving several promotions, until his retirement in 1987.

Altogether, Chief Ilesanmi was away from home for forty-two years, although he came to Ilesa on a regular basis and built his house there in 1978. He owned his first car by 1957, but the roads were bad; he came home about twice a year for the weekend. During most of those years, his parents were still living in Ilesa. In 1981, following a visit to a brother who lived in Atlanta, Georgia, he began building a hotel in Ilesa, which he called the Atlanta Hotel. He opened the hotel in 1985, before his return to Ilesa, but he has become more involved supervising it since his return home. His daughter runs the hotel.

During the years that he lived in Lagos, Chief Ilesanmi was involved in a variety of Ijesa social and organizational activities. He was the assistant general secretary of the Council of Ijesa Societies in Lagos from 1947 to 1955, president of the Ilesa Grammar School Old Students Association in Lagos for twenty-five years, and secretary of the Ijesa Club. And for about six years he was on the Ijesa Planning Council, a committee based in Ilesa, which was formed to discuss the economic and commercial progress of Ijesaland. He also belonged to two societies in Ilesa—the Egbe Atunluse Ile Ijesa and the Ilesa Progressive Circle—and has continued his active membership in these organizations since his return home.

In recent years, Chief Ilesanmi has worked with other key Ijesa men to try to resolve local conflicts as well as to promote efforts that he believes would improve Ijesaland, such as new educational institutions and improving the electricity supply. He explains his deep involvement: "Part of me all along loves to subscribe in social development efforts, to take a keen interest in these things." In 1981 Chief Ilesanmi was given an honorary chieftaincy title, Owamuwagun ("the *oba* enhances one's manners") by Agunlejika, the *owa* of Ijesaland at the time.

Radio Personality and Chief in Lagos

Oluremi Onasanya, better known by her chieftaincy title, Yeyebokun, or her radio title, Omo Obokun, lives at the corner of a busy intersection in the Surulere section of Lagos. Although she is from Ilesa, she has lived nearly her entire life in Lagos. Nevertheless, she made her reputation telling folk stories on the radio, as Omo Obokun (child of Obokun), which clearly identified her to listeners as Ijesa. Born in 1914, she began living in Lagos in 1926. She attended primary school in Ilesa, then came to Lagos, where she lived with her grandmother; she attended secondary school in Lagos, then returned to Ilesa to work at Wesley Guild Hospital.

She worked for many years as a trader and caterer in Lagos, beginning her radio program in 1953. She had learned many Yoruba stories and proverbs while living with her grandmother as a child and used these as the basis for her popular radio show, which she continued to broadcast into the late 1980s. She also published some of her stories for schoolchildren.

She has long been active in Ijesa organizations in Lagos, especially the Ijesa Women's Association, of which she was the president at the time of our interview in 1992. The organization helps other groups in Ilesa with activities they want to carry out; for example, they helped raise money for a project headed by Olori Agunlejika, the wife of the late *owa*, when she worked with Save the Children. The group also tries to undertake activities of its own; one goal is the building of a student hostel in Ilesa. As an individual, Yeyebokun also tried to help other Ijesas who came to Lagos, such as those who were looking for work. In recognition of her activities, she was given a traditional chieftaincy title in 1970, Yeyebokun, meaning the "one who takes care of the palace and who looks after the welfare of everyone."

At the same time, Yeyebokun was very active in Lagos-based organizations, especially in the Methodist church at Tinubu Square in central Lagos. Although she was also a member of the Methodist church in Ilesa, she said that she "couldn't leave Lagos" to settle "at home" because of her involvement in the church in Lagos. Yet she also says that "no matter where you are, you have to maintain contact with home." She has a house in Ilesa and stated that she goes there regularly.

A Lagos Engineer

J. O. Agbeja is managing director of an engineering company in Lagos; he has lived and worked in Lagos for most of his adult life and has spent more than twenty years with his present company, which he owns. Born in Ilesa in 1940, he attended primary and secondary school there and left to further his education in London. Later he lived and worked in Ibadan for a short time. He continues to live in Lagos and expects to do so for the immediate future. Among his children, two, a son and a daughter, were living in Great Britain at the time Agbeja was interviewed in 1992; the rest were students living in Lagos. Like other elite Ijesa living and working in Lagos who were interviewed, Agbeja is active in several Ijesa social organizations in Lagos—the Ilesa Social Elite, the Ijesa Society of Lagos, and the Council of Ijesa Societies, all of which, he states, work to "enhance the progress of all Ijesas."

While living in Lagos Agbeja visits Ilesa very frequently, "as a matter of course," going to see his brothers and sisters who live there, as well as various family elders such as aunts and uncles. He regularly brings money to those he visits and brings back foodstuffs with him to Lagos. He has built a house in Ilesa and thinks that that is one of the reasons why his own children continue to go home; by building a house at home "the children will know the family." However, he is unsure whether he himself will retire to Ilesa; he expects to establish a farm and go home more frequently. On the one hand, when he goes home on weekends, there are many people to see. On the other hand, he says that "the people I grew up with aren't there, so except for junior members of the family, and friends who are also visiting at home, there isn't anyone I know there, so it's lonely." He asked whether it is possible to retire and go home, saying that when you do, "with whom do you relate? You don't have friends there."

Despite his involvement in Ijesa organizations, Agbeja is highly critical of the efforts Ijesas make to develop the community and region. He has contributed money to help build a hospital ward and for several other activities yet argues that Ijesas lack the cohesion that they need to really make a significant difference. In his view, "People in Ilesa are dynamic and industrious. They believe that individuals make themselves, and many are successful, as engineers, lawyers, doctors, and so on. All of them got where they are by hard work." But then he asks, given this dynamism, why is Ilesa still the way it is: "Why is the town not developed?" His answer is that Ijesas are too individualistic. Despite the fact that members of his own family, such as his father and uncles, worked as *osomaalos* for many years, he believes that "the *osomaalo* doctrine of individualism has eaten deep into the people." He continues, "An *osomaalo* is an individual who goes about trading and makes himself. The Agbeja family is famous because they have worked hard and made themselves.... People don't believe they need anyone else to get on." He compared Ijesas with other Yoruba groups such as the Ijebu and Egba, saying that the others form a group and develop a project or an industrial concern, but that in Ilesa "to harness the ingenuity and skill of our people into a formidable industrial force is almost an impossible task." He referred to several instances where a group had begun to organize an effort but then had not continued. Yet there are many problems in Ilesa, such as joblessness, and he would like to see organizations undertake projects that would assist those without jobs. But, according to him, most are too busy with their own businesses and too individualistic to pool funds for a joint effort that would benefit others. In his view, "Ijesas like to say that they did it on their own, that no one helped them get where they are. Yet at the same time, everyone goes home, they guard their family connections jealously."

A Migrant to Iloko

Abdulraman Abidoye Adeniyi is a young man from Iragbeji, a town in the northern part of Osun State. He was living and working in Iloko at the time he was interviewed in 1995. He had been there for about six months, working as a security guard at Olashore International School and renting part of a house with two other employees at the school. He had already joined the hunters' association in the town and said that he participated in all of the activities in which townspeople are involved. For example, he said that if they ask people to come help repair the road, he would join them, or if

there is a meeting for the unity of the town, he would attend. "If someone dies, because of the love people have for the town, they will all help dig the grave and bury the person." He said that they had not asked him to contribute any money for projects in the town. He said that nonindigenes are invited to most meetings, especially if the meeting is about the development of the town or about protecting the town. The townspeople "take you closer to themselves" if you're a person of good behavior.

He thought that Iloko was somewhat different from other towns in its willingness to accept people who had moved there from elsewhere, as well as in the extent to which people from the community worked together. In his view, "The people here so much love themselves" that if anyone is doing anything they will help each other. "If someone is doing something, the others don't just leave them alone, but they help them. In other towns, people don't have time for one another." He thought that perhaps Iloko was this way because it is small.

In these life histories of specific people, we see a range of patterns of movement, as well as some of the varied—and often complex—reasons for migration. Some, such as P. A. Olashore and Janet Famurewa, moved to one place or one region of the country, then later moved back home. Others, such as the Falobis, moved around to a large number of different places. The decisions on whether and when to move were not necessarily voluntary. Clearly, in the cases of the Falobis and Chief Ilesanmi, job transfers led them to go to specific places at specific points in their lives. Yet Falobi himself decided that he wanted to return to his home area before retiring, as he worried that he would have difficulty collecting his pension if he retired in another part of the country.

When the response in a survey is that someone moved for family reasons, that can in fact mean many things. For P. A. Olashore, he went as a young child to join his uncle in the north; likewise Yeyebokun began living in Lagos with her grandmother when she was very young. Yet their reasons for staying on in these places were not simply that family members were there. Clearly, Olashore established himself in a successful business, learned Hausa, and seems to have had no real intention to return to Ijesaland except for the call from family members for him to come home as head of the family. Yeyebokun has lived nearly her entire life in Lagos, and although she has a house in Ilesa and a chieftaincy title there, she does not seem to have any desire to return there to live. Janet Falobi might well tell an interviewer that she first went to northern Nigeria to follow her husband. But she was also working there as a teacher and returned to Iwoye later than her husband did, then went off again, to Kontagora, for three years' additional training. Yet her husband states that one of his main reasons for returning to Iwoye was that his wife wanted to do so.

The pattern of Chief Ilesanmi's activities might seem to be the most like what one would expect to find among migrants: someone who had a relatively high level of education for that time, who went to Lagos to look for work, finding a job as a clerk for a major company and receiving further training that enabled him to have managerial positions. Eventually, he established his own business, a common pattern for many Nigerian professionals, although he returned to salaried employment later. Again, like many professionals, he was based in Lagos most of the time, except for a brief period in Kano. And then, after forty-two years away, he came back to Ilesa to retire, again establishing a business in the form of a hotel. Like others of his background and status, he is very involved in Ilesa organizations and activities.

But we see much the same type of pattern in Janet Famurewa. Not highly educated or with a professional background, she worked for many years as a tailor in Bendel State. She returned to Osu because she wanted to come home and, since returning, has been active in several organizations and has contributed small amounts of money for local improvements. Even though the level of her contributions may be considerably lower, and her visibility in the community much less, she shares many of the goals of others who are better off and more visible: she would like to be able to contribute more to the improvement of the town and is very aware of what the local needs are, such as an improved water supply.

Some individuals with strong connections and interests in their hometowns would not be considered migrants at all, that is, they have always lived away from home and are likely to continue to do so. For example, a well-known Lagos-based doctor, Irene Thomas, is an example of someone who has never lived in Ilesa but nevertheless considers herself Ijesa. Her biography in the *Ijesa Year Book* describes her as follows: "She has, throughout her life, been a worthy ambassador of Ijesaland. She has served with love and devotion" (1997: 294). Born in Lagos to a father who was also born in Lagos (her grandfather was part of the Ilesa royal family), she has taken a chieftaincy title in Ilesa and makes contributions to activities there, but she is unlikely to ever live there. Asked why Ilesa is still so important to her even though she hasn't ever lived there, she responded simply "it is still home." Others, such as Agbeja, don't know if they will ever return to Ijesaland to live but are very involved and concerned about events there.

Finally, migration in Ijesaland also includes people, such as the young man in Iloko, who are not from there but who have moved to the region for work or other reasons. They, too, are in some cases involved in local activities while also being engaged in maintaining connections to their own home communities.

Family and Kinship Links: Visiting and Remittances

In these brief case studies we see not only patterns and reasons for movement but also some of the ways in which migrants participate in hometown activities. The question must be asked: Are such individuals exceptional in their dedication to their hometown and its improvement? Or is this what one finds among the majority of Ijesas, including those who have returned home to live as well as those who are outside their home communities? And are these community ties established within the context of other family and kin connections, or are they separate? If someone's entire family is outside the hometown, are they still engaged in that community? Do they maintain ties with family regardless of where they are located? And do they encourage younger family members to continue to regard the hometown as home?

In this final section, some answers to these questions will begin to emerge. I will return to the survey data to consider evidence of the connections that individuals maintain with family and kin elsewhere, focusing on data on visiting and remittances.[12] Evidence of links to and involvement in the hometown as a whole is discussed in chapters that follow (Chapters 5 and 6 describe hometown organizations and celebrations; Chapter 8 discusses specific community development activities, including survey data on the extent of participation in such activities).

Despite, or perhaps because of, the extensive amount of migration of Ijesa people, nearly everyone keeps connections with family and kin elsewhere. Those who are now living in their hometowns maintain links with family members living outside the hometown; likewise, those now living outside their hometown also maintain such connections. Of particular significance, and unlike the pattern in some other regions of the world, movements of people and of remittances go in both directions—from those outside their hometowns to those at home, and from those at home to those outside.

The vast majority of the respondents in the survey indicate that they visit and/or receive visits from family living elsewhere. Of the 191 currently living in their hometowns, 173 (91 percent) receive visits from family living outside the town; likewise, of the 89 living outside their own hometowns, 86 (97 percent) reported that they visit it. Those living at home also pay visits to family elsewhere, with 127 (70 percent) reporting that they do so, and those living away from home similarly receive visits from home, with 78 (88 percent) reporting such visits. For those living at home, siblings are the most frequent visitors;[13] 139 (80 percent) reported that brothers or sisters visit them. Children account for many other visits; 109 (63 percent) receive such visits. More distant relatives also visit, including aunts, uncles, and cousins. Similarly, when those who are living at home pay visits to family elsewhere, they are most likely to visit their siblings and children; of the 127 who reported such visits, 99 (78 percent) visit siblings and 50 (39 percent) visit children.

The visiting patterns are slightly different for those living outside their hometowns. When they visit the hometown, they are able, of course, to visit a variety of relatives living there. When they receive visits from hometown-based relatives, their most frequent visitors are their parents and siblings; relatively few reported visits from children. Of the 78 who reported visits from home, 61 (78 percent) received visits from siblings and 30 (38 percent) had visits from parents, while only 10 (13 percent) had visits from children. To a considerable extent, these differences are related to the age of respondents—those living outside their hometowns tend to be younger (only two are over 65) while those living at home are much more likely to be elderly and therefore to have children rather than parents living elsewhere.

Visitors in all directions bring gifts to those they visit; they also receive gifts from them. When family members living outside visit those living at home, the most common gift is money. Of the 136 respondents who reported receiving gifts from visitors, 85 (63 percent) received money from at least one visitor, while 47 (35 percent) reported getting some type of food item; about half receive money and/or food from more than one visitor.

Although many who reported getting money did not specify amounts, and others indicated that they got small amounts, about one-third indicated that the amounts they receive from regular visitors are over N100, and a few reported receiving over N1,000. These larger amounts should clearly be considered remittances, in that they are more than just the small amounts of money that are regularly given out in a wide variety of social circumstances among the Yoruba. These gifts represent sums of money that can be used for a variety of needs, from basic survival to purchase of items that individuals would otherwise not be able to afford. The importance of money as a gift or remittance to those living at home becomes clearer when we consider gifts received when respondents visit their relatives living elsewhere. Of the 104 respondents who reported that they visit and receive gifts from at least one relative, 84 (81 percent) reported receiving money. Again, in some cases the amounts received are fairly substantial. Food items account for a relatively small proportion of the gifts received when respondents living at home visit family elsewhere.

In contrast, the items given to those who visit from outside by those at home are much more likely to consist of foodstuffs rather than money. Of the total number of visits (120) in which family members are reported as taking something back from the hometown, 101 (84 percent) involve receiving food items; only 24 (20 percent) involve gifts of money. Similarly, when respondents visit family outside the hometown, they are likely to bring food items with them rather than money. Of the 136 visits in which respondents reported that they bring something with them, 116 (85 percent) involved bringing foodstuff, while only 27 (20 percent) involved money. Further, no one reported bringing a sum of money larger than N100.

Similar patterns exist for those respondents who are currently living outside their hometowns. Those living outside the hometown tend to give money to family members from home, and they tend to receive food items from those family members. When visitors from home come to see respondents living outside their hometowns, the large majority bring food; of 83 visits reported in which gifts were brought, 60 (73 percent) of the visitors brought food, compared to 24 (29 percent) who brought money. When these visitors go back home, the reverse pattern occurs: they mainly take money back with them as a gift from the respondents living outside the hometown. Of the 95 visits in which respondents reported sending gifts back home with visitors, 58 (61 percent) consisted of money, while 31 (33 percent) involved food.

Even when people do not visit, they send things to relatives elsewhere. Fifty-two of those respondents living outside the hometown (58 percent) reported that they send things to relatives at home, with their mother the most commonly mentioned relative. Similarly, of those who reported that a relative at home sends them something, the most frequently mentioned family member is their mother. Thirty-four (65 percent) say they send money to a hometown-based relative, and 28 (54 percent) send food items; 10 respondents reported sending both money and food. Of those 37 who reported having a relative sending them something from the hometown, only seven (19 percent) receive money, and 26 (70 percent) receive food.

These patterns of flows of people, money, and food reflect continuing interactions between those living at home and those living outside the hometown. Unlike the patterns that have been described in other regions of the world, the flows here are two-way. But there are significant differences between the situations where money is given and those where the gifts consist of food items. Money comes from those outside the hometown to those living at home. For those respondents currently living in their hometown, they receive money from children and other relatives when they visit. For those respondents not currently living in their hometown, they give and send money to relatives at home, especially their mother. Foodstuff goes in the opposite direction—from those at home to those outside the hometown.[14]

Monetary remittances are important to those living in the hometown and can be used for a variety of purposes by the recipients. The fact that many respondents voluntarily specified the amount they receive suggests that these gifts have considerable significance. Data were not collected on the specific uses to which people put the money received as remittances. Whatever they are used for, they have an important impact on the individuals and families that receive them. In response to other questions, for example, some of those interviewed indicated that they were affected by adverse economic circumstances because their livelihood depends on the earnings of children living elsewhere. Overall, such remittances have an aggregate effect as well on the income levels in the hometown communities.

The flows described here take place between individuals and within families. They do not represent monetary or other donations to the community as a whole, or to overall community development. For activities at that level, we need to consider contributions to overall community efforts; this is the focus of the chapters that follow.

Notes

1. Lifetime migrants include people whose residence at the time of the survey differs from the place of birth, as well as those who are currently living in the birthplace but who had lived elsewhere for at least six months (Federal Republic of Nigeria 1989: 38).

2. In the Nigeria Migration and Urbanization Survey (1993), 51 percent of a nationwide sample were either migrants or return migrants; in Osun State 63 percent of males and 54 percent of females were migrants (Nigerian Institute of Social and Economic Research [NISER] 1997: 45, tables 5.30 and 5.31). However, the sample for that survey was stratified "to reflect the importance of migration to the urbanization process" as well as to include areas known for rural out-migration, rural in-migration, and international migration (NISER 1997: 22).

3. According to Aluko, the word *osomaalo* is a shortened version of *Oso ni malo ki mi to gboo mi*, meaning "I shall stay here in a squatting position until my money is paid." This refers to a system whereby the trader sold goods on credit, returning later for payment (Aluko 1993: 11).

4. The 280 people were selected by sampling residential buildings in each of the five towns. In Iloko and Iwoye, a 10 percent sample of all buildings in each town was selected. In Osu and Ijebu-Jesa, the sample was taken in several specific sections of the town. And in Ilesa, five named quarters—Ifofin, Ikoti, Ijoka and Egbe Idi combined, and Imo—were used for the sample (see Map 3.3). These represent older, central areas of the city as well as areas that have been built up in more recent years. Interviewers were instructed to conduct one interview in every tenth building; many buildings in Yoruba communities contain more than one household, but it would have been very difficult to first ascertain the number of households in a building. Therefore the numbers do not represent a 10 percent sample of all house-

holds in the towns. One adult, not necessarily a household head, was interviewed in each of the buildings selected. This individual provided information not only on himself or herself but also for other members of the immediate family, regardless of where they were living, as well as information on the other household members living in the same residence. Originally I had planned to use maps drawn of the towns for the census that was conducted in late 1991, but when this turned out not to be feasible my research assistant and I drew our own sketch maps for the interviewers. Some of the data for the towns of Osu and Ijebu-Jesa provided the basis of analysis in Trager (1995a, 1995b, and 1997).

5. The five who move back and forth help reveal some of the patterns of movement in which people regularly engage: two are young men, university students who were at home on holiday. Of these, one's hometown is in Lagos State, but his parents have lived in Ilesa for many years. The other three, two men in their fifties and a woman in her eighties, were visiting children or other relatives in their hometown at the time of the interview and stated that they come home very frequently for visits although they live elsewhere.

6. The discussion below is based on two sets of questions in the survey. One set inquired about others living in the same household as the respondent; the other asked about specific family members (spouse, children, parents, and siblings) living in other households.

7. Clearly, parents, siblings, and adult children are likely to be in different households even if living in the same town or city. The figures reported here refer only to those whose residence is in a different town from that of the respondent.

8. This discussion includes all respondents whose hometown is one of the five communities studied, including those living in another of the communities. For example, someone from Iloko currently living in Ilesa is included here, whereas the earlier discussion of the 191 living in their hometown included only those whose hometown and current residence were the same.

9. Children living in other households and locales are primarily adult offspring who are working in those places; Lagos and Ibadan predominate, as they are the large cities to which people go to find work.

10. I would like to thank my former student, Jackie Handford, for drawing my attention to the number of spouses living in different locales; she focused on this issue for her project under a National Science Foundation Research Experience for Undergraduates grant. Geschiere and Gugler (1998b) call attention to this issue, pointing out that there has been little discussion of this pattern in the literature.

11. As with all of the life histories in this section, the information was provided by conducting interviews with the individual whose life is described. In the case of P. A. Olashore, other information on some of the events in his life is given in a book by his cousin, Oba Oladele Olashore (O. Olashore 1998).

12. Heather Spencer, my student at the University of Wisconsin–Parkside, did the initial analysis of the data discussed below. The extensive literature on the role of remittances and implications for rural development includes research elsewhere in Africa (e.g., Johnson and Whitelaw 1973/1974; Rempel and Lobdell 1978) and in Asia (Trager 1984, 1988b; Oberai and Singh 1980), as well as theoretical statements (Stark 1980). The major contribution on this topic in southwestern Nigeria is Adepoju (1974).

13. The respondents were asked to name up to three relatives who visited; the results reported here combine the responses. Similarly, respondents were able to indicate more than one type of item brought or sent as remittances; those responses are also combined in the discussion that follows.

14. The Nigeria Migration and Urbanization Survey (1993) reports that about one-third of male migrants and one-fourth of female migrants nationwide sent remittances, mainly to their places of origin. This survey does not include information on flows of goods or money from those at home to migrants (Nigerian Institute of Social and Economic Research 1997: 97–101).

5

"We Love Ourselves Abroad": Hometown Organizations and Their Members

The May 1992 meeting of the Ilesa Social Elite took place at the Lagos residence of one of its members, Ayo Oni, an accountant. The members gathered at about 4:30 in the afternoon; as they arrived, they began to take seats in the rows of metal chairs that had been set up in an outdoor area that was covered by a canopy. Beer and soft drinks were served, and the men, all in their fifties and sixties, greeted one another warmly and chatted among themselves. By the time the meeting began, around 5 P.M., about twenty members had arrived; more came later, with about thirty attending in all. During the business meeting, the officers—president, past president, general secretary, and publicity secretary—sat at a table facing the chairs. The meeting, which was conducted in English, began with a reading of the minutes of the last meeting. Then the men discussed their current project, the building of a maternity ward for the Wesley Guild Hospital in Ilesa, and the importance of making their contributions. They then considered a set of recommendations about the group's clubhouse in Ilesa. After lengthy discussion of these issues, the president made some announcements, then adjourned the meeting at 7:30 P.M.

As soon as the meeting ended, food and drinks were served; a few people moved into the house to eat, but most stayed outside while they ate pounded yam and visited with one another. After everyone ate, the president called all inside the house to thank the host and his wife. The president made a brief speech thanking Mrs. Oni, then told her husband to sit next to her while the members all sang "For he's a jolly good fellow." Most members departed soon afterward.

On the evening of April 5, 1997, following the coronation of the new *oba* of Iloko, the Iloko Women's Forum met in the entrance court-

yard of the palace in Iloko. All of the women had attended the coronation earlier in the day, many of them coming to Iloko specifically for
the occasion from the other towns where they reside. The meeting was
scheduled to begin between 8 and 9 P.M. At about 8:30, two of the leaders began to go around to houses of members to remind them of the
meeting. Others arranged some tables and chairs in front of the palace
and brought out several large metal pots with snacks that were to be
served at the end of the meeting. The meeting got under way at about
10 P.M., with about twenty-five women who were joined later by several more. They began by singing religious songs, and one of their members led the group in a prayer. Then reports were given on the activities
of the zonal groups—members residing in Abeokuta, Oshogbo, Ibadan,
and Lagos, as well as Iloko. Most of the reports focused on efforts connected with the coronation and with raising funds at the coronation by
selling rosettes, small badges made of ribbon and paper that commem-
orated the event. Then all members were asked to introduce themselves, and each briefly described where they live and the work they
do. Most of the women reported in Yoruba, or in a mixture of Yoruba
and English. While the meeting went on, children played around the
edges, and some other adults, not participating in the meeting, sat elsewhere in the courtyard drinking beer. Toward midnight, the snacks—
doughnuts and soft drinks—were passed around to the children, and
eventually, before the meeting ended, to the women themselves, most
of whom packed them in plastic bags to take home. The meeting broke
up at midnight, with most returning to their homes and some stopping
by at the night party being held to celebrate the coronation. Many
planned to be in church the following morning for the thanksgiving
service that was also part of the coronation celebrations.

The tendency to form associations and corporations is very strong among
the Yoruba.... They are formed for the purpose of promoting and protecting common interests in the field of politics, economics, religion, recre-
ation and enjoyment.... One interesting result of this tradition of associations is that wherever there is an appreciable community of Yoruba, either
outside Yorubaland or even only outside their own particular communities, an organisation will spring up complete with officers. This organisation will certainly have judicial functions, and will have its convivial and
mutual help features strongly developed.... The Yoruba equivalent for
association is *Egbe*.... Although membership of an *Egbe* is not compulso-
ry, it was the rule and not the exception to belong to one. A person who
had no *Egbe* was not a properly adjusted and socialised being. (Fadipe
[1939] 1970: 243, 260)

As Yoruba sociologist N. A. Fadipe makes clear, Yoruba people are involved in organizations of all types, and this has long been an important part of their culture. One might argue that the Yoruba are the original "organization men" (or people); long before Vance Packard called attention to Americans' involvement in and commitment to business organizations, the Yoruba were involved in numerous organizations and societies, ranging from occupational groups to religious groups to age groups and social clubs of all types. These *egbe* include adults of all ages, both men and women. In contemporary Yoruba society, large numbers of people in all types of communities participate in at least one such organization. For example, women who are traders usually belong to a market women's organization, either based on the commodity they sell or the market in which they sell it (Trager 1976–1977, 1981). Men, too, are involved in occupational associations, some of which regulate the commercial activity; others provide assistance through the formation of credit-and-savings groups. Many men and women belong to groups associated with their church or other religious organization. On Sunday afternoons, both men and women are likely to spend part of their time in meetings of an *egbe*, such as the Ilesa Social Elite whose meeting is described above.

Elite and wealthy Yoruba are typically involved in multiple organizations: church groups; professional societies; organizations such as Rotary; social clubs; groups of people who attended the same schools ("old boys" associations); and organizations whose membership is based on community of origin. These last groups, commonly referred to as "hometown organizations," are also likely to have multiple and overlapping memberships. Some are social clubs, usually made up of people who have grown up together; others have a more practically oriented agenda; and some seek to encompass everyone from a particular community or region. What is striking about the biographies and activities of many individuals is how many different organizations they participate in, as well as the range of leadership roles they play in these organizations.

Hometown organizations have been the focus of considerable attention in recent years, as it has become apparent that in many Yoruba communities these organizations are a significant source of local-level development activities (Barkan, McNulty, and Ayeni 1991; Honey and Okafor 1998; Trager 1992). Several scholars have argued that these organizations are a significant and often overlooked part of civil society in contemporary Nigeria, an issue that I will return to in Chapter 10.

This chapter focuses on hometown organizations in Ijesaland. I first consider the cultural and historical contexts for contemporary hometown organizations; I then move beyond a general discussion of all the Ijesa hometown organizations (so many that such an effort would be impossible) to focus on several specific groups. In particular, those organizations that are primarily concerned with development in their communities are examined. I conclude with a case study of one organization—the Ijesa Solidarity Group—a relatively new organization, which differs in some important respects from other organizations in the region.

Hometown Organizations in Ijesaland: Cultural Context and Social Organization

Hometown organizations need to be considered in their wider cultural context; at the same time, variation among different types of hometown groups is also important to note.[1] As has already been mentioned, many individuals belong to at least one *egbe;* hometown organizations are part of a much larger array of societies and associations in which Ijesas are involved. The types of groups in which individuals participate, and the extent of their participation, vary considerably and may be affected by gender, age, social status, occupation, and residence. For example, most men and women may be at least nominally members of an occupational association: traders in a particular commodity; taxi drivers or motor mechanics; and so on. However, these organizations are not always active on a regular basis. Many men and women also participate in small social groups that act as credit-and-savings groups *(esusu).* Many are also members of groups associated with their religious practice. And in recent years, some communities have established what are called "vigilante" groups for guarding the community, and some individuals have made that their primary organizational commitment.

Two women in Osu are good examples of the types of involvement that many people have in associations based in their community. The first, Chief Florence Alegebeleye, is a farmer who grows corn and cassava with the help of her adult son. She became one of the women chiefs in the town about a year before the interview (1992) and participates in the meetings of women chiefs. The only other organization that she belongs to is the Methodist Irepodun Society, a church group that meets regularly and where members contribute money, some of which is used to buy the same cloth *(aso ebi)* so that they can wear it to church at the end of the year. She has also made contributions in the town for the building of the town hall, which had not yet been completed at the time of the interview. The second, Janet Famurewa (see Chapter 4), returned to Osu about ten years ago. She is a member of the Egbe Cooperative Alajeseku, which has both men and women as members. She explained that members contribute money, then can borrow money: "For example, if you contribute N200 then you can borrow N400. The amount people contribute and borrow depends on the business they are doing." She explained further: "If you return the money you borrow after two weeks, you can borrow more. The society meets every two weeks, and people make their contributions; some contribute N100, some N20, some N50. People can borrow at these meetings, and then after getting a loan you have to wait six months before you can borrow money again." Famurewa also makes contributions in the town, helping to pay for the nightwatchmen that are hired to protect the town.

Older people, as well as those of greater wealth and social status, tend to be involved in a multitude of organizations. In particular, those individuals residing outside their home community are likely to be members of organizations both in the communities where they live and in their hometowns. For example, a Lagos-based lawyer or businessperson may well belong to several organizations: a professional society; Rotary; an "old boys" association; a group from the same Ijesa town of similar age and background; and a church-based group in the city as well as back home. As this individual becomes more senior and prominent, he or she is likely to be selected for leadership positions in one or more of these organizations. In addition, he or she may be given either an honorary or traditional chieftaincy title in the hometown, or in another town where a friend is in a position of leadership. The result of this complex involvement in organizations is an overlapping and extensive web of social connections, which are reinforced and maintained through meetings and social events and celebrations. On a given day or weekend, someone such as this may attend several functions—weddings, funerals, meetings, church—not only at home but also in the communities of friends.

For example, a Lagos-based engineer, who was described by a friend as the "bedrock" of the Ilesa Frontliners (described below), is the past president of that organization. He is also active in the Ilesa Social Elite and is the representative of that group on the Council of Ijesa Societies. He explained that he is also a "foundation member" of two newer organizations, the Ilesa Cultural Foundation and the Ijesa Solidarity Group. He was also about to become the *baba ijo* (father of the congregation) of St. Peters Church in Ilesa. On one occasion, he described a typical weekend, when he was supposed to attend four events on a single Saturday: a meeting of his church synod in Ilesa; a wedding in Benin, and another in Oshogbo; and the meeting of the Ijesa Solidarity Group, which was expected to last a good part of the day.

Women, likewise, tend to be involved in multiple organizations. Funke Omoniyi, a Lagos-based woman who is from Ilesa and whose husband is from Iloko, participates in organizations in all three places. She is a member of the Iloko Progressive Ladies–Lagos Branch, an organization for all wives and daughters of Iloko. She also participates in (and helped start) the Council of Iloko Women, which includes all of the women's societies in the town. In addition, she is the past president of her Lagos chapter of the Inner Wheel Society (the women's group affiliated with Rotary). And she has family ties to Ilesa and is a member of a social club there, the Ijesa Ladies Friendly Society. She was the president of that group at the time of the interview in 1996. She described the difficulty in keeping up with all these activities; just letting people know about a meeting, distributing notices, and actually attending meetings was becoming increasingly difficult, especially during periods of fuel shortages and price increases. One way of countering these difficulties was to hold meetings during the weekends when other major events were occurring in the town. In Iloko, for example, the women's organization met following two celebrations in spring 1997; one meeting, described at the beginning of this chapter, took place on the weekend of the coronation of the new *oba*, and the other occurred a few months later, when the funeral of the *oba*'s mother took place. These examples—and many more could be found—suggest the ways in which multiple demands can be placed on the time, energy, and resources of key individuals, both men and women.

Within the wider array of organizations, hometown associations are particularly important for those who are not residing at home, and, to a lesser degree, for those who have returned home after having lived outside the community. Like other organizations, most tend to be formed by people with common social characteristics or backgrounds and to be organized in terms of gender, age, social class, and status. The names of organizations provide a sense of this: the Ilesa Social Elite; the Federation of Ijebu-Jesa Students Union; the Ladies Improvement Society. In addition, some organizations seek to link together several smaller groups, such as the Council of Ijesa Societies, and others seek to represent the entire community, such as the Iwoye-Ijesa Descendants Union, or to join together as a development council.

To describe, or even list, all hometown organizations in Ijesaland would be impossible. Each town has numerous organizations, with varying and overlapping memberships. There are also regional organizations, which bring together people from all Ijesa communities; these include both membership organizations and organizations of organizations—that is, councils or groups of smaller organizations. The following discussion uses descriptions of specific organizations to provide a better understanding of how the various Ijesa organizations operate and interact. It will be clear from this discussion that these organizations have a variety of functions, from the purely social to efforts at community and regional development. Following the discussion of several contemporary organizations, I will consider some historical antecedents—Ijesa hometown organizations that played important roles in the region in an earlier period. I will conclude with an extended case study of one organization, the Ijesa Solidarity Group, which formed in the 1990s and has focused on local development.

Specific Organizations: Age and Gender

Two of the most common ways in which hometown associations are organized is in terms of the age and gender of the members. Some are essentially groups of friends who have given themselves a name; for example, Club 72 and Club 77 are groups of men from Ilesa whose name refers to the date when they graduated from school. These are, in effect, small age groups, people brought together through a common experience. Such groups are primarily defined by their members as social clubs, although they may take on a project having some wider visibility and impact, such as putting up street signs in the town. Some groups of this type will put up a welcome sign at the entrance to the town—"the [name of group] welcomes you to Ilesa" or "wishes you safe journey" on leaving the town.

Similarly, gender is the basis of organization for many groups; most hometown organizations, like most other Yoruba associations, are single-sex organizations. Women, like men, have organizations that are primarily social groups, based on common interests and experience. There are also groups that have formed as complementary groups to a men's organization, and other groups that are all-inclusive, including all the wives and daughters of the town.

Two organizations that are examples of men's hometown groups are the Ilesa Social Elite and the Ilesa Frontliners. The Ilesa Social Elite has about 200 members, men who primarily live in Lagos, although some live elsewhere and some have moved back to Ilesa. There is also a branch based in London, the Ilesa Social Elite–London Branch. The organization was founded about thirty years ago. According to the publicity secretary, Chief Alex O. Adagunodo, it is "basically a social club, concerned with the social interests of the individual members. For example, if someone is doing a marriage ceremony [e.g., of his daughter], they need a group to come; the members of the club will come. The same thing for a funeral. The social aspect is primary." In addition, "members who have problems, for example, matrimonial problems, will discuss them privately with the executive and the president. If someone has financial problems, the club may find ways to help. If they have a court case, there are lawyers who are members, they can advise and give representation where possible. These are the types of things that individuals enjoy from the group."

Chief Adagunodo also describes how the hometown benefits from the organization. He said that they try to give honor to the town from a distance: "Everyone should act as an ambassador from Ilesa and put the town on the pedestal of fame. The value of the individual members put together is the value of the group." They encourage members to build houses at home and to improve the quality of the town. They also assist children from Ilesa to find jobs, thereby trying to reduce unemployment of people from Ilesa.

One of the major activities of the Ilesa Social Elite has been to build a clubhouse, which can be rented for functions such as receptions. Once the group built the clubhouse, they realized that "it is the elite at home and abroad who use the club." They then began to develop a project they felt would benefit the "grassroots people"—the building of a maternity ward at Wesley Guild Hospital (one of two large hospitals in Ilesa), which they expected would cost more than N1 million. In 1992 they began collecting money for that project, anticipating that it would take about two years, depending on how quickly they got the needed contributions.

The Ilesa Social Elite meets every two weeks in Lagos, at members' houses; about forty to fifty members attend each meeting. Discussion focuses on current issues of concern to the members: the management of the clubhouse, the collection of money for the maternity ward project. At the meeting described above, announcements were made about recent and upcoming events: the death of the club's first president; the funeral for the mother-in-law of a member, with a reminder that members should attend even if the member hasn't been attending meetings; and the celebration of the tenth anniversary of the coronation of the *owa* of Ilesa the following week. Meetings end with refreshments and conversation among the members.

The members of the Ilesa Social Elite are all about the same age, men now in their fifties. They have tried to organize a separate group for their children, since the younger people don't want to belong to the original group. There is also a complementary group of women, the wives of the members of the group.

The Ilesa Frontliners is another group of men, some of whose members are also in the Social Elite. It is a smaller organization, with fewer than forty members. The founders are friends and former classmates; many went to primary and secondary school together in Ilesa. The membership has expanded since, but it is basically a group of "people of like minds," according to B. A. Ibironke, who was the president of the group in 1992. The members are professionals—lawyers, engineers, accountants, businessmen, teachers, and bankers. As one of the members explained, they are basically an "age group" with all the members five to eight years apart in age. They formed in 1982 when they decided that the earlier generation, members of the Egbe Atunluse (described below), had done a lot for the town but that the younger generation had not. They wanted an organization that would do something for the community. Unlike the Social Elite, the Frontliners see themselves less as a social club; they hold meetings in a meeting room rather than at members' homes, and there is no entertainment and less socializing. Rather they are a service group that raises money for specific projects. Their first project was the repair of the clock at the town hall in Ilesa; then they financed street signs for the whole town, and they bought chairs for the town hall. Their project in the early 1990s was to collect money to build a public library in Ilesa. The Frontliners tax themselves to raise the funds to finance these projects.

Like the Ilesa Social Elite, the meetings of the Frontliners provide an opportunity to discuss issues and bring members up to date on events occurring in Ilesa. For example, in 1992 topics of discussion included the upcoming celebration of the anniversary of the *owa*'s coronation; the formation of new local government areas and states; and chieftaincy disputes in Ijesaland. The latter, a topic of considerable concern to many Ijesas, is an issue on which several organizations and individuals sought to play a role in an effort to reduce and prevent conflict both within Ilesa and between Ilesa and other Ijesa communities; chieftaincy disputes as a source of conflict in the region are discussed at greater length in Chapter 9.

Women's groups are also organized in a variety of ways and take on various activities. Some formed as complementary organizations to men's organizations. The Ijesa Young Women Progressive Society was organized in 1970 as a complementary group to the Ilesa Social Elite. By 1992 the group had about thirty members between the ages of thirty and sixty. Unlike some other organizations, they were trying to recruit younger members, so that there would be continuity and so that they could get "bright new ideas," as one of the members put it.

The aims of the group are stated in their written constitution:

> (a) to foster the unity, progress, and advancement of Ijeshaland; (b) to participate actively and cooperate with other women organizations in educational, social, or cultural matters relating to Ijeshaland; (c) to promote the spirit of sisterliness among members and to render to them possible assistance as and when necessary; (d) to render moral and financial support to cases deserving it in matters calculated to enhance the progress and advancement of Ijeshaland. (Constitution of the Ijesa Young Women Progressive Society 1970 [rev. 1986]: 1)

The members are married women who are literate; they are Ijesa either by birth or marriage. They meet monthly at members' homes. The organization includes people from other Ijesa towns, although many are from Ilesa. Most members live in Lagos, although some have moved back home.

According to its leaders, the society is concerned with the affairs of Ijesaland. If there is anything that needs attention at home, such as chieftaincy issues, they communicate with people at home and send delegations home to convey their viewpoint. If there is an important chieftaincy matter to be settled, such as a vacant position, they can intervene to see that the right candidate is chosen, not necessarily someone with lots of money. They write letters and give advice in such circumstances. The organization is also concerned with improving the lot of women and children. They have land in Ilesa and want to build a hostel for students in the community. They also wanted to build a place where people can go for relaxation. The members feel that their children don't like to go home with them, because there's nothing there to do for fun, so they wanted to provide somewhere for them to go. The organization also provides assistance to its own members, with amounts stated in the constitution that are to be given to members engaged in family or other ceremonies; for example, a sum of N50 is to be given to any member whose son or daughter is getting married, another N50 to the couple; N200 is to be paid to any member whose husband dies; N50 to a member celebrating a special birthday, having a housewarming, or taking a chieftaincy title (Constitution, p. 11). Like many other groups, the organization is also a member of the Council of Ijesa Societies–Lagos, and acts with that larger body on issues of general concern.

An older women's organization is the Ijesa Ladies Improvement Society, which began in 1945 with eight members as a complementary organization to the Egbe Atunluse Ile Ijesa (Ijesa Improvement Society, described below). Chief V. A. Thompson, one of the founding members, became the life president in the late 1980s. Unlike the other organizations described so far, many of the members of the Ladies Improvement Society reside in Ilesa; of the seventy members, about fifty live at home and the rest live elsewhere. Some have retired back to Ilesa. Many of the members are now in their seventies, and the youngest are between fifty and sixty years old; membership is open to "all educated daughters and wives of Ijesa who are of fine strength of character" (Constitution of the Ijesa Ladies Improvement Society–Ilesa 1987: 1).

The organization has a strong religious orientation, emphasizing that all members should be active in the churches to which they belong; its activities include lectures on religious subjects and prayer meetings. But the organization has wider aims as well. Its stated objectives include seeking "the progress of Ijesa-land and to foster the spirit of mutual assistance among its members" (Constitution, p. 1). At monthly meetings, held in Ilesa, there are talks on subjects such as polygamy and monogamy, female circumcision, and the care of the elderly. In addition, the organization runs a day-care center and gives scholarships to students at two of the secondary schools in Ilesa. In the 1980s they helped to organize a new marketplace in Ilesa, a weekly market for the sale of farm products and palm oil. The group also had plans in the early 1990s for building a hostel for local students but had no money to carry out the plans at that time.

Most of the founding members are retired from occupations such as nursing, trade, and teaching, and some have died. By the early 1990s members were finding it increasingly difficult to support their activities, such as the day-care center, and even to attend each others' ceremonies. As the president of the group pointed out, when an event took place in Ilesa it was relatively easy for those living at home to attend; but when the event was outside the town, it was difficult to obtain transportation, and everything was becoming increasingly expensive.

As a complementary organization to the Egbe Atunluse, the Ijesa Ladies Improvement Society also attends events organized by the other group; for example, when the Egbe Atunluse celebrated its seventieth anniversary in 1992, the women's organization was well represented.

Some women's groups restrict their memberships to those who are from the hometown; others are open to women from other places. For example, in Ijebu-Jesa, one group, the Friendly Mothers Society, is primarily a social group that is open to women from places other than Ijebu-Jesa, but the Ladies Friendly Society is restricted to those who are "daughters" of Ijebu-Jesa, either by birth or marriage, whether they are living in the town or outside. However, it is based in the town, and the two women who were its officers in the early 1990s were living in Ijebu-Jesa, although they had previously lived elsewhere. At that time, the group had just started up again after some years of dormancy, and it had plans to "do something for the town." They were at the initial stages of planning, with the goal of obtaining a piece of land to establish a park, with playground equipment and other facilities. The officers were unsure whether they would be able to carry out this plan because of the economic situation.

Similarly, the Iloko Progressive Ladies–Lagos is an organization of wives and daughters of Iloko; anyone age fifteen and up is qualified to join. The organization is concerned with identifying ways in which Iloko can progress, especially things that will assist the women. They discuss whether there are trades that women could engage in, and they interact with women living at home when they go there on weekends and for ceremonies. They also encourage members to patronize one another's businesses; if a member is a seamstress or caterer, for example, the other members will utilize her services. They have also been considering establishing a career center in Iloko to train those who have finished primary school in trades such as hairdressing and sewing.

As these descriptions indicate, there is a great deal of variation among Ijesa hometown organizations. Some are almost entirely social and exist primarily for the benefit of their own membership. Others have wider goals, seeking to assist the larger community in one way or another. Some have successfully raised money to carry out projects, whereas others are engaged in trying to develop projects but may not actually have the resources to carry them out. Some Ijesas are highly critical of contemporary hometown associations, arguing that they talk a lot about doing things but accomplish little; unfavorable comparisons are made with the older organizations, such as the Egbe Atunluse, that were very active in the past (see below). Some view the women's organizations as less active and less successful than the men's organizations, yet others stated that the women made important contributions even if they were less visible.

One of the issues raised is the narrow focus of many of these organizations—on one specific community rather than the region, and on the concerns of the members rather than larger issues. In recent years, there have been efforts to broaden the impact of the individual associations by bringing them together in larger groups; in addition, new organizations have formed that focus on the entire region rather than on one community.

Community-wide and Regional Organizations

In smaller towns, there have been relatively successful efforts at bringing together groups of associations into larger organizations. Such efforts have been much less successful in Ilesa; given Ilesa's size and diversity, it is probably unrealistic to expect such an organization to emerge there. An example of a community-wide organization is the Iwoye-Ijesa Descendants Union; it is open to all from Iwoye—men and women, literate and nonliterate, those living at home and those outside. In the past, this organization was involved in the construction of the grammar school in Iwoye. In the early 1990s, the organization's main project was rebuilding the *oba's* palace; everyone from the community was asked to contribute to that effort, and a community-day celebration, Iwoye-Ijesa Day, was organized in 1992 to raise money to finish the palace. At that time, there were plans for another project, the building of a palm-wine factory, to be owned by the community, as well as plans to open a community bank. The bank, described further in Chapter 8, was opened in 1995.

In Iloko, there are two organizations that are meant to encompass people from throughout the community: the Iloko-Ijesa Development Committee and the Council of Iloko Women. The latter was established to bring together all of the women's societies of the town. It is not a membership organization; rather, it includes representatives of each of the other women's groups. It was started by a woman who resides in Lagos, Funke Omoniyi; her husband, J. I. Omoniyi, is the chair of the development committee. The council works with the development committee. The latter organization "tries to involve everyone ... especially the educated people." Beyond its five officers, it does not have a fixed membership; anyone who is interested can participate. They try to involve those living at home as well as those living outside, but those at home form the core group because they can meet more easily. Those who are educated and those who are "financially strong" are the key participants. According to Omoniyi, there are relatively few people who "have the spirit of giving," and they are the ones taking the leadership roles in the activities of the development committee.

The committee seeks to operate by consensus, undertaking extensive discussions with a cross-section of the community before undertaking any project. Sometimes they hold meetings to which everyone is invited; the committee also makes decisions about levies to be paid by community members for the projects they undertake (see Chapter 8).

In Ijebu-Jesa, the Ijebu-Jesa Unions' Conference is the organization that plans activities such as Ijebu-Jesa Day and undertakes other community efforts. It is an umbrella group of the organizations in the town, with seventy-six organizations registered as part of it. This is the most recent of several efforts at bringing together groups in the town; earlier groups undertook projects such as building a marketplace with permanent stalls and building the town hall, which was completed in 1982. The project in the early 1990s was the building of a new palace for the *oba*. The community-day celebration, Ijebu-Jesa Day, was organized by the Union Conference (see Chapter 2).

In Ilesa, as in the smaller towns, there have been efforts to bring together the many organizations into larger groups—the Councils of Ijesa Societies. Several such councils exist in Lagos, Ibadan, and Ilesa itself. According to the president of the council in Ilesa, the councils outside Ilesa have been larger and more successful because "we love ourselves abroad more than we do at home." Nevertheless, the Council of Ijesa Societies–Ilesa reorganized in 1991, with two representatives from each member organization, and began to hold monthly meetings; by 1993 they had established an office in Ilesa and had twenty societies as members. Despite calling themselves the Council of *Ijesa* Societies, the member groups are limited to organizations from Ilesa. The council includes people such as Chief A. O. Lamikanra, the president, and the vice president, Chief Ilesanmi, who have lived and worked outside Ilesa much of their lives but who have now retired home to Ilesa. They want to encourage others to do the same—"to come home, to start industry and commerce." Therefore, one of their efforts in the early 1990s was to explore possibilities for industrialization in Ilesa; their idea was that the council would make suggestions of specific industries that might be possible to develop locally, then try to encourage individuals to follow up on these ideas and develop industries. As we shall see below, another new organization, the Ijesa Solidarity Group, was also trying to explore industrial development at about the same time.

The major activity of the Council of Ijesa Societies–Ilesa in 1991 and 1992 was to organize an award ceremony, honoring several distinguished Ijesas. This ceremony, like others described in Chapter 6, emphasized Ijesa unity and progress. In 1993 the council was involved in efforts to organize an Ijesa National Day; unlike other community-day celebrations in other towns, this one generated considerable controversy and was deemed to be less successful than had been hoped by the organizers. This event is considered in more detail in Chapter 6 and demonstrates some of the limitations of such celebrations.

The hometown organizations described thus far mainly involve people based in the large southern cities, such as Lagos and Ibadan. There are also organizations that bring together people living in other parts of the country. Since many Ijesas live in northern Nigerian cities, such as Kano and Kaduna, where they have gone to work as traders and in other occupations, they have formed organizations there, which not only represent Ijesas but also other Yoruba. Unlike most of the organizations elsewhere, these groups are concerned with issues affecting their residence in the north, as well as issues in their home areas. The groups are organized in hierarchical fashion according to town, local government, and state. For example, those from Ijebu-Jesa have an Ijebu-Jesa Union in Kaduna, which is then represented in a group of associations from the Oriade LGA. The Oriade association has a representative on the Osun State Indigenes Association in Kaduna, which is part of a still larger group, the Yoruba Association. According to the Oriade representative, the Osun State Indigenes Association undertakes activities such as trying to improve transportation between Kaduna and the south. They also planned a Yoruba Day and an Osun Day and were raising money in 1995 to build an Osun House in Kaduna (Osaghae 1994, 1998 describes both Igbo and Yoruba unions in the north).

In the early 1990s two new Ijesa-wide organizations formed, with goals different from those of other hometown organizations and with rather different agendas from each other. One was the Ijesa Solidarity Group, described in detail in the last section of this chapter. The other was the Ijesa Cultural Foundation, which was formed by several academics and others interested in the history and culture of the region. Their goal was to spread knowledge about historic sites, festivals, and other aspects of local culture, both for their own residents and for the development of tourism. The most ambitious goal was to establish a museum, for which the foundation stone was laid in 1992 by President Ibrahim Babangida. The major accomplishment has been the publication of a book on the cultural resources of

Ijesaland (Agbaje-Williams and Ogundiran 1992), and there were plans for other publications.

The community-wide and regional organizations described here include several different types of organization; some are membership organizations, whereas others are associations of smaller organizations. Some try to include everyone from a specific community, whereas others include people from throughout the region but make no pretense of being all-inclusive. Their goals and agendas also vary. Most of the community-wide organizations are primarily concerned with the development of their community, but how *development* is defined—and what it includes—varies considerably, ranging from the building of town halls and the *obas'* palaces to the installation of electricity to more specific efforts at economic development. (See Chapter 7 for a discussion of the meaning of development in Ijesaland.) The regional organizations also vary, with groups such as the Ijesa Cultural Foundation having a specific focus; others, such as Ijesa Solidarity Group, have a much broader set of goals. The success or failure of these organizations in achieving their goals also varies.

Historical Precedents:
Hometown Organizations and Development

In articulating the goals and establishing the structure of contemporary organizations, many Ijesas are conscious of several historical precedents and point to them for lessons, both positive and negative. Three specific examples, all quite different from each other, are frequently referred to in conversation about the activities of hometown organizations. The Egbe Atunluse Ile Ijesa, considered to be the oldest hometown organization in the region and still in existence, is referred to as a model of what "our fathers" accomplished, one to be emulated. The second, the Ijesa United Trading and Transport Company (IUTTC), is usually referred to as exemplifying some of the problematic aspects of undertaking economic activities. And the third, which did not involve an organization but rather a small group of individuals, is International Breweries Limited, established in 1978 in Ilesa and widely seen as the one example of successful industrial development in the region.

The Egbe Atunluse Ile Ijesa, or Egbe Atunluse, was founded in 1922.[2] In 1992 it celebrated its seventieth anniversary with a symposium and book-launching. The title of the book reflects the image of the Egbe Atunluse: *Egbe Atunluse Ile Ijesa: The Flagbearers of Ijesa Enlightenment in the Twentieth Century* (Ifaturoti and Orolugbagbe 1992). Most people point to the early years of the organization as the period of its greatest impact. Most of the current members are elderly men, and although some younger men have joined in recent years, these are mainly children of the original members. For example, one of the youngest members, a man in his fifties, explained that his father was one of the founders and that he decided in 1985 to join the organization because of his father. His view was that they needed to get more young members and to "rejuvenate" the organization with new projects. Others, however, see the Egbe Atunluse as no longer central to activities in Ijesaland and have joined other organizations.

According to the authors of the book on the Egbe Atunluse's history, the "sole aim" of the Egbe Atunluse is "to ensure progress and development for the land and people of Ijesaland" (Ifaturoti and Orolugbagbe 1992: 13). The organization realized "from its early beginnings that ... they must have the intellectual capacity to understand the meaning and scope of 'development' and [that] ... the key to 'development' ... lay in Western education" (p. 13). Many of the early members were *osomaalo* traders, and since they were predominantly Christian, they also emphasized Christianity. Membership was open to "all sons of Ijesaland who in the opinion of the society are deemed qualified" (p. 14), and there was also a provision that non-Ijesas could be admitted; one man with origins in Ibadan became the fifth president.

From its early years, the Egbe Atunluse placed major emphasis on education. In 1924 the organization decided to obtain land for an educational project, as well as to make contacts with Ijesas living outside Ijesaland to collect funds (Ifaturoti and Orolugbagbe 1992: 31). By 1928 they were making efforts to establish a secondary school; this led ultimately to the founding of the Ilesa Grammar School in 1934, still one of the most important secondary schools in Ilesa. The Egbe Atunluse continued to support the school in a variety of ways, finding the principal and teachers and helping to provide accommodations for them. Much later, in the 1960s, the school was taken over by the government. In the intervening years, the Egbe Atunluse was instrumental in the founding of another secondary school, the Obokun High School, founded in 1954 as a coeducational school; later the Ilesa Grammar School also became coeducational (Ifaturoti and Orolugbagbe 1992: 31–40). The founding of these two secondary schools by the Egbe Atunluse is usually referred to as the most significant contribution made by the organization to the community. Although it was also involved in a variety of other issues, it became less central to the development of Ilesa over the years. By the time of its anniversary celebration in 1992, many questions had been raised over its lack of continuing influence and effectiveness, and in their book published in connection with the anniversary, the authors call for a renewal of the organization and suggest in particular that the Egbe Atunluse should work with hometown organizations from other Ijesa towns, noting that the Egbe Atunluse was seen as largely an Ilesa-based organization (Ifaturoti and Orolugbagbe 1992: 63–65).

Among the themes of the 1992 celebrations was the continuing need for Ijesas to unite and work for progress and development. The symposium that was part of the seventieth-anniversary celebration was entitled, "The Unity of Ijesaland—the Concept: Is It Worth Working For? What Method to Achieve It?" Although the event, which took place on a rainy weekday afternoon, was not well attended, the speeches given provide an indication of not only the concerns of the Egbe Atunluse but also of broader issues in Ijesaland at that time. (This event is discussed in greater detail in Chapter 9.) At the book-launching that was also part of the anniversary celebration, the theme moved from the need for unity to the necessity for the Egbe Atunluse, and others, to work for the development and progress of the region. One speaker, referring to the past successes of the organization, said that there is disappointment that they are not doing more now, asking, "If small towns all over are raising funds for development, why not Ilesa?" Another speaker, Lawrence Omole, considered to be one of the most successful Ijesa entrepreneurs, was equally critical, stating that the Egbe Atunluse had "failed to deal with some problems, such as the unity of Ijesaland, the place of Ijesaland in Nigeria, and the economic development of Ijesaland." He said that these are "linked issues" and that "it is time for self-examination and hard work. We must protect the values we cherish and which are now threatened."

These comments and criticisms are voiced in several different contexts, not only about the Egbe Atunluse but also the situation in Ijesaland in general. In Chapter 9 I will consider in greater detail the ways in which chieftaincy and intertown disputes affect the perceptions of unity and development in Ijesaland. At the same time that the Egbe Atunluse itself is trying to reassert its influence on these issues, through activities such as the 1992 celebration, other organizations are pointing to the Egbe Atunluse as an example, both for its successes and failures.

Although the Egbe Atunluse had a broad focus—its motto is "Progress and Improvement"—and made its major contributions in the development of secondary schools, other organizations took a more narrow economic focus. There have been several efforts at promoting economic development and industrialization, including one in the 1960s by a now-defunct group called the Ijesa Planning Council, headed by Lawrence Omole (Omole 1991: 103). Two of these efforts are frequently referred to, one as a negative example, the other as a successful model of industrialization. Together, the two inform much of the current debate about the appropriate way to pursue economic development in Ijesaland and the appropriate role for hometown organizations in those efforts. For example, one of the speakers at the Egbe Atunluse symposium described above stated that the "IBL [International Breweries Limited] shows the possibility for investment here" and added, "Thank God that IBL came along twenty years after IUTTC."

IBL was established by several local entrepreneurs in 1978; the IUTTC was a much earlier effort at economic and industrial development.

The IUTTC formed in the early 1940s when a group of Ijesa business-men came together in "the first major cooperative effort on the part of Ijesa to pool their resources together to establish a company which was expected to serve as an intermediary between the local people and the big British trading companies. By so doing, it was hoped that it would greatly assist in promoting the economic development of Ijesaland" (Omole 1991: 53). The founding members were mainly involved in cocoa-buying and transporta-tion enterprises on their own, and the IUTTC was engaged in the same eco-nomic activities. For a time, the IUTTC was successful, and it owned sev-eral buildings in Ilesa and Lagos. It still exists in limited form and owns a building in Lagos; the current members are the sons of the founders. However, the general view among people in Ilesa is that the IUTTC encountered problems early in its history. These involved disagreements and accusations among the members and the fundamental problem that the members were in competition with themselves; that is, as the son of one shareholder explained, his father had an independent produce-buying com-pany so he, and most of the others as well, were directly competing with the IUTTC. One of the issues raised when people today refer to the exam-ple of the IUTTC is whether a group, or organization, can successfully engage in investment and industrial development.

In contrast, IBL is seen as an example of a successful industrial invest-ment effort undertaken by a small group of individuals, not by an organiza-tion. The process of establishing the brewery, which took most of the 1970s, is described in some detail in Lawrence Omole's autobiography (1991: 106–119), as Omole was one of the leaders in this project. The brewery opened in 1978 and has expanded since then. In addition, it has led, according to Omole, to the establishment of several related industries (1991: 119–120). However, it is the brewery that nearly everyone refers to when they discuss the need for industrialization in Ijesaland, an example that proves it can be done. IBL is seen as having had a significant impact on Ilesa, not only on those who are its investors and employees but on the entire community, demonstrating what can be done and encouraging others to undertake industrial projects there. (See Trager 1985b for analysis of the brewery's economic impact on market women.) People discuss why the brewery was successful when other efforts have not been and argue about whether it is a unique case or one that provides a model for others. And since it was established by a small group, rather than by a larger organization, people refer to it to support the view that organizations cannot suc-cessfully engage in economic development. This has been a major debate in the Ijesa Solidarity Group, the newest organization to work for the develop-ment of Ijesaland (discussed below).

Fathers, Sons, and the Lessons of History

The historical precedents considered here are relatively recent, from the 1920s, 1940s, and 1970s. Ijesas also point to more distant events as provid-ing examples from history. For example, the Kiriji War of the nineteenth century is given as a case of Ijesa unity and has been the focus of celebra-tions in the 1980s and 1990s (see Chapter 9). In the organizations discussed here, many of those involved were the fathers of men who are today engaged in Ijesa organizations. This has significant implications for how people perceive the efforts being made today. Yet many men point to their fathers' generation as having done more than they (e.g., the Ilesa Grammar School by the Egbe Atunluse). They criticize themselves for not having come together in as effective a manner as the earlier generation did, and they seek to emulate the model provided by their fathers' generation. At the same time, there were disagreements and conflicts among the fathers, and their sons are well aware of these; in many cases they continue to be influ-enced by their knowledge and perception of the past, of specific events and the roles played by their own and others' fathers. As Justice Kayode Eso put it in a conversation in 1994, "The modern past is a catalyst to what is going on now." He referred to both political and economic disputes and divisions of the 1940s and 1960s—especially the 1941 riot in Ilesa and party politics in the 1960s—as still affecting how individuals today interact (see Peel 1983 for information on these events). The same is true with regard to the efforts at economic development and industrialization, as these involved specific individuals who had specific relationships with each other, relationships that continue to affect how they, or their sons and daughters, view one another and interact today.

The Ijesa Solidarity Group:
The Emergence of a New Organization

In July 1991, a new organization formed in Ijesaland, the Ijesa Solidarity Group. It had a broader agenda and sought to have a more inclusive mem-bership than many of the other Ijesa hometown and regional organizations. Its founders were highly conscious of the problems encountered by other organizations in the past and saw the new organization as different in several crucial aspects. Examination of the formation and activities of this organization provides a view of the current debates and problems, as well as prospects, for locally based organizations in the current period. It makes clear that these groups, like organizations everywhere, are involved in a process, with changes in the goals and focus of the organization as changes occur in the surrounding environment, and as members' ideas of what is important take shape and change over time.

Osun State and the Formation of the Ijesa Solidarity Group

The impetus for the formation of the Ijesa Solidarity Group came from the expectations that a new state, Osun State, was about to be established, which would encompass the Ijesa area, Ife, and other areas of the former Oyo State. In July 1991, a group of Ijesa men, called together by business-man Lawrence Omole, met to discuss ways in which they could influence the outcome. In particular, they were concerned with the location of the state capital; they decided to form an organization to act as a pressure group to lobby for Ilesa as the new state capital. Although they were unsuc-cessful in that effort (Oshogbo was named the state capital), those who met decided to continue as an organization, which they then called the Ijesa Solidarity Group.[3]

By October 1991, the group had decided that the Ijesa Solidarity Group should be a membership organization "to continue working for the develop-ment of Ijesaland and all of Osun State," as one of the founding members put it. They issued a call for members and began to raise money, which was seen as the foundation for the activities they expected to carry out. A pro-tem chairman was appointed, E. A. Ifaturoti, one of the original group, and Lawrence Omole became the patron; a pro-tem council was formed, and plans were soon under way for publishing a newsletter, drafting a constitu-tion, and establishing a set of broad goals for the organization. Forty-three people attended a meeting that month; the list of those who attended included prominent Ijesas residing in Lagos and Ibadan, as well as several living at home in Ilesa.

During the first year of its existence, there was considerable activity, including committee appointments, meetings, and publication of the newsletter. The first newsletter, published in December 1991, reported on the July meeting, referring to it as a meeting of a "representative" group from all four LGAs in Ijesaland "to discuss non-partisan aspects of the political fortunes of Ijesaland." This group decided:

- that we of Ijesaland should resolve to be the keepers of our broth-ers;
- that pooling our resources, we should focus on developing every nook and corner of Ijesaland; and

- that through achieving complete social integration in our community, we can show the way to the attainment of this same noble objective nationwide. (ISG Newsletter 1991: 1)

In his letter to members, the chairman described the problems facing Ijesaland, saying that over the past fifty or sixty years there had been "stagnation in Ijesaland" and that even though the government may have neglected the region "there can be no reason why we should ignore to do the little that lies within our own powers to improve Ijesaland" (ISG Newsletter 1991: 2). He referred to so-called stateism—the efforts of various organizations to work for new states for their own ethnic group and region and to oppose those seen as "nonindigenes" of the state. He argued that Ijesas should oppose this trend:

Coming together is the other side of the coin. One side is the one represented by Stateism and hatred of, and discrimination against those who are not of the same ethnic group as ourselves. Coming together means: recognising ourselves as brothers and sisters and doing things together which would be difficult to achieve individually or in smaller groups.... Coming together would show other groups the example of what can be done by love and the futility of sectionalism and hate. (ISG Newsletter 1991: 3)

He ended by emphasizing the nonpolitical nature of the ISG: "The Solidarity Group is not a political party but stands for those things affecting Ijesa people upon which there can be no political difference among us. They represent issues which are above politics" (ISG Newsletter 1991: 3–4).

This first newsletter also described the broad goals of the ISG, which were later modified somewhat and stated as follows in the organization's first constitution:

(i) To promote unity, social, economic, educational, and cultural integration among all people who are Ijesa or are of Ijesa origin or descent or by marriage.
(ii) To harness the resources of the people and territory of Ijesaland to promote rapid economic and sustained economic growth and effect development and modernisation of Ijesaland.
(iii) To always act, with due cognisance being paid to the necessity for the continued integration of the diverse peoples of the Federation of Nigeria, to foster brotherhood and oneness among all Ijesa. (Ijesa Solidarity Group Constitution n.d.)[4]

In elaborating on the second of these goals, the first newsletter referred to the development of an investment corporation for the establishment of industry; as will be further discussed below, this became a central point of debate within the organization.

By July 1992, one year after the organization first formed, the group had focused on several of these organizing themes and discussed them at a meeting that month. One theme was unity. Justice Kayode Eso had been asked to look into "the problems of disunity in Ijesaland." He reported on the distrust that exists among Ijesas, and the historical roots of that distrust, saying that some people wanted to focus on tradition—on the past—whereas others say that they should "talk about what we should do in the modern day without reference to tradition." He advocated a middle course, saying that they must pay attention to history but also find a basis for moving ahead, that Ijesas should recognize that "we are all Ijesas" and that people outside the area don't distinguish among them. These comments, and others at the meeting, were expressed in the context of chieftaincy disputes that were taking place at the time, as well as in the context of the feelings that exist among those from Ilesa and those from other towns. (These issues, and the overall question of unity, are discussed further in Chapter 9.) Several speakers made practical suggestions for overcoming some of the barriers among those from different Ijesa towns; beyond encouraging membership from the whole region, one idea that was later adopted was to hold some of the meetings in other Ijesa towns rather than in Ilesa.

The members at the July 1992 meeting also discussed proposals for an Ijesa National Day, which was then in the process of being organized. Several speakers pointed out that such a day was not likely to be successful given the problems of disunity, and ISG did not participate as an organization in this celebration, although an Ijesa National Day did take place in 1993 (see Chapter 6).

The second major theme reflected in the goals of the organization and considered at some length at the July 1992 meeting was economic development. By the time of this meeting, what had originally been termed an investment corporation was now being referred to as an "endowment fund." The leading role in this discussion was again taken by Justice Eso, the chairman of the organization's Ways and Means Committee. He talked about getting N1,000 contributions from each of 125,000 Ijesas, resulting in a fund of N12.5 million. More important, he discussed what they should do with that kind of money: "Do we want it to build palaces for the *oba*? Or to build marketplaces? Or for town halls? Let us use it for a purpose that will bring our children to Ijesaland, to create employment.... We should use the money in a way that will bring a future to Ijesaland." In the discussion that followed, other speakers argued that there was a problem with a broad endowment fund, pointing out that people will want to know "exactly what it will be used for before they put in their money" and that "it's not enough to say that we're all Ijesas and the money is for the development of Ijesaland." One speaker called instead for an investment fund, through which contributors would receive dividends on their investment. The issue of how to create a fund for economic development became a key debate in the organization (see below). Despite the questions about what type of fund to establish, and how to go about the process of economic development, members did begin to make contributions.

Membership

In the first year of its existence, the ISG issued a call for membership which began, "DON'T SIT ON THE FENCE!" and continued, "DO YOU CONSIDER YOURSELF TO BE AN IJESA? IF SO, DO YOU FEEL PROUD TO BE ONE? ARE YOU EAGER TO PROMOTE THE GROWTH AND DEVELOPMENT OF IJESALAND? THEN BE PART OF THE IJESA SOLIDARITY GROUP."

Three differences separated ISG's membership from the other organizations discussed above. First, unlike most other associations, the ISG wanted both men and women as members, although most of the early active members were men. Second, they did not want a membership restricted by age, and although the founders were mainly men in their sixties and seventies, they actively sought the involvement of younger Ijesas. Third, from the beginning the group tried to recruit members from throughout Ijesaland, and the founders were concerned that it not be seen as simply an organization of people from Ilesa.

Despite its statement that "it is hoped that *all* Ijesa persons will eventually join" (ISG Newsletter 1991: 6), the organization focused its attention on professionals. This is clear from the call for membership, where not only titles but also occupations and areas of competence were requested. The list of those who attended the first meeting and the members of the council reflect this emphasis, with businessmen, professors, engineers, and lawyers being named. As one of the organizers explained, they wanted to have members from a wide variety of fields, with prominent people who could "influence decisions" and work to benefit the development of Ijesaland. As a person active in one of the other Ijesa organizations but not in ISG saw it, the ISG was an "elite organization."

By the end of June 1992, the organization had about 200 members, with more than half from Ilesa and the rest from the other LGAs in the region; about a third resided in Lagos and another third in Osun State; the rest lived in other parts of the country. All members were required to pay a membership fee of N200 per year; in addition, they were asked to subscribe to the investment fund with a minimum of N1,000 per person, and later they were asked for other contributions as well. Clearly, only people with reasonably large incomes could afford these fees.

Differences from Other Organizations

Those involved in establishing the Ijesa Solidarity Group saw it as being very different from other organizations and societies. In addition to its efforts to be more inclusive in its membership, there were fundamental differences in goals and emphasis. It started out with two major concerns—the unity of Ijesaland, and economic development in the region. For example, one founding member from an Ijesa town outside Ilesa commented that it had "a completely different purpose [from other organizations], to try to foster unity and get away from the chieftaincy problems which are splitting Ijesaland. They are trying to find common ground." Another member, a woman from Ilesa but based in Lagos, commented that ISG is "concerned with the development of Ijesaland—economically, industrially, socially." She said that it is "concerned with the whole of Ijesaland, not just Ilesa" and that they "want to get as many people involved as possible and spread things around Ijesaland." An Ilesa-based businessman saw it as "a catalyst that will help to find areas of investment and help provide infrastructure" so that more industry would come to Ilesa and Ijesaland. And a young engineer, working in Lagos, also spoke of the need for economic development, noting that although he didn't grow up in Ilesa, he always comes back and is concerned "about the state of the economy [in Ilesa], the joblessness." These and other members were determined to see the organization take effective action, not to become like other organizations that they saw as being merely social clubs—good for talk but no longer effective in working for the development of the region.

The group hired an executive secretary to handle administrative matters and established three committees that were supposed to carry out most of the activities, along with the council; the organization thus differed structurally from other societies.

At the same time that there was broad agreement about these goals, however, there were also different interpretations and understandings among the members about how to actually go about achieving their objectives. Three issues stand out in the discussions and debates that took place within the organization in the first several years of its existence: economic development; leadership; and broadening the original goals. At the same time, it quickly became clear that it is much easier to talk about the need for unity than to actually resolve the various conflicts that existed.

Debates

The Ijesa Solidarity Group started out with an ambitious agenda. Not only did it want to solve the problem of distrust and lack of integration among the people of various Ijesa towns, as well as disputes among their chiefs; it also wanted to find ways to pursue economic development for the towns and region and, more generally, for Osun State. Later on, additional objectives and concerns were added to the activities of the organization. During the first five or six years of its existence there was a broad consensus among the members about their goals, but it quickly became apparent that there were several areas of disagreement as well.

The first and most important issue was how to go about the objective of economic development. Initially, some members spoke of the formation of an investment corporation that would involve the pooling of financial resources in order to "cause feasibility studies to be carried out and promote the establishment of several cottage industries spread throughout Ijesaland" (ISG Newsletter 1991: 7). Furthermore, these cottage industries would be "jointly subscribed by the corporation and the local inhabitants who shall have substantial holdings in such industries" (ISG Minutes of Pro-Tem Council Meeting, May 9, 1992). Later, the concept of an endowment fund was introduced. There were also some specific ideas about types of economic activities that might be developed. Many thought it best to develop industry based on local agricultural products. For example, one suggestion was that a rice-processing mill be established in one of the smaller towns, Erin-Ijesa, an area where rice production had increased in recent years. Another idea was for the organization to buy land-clearing equipment to lease to farmers. There were also discussions of providing infrastructure, perhaps in the form of an industrial park, as well as of establishing banking facilities such as community banks.

There was broad agreement that they wanted to help generate employment, develop industry of some type, and spread economic activities more evenly around Ijesaland. People spoke of "cottage industries," but there was no agreement on specific industries that would be suitable. More basic, there was no agreement on how to go about establishing these industries. The differences of opinion revolved around several issues. One issue was whether it was best to have an endowment fund to which people would contribute for broad goals of economic development versus establishing an investment fund where people would own shares. A related issue was whether there would be investment for specific projects or a general fund that could be tapped when needed. Another issue was whether the organization, as an organization, should get involved directly in economic development at all, or whether they should simply work to provide infrastructure and suggestions of appropriate industries and let individual entrepreneurs develop the industries. For example, one member said that at first he thought that the organization should establish industries but that later he and others decided that it would "be better to provide the infrastructure for industry, such as water and electricity"; he thought they should establish an industrial park in a town such as Ijebu-Jesa or Ibokun and encourage people to establish industries there. Others thought that an investment fund, with members and others holding shares, would be best: "People should feel they are investing in something, and they can either increase the amount they invest, or they can sell their shares if they don't see things happening."

The fundamental problem in this debate was the difference between those who were willing to contribute money to an organization for economic development versus those who preferred to operate as individual entrepreneurs. In effect, this debate goes back to that raised by the experiences in the Ijesa United Trading and Transport Company and the brewery— depending on how those involved saw the failure of the first and the success of the second. One member, a successful businessman himself, argued that it isn't possible "to have joint ventures and investments in industry from a community group." Although he recognized the success of the brewery, he felt that was due mainly to the efforts of one individual, Lawrence Omole, and he gave counterexamples of other unsuccessful attempts. In his view, "The problem with economic development is that people don't trust others; if they want to invest in something they want to do it on their own, and not have others involved who might misuse the money." Furthermore, in his view, "When people contribute to something, they want to be able to come back later and ask how their money was spent, and see something that it was spent on, something visible." In sum, this individual argued, "joint ventures can't work in this environment."

A second issue that became the focus of debate in the organization was leadership, in particular whether the founding members should continue to lead the organization after several years or whether new, younger members should take on leadership roles. The most active early members were men in their seventies, including some who had already retired and others who were still working. The man who was the first chairman, E. A. Ifaturoti, began talking about handing over to someone else as early as 1992. In fact, however, he became the first president and was still the central figure in the organization by 1996. By that time, however, he and other early leaders were arguing that younger members should take the lead: "It's time for the 'younger element' to take charge. Those who started the organization have done what they can, in getting it organized, and now a younger element must take over if it's going to continue." At the same time, some of the younger members, although believing it important to be involved in the organization, felt that they didn't have time to devote to it, that they were still too busy with their own professions and businesses. Underlying this debate was the issue of respect for age in Yoruba culture and the fact that in most other organizations—established as age-based groups—the same people tend to remain the leaders for very long periods.

The issue of changing leadership became a central point of discussion at the meeting of the organization that took place in April 1996, a meeting not attended by the president, who was out of the country. One of the committee chairmen spoke forcefully, arguing that "those of us who are over sixty-five" want young people to run the organization; "it is high time that young people run the organization." He went on to note that younger people may not feel comfortable disagreeing with the founding leaders and that it may be difficult for "you people to sack us" but said that they needed leaders who could travel around more easily, who could better represent the organization. Several younger members, men in their fifties, responded to this argument; one said that he was "appealing to the elders" that they shouldn't abandon the leadership and that they shouldn't "hand over to the younger generation who would kill the organization in a year or two." Others proposed a gradual increase in involvement of younger members, saying that they should be given assignments, such as representing the organization in meetings with government officials. Later, one of the older members analyzed the debate in cultural terms: "The reason that the young won't take over is that there is respect for those older, and if a young person says he wants to be head of the organization in place of an older one, people will view him as an upstart." He said,

> Younger people may have ideas and feel that they won't be listened to. If someone younger presents ideas at a meeting, older people don't pay attention to them. The older people tend to be more cautious and conservative than the younger, and may view the younger ones as having "revolutionary" ideas, and so they may react negatively to ideas presented by younger people. The result is that younger people don't bother attending meetings because they feel that they won't be listened to.

This man, like many of the others at the meeting, felt that there should be no immediate change in leadership but that ultimately they needed to find a way to bring in younger officers for the organization. In fact, by 1998 a new president, and other new officers, had taken office.

A third area of some debate in the early years of the Ijesa Solidarity Group focused on the goals of the organization. Although there was broad agreement on the goals of fostering unity and undertaking economic development, over time other issues and objectives were undertaken. For example, since the organization had begun as a pressure group to lobby for Ilesa as the capital of the new Osun State, it is not surprising that people expected it to continue to lobby for Ijesa interests. When civil servants in the new state felt that they were being discriminated against as Ijesas, they came to the ISG to ask for assistance. Later, in 1996, when there was again the possibility of new states being formed, the organization took an active role in working for the formation of Oduduwa State and in again arguing for Ilesa as the capital; this time, however, a new state was not established.

As part of the effort to foster unity, members became involved in helping to resolve disputes in the region, including chieftaincy disputes among the Ijesa towns as well as factional disputes within specific communities. For example, a special committee was formed to look into the situation in one community where there was a serious dispute involving two factions (see Chapter 9).

Another project was the establishment of a historical research fund, which began in 1995. The leaders in this effort argued that it was necessary to undertake historical research as a basis for both of the central goals of the organization—unity and development. As Bolanle Awe put it in the article she wrote for the launching of the fund, *"The Ijesa have a history of which they can be proud*. It is a past that should inform their present" (Awe 1995–1996: 5; emphasis in original). Others, however, felt that the organization was trying to do too many different things and that it would be better if it remained focused. As one member put it, the group had "undertaken too many different things more or less simultaneously." Instead, he said, "they should choose one cause, and do it well, and pursue other issues later." That cause should be economic development; "it is economic development that will help the people, and that is what they should be focusing on." History is important, he added, but it can be done later.

Activities, Results, and Criticism

Over the first several years of its existence, the Ijesa Solidarity Group had some accomplishments as well as some disappointments; members themselves were actively engaged in critically evaluating the problems that had occurred and were trying to find solutions. The organization was successful in establishing itself as a new group, most of whose members were professionals, primarily living outside Ijesaland but concerned about the region. With a membership of between 400 and 500, they had not come anywhere near the original ambitious goal of thousands of members. But they had been successful in attracting both men and women, as well as those of varying ages. By 1998 the debate over leadership had been resolved, and a younger man had become president of the organization. The organization had adopted a constitution and considered some changes in its structure, with the hope that it would become more effective.

They had had some success in addressing the problem of unity among Ijesas. Members came from several different towns and were highly conscious of the importance of not appearing to be dominated by those from Ilesa. To address this issue, a meeting was held in March 1995 in the town of Ibokun, which included a courtesy call on the *oba* there, as well as recognition of others of importance from that town and nearby ones.[5] The group had become involved in attempts to resolve some chieftaincy disputes, although members recognized that these were not issues that could be resolved in a short period of time.

The organization had also successfully mobilized some resources and had established an office and hired administrative staff. Funds had been collected for the endowment fund, and other funds were collected for the historical research fund. ISG had begun to be recognized as a group different from other societies in its concern with economic development and with trying to do something for the "common people."

However, no economic activities had been undertaken, and there was considerable criticism and disappointment about this failure. For example, at the December 1994 meeting of the organization, the president referred to the "lofty objectives" with which the group had started. But he said, "If we are to claim success, the net beneficiaries of our activities would be the ordinary peasants—to bring them something that would make their position better. So the economic committee was established to examine how to get economic growth in Ijesaland. But it hasn't happened, we haven't moved forward." Later, at the same meeting, he said, "We've existed for three years and we haven't done anything. The man in the village doesn't know we exist." A few months later, he expressed the view that the ISG had been successful in "raising people's consciousness" but that they hadn't succeeded in actually doing anything, such as establishing an industry. He also noted that they needed more information about "what is needed at the grassroots," to find out what people want and what the problems are. (The debate about economic development is examined at greater length in Chapter 8.)

By 1995–1996 some of the founding members had become disenchanted and were less involved than they had previously been. Others, including some of the younger members, continued to see the ISG as an important organization, one they wanted to continue to support as members. Some recognized that expectations had probably been too high; one woman commented after the 1996 meeting that some of the people involved expected too much to happen too quickly.

In the evolution of the Ijesa Solidarity Group in its first few years, we see a process similar to that which occurs in many new organizations: First, a group of interested people came together around some fairly specific, but broad, goals; then, as more people got involved, the goals became more diffuse and there were different understandings about how best to achieve them. In the process, changes occurred in organizational structure; some members lost interest while others became more involved. The emergence of the ISG occurred in a particular economic, political, and historical context, a time when Ijesas were seeking to improve their situation within the new Osun State while also trying to respond to the economic difficulties many in the area were facing. Members were conscious not only of the contemporary context but also of organizational efforts in the past in which they, or their fathers, had been involved, as well as the successes and failures of organizations like the Egbe Atunluse and the IUTTC.

❧   ❧   ❧

The last section of this chapter has focused on the internal evolution and debates in the development of the Ijesa Solidarity Group. However, these debates and developments did not take place in a vacuum. Rather, the ongoing economic and political crises in the country informed the perspectives of the members, affecting their perceptions of what was feasible and worth undertaking. Chapters 7–9 examine the changing economic and political contexts for local development efforts, considering not only those of the Ijesa Solidarity Group but also those discussed and undertaken by other organizations and communities.

Notes

1. I use *hometown organization* and *hometown association* to refer to all groups with a hometown or home region base. Others (e.g., Honey and Okafor 1998) use the term *hometown association* only to refer to "apex" organizations that encompass other smaller groups.

2. A study of the history of town unions in Ijesaland emphasizes still another organization, the Egbe Omo Ibile Ijesa, which played a key role in political disputes in the area in the 1940s (Omoni 1984).

3. Several years later, in 1996, the issue of formation of new states and capitals arose again; efforts were made by the Ijesa Solidarity Group and others to influence the government to establish Oduduwa State, encompassing Ijesaland and Ife, and those involved in ISG again were working to have Ilesa named the state capital; however, Oduduwa State was not established. See Chapter 9 for additional discussion of this process.

4. A new constitution was drafted in 1998, but the statement of aims remained the same.

5. Later, a meeting was held in Ijebu-Jesa but the *oba* there had just suddenly died, so that meeting was less successful than the one in Ibokun.

6

Ceremonies and Celebrations: The Symbolism of Hometown Links

The Council of Ijesa Societies–Ilesa First Merit Awards Day for Distinguished Ijesa Sons/Daughters and Corporate Bodies took place on a Saturday afternoon in April 1992. The large cafeteria of International Breweries was festooned with balloons and banners; the tables were set with white cloths and place settings, and a long table at one end of the room served as the "high table" where all the honorees and speakers were to be seated. By 2:00 P.M., when the occasion was scheduled to begin, many prominent Ijesa men and women had arrived and taken their seats. Some had traveled from Lagos and Ibadan for the weekend, others from Ife and other nearby communities, and others came from within Ilesa. The roster of those to be honored—twenty people, as well as four organizations—included some of the best-known Ijesas in the country, including past government officials, academics, and businesspeople. A large glossy brochure, sold for N30 each, not only gave printed citations and photos for each honoree but also contained many congratulatory advertisements from other organizations and individuals.

Shortly after two o'clock, the honorees and speakers were called to sit at the high table. Later, both the Owa Obokun of Ijesaland and the deputy governor of Osun State, Prince Adesuyi Haastrup, who is from Ilesa, joined the others. A professional orator, Baba Ijesa, greeted and welcomed everyone; then a prayer was given by an Anglican priest, emphasizing our "fatherland" (Ijesaland) and the children of Ijesaland. E. A. Ifaturoti, the chairman of the occasion, read his speech, which was printed in the commemorative brochure. After greeting everyone, he began by saying, "What we celebrate today can be summed up in the word GREATNESS." He went on,

> *I have asked myself what the Council of Ijesa Societies is trying to tell us. I find that in a very objective way, they are telling us that we do have illustrious men and women in Ijesaland and*

119

*therefore, that we should rally these and others in a bid to save,
if not the whole of Nigeria, at least Ijesaland. If Ijesa people
succeed in saving Ijesaland, the Egbas, Egbaland, and Ijaws
their part of Nigeria and so on, we will succeed in arresting the
speed of decadence and deterioration that is apparent in
Nigeria.... Our Guests of Honour by their industry and character, by dint of perseverance and absolute faith in themselves,
have added a definition to the name tag we wear [Ijesa]—industrious, highly principled and highly motivated people. These
qualities of the Ijesa people are acknowledged and recognised
nationwide....*

*Today we live in a country in which everything is losing
value and the future is unsure. We live in a country in which
mediocrity is encouraged and promoted and qualities such as I
have extolled are shunned.... By a continuous process of bad
governance, life has become increasingly difficult for most people, even salary earners. The peasants, worst of all, are suffering and quality of life is deteriorating and life expectation
diminishing. In circumstances such as this, of necessity patriotic
elements in every community should rally under the leadership
of their great men. Only in that way can the evil effects of our
economic situation be ameliorated. It is to the credit of many of
our award recipients that they have pioneered the founding of
an Ijesa Solidarity Group precisely to take care of this.... In my
view, what the Council of Ijesa Societies–Ilesa is telling us
today is that those of us who are privileged through education
and exposure should rally to save Ijesaland and make it great.
We should be the voice of our voiceless peasants who number
hundreds of thousands.*

He concluded by noting that those being honored had "served
Nigeria well" and that they should "complement ... service to the
Nation with service to Ijesaland"; then he referred to the great men of
the past as well as the "great men and women of the coming generation
who will actualise our Ijesa dream" (Ifaturoti, 1992a).

Next, the president of the Council of Ijesa Societies, Chief A. O.
Lamikanra, gave his speech, repeating some of the themes in the first
speech and adding new ones. He first noted the wealth of talented people in Ijesaland:

*My pleasure on this occasion is matched by my pride in the abil-
ity of the Council of Ijesa Societies to bring together under one
roof the very cream of Ijesas at home and abroad. It is my sin-
cere wish that this is a new beginning in the social intercourse
between all Ijesa sons and daughters.... Looking at the illustri-
ous names on our list of awardees as well as the calibre of our
invitees one can only be impressed by the quality of talent which
is available to us in Ijesaland. It is unlikely that any other section of Nigeria can boast of so many achievers in so many
diverse fields as we have in this hall today. The combined tal-*

ents of those of you present here represent a vast potential that can be tapped for the development of Ijesaland.

But, he noted, in order to do anything, there needs to be unity:

Before we get to the stage of actually doing anything however, we must have UNITY. All Ijesas must be prepared to think in terms of the greater Ijesaland, where all Ijesas will feel truly at home and consider that they belong in body, mind and soul.... The need for unity and clarity of purpose cannot be overemphasised especially at this time when the states of the Federation are getting progressively smaller in size and the possibility of an IJESA STATE cannot be dismissed out of hand.

He then challenged everyone to make contributions for development and to work for industrialization of the region:

The Council of Ijesa Societies–Ilesa is hereby giving an undertaking that it will continue to challenge all Ijesas with ability in any form of human endeavour to come forward and make a positive contribution toward the development, physical and otherwise, of our fatherland. We are talking directly to all of you present here today and through you to all sons and daughters of Ijesaland where ever they may be....

The special message for this year's award ceremony is INDUSTRIALISATION. Our land, Ijesaland, is richly blessed with natural and mineral resources. Our agricultural land is fertile and abundant with untold wealth in the form of precious minerals. The climate over Ijesaland is healthy and we are centrally placed, especially in Western Nigeria and beyond so we have access to a large market for our industrial goods. More than all these we have accomplished people who by their training can supply the brains and sophisticated man power needed to drive the engines of Ijesa Industrialization. ALL THAT IS REQUIRED IS THE WILL. There are many of us who have devoted a whole production life time to the development of other parts of Nigeria. Now is the time to think of the fatherland and the immense benefit which will accrue to our youths who will no longer have to leave home in search of the proverbial golden fleece. Now is the time to think of Ijesaland as a place where we wish to live and not simply as the place where we wish to be buried.... The example of the International Breweries is one we can see and learn from. There is no doubt whatsoever that this single industrial concern has been able to change the face of Ijesaland for the better in the last ten short years.... It is good to dream of the time when this company [i.e., IBL, where the ceremony took place] will be only one of many employing thousands of people in Ijesaland. That time will come only through the efforts of each one of us (and many other Ijesas) present here today. (Lamikanra 1992)

Toasts to Nigeria and to Ijesaland were made by two speakers, although drinks had not yet been served to most of the tables. The Owa of Ilesa arrived, and at about 4 P.M. the award presentations began. Each citation was read aloud, and each awardee was given a plaque; Olori Remi Agunlejika, the wife of the late *owa*, was called on to present the plaques to the first honorees, and later the wife of the deputy governor presented plaques. Those honored ranged from Lawrence Omole, Oladele Olashore, and Kayode Eso—people we have discussed in earlier chapters—to others such as Christopher Kolade, then chief executive of Cadbury, a large food-processing corporation, and Bolaji Akinyemi, former foreign minister of Nigeria. Women were honored as well, including Bolanle Awe, Irene Thomas, and an engineer, Joanna Olatunbi-Maduka. Each citation provided a summary of the individual's accomplishments, usually pointing out the difficulties they had surmounted in their early life, and emphasizing how much he or she had done for Ijesaland. For example, the citation for Chief I. O. Akinmokun stated that he built the market stalls in Ikeji-Ile, his hometown, and supplied books to primary school students there, as well as scholarships for university education. The citation for Prince Michael Adewale-Adediran begins by stating that "the pathway to glory and success has been very rough and tough." After describing his schooling, it goes on: "young Adewale could not go beyond secondary school due to abject poverty." It then describes his business success in establishing Adediran Steel and Wire Industries Ltd. in Ilesa and concludes by describing his contributions to Ijesaland, including paying for the electrification of Iyinta, where his father had been the chief, and listing all of the organizations he belongs to and awards he has received. The testimonial for Bolanle Awe, who at the time of the ceremony was the director of the Commission for Women's Affairs in Nigeria, describes her as "renowned the world over as an academician of the first order" and points out that she "has always been a woman of the people, always ready to make practical contributions to the development of this nation." The citation for Irene Thomas emphasizes that she is an Ijesa "abroad," who, like others from Ijesa families who settled in Lagos, was born and grew up in Lagos, where she still lives:

> *Dr. Thomas may in purely physical terms be regarded as an Ijesha abroad but the heart which beats so strongly in her is totally Ijesa and her spirit is forever in the land of her fathers.... [She] has throughout her life been a worthy ambassador of Ijeshaland in many foreign places. She has served the fatherland with love and devotion and is a shining example to the many thousands of Ijesha sons and daughters who in response to the adventurous spirit in that very blood have gone abroad to seek their fortune. The future of Ijeshaland would be nothing short of glorious were*

such Ijeshas "abroad" to follow the trail blazed by Dr. Irene Modupeola Thomas. (All quotes from citations are from the brochure for the First Merit Awards Day, April 18, 1992.)

Midway through the ceremony, the Owa spoke, one of the very few speakers of the day to use Yoruba rather than English. Then a meal was served to everyone as the ceremony continued. The last awards were presented to organizations—the Egbe Atunluse, International Breweries, and the Councils of Ijesa Societies in Lagos and Ibadan. One of the award recipients gave a brief speech on behalf of the awardees, stating that "by honoring us Ijesaland is honoring itself." Finally, the deputy governor spoke, pointing out that Ijesas are prominent in all fields and all over the country but that they have not worked for their own unity. Some donations were announced, and the event ended five and a half hours after it began, at 7:30 P.M. By this time, many who had been there earlier had left; one of the key participants referred to the day as an "endurance contest."

❧ ❧ ❧

This award ceremony was one of several events organized to honor specific Ijesas, in which common themes of unity, progress, and success were articulated. These events, like many life-cycle celebrations—birthdays, weddings, funerals—reflect the Yoruba appreciation for ceremony and display while also providing opportunity to symbolically reinforce the themes articulated by hometown organizations and others. In addition to ceremonies honoring individual Ijesas, there are communal celebrations, such as the community-day celebrations (see Chapter 2).

This chapter will examine several ceremonial and celebratory events. Those that honor individuals, such as birthday parties and award ceremonies, demonstrate how an emphasis on individual success is used to articulate communal goals. In addition to the community-day celebrations, there were also efforts during this period to hold an Ijesa National Day; these efforts had varying degrees of success and reflect some of the difficulties that exist in achieving the unity so constantly advocated. Finally, the chapter considers a "traditional" ritual in modern form: the installation and coronation of a new *oba*.

Award Ceremonies

The award ceremony described above took place in April 1992; just a month earlier, another celebration honored four of the same individuals: the successful entrepreneur Lawrence Omole, professor Bolanle Awe, Justice Kayode Eso, and businessman I. O. Akinmokun. This earlier ceremony took place in Lagos and was organized by one of the hometown organizations based there—the Ijesa Society–Lagos. It took place in the evening, with a buffet dinner served around the swimming pool of a private club. Those who attended came not only from Lagos but also from Ilesa and other Ijesa towns; all were clearly identifiable as "elite" Ijesa, and all were dressed in expensive *agbadas* for the men, and *iro* and *buba* for the women, dress appropriate to a grand occasion. Speeches at this event, like those at the other award ceremony, emphasized patriotism and being Ijesa, individual success, and doing good things for the community. The president of the sponsoring organization, Ambassador O. O. Fafowora, pointed out in his welcome address that his organization, the Ijesa Society, is an organization of all Ijesa, from any part of Ijesaland. He said that they are all concerned with Ijesaland but that they are also "patriotic and nationalistic." In fact, in his view, being patriotic and nationalistic also requires that one is "concerned with one's own community." Each speech for the award recipients emphasized how well known the individual is, both nationally and internationally, as well as how much they have done for Ijesaland. For example, that for Chief Akinmokun discussed his generosity and the things he has done for his hometown, such as building market stalls and giving scholarships, many of the same things that were mentioned a month later in the award ceremony.

A year later, still another award ceremony took place to honor several Ijesas, but this one had a somewhat different focus. It was organized by a local government council, the Oriade Local Government, rather than by a hometown organization. As a result, those honored were from communities in that part of Ijesaland rather than from the whole region. Nevertheless, some of the same people were again involved: Chief Akinmokun was the chairman of the event, and Prince Oladele Olashore was one of the three men honored. The others were a lawyer, Chief Bamidele Aiku, and a judge, Justice Oyerinde Iyanda. The ceremony took place in June 1993—a time of considerable tension in the country—shortly after the June 12 election results had been annulled by the military president but before it was known what would occur next. In fact, a radio address by President Ibrahim Babangida was scheduled for that day. As a result, many of those who attended wondered if the ceremony would take place as planned and whether Prince Olashore, who was then minister of finance in the federal government, would be able to attend. In fact, the ceremony went ahead as scheduled, with all the honored guests—"eminent personalities," as they were called in the program for the day—arriving shortly after noon, along with several *obas* from the towns within the LGA, several elected officials, and other townspeople.

The chairman's speech noted that this was the first time that the local government had honored some of its "sons." He then pointed out that those being honored are "not only eminent in this local government area, they are eminent Nigerians, they are eminent throughout the whole world." As in other award ceremonies, citations were read for each man; each citation gave the man's family and educational background and a list of accomplishments, and emphasized what he has done for Ijesas. For example, that for Chief Aiku mentioned that he is the secretary of the Ijebu-Jesa Group, a hometown organization in that town, and on the board of directors of the community bank there (see Chapter 8). In the case of Oladele Olashore, the speaker, professor Kunle Odeyemi, focused on contributions at home as well as successes nationally: "Back home, at the grassroots level, where we assess critically, he has scored very high.... He has complete identity with your people, the rural folk. To you [Olashore], Iloko is the biggest city in the world; life has full meaning to you when you are around your own people." Olashore's contributions to the town, and his development of the Olashore International School, were then noted (see Chapter 8). The speaker then declared that one of the stretches of road between Iloko and Ijebu-Jesa was to be renamed Prince Oladele Olashore Way.[1] Each awardee was decorated with a wide blue sash that read "Eminent Personality Award Ori Ade Local Government."

In addition to giving the awards, this ceremony provided an occasion for the commissioning of six local-government projects and laying the foundation stone for a seventh. Therefore, before giving the awards, everyone present moved from place to place around Ijebu-Jesa and its outskirts to visit the sites of these projects, including a library in Ijebu-Jesa, a piggery, and an automobile workshop.[2]

Toward the end of the ceremony, one of the *obas* spoke, followed by Oladele Olashore, who spoke for the recipients of the awards. He pointed out that there are many others in the LGA, both men and women, who "are men of achievement" who could be honored. He then discussed the challenges ahead of them, noting that "we have quite a lot to do in [the Oriade LGA] and a lot to do in Ijesaland." He referred to the increasing numbers of smaller local-government units but emphasized the need for overall unity: "We want to continue to unite, and to ensure that we have a more vibrant Ijesaland to fight for."

Each of these three events was the "first" of its particular type—organized by a Lagos-based society, in the case of the Ijesa Society dinner; organized by a group of associations, in the case of the Council of Ijesa Societies; and organized by a local-government council, in the case of the Ori Ade LGA ceremony. All three took place in 1992 and 1993. What were the reasons for this sudden interest in award ceremonies, and how were these events viewed by those involved?

These were not the first events, or the only ones in this time period, to honor individual success. There had been earlier occasions where a single person was given a reception; for example, when Justice Kayode Eso retired from the supreme court in 1990, a reception was given for him. The Ijesa Solidarity Group gave a reception for Oladele Olashore when he was appointed finance minister in 1993, and other similar receptions and dinners took place in connection with other high-level appointments. As one person pointed out, it "honors the town" to have someone like Olashore in such a position, and therefore people from the community want to honor him.

Yet the award ceremonies seem to be on a different scale, with many more people being honored and with greater symbolic weight in their emphasis on the twin goals of unity and progress. Each of these ceremonies focused on individual success, with long citations about the many accomplishments of each of those honored. But much of the rhetoric in these citations elaborated communal values: how good an Ijesa the person is; how much he or she has done for the community and Ijesaland; how he or she is an excellent example for others of contributions everyone should make for the "fatherland." Even in the case of those who have never lived in Ijesaland, such as Irene Thomas, we get statements such as that quoted above, that she is "totally Ijesa and her spirit is forever in the land of her fathers." Furthermore, she is seen as an example "to the many thousands of Ijesa sons and daughters who ... have gone abroad to seek their fortune." In other words, these successful Ijesas are being honored not only for their success but also because they provide symbolic examples of the way in which Ijesas wish to be perceived—working for the progress and development of their home.

Much of the rhetoric at these celebrations also emphasizes the goal of Ijesa unity. The fact that the awards are given by organizations representing people "from all of Ijesaland," and that in each ceremony the award recipients were selected so that they came from several different Ijesa towns, was crucial to the success of the celebrations. Had those recognized come only from Ilesa, there would have been complaints. Beyond this, the speeches and citations pointed to what had been done for Ijesaland; even when the contributions were mainly for a single community, this was portrayed as assistance to the whole region. Some speeches, such as the concluding speech made by Oladele Olashore at the Oriade ceremony, quoted above, were explicit in calling for unity, for "identifying ourselves as Ijesa."

These occasions were seen as important; those involved felt that it was important to recognize individual success and to do it in a way that honored people from the whole region. As one of those involved in the Council of Ijesa Societies ceremony noted, "They don't easily give out awards in this place [Ijesaland], you really have to work for it, so it is very important."

And he pointed out that the awards covered all of Ijesaland, with people honored from many different Ijesa communities. Each event was well attended and was taken seriously; people made an effort to be present even when there were difficult circumstances, such as the situation at the time of the Oriade awards.

At the same time, however, people also worried that their hometown organizations would simply become groups that give receptions and award ceremonies, and they did not want this to happen. Interestingly, after the spurt of such ceremonies in 1992–1993, the interest in these events declined in subsequent years, probably because of the changing political and economic climate, which affected people's interest in recognizing achievement as well as their ability to provide the resources for organizing events of this type.

Life-Cycle Celebrations

Changes in status and major events in the life cycle are marked by ceremonies and celebrations among the Yoruba, as in many other cultures. Naming ceremonies take place a week after the birth of a child; weddings mark marriages; funerals are key occasions for celebrating the life of a person who has died, especially one who has led a long and successful life. Changes in status, such as the taking of a chieftaincy title, are also occasions to be marked by ceremony. Among Ijesas today, such events, and others, become opportunities for display, celebration, and parties. On weekend evenings, it is not unusual to find major streets in Ilesa blocked off by the chairs that are set out for such a party, although in recent years such events have become less common, and fewer last all night than was the case a few years ago. Some Ijesas have begun to criticize what they feel are ostentatious displays of wealth and status at parties and have voiced concern about the pressure on people without much money to put on a large celebration, especially in the case of the death of a parent. At the same time, when there is an occasion to be marked, it would be very difficult to *not* do so in the ways that are considered appropriate; others in the family and community will insist, for example, that a large funeral must be held even when an individual prefers a smaller event. Furthermore, in recent years, some events have become the occasion for noting individual contributions to the community and, like the award ceremonies described above, draw on the symbols and rhetoric of Ijesa unity and progress while celebrating an individual's life.

This section describes some of the celebrations that mark life-cycle and status changes, particularly those that are used to emphasize larger contributions and communal goals. Funerals are typically the most elaborate of the life-cycle ceremonies, although weddings are sometimes also very large and elaborate. Families sometimes wait weeks or months to bury an important person who has died after a long and successful life, waiting until all members of the family can gather and until they have accumulated sufficient funds to put on an appropriate celebration. For those who are Christian, a funeral may involve several days of activity, beginning with a Christian wake the evening before the funeral; then there is a church service, followed by a reception or receptions for those who attend, where a meal is served, and usually with a band and dancing; in some cases, the festivities last into the evening and even through the night. There may also be another church service, a thanksgiving service, on the following day.[3]

In the case of prominent individuals, and of those from important families, a pamphlet is printed containing the funeral service and prayers to be said, as well as a biography of the individual. Those biographies, as well as the sermons given as part of the service, not only relate the highlights of the deceased's life but also point out the contributions he or she made to the community and larger society. For example, the biography of Dorcas Takuro, who was a cloth trader in Ilesa and whose funeral took place in September 1991, gives her lineage and schooling, then describes her textile trade, noting that she was one of the "pioneer textile traders" when the new Atakumosa market opened in Ilesa in 1968, and that she "was often commissioned by the various clubs and societies in Ilesa to help select the outfit for their anniversary celebrations each December." The biography also describes how she became "one of the pioneer distributors for International Breweries" and then ends by describing her family and church activities. In another case, the funeral of Chief Samuel Olatunde Thompson, his active involvement in both church and community was emphasized. The sermon described the things he had done for the church, such as setting up a fund to maintain the organ; what he had done for people, such as helping others with their schooling; and what he had done for the town and Ijesaland, such as helping to improve the roads.

Birthday celebrations have become another important means of marking an individual's success and contributions to the community. One of the more elaborate such celebrations in recent years honored Lawrence Omole, for whom there were two eightieth birthday ceremonies in October 1995. The first was a large party with music, food, drink, and speeches, held on the grounds of his house in Ilesa. The second was a one-day conference, "Entrepreneurship within the Nigerian Economy: Past, Present, and Future," organized by a group of his friends together with the Center for Industrial Research and Development at Obafemi Awolowo University, located in the nearby city of Ile-Ife. Both events brought together many Ijesas, but the first included a wider range of people; the second, held in the

University's conference center, attracted mainly academics and other professionals.

Many of the comments and speeches at these two events again emphasized the themes of individual success, community progress, and Ijesa unity. In a lengthy toast at the birthday party, Justice Kayode Eso spoke of Omole's success in business as well as his success at assisting people in Ijesaland. He referred to the contributions he had made to educating "thousands" (through financial support), and to the fact that he had demonstrated that it is possible to "stay in Ijesaland and make good." He said that Omole had become a "giant in economics" and that through International Breweries he had given employment "to thousands." He continued by emphasizing that there is "not a single area in Ijesaland that does not benefit from IBL." But then he went on to say that what Omole has not yet achieved is "the unity of Ijesaland" and that the "unification of Ijesaland" is now his major goal, that he will bring everything he has—"his might, his money, his kindness"—to the effort to unify Ijesaland.

In his own brief comments, Omole focused on the same theme, saying that everyone "should come together and work hand in hand to develop Ijesaland." He said that the first thing to do is to create jobs for people, and the second is working hand in hand; he added that "there is love between them in Ijesaland, but it is not enough."

Speeches at the entrepreneurship conference, although more academic in tone, also celebrated both individual success and community contributions. The keynote address related Lawrence Omole's biography in some detail, emphasizing both his early difficulties and later successes in business. But these were seen not simply as demonstrating the business ability of an individual but also as assisting in the development of Ijesaland: "[Lawrence Omole's] commercial and industrial conglomerate is needed to generate employment, increase output, and industrialise Ijesaland" (Tomori 1995: 12). Even the notepads handed out to conference participants emphasized these themes, with a heading at the top of each page reading "Omole—A Vision of Industry and Philanthropy."

Communal Celebrations: Community Days, National Days, and Coronations

Award ceremonies and life-cycle celebrations of individual success represent just a few of the ways in which Ijesas have promoted the goals of unity and progress. Communal celebrations have also been an important arena for the display of symbols of unity, success, and development of the hometown. We have already considered community-day celebrations in Chapter

2, where we noted the major themes articulated in these efforts to create a new ritual tradition to bring people back to their hometowns: self-help; unity; returning home for development. In addition to the community-day celebrations in individual Ijesa towns, there have been attempts to organize Ijesa-wide celebrations, in the form of an Ijesa National Day. As is described below, these efforts have had more limited success than the community-day celebrations described in Chapter 2.

At the same time that new ritual traditions have been created, older rituals and ceremonies have continued, often with crucial modifications; one of the most important of these is the coronation of a new *oba*, or king. These events, like the newer ones, again become contexts for reemphasizing the themes of unity, progress, and returning home to develop one's hometown. In the remainder of this chapter, I will consider new as well as old communal celebrations by examining two types of events: the attempts to create an Ijesa National Day, and the installation of a new *oba* in Iloko.

Community Days and National Days

As we have seen in Chapter 2, one of the main themes of community-day celebrations has been unity, especially the unity of the town where the celebration is taking place. The closing statement of Prince Olashore at the second Iloko Day exemplifies that emphasis: "I think you have seen what it is like to be united. I believe you will continue to be united in all your endeavors." However, despite the rhetoric and symbols, not all efforts at communal celebration actually work to bring people home and unify the community. Although the celebrations in some smaller towns, such as Iloko, seem to have in fact brought members of the community together, and to have been meaningful for those involved, others have been much less successful. In particular, attempts to create Ijesa-wide celebrations, with the goals of unifying Ijesaland and bringing progress to the whole region, have created controversy and difficulties. Two more or less simultaneous efforts help to demonstrate the conflict between the rhetoric and symbols of Ijesa unity and the reality of continuing divisions.

In 1992 and 1993, two sets of individuals and organizations sought to organize events to celebrate Ijesa unity. One group promoted the concept of the celebration of a key event in Ijesa history as the basis for renewing and reestablishing unity in the region; the other promoted the idea of an Ijesa National Day. Although there was some contact between the two groups, and some individuals met with both, they were unable to agree on a common theme or event; in the end two separate events took place, one in March 1993 and the other in April 1993.

In 1992, after the civilian governor and deputy governor of Osun State were elected, the deputy governor, who was from Ilesa, discussed the idea of an Ijesa Day with one of the Ijesa hometown organizations; he promised to give N100,000 if such an event were organized. The first effort was unsuccessful; rather than organizing an official Ijesa National Day, an alternative Ilesa Day took place in December 1992, which was, according to one observer, "a washout, a complete failure." They did not get the N100,000 promised by the deputy governor. He then brought together another group of people, including the chairmen of the LGAs as well as leaders of some of the hometown organizations. According to Chief A. O. Lamikanra, one of the key participants in his role as president of the Council of Ijesa Societies, the "objective of having an Ijesa National Day was to create awareness in the whole of Ijesaland so that Ijesas everywhere begin to take pride in being Ijesas." According to him, "The Ijesas never do anything together; each town has its own events, its own community days, and so forth," and they "wanted to try to break down that situation."

An advisory committee was established consisting of Chief Lamikanra and the government officials. In addition, there were plans for a larger committee that would have representation from hometown organizations and local government areas. Instead, however, the organizing committee consisted of LGA officials, women associated with the local government, including the wives of the LGA chairmen, and several other prominent people, many of whom were from Ilesa.

From the beginning of this planning effort, questions were raised about the appropriateness of an Ijesa National Day. For example, at the Ijesa Solidarity Group meeting in July 1992, the issue was debated, with some arguing that "it is premature to have a national day for the whole of Ijesaland." Some took the view that "when we have resolved all outstanding problems, when we have resolved all issues affecting Ijesa unity, then we will go into the question of having a national day." However, others felt that it was appropriate and argued that an Ijesa national anthem should also be written.

Still another view was that if there were to be such an event it should be in connection with a traditional festival such as Ogun, one of the major festivals associated with Yoruba religion, which in the past brought a lot of people home. Eventually, E. A. Ifaturoti proposed to the Ijesa Day planning committee that the best way to have a successful national-day celebration would be to connect it with something that "represented a national event for Ijesaland." He then proposed that Ijesa National Day should be celebrated in connection with another celebration that was already being organized to mark the centenary of the return of Ijesas from the Kiriji War, which the Ijesa had fought against Ibadan in the late 1800s. The Kiriji celebration was already scheduled for March 1993.[4] Because people from all over Ijesaland were part of the Kiriji effort, and because Kiriji provides a key historical example of Ijesa unity, with war heroes whose lives are still celebrated, the organizers of that commemoration thought it would provide a fitting base for the establishment of an Ijesa National Day. However, when the local-government chairmen were approached with this proposal, they decided instead to go ahead with the Ijesa National Day as originally planned. Other events around the same time, including conflicts between Ilesa chiefs and the Owa, also affected the organization of the Kiriji event and the possibility of a jointly organized Kiriji-Ijesa National Day.

The Kiriji celebration took place in March 1993 as scheduled but primarily involved those who were descendants of war heroes. Profiles of the heroes were presented by their descendants, and an advertisement was placed in one of the newspapers, stating that the Kiriji descendants are "committed to peace with all" and proposing the formation of an association to keep alive the sentiments that brought the allies together during the wars of the 1800s. This proposal was later criticized by others who felt that such an association would exclude others and promote conflict rather than unity.

The Ijesa National Day also took place in April 1993, with a weeklong schedule of events that included a competition among secondary schools; an agricultural/industrial show held in another Ijesa town, Ibokun; a lecture on Ijesa history held in Ijebu-Jesa; and a symposium on "Strategies for Rapid Development of Ijesaland" held in the town hall in Ilesa. The main event of the week was on a Saturday in Ilesa; as at many other community-day celebrations, a program booklet was published containing speeches and advertisements for the occasion. A central part of the day's activity was the launching of a N50 million industrial development fund, for which the chief launcher was to be Chief Moshood K.O. Abiola, who at the time was a prominent and important participant in many such events around Nigeria.[5] Although Chief Abiola did not in fact attend, he did make a contribution, as did many other people. The written statements and speeches reflected once again the goals of unity and development; in addition, some also focused on the idea of an "Ijesa Nation." For example, one of the statements in the program booklet reads:

> The first Ijesa National Day which is being celebrated between 6th and 10th April 1993 marks the continued existence of the Ijesa Nation. This is the time for all patriots to rally round and raise the flag of our nation so that we can build on the collective achievements of our illustrious forebears many of whom laid down their lives to the glory of the fatherland. In remembering our heroes we must come together to lay the foundation for a brilliant future.
>
> There is no doubt that the cornerstone for our future lies in our unity and oneness of purpose, hence the great need to come together as a people with a common destiny. This is the main reason why the Ijesa National Day Celebration has now become mandatory and the success of activities connected with this occasion is the primary responsibility of all Ijesa sons

and daughters from all walks of life.... The success of this programme depends entirely on the enthusiastic Co-operation of all Societies and prominent personalities within the length and breadth [of] Ijesaland as well as all Ijesa both the inner and wider diaspora.

The Celebration of Ijesa Day is meant to serve many useful purposes but first and foremost, it will serve as an eminent forum for a meeting of minds. There is no doubt that Ijesaland is blessed with an impressive abundance of natural and human resources which can [be] utilised to the greater glory of Ijesaland and it is now time to work out a viable means of realising our enormous potential for meaningful development. It is in this respect that the Ijesa National Day Planning Committee is calling on all Ijesa Students, Artisans and indeed all Ijesas to make their contribution in terms of time, talents, abilities, money and ideas to the successful execution of plans for the first Ijesa National Day.

Following the deregulation of the Capital Market and subsequent privatisation of all public establishments, the only rational way to develop one's environment and provide meaningful and gainful employment opportunities for our teeming population of unemployed graduates and others is to establish Companies and Industries on a communal basis. One prominent and essential utility, that can facilitate the take off of such industries is the provision of Infrastructures such as Land, Electricity, Water and effective Communication Network.

It is against this background that we have chosen Industrialisation and industrial development as our theme and project for now. All monies realised therefore from the launching will be utilised to develop industrial estates in the four Local Government Areas of Ijesaland and provide infrastructures for the takeoff of industries.

It cannot be said too often that the success of the Ijesa Day Celebration depends on the efforts of all Ijesa patriots. Your particular interest and active participation in this project is indispensable to its success. Please rise up to this noble occasion with great vigour. ("Write Up on the First Ijesa National Day and Launching of a N50M Industrial Development Fund," in program booklet of the first Ijesa National Day, April 10, 1993)

Although many people did attend the Ijesa National Day celebration and a considerable amount of money was collected, the event was not attended by people from all Ijesa communities. In fact, two other Ijesa towns had their own separate community-day celebrations on the same date as Ijesa National Day. Not enough money was collected to actually begin any industrial development efforts, so what was collected was put in a bank account with the intention of adding to it from subsequent fund-raising efforts.

Subsequent efforts to organize either an Ilesa Day or an Ijesa National Day were not successful. The symbolism and rhetoric of Ijesa unity confronted the reality of continuing divisions among the various towns; conflict among different organizing groups with differing ideas; and conflict among the chiefs and *obas*. In addition, efforts at fund-raising have confronted the political and economic realities of the latter part of the period under study. Both the local conflicts and the political and economic realities are considered in depth in subsequent chapters.

"Traditional" Communal Celebrations: The Coronation of an Oba

Whereas community-day and national-day celebrations represent new traditions, other ceremonies are based in the continuation and modification of older traditions. One of the central traditions of all Yoruba towns is the installation of a new *oba*, the king or traditional ruler (see Olaniyan 1997). Both Iloko and Ijebu-Jesa installed new *obas* in 1996–1997; however, one was made into a much bigger event than the other, attracting people from all over the country to the final part of the ceremony. This was the installation and coronation of Oba Oladele Olashore in Iloko-Ijesa, ceremonies that began in February 1997 and culminated in early April. In this event, we are able to see the successful bringing together of much that we have discussed in this chapter: the return home of a highly successful individual from the town, as well as the celebration of the town's progress, development, and unity. We see as well how traditional events are being modified in significant ways to enable an emphasis on the key themes of progress and unity.

In April 1997, at the final set of events marking the accession of Oladele Olashore to the position of *oba* in his hometown, the new *oba* made a speech toward the end of the day, in which he stated: "Royal fathers should not be misled by the unbridled authority by which our forefathers exercised as rulers; while upholding and promoting our culture, we should nonetheless continue to re-evaluate and change those age long traditions that are dehumanizing or inconsistent with modernity."[6]

The installation and coronation of Oba Olashore as the Ajagbusi Ekun, the Aloko of Iloko-Ijesa, was the culmination of a long process, which took place over several months, even years. The previous *oba*, Olashore's father, had died in 1989; in the interim another chief had acted as regent. However, there had been considerable discussion about and pressure on Olashore to become the new *oba*, and in 1996 he accepted. The actual installation and coronation events began in February 1997, with several ceremonies and rituals, and concluded with a large public ceremony in April.

To some, the institution of *oba*ship—and chieftaincy in general—is seen as archaic, with little relevance to the contemporary situation. For others, in contrast, the institution is taking on new meaning; as Olaniyan (1997: 9) recently pointed out,

> The institution of *oba*ship rather than showing signs of atrophy or falling into desuetude in the face of fiercely contending forces of modernization which could have rendered it an irrelevant feudal relic, appears to be

deriving new vigor and stronger influences. Today in Yorubaland, men with varying backgrounds in the public service and the private sector with impressive educational attainments can be found in palaces wearing beaded crowns and upholding their heritage and finding favor with government.

Oba Olashore is an excellent example of this type of person, and his installation and coronation are an example of the modernization of the institution.

As with traditional installations, the process involved several stages; these included traditional rituals and practices, as well as new rituals and ceremonies. The first ceremony was a Christian anointing ceremony; this is a new element in the installation of an *oba* and linked contemporary religious beliefs (Christianity) of the individual being crowned with a tradition that is rooted in Yoruba religion. The *oba* is a sacred personality who is expected to have gone through several rituals through which "the new *oba* receives sacred empowerment from all his predecessors" (Olaniyan 1997: 3).

On the evening of the same day as the anointing ceremony, the *oba*-elect followed traditional practices by being installed as a chief, the *saloro* of Iloko. This was followed by a candlelight procession of staff and students from the Olashore International School. A week later, the first part of the traditional installation as *oba* took place, with homage being paid at traditional shrines. Then Oba Olashore moved to the house of one of the other chiefs; however, instead of spending three months there, he spent three weeks. During this time, he was expected to learn the traditions of the town and to undergo various rituals; this was the most traditional of the periods of the installation, and the *oba*-elect was required to stay in the chief's house for the entire time. He later reported that he had learned the history of the town and of his forefathers, but most of the events and rituals of this period take place in secret. Then, on March 16, 1997, the new *oba* moved to the palace in a procession with townspeople; at the palace, many groups in Iloko came to pay homage. Many of those who participated felt that this was the highlight of the process, as well as the real, or traditional, installation. However, in contemporary Nigeria, the installation of an *oba* also requires government approval; hence, there was an additional ceremony— the coronation and presentation of staff of office, which attracted enormous crowds and became the occasion for great celebration in early April. The coronation—presentation of a beaded crown—was carried out by the chiefs of the town; the presentation of the staff of office was conducted by the military administrator of Osun State. The coronation was preceded by a service in the local mosque and followed the next day by a thanksgiving service at the Methodist church in Iloko.

The symbolism of these varied ritual events is notable for the joining together of the traditional and the modern: Yoruba religious beliefs and

Ijesa *obas* and other guests at the coronation of Oba Oladele Olashore

Christianity; indigenous political institutions and the contemporary military government; the success and stature of an individual who has participated in government and business with the status ascribed to the highest traditional position in a Yoruba community; and success beyond the confines of one's hometown with coming home to develop the community. As with the other ceremonial events described in this chapter, language itself was a major marker of the modernity of the ceremonies; whereas the activities associated with those stages that are part of traditional installations were conducted in Yoruba, those associated with the contemporary aspects of the role—the Christian anointing and the coronation and presentation of staff of office—were conducted in English. All speeches at the April 5, 1997, coronation, including those by other *obas*, the Ooni of Ife and the Owa of Ilesa, were given in English.

These speeches reflect the significance placed on having someone become *oba* who has succeeded beyond the hometown; they emphasize the expectations people have for a contemporary *oba*, as well as the expectations that the *oba* himself has for the role he has agreed to take. The Owa Obokun of Ijesaland spoke of his concern that "we attract the likes of Oladele Olashore to positions of traditional rulership," declaring in addition that "the Aloko is too big for Iloko." The Ooni of Ife, generally viewed as the most influential of contemporary Yoruba *obas*, declared that "history is being made in Ijesaland today." Oba Olashore is "our pride" as well as the *ooni*'s own "personal friend"; in addition to reviewing his many accomplishments, the *ooni* stated that all could see "the good work he has been doing in this town." Similar statements came from the military authorities; Chief of General Staff Oladipo Diya, in a short speech, stated that "the ancient town of Iloko is lucky to have you as traditional ruler" and added that "you will surely serve Iloko well in its quest for modernization."[7]

Similar comments appeared in the numerous publications that focused on the coronation: all of the major newspapers in Nigeria published articles, interviews, and photographs, and the Iloko community itself put out a magazine, *Iloko Chronicle*, published by the Federation of Iloko Ijesa Students Union. The front-page headline of one newspaper, the *Daily Monitor*, conveys a sense of how the event was portrayed: "Historic Day at Iloko: OBA OLASHORE'S MOMENT OF GLORY" (April 5, 1997). Inside, opposite a congratulatory full-page advertisement from the newspaper's publisher, the first page of a three-page article about the coronation began:

> To say Oba Oladele Olashore, the Ajagbusi-Ekun of Iloko-Ijesha in Oriade Local Government, Osun State is adored by the whole of his community sounds hyperbolic but its true. According to various people interviewed in Iloko, and environs, they said the outstanding financial guru and administrator per excellence had to be begged, persuaded and convinced to assume the traditional position of his father, which became vacant seven years ago....
>
> As evidence of collective acceptance of the new *oba*, the four ruling houses in the town ... all came together in unison to choose him as their leader without any sentiment, rancour opposition or court cases.
>
> Moreover, most of the indigenes who spoke with *Daily Monitor* agreed that he has been divinely chosen to lead Iloko people, they also referred to his developmental activities in the town, ever before this present elevation. They pointed to the Olashore International School which favourably compares with any standard private school in the world, in terms of structure, personnel and facilities.
>
> He was also said to have engineered the N2 billion step down 33 KV transformer leading into the town, when he was the secretary of finance during the Interim National Government era. In addition, he was said to have made possible, the digital telephone lines between Iloko and Ijebu-Jesha with the construction of the highway from Ife to Ilesha. He was said to have done all these during his brief stay at the federal level.
>
> All these add up to his philanthropic gestures within and outside his domain, brought him greater recognition from people far and near. His effects at motivating others to come and build the town to a befitting level was also commended just as Oba Olashore himself also promised to construct markets for the town to encourage business transaction with people

from different areas. (*Daily Monitor*, April 5, 1997: 11–12; original printed in italics; all spelling and punctuation as in original)

The article continued with quotes from various prominent people,
pointing out Oba Olashore's accomplishments and commitment to the community and concluding that "a king is not only an embodiment of ... traditional values, he is a symbol of people's collective resolution" (p. 15).

Another newspaper on the same day headlined its article on the coronation "All hail the New Aloko of Iloko":

> Today, the small serene town of Iloko in Oriade local government area of
> Osun State will suddenly become large not just on the map of Nigeria but
> also on the map of Africa. As dignitaries, distinguished royal crop, accom-
> plished diplomats and the nouveau rich converge on the Iloko soil, the
> town will nearly burst at its seams for this unprecedented conglomeration
> of distinguished personalities....
>
> For a man who has clearly distinguished himself in his chosen career
> with a well built professional image, it is a glorious ascendance to the
> throne.
>
> And as a mark of his accomplishment in both business and social cir-
> cle, the celebrating audience shall comprise of a powerful government
> delegation led by no less than the Chief of General Staff, Lt. Gen. Oladipo
> Diya, Emirs, Obas, Obis, honourable ministers, military administrators,
> commissioners, directors general and accomplished businessmen and
> women representing the cream of the Nigerian society are expected at the
> once-in-a-life-time ceremony to hail the new Aloko who is equally well
> hailed at home. (*Tribune on Saturday,* April 5, 1997: 15)

Saturday Punch, another newspaper, had a supplement section focusing on the coronation, including quotations from friends and colleagues.
One described Oba Olashore as "a typical Ijeshaman, a brilliant and very
hardworking and honest leader" (*Saturday Punch*, April 5, 1997: 12). In an
article entitled "From the Boardroom to the Palace," J. I. Omoniyi, head of
the Iloko-Ijesa Community Development Committee, was quoted as saying,
"We all realise the Oba-elect's noble contributions to the development of
the community. He has been one of the moving forces of the developments
recorded so far in the history of Iloko" (p. 5). He then went on to describe
the community expectations: "The people expect improvement in the provision of good roads, pipe-borne water and availability of drugs in the town's
maternity centre. There's no doubt about all these and the people are eager
to see them addressed. I think the Oba has a major role here" (p. 5).

The same newspaper reported on the event a few days later:

> He had gone round, conquered every terrain he had crossed. A former
> minister, or what was referred to as secretary in the defunct Interim
> National Government; at various times, chairman of important business

concerns, one of the most successful bankers in the country. Last week, Oladele Olashore, returned to his place of birth to ascend the throne of his fathers.

His coronation could have passed for the inauguration of the country's president. His town, Iloko-Ijesha was aglow. The glory that came to the town was so great that a nursing mother had to declare to her elderly mother, who was protesting at her having abandoned the baby, that "*maa foju mi lounje*" ("I will feed my eyes")....

The return of Oladele Olashore to the throne of his fathers was indeed a glorious moment for the Iloko-Ijesa community, which now has an Ajagbusi-Ekun that the whole world is intent on claiming for theirs. (*Punch*, April 10, 1997: 15)

The same paper, in another article, referred to the expectations for the new *oba* to work for the community's development:

The interest the people displayed in the coronation is better appreciated when it is realised that courtesy of the new *oba*, while the rest of the nation is going down the slope in civilisation, Iloko, in spite of its size, is not only climbing the ladder of development but has shown an inkling of being a part of the re-discovery of the sane road to development in the nation. (p. 14)

[Quoting from the speech that Oba Olashore gave at the coronation:]

Said he: "I come to serve the local community, I come to serve the Ijesa people, I come to serve the Yoruba race and indeed the Nigerian polity." A priority area for him is the mobilisation of the Iloko people for self development. His own expectation in this direction is that "the success that we will achieve in Iloko will be worthy of emulation by our neighbouring communities."

The town, during his reign, will have as priority, the "inducement and attraction of investors, both indigenes and non-indigenes, to extend their business interest to Iloko, to Ijesaland and Osun State in general, for the development of industry and commerce which will sustain the use of local labour and raw materials." (*Punch*, April 10, 1997: 14)

The article, like others published in the same period, also noted Oba Olashore's emphasis on ensuring "peace and tranquility" of the community and, more broadly, among Yoruba communities:

On peace among the royal fathers, Oba Oladele Olashore whose coronation witnessed the converging of most of the leading traditional rulers in Yorubaland, such that had not occurred for a long time offered, "I volunteer the rest of my life as the messenger to the royal fathers for the promotion of peace and the development of our communities and the nation at large." (p. 14)

Prior to the coronation, in January and February, another major Nigerian newspaper, *The Guardian*, published both a lengthy article on

Olashore ("From the Vault to the Village," January 18, 1997) and an interview with him ("My March to the Throne," February 8, 1997). The article,
which emphasized Olashore's accomplishments as a banker and public official, pointed out that he would be joining "the blossoming rank of highly-
bred, well-informed successful professionals installed as traditional rulers
in Nigeria" (January 18, 1997: 9). The interview presents the views of the
new *oba* on the role of traditional rulers. In reply to a question about why
he decided "to leave the world of banking for the traditional assignment,"
Olashore began his response:

> Well, you should realise one thing, that Obaship is not available to every-
> body. You can't buy it. It's not because you are wealthy or a big man that
> makes you an Oba. Certainly, you must belong to the royal institution
> before your people can ever consider you for that position. Secondly, indi-
> vidually, you would assess your own relevance to your own society and in
> what way you can play a better role to enhance your own society.... I saw
> my appointment as serving my immediate community, that is Iloko people
> and Ijeshaland. I saw my role in the entire traditional institution in
> Yorubaland. How can I enhance the status of traditional institution, how
> do I relate with other Obas in various parts of Yorubaland...? I saw my
> appointment too as serving Nigeria in a new capacity. I also see that the
> role of Obas has since changed from the time they were ruling, when their
> people were serving them, to now, when they have to serve their people.
> There is a lot of difference today. Today, any Oba that goes to the throne
> because he expects his people to come and serve him, he will die in
> hunger. In fact, they can neglect him in his palace.

He was then asked about the "sanctity of the traditional institutions."
He responded:

> The traditional institution will continue to be sacred.... In the years gone
> by, traditional rulers were really rulers but today, ... you have no real
> executive authority beyond those conferred on you by the government of
> the day and that makes the difference between current position of the tra-
> ditional rulers and the old position. But having said that, they are the lead-
> ers of their people. They are the spiritual leaders of their community. So,
> their people look up to them for guidance in every aspect of their own life.
> This is why the sacredness of the traditional institution will continue to be
> relevant at all times....

Finally, he noted what he sees as the role of traditional rulers, "as the
inspiration to their own people. I personally see the need to mobilise the
people for self-actualisation and development" (*The Guardian on Saturday,*
February 8, 1997: 8).

Publications from the Iloko community itself also emphasized the view
of the *oba* as someone who can assist in the town's development and who
has the personal characteristics requisite for doing that. The *Iloko*

Chronicle, published in conjunction with the coronation, has several articles that emphasize these points. One points out the accomplishments of Olashore's father when he was *oba*, especially in encouraging education in the community. Another, an interview with Chief 'Sola Ogunsanya, a leading chief and formerly the regent (after the death of Olashore's father and until the appointment of the new *oba*), details the efforts that he made toward community development. He also reflects on the characteristics necessary for someone to become *oba*. He describes three criteria: "You must be educated... you must be able to speak, read, write fluently or speak fluently at any occasion.... Number two criteria, we don't want someone who will come there and ... start to tax you, [ask you to] bring twenty Naira to buy a car for him.... Then the other criteria is that he must be somebody who has some reasoning, some vision in his head...." (*Iloko Chronicle*, "Exclusive Interview with the Orisa and Former Regent of Iloko Ijesa, Chief 'Sola Ogunsanya, n.d.: 22). An interview with another chief, Chief Ajewole Ifaloye, emphasizes the major criterion in selecting Olashore as *oba*, that "opinions of the people were sampled, oracles were consulted and all the prophets and the Imams visited singled him out as the Oba that will bring Iloko-Ijesha community development." He went on:

> Looking at the past records of the new Oba, one can not but agree that he has contributed immensely to the development of the town.... He has been a front-line influence, talk of when we wanted to install the electricity, the Aloko's palace, the tarring of Iwaraja-Iloko-Ijebu Road, not to talk of Olashore International School and other things aimed at bringing development into this community.
>
> Another reason for selecting him is that this town has developed up to a certain level. We want somebody who will bring more development, somebody whose reign will encourage construction of industries to provide employment for our children, improve the market situation and bring more development than ever before. We don't want an Oba who will be a burden to the community, who can't feed unless he gets returns from farms or salary from the government. We want somebody who rather [than] being a burden will bring us development. (*Iloko Chronicle*, "Interview with the Saba of Iloko Ijesa Chief Ajewole Ifaloye on the Selection of the New Aloko of Iloko-Ijesa," n.d.: 37)

This same chief appears in a video about the coronation; there, Chief Ifaloye speaks in Yoruba, commenting that "he [Olashore] comes to Iloko regularly and we observe that the love of the people and the progress of Iloko is in his heart" (NTA Ibadan Presents 1997).

This emphasis on "progress" and "development" and on the role of the *oba* in bringing it about appears in the published program booklet of the coronation itself. A section entitled "The People" describes the people of Iloko as "very industrious and development conscious." Another section on

Oba Oladele Olashore in his palace on the day of his coronation,
April 1997

the Iloko Traditional Council describes the council as being made up of "a mixed grill of both elderly persons who are highly experienced and younger crop of chiefs who are very educated and well travelled." And a section entitled "Development" states that most of the development activities that have taken place there have been "through collective self-help or individual efforts" rather than by government. It lists major projects, such as electrification and the town hall, and concludes, "Iloko is indeed an ancient town with potentials for developing into a modern city because of the self-help spirit of the citizens and their dogged determination to transform their village into a model town" (all quotes from coronation program booklet, April 5, 1997).

Oba Olashore's own speech at the coronation, as well as his other comments quoted above, reflect these same expectations. In his speech, he followed the statement quoted above—that is, about changing those aspects of tradition that are "inconsistent with modernity"—with the statement that his goal is "to make my reign worthwhile and beneficial for the progress and happiness of our people" and that he wants to work "for the promotion of peace and the development of our communities and the nation at large."

In examining a variety of ceremonial and celebratory events in this chapter, we see how Ijesas have emphasized individual success as well as communal progress and development. We have also observed how the rhetoric of unity and development is not always matched by the reality. And finally, in considering the coronation of Oba Oladele Olashore at some length, we see how a major traditional institution—the *oba*, the traditional ruler—is being transformed to incorporate new symbols and meanings. Rather than view "tradition" as only a link to the past, it is seen by Ijesas as an instrument for pursuing development and modernity.

Next I will consider in greater depth what people mean when they advocate "development" and then examine several current local development efforts in the context of the contemporary economic and political situation in Nigeria.

Notes

1. Around the same time, two other roads in the area were also renamed in honor of Prince Olashore.

2. At the time, these projects consisted of buildings that had been constructed, but there was nothing actually in them. The elected local government council that organized the ceremony and erected the buildings was soon afterward disbanded by the government (as were all elected local councils in the country).

3. Yoruba who practice Islam follow the traditions of that religion and carry out the burial almost immediately, but they may hold additional ceremonies later on.

4. There had been a ceremony and symposium to commemorate the one-hundredth anniversary of the ending of the Kiriji War—the National Conference on the Centenary of the Kiriji/Ekitiparapo Peace Treaty—which took place at the University of Ife in September 1986. The 1993 event was to mark the return from the war camps of the Ijesa soldiers. The importance of the Kiriji War and the formation of the Ekitiparapo—the organization that fought it—in Ijesa history are considered further in Chapter 9.

5. Abiola was a presidential candidate at the time and was later elected in the June 12 election that was later annulled; he was a very wealthy businessman and prominent donor for many fund-raising events.

6. Quotes here are taken from my video of the event, although this statement was also quoted in newspaper articles; Olaniyan (1997) also refers to it.

7. Again, all quotes are transcribed from my video of the event.

7

Local Development
and the Economic Crisis

*[The Structural Adjustment Program] has destabilized everything. Things
are getting difficult with every passing day.*
　　　　　　　　—An interviewee in Iwoye-Ijesa, May 1992

The task of community development cannot be left to government alone.
　　　　　　　　—Isiaka Adeleke, governor of Osun State,
　　　　　　　　in his speech at the Second Iloko Day, 1993

At the Ijesa Solidarity Group meeting on July 11, 1992, members
debated the best way to raise money for economic development projects. One speaker proposed establishing an endowment fund, arguing
that they should be able to raise N1,000 from 125,000 Ijesa people,
yielding N12.5 million.

> *Even in our currency now, that's a lot of money. Even in other
> currencies, outside currencies, Lillian Trager's currency, that's
> a lot of money. If you think of raising that kind of money, you
> have to think about what it is for. Do we want it to build palaces
> for the* oba? *Or to build marketplaces? Or for town halls in Osu
> or Ibodi? Let us use it for a purpose that will bring our children
> to Ijesaland, to create employment. We've all gone out from
> Ijesaland, we probably wouldn't have gone out if there were
> work here, if there had been something like IBL [the brewery]
> here, some of us, some of our children would have stayed here.
> We should use the money in a way that will bring a future to
> Ijesaland.*

Another speaker said "we should tackle this problem at a grassroots
level." He argued that instead of an endowment fund, they should create an investment fund.

> *People want to know exactly what it will be used for before they
> put in their money. It is not enough to say that we're all Ijesas*

*and the money is for the development of Ijesaland. When you
can't identify what you will get out of it, it's not all that easy to
get contributions. If we call it an investment fund, whatever
someone contributes, no matter how little, is invested in savings
or fixed deposit, and whoever has contributed knows that his
money is yielding dividends. Then they know they are earning
interest on their contribution.*

Another speaker suggested that ISG should "establish a limited liability company whose objective would be to establish some economic projects. People would subscribe to shares, not just contribute to a fund. That fund would yield money; this is a way that people can be encouraged to part with their funds. The money shouldn't be for some nebulous activity like building palaces. The fund should be for investment."

⚝   ⚝   ⚝

In previous chapters, we have considered ways in which individuals remain connected to their hometowns, and some of their motivations for doing so, as well as the ways in which groups of people come together in hometown organizations to assist and celebrate their communities. In Chapters 7–9, we consider the activities of individuals and groups within the broader contexts of economic, sociopolitical, and cultural dynamics. We examine ways in which the Nigerian economy and society affect the dynamics of local development, how the activities of individuals and groups in hometowns are shaped by broader social and cultural forces, and how those activities help to frame the debates and people's perceptions of their situations. When the governor of Osun State calls for people to "come home to develop their community," as he did at the Iloko Day celebration in 1993, or when the appointed administrator states that "government cannot do everything alone," as quoted in a newspaper article in 1992, what do they really mean? What is the economic and political context of such statements, and how is the local response affected by that context? At the same time, what do people consider development to be, and how do they seek to "develop" their communities? How do the social and cultural dynamics of the region and its communities, including conflicts within and among them, affect the approaches that people take in their efforts to develop their hometowns? Who decides what activities to undertake, and to what extent is that agenda shared throughout the community and region?

Chapters 7, 8, and 9 approach these questions from several different angles. Chapter 7 focuses on the economic context of local development. It begins with a discussion of the meaning of *development* in Ijesa communities and what types of problems are seen as central to local development. It then provides an overview of the broader economic context in which these problems and perceptions have arisen, a context that has frequently been portrayed as a near-total collapse of the Nigerian economy. The continuing economic crisis of recent years, including the period known as the Structural Adjustment Program (SAP), has worsened the individual economic situation of many, but by no means all, Nigerians. The chapter then examines the impact of that crisis at the local level and the perception of the economic situation by people in the Ijesa region.

Chapter 8 considers how and why people continue to address local development problems in such a context. What, specifically, do they try to do? It considers specific efforts, including the establishment of community banks and women's income-generating projects, as well as the articulation of goals for local development that have not been attained, including the Ijesa Solidarity Group debate about how to go about the process of economic development and industrialization. It also considers the extent to which people have been involved in these efforts, as well as their views of whether the local development activities that have taken place are beneficial for them.

Chapter 9 then considers the political and sociocultural context in which local development efforts are taking place, including both the broader, national-level political arena and local political issues. It shows how elusive the often-articulated goal of Ijesa unity really is, despite the fact that many view unity as essential to the success of local development.

What Is Development?

In Chapter 2, we saw that at community-day celebrations there are repeated calls for the development of hometowns, noting the related themes of self-help and the inability of government to carry out development efforts alone. Chapters 5 and 6 examined the ways in which hometown organizations seek to bring people home, not only to celebrate their communities but also to help develop them. But when Ijesa people advocate development, what do they really mean? Are they using the word in the same way that social scientists use it? And what is the relationship of the English word *development*, and its multiple meanings, to Yoruba concepts?

One of the striking aspects is the fact that the English word is commonly used when Ijesa discuss development, even in conversations and statements that are otherwise in Yoruba. Yet there are related Yoruba concepts. J.D.Y. Peel has argued that the most important of the Yoruba concepts is *olaju*, literally meaning "to open the eyes," but with the metaphorical meaning of "'enlightenment,' a social state or process of increased knowledge and awareness, which is a condition of greater effectiveness and prosperity" (1978: 144). He notes several other related terms: *ilosiwaju, itesiwaju, idagbasoke*, and *atunluse* (p. 141). More recently, D. Warren, R. Adedokun, and A. Omolaoye include two of these terms in a list of Yoruba development concepts: *ilosiwaju*, defined as "progress," and *idabasoke*, defined as "development" (1996: 49); as Peel points out, the latter term has the sense of "rising up" or "growing," similar to the English concept of development as maturation (1978: 141). Yet when I asked individuals in Ilesa and the other communities studied what they meant by development, only one responded with a discussion of Yoruba terms. He first responded with the word *ilosiwaju* but then stated that the better term was *itesiwaju*. According to him, *itesiwaju* means to bend forward, or to inch forward. "*Ilosiwaju* also means to move forward but *itesiwaju* is better because of its implication of inching, moving slowly. *Development* and *progress* are the same word in Yoruba; it means to progress in every facet of life, to move toward attaining one's goal." He gave the example of a farmer who produced ten tons last year and this year produces twelve tons; that is progress.

The governor's speech at Iloko Day in 1993, quoted in Chapter 2, captures much of the range of activities considered to be development in Ijesa communities. To quote parts of that speech again:

> There is quite a lot you can do individually and as corporate bodies to bring development to our doorsteps. Indeed, I wish to commend the self-help spirit of the people of Iloko, who have not waited for the government to provide everything for them, but decided to find avenues of solving some of the problems themselves. During the first Iloko Day, I learned you realized over 1 million nairi, which you have utilized to provide two boreholes for the community. You have also commenced work on the construction of the community center which incorporates a multipurpose community hall, library, and a police post. All these are commendable efforts. I believe by the next Iloko Day, I will be here to commission the community center. The Nigerian economy, having been deregulated, reduced the public-sector participation in business and industrial ventures. It is the private sector that is being encouraged to take up the task of setting up viable industries and businesses.
>
> The government is primarily concerned with the provision of a conducive atmosphere for industrial and business activities. I therefore use this medium to call on all our industrialists and businessmen and women to come to Osun State to aid our industrial and business development by way of setting up viable ventures. The state has what it takes to set up industrial concerns. I will also seize this opportunity to call on all wealthy sons and daughters of not only Iloko but the entire Ijesaland to come *hooome* [his emphasis], and invest to make their birthplace a worthy and proud place to live in. Abuja or Lagos is not your home. Come home and join hands in development of your motherland.

The types of activities mentioned—buildings, infrastructure, and industry—reflect what many consider to be development. They also reflect some of the disagreements that exist among key Ijesas in determining the types of projects to undertake, as well as some of the differences among the communities studied.

For some, the most important type of development effort is building things—town halls, *obas'* palaces, and infrastructure such as roads. For example, one leading individual described the importance of buildings and infrastructure. To him, "Development is building: building things like town halls and houses, building roads and other infrastructure, and building communities." He said that buildings are the most potent example of storing wealth and gave the example of the money spent on his house when it was built versus what it costs now to build. He noted that when people contribute to something they want to be able to come back later and ask how their money was spent, to see whatever it was spent on, something visible. Town halls, in particular, are important for community unity, as they are a place for people to get together. And, he added, not only town halls but also other things like maternity centers are built.

Similarly, a group of men attending a meeting of the Iwoye Development Union emphasized the importance of infrastructure and buildings. They noted that they were in the process of rebuilding their *oba*'s palace and that although they had "already fought for" electricity and water, neither worked very well, so they were still interested in improving them. They had also built a community health center and a grammar school, with the intention of having the government operate them.

Others criticized the emphasis on building things, arguing that town halls and other buildings do not constitute development. Some focused on education, stating that they thought education was the key aspect to development in their communities. Whereas in the past many groups sponsored the construction and funding of schools, as the Egbe Atunluse did with the Ilesa Grammar School in the 1930s (see Chapter 5), education is much less emphasized today. As Peel points out, the concept of *olaju*, meaning "enlightenment," was specifically linked with education among those he interviewed in the 1970s (1978: 144). It is not that education is viewed as unimportant today. But it is not the major focus for most when they use the term *development*.

Rather, the major focus of those who discuss development is *economic* development, with most concentrating on the need for industrialization. Interestingly, only a few refer to the importance of improving farming, despite the fact that the majority of those in the smaller towns continue to be farmers. One who did mention farming discussed it in a rather general way, arguing that the farmers need to be willing to change their methods in order to be able to use the land more productively. However, even though

he has established his own small farm, this man still emphasized the importance of industrialization. He would like to have investment in industry that
would provide employment for people. According to him, it should be
something based on food, on processing, suggesting that there are various
locally produced foods that could be the basis for industry.

As one man put it,

> The question is, what is development? In the past, schools were built,
> such as Ilesa Grammar School, and that was educational development.
> Now, the emphasis should be on economic development. The Council of
> Ijesa Societies [of which he was a leading member] is talking about vari-
> ous economic activities, including cottage industries, small-scale indus-
> tries, and large industries. These should be based on local raw materials.
> The goal is to expand employment.

According to him, the council wanted to propose ideas for possible industry
and then to encourage individuals to invest; the council was not planning to
actually establish industries itself but rather to promote industrial investment by individuals.

At about the same time, members of the Ijesa Solidarity Group were
also debating whether the organization could establish industries or some-
how provide the context for industrial investment by others. Although they
debated how to go about promoting economic development, there was little
debate about the meaning of development; for the leaders of Ijesa
Solidarity Group, "development means industrialization and economic
development," as one put it. They first thought that the organization itself
would try to establish industries but later decided that it would be better to
provide the infrastructure for industry, such as water and electricity,
because these were not being provided by government. One possibility was
for ISG to establish an industrial park where they would encourage individuals to set up industries.

This focus on industrialization as the key to development was not limited to men; one of the women who discussed the topic likewise emphasized the importance of establishing industries but emphasized that they
should be industries that would employ women. As we shall see in Chapter
8, some of the efforts that actually got under way did involve the establishment of very small-scale processing industries involving women.

In his discussion of the concept of *olaju*, Peel points out that trade was
an underlying aspect of that concept historically. As we have seen, many
Ijesas had been involved in trade as *osomaalo* traders, who traveled outside
of Ijesaland and brought back the knowledge that was key to enlightenment. Today, the concept of development has shifted away from the knowledge and individual advancement associated with *osomaalo* trade to an
emphasis on economic development based on industrialization, as a way of

employing Ijesas and encouraging them to stay in the region. When I asked one man whether he thought that people would put their money into industry, he responded, "We're traders, and trading leads to industry." Others, however, see the *osomaalo* tradition as an impediment to development. As discussed in Chapter 4, these people think that the tradition of trade among Ijesas has overemphasized individual success to the neglect of communal advancement. They argue that there will be no development in Ijesaland without greater unity among the people and communities of the region; I will consider the theme of unity at greater length in Chapter 9.

The point here is that for Ijesas the concept of development, like the Yoruba term *olaju*, can shift in meaning and implications depending on the current context and current views of how to gain access to the resources that are seen as key to the success of the community and region. In an earlier period education was central, and organizations such as the Egbe Atunluse established schools. Today, the answer is seen in development more than enlightenment. And development can include buildings, infrastructure, and especially industry.

One interview, with the *oba* of Ido Oko, a small Ijesa town located a few miles outside Ilesa, demonstrates how key leaders see the links between the various elements of development.[1] J. A. Adeyeye II came back to his hometown in 1988 to become *oba* after many years in Lagos and elsewhere. He described what the town was like then: "Ido-Oko was a place where there was no all-weather motorable road, no social amenities such as water, electricity, or medical care. There was no hospital or dispensary or maternity. There was no source of good drinking water, no pipe-borne water." He decided that in becoming *oba* he would "dedicate his life to the development of the town." He said that the first task was to ensure that there was electricity in the town, and they therefore undertook a rural electrification project. By using a connection with someone in government, he was able to get government financing for electrification. The next target was water. They put in deep wells where people can fetch water. This was paid for by community contributions, as well as by contributions from friends outside the community. A health center is being built. This is a joint project of the community, local government, and state government. Then there are the roads. He said that at times during the rainy season they would be cut off for days. He constructed the road from Ilesa in 1987 and is maintaining it. They were also concerned about education. Together with the neighboring communities they built two buildings for a secondary school. The state took it over after it was built and provides the teachers.

The community is also encouraging economic activities. A small *gari*-processing factory (*gari* is a staple food made from cassava) was established to encourage the farmers to plant more cassava. They can produce more *gari*, and this will provide employment. He said that there is a ready market for the *gari* that is produced; it is sold in the town. They also have a palm oil–processing factory, which provides employment for women and those who have finished primary school. They are also processing palm-kernel oil and making soap. The *oba* believes that if they have these small things, the aggregate of all of them will improve things in the town. In the view of Oba Adeyeye, "The outlook of people here has completely changed from before; I have been able to mobilize and educate them, motivate them. They don't think that something is impossible to do; they don't say I fold my hands, government will do this. Now they know god helps those who help themselves, and the government will help those who do things for themselves." He also wants to improve things for the children. "We have been able to open their eyes. Before, boys in secondary school didn't live here; now they are here and can see that they can be farmers, and do other small-scale things, and in that way, it will help to reduce rural-urban migration." The town is now trying to build a community hall, with contributions from friends outside as well as those of townspeople. His belief is that "this community brought me up, and therefore I should do something for the community."

Ido-Oko is somewhat unusual in that it is attempting to undertake this range of activities in a short period of time. Some of the different views expressed about what constitutes development depend not only on individual perspectives but also on where those individuals are located. Those from Ilesa, which built a town hall long ago and has several sites for meetings and ceremonies, are much less interested in building things—whether schools or town halls—than those in the smaller communities that still have little infrastructure. In addition, those in Ilesa can point to the successful example of the brewery to emphasize the importance of industrial development. As we shall see in Chapter 8, the actual development activities undertaken span the range from buildings and infrastructure to small-scale processing and other economic development efforts.

It is not only *obas* and leaders of community organizations such as Ijesa Solidarity Group who comment on the need for development of their communities. Although others may not express their ideas with as much sophistication, there is a common set of concerns shared by nearly all. When people are asked about what they consider to be the major problems faced by their town and by the region as a whole, the answers fall into the same categories: the need for infrastructure such as water, roads, and electricity; the need for industry; and the need for social amenities such as schools, health centers, and town halls. In the survey taken in May 1992, respondents in all five communities were asked what they considered to be three problems facing their hometown and three problems facing Ijesaland.[2] Of the total responses (645) about problems in the hometown, 50 percent dealt with infrastructure; 20 percent mentioned water; 14 percent roads and transportation; and 12 percent electricity. The need for industry was also high on the list with 20 percent of all responses. Several social amenities make up the next largest category of responses, at 18 percent; these ranged from simple statements that there is "a lack of social amenities" to specific mention of facilities, such as institutions of higher learning, hospitals, marketplaces, and town halls. Finally, the remaining 12 percent of responses about the hometown referred to a range of other problems, from "no money in town," the cost of living, and overall living conditions, to more specific issues such as the need for government loans to farmers. Many of these responses concern the overall economic situation, whereas some refer to political and social issues. Interestingly, very few people indicated that they expected more assistance from government in solving any of the problems; only one person referred to the need for "government enterprise," contrasting sharply with Peel's earlier results, when many said "let the government set up a factory" (1983: 158).

The responses to the question about three problems facing the entire region of Ijesaland were similar, although with slightly different emphasis. Of the total of 412 responses, 39 percent referred to infrastructure; 27 percent to the need for industry; 18 percent to social amenities; and 16 percent to other needs. Again, water, roads, and electricity were high on the list of infrastructure, although two people stated that the area needed an airport. The list of amenities was similar to that for the hometown, although no one mentioned town halls, whereas the list of other problems referred not only to economic conditions but also to political and social issues in the region, such as the need for unity and cooperation and the problem of local boundary disputes.

The responses given by those surveyed in answering an open-ended question about the problems of the area suggest that their views are fairly congruent with those who talk about the need for development. However, they place considerably more emphasis on practical needs, such as water and reliable electricity, and on economic concerns, such as industry and employment, and less emphasis on buildings such as town halls (mentioned by only 2 respondents) and *obas'* palaces.

The Economic Context for Local Development: Crisis and Adjustment

What was the economic context for these views of the need for local development? How were changes in the Nigerian economy affecting people in local communities? And how did people respond at both the individual and community levels? This section provides an overview of the period from the mid-1980s to the mid-1990s, a period when the gross national product

(GNP) per capita declined from U.S.$800 in 1987 to U.S.$340 in 1993 (World Bank 1993) and still further to U.S.$240 in 1996 (World Bank 1998). In 1992 the president of the country, General Ibrahim Babangida, was widely quoted as having said that he didn't understand why the Nigerian economy hadn't completely collapsed. Another senior official was reported to have said, "The state of the Nigerian economy is still anything but promising. All the relevant macro-economic indices portend problems, and a steady deterioration in the standard of living of the populace" (*The News*, October 11, 1993). It was also a period when some Nigerians accumulated considerable wealth, while the vast majority became poorer. As a World Bank study summarized the situation in 1995: "Most Nigerians both feel and are worse off now than only three or four years ago.... The perception of many Nigerians ... that poverty has been continuous and worsening is totally realistic" (World Bank 1996a: vii).

It is useful to consider the economic context from two vantage points. First, the major developments in the Nigerian economy are considered: the situation prior to the imposition of the Structural Adjustment Program in the mid-1980s, the SAP itself, and the situation of the early 1990s. Second, the perspective of people in Ijesaland itself needs to be taken into account: How did those in the Ijesa communities studied perceive the economic situation and how did it affect their lives? This section examines the major economic changes and their impacts; the next section considers the local perceptions of these changes.[3]

In the early and mid-1980s, the Nigerian economy went from oil-based boom into rapid decline. The following statement by a leading businessman in 1985 summarizes the situation at that time:

> Our economy became dominated by a single commodity—oil and ... it provided 25 percent of our Gross Domestic Product, 95 percent of our foreign exchange earnings and 60 percent of Federal Government revenues in 1985. At the same time the world economy reflected a fall in oil prices and Nigeria's earnings from oil exports became less than half of what they used to be. Nigeria had a crushing debt service burden which was consuming 40–50 percent of the foreign exchange and part of the remainder was swallowed by imports of the agricultural products which were necessary to feed the population but which we should be capable of producing in the country. (Shonekan 1985: 1–2)

During the period of the oil boom, the country had become heavily dependent on imports; this was exacerbated by policies of the civilian government in the second republic (1979–1983), which included the importation of cheap rice and other grains. Nigerian agricultural production declined substantially, and commodities that had been major exports and earners of foreign exchange, such as cocoa, became much less important. In addition, the currency was greatly overvalued; for a time in the early 1980s the exchange rate was fixed at N1=U.S.$1.50; up until 1986, just prior to the introduction of SAP, there were very strict currency regulations, and the rate was N1=U.S.$1.

The Structural Adjustment Program was not the first effort to institute economic reforms; there had been earlier attempts by previous governments (Phillips 1987: 1). In the late 1970s, the regime of General Olusegun Obasanjo responded to a decline in oil revenues by introducing a variety of austerity measures, which included banning various imported consumer goods; likewise, the civilian government of President Shehu Shagari introduced austerity measures to reduce imports in 1982. These regimes also introduced programs that were supposed to increase agricultural production; Obasanjo introduced Operation Feed the Nation, and Shagari had his Green Revolution program. The latter "could hardly be identified except in the form of preferential tariffs,... panel vans and agricultural implements. The ... regime presided over the collapse of the programme as it embarked on massive politically motivated importation of food stuff, the most notorious of which was rice" (O. Olashore 1991: 30).

By 1984, when Nigeria returned to a government under military rule, there were further cutbacks in government expenditures and additional efforts to reduce imports. Despite the considerable debt burden and the decreasing revenues available from oil, however, the Buhari regime was not able to come to an agreement with the International Monetary Fund (IMF) for a loan, as it refused to fulfill IMF conditionalities of trade liberalization, removal of petroleum subsidies, and devaluation of the currency (O. Olashore 1991: 51).

In June 1986 the Babangida government began its Structural Adjustment Program. What was most noteworthy at the time was the debate that preceded the announcement of the SAP policies, a wide-ranging public debate about whether the country should take a loan from the International Monetary Fund and meet the IMF's conditions. The newspapers and magazines at the time were filled with articles containing many viewpoints, there were public speeches and debates, and in general it was probably a period of some of the most open debate that has been seen in the country.[4] In the end, the decision was made not to take an IMF loan. However, many of the same policies that would have been adopted under an IMF loan became part of the SAP program. Nigerian commentators have therefore argued that the SAP program was in fact basically a conventional IMF/World Bank–mandated set of policies. For example, one academic analyst argues:

> Although Nigeria presents us with an interesting, even unique example of
> a state that is undergoing market reforms without actually taking an IMF

loan, it would be too far fetched and too misleading to suggest that these reforms were themselves the exclusive creations of Nigerians.... What structural adjustment represented when it was formally launched in 1986 was the total capitulation of the state to the conditionality clauses of the Fund.... It was only after the Nigerian programme was launched that various social forces in the country began to struggle to stamp their own influence on it.... If, therefore, there is anything authentically Nigerian about the adjustment programme which the state has been implementing, it is the stamp which the reality of the domestic politics of adjustment has imposed on what is essentially an orthodox IMF economic recovery package. (Olukoshi 1991b: 77–78)

Even those who argue that Nigeria's SAP was unique and its "own creation" agree that the basic orientation was directed and supervised by the IMF and the World Bank (Phillips 1987: 6; see also Callaghy 1993: 489–491 for discussion of the role of the World Bank in developing these policies).

The policies mandated under SAP included devaluation of the currency; deregulation; reduction of administrative controls and greater reliance on market forces; trade and payments liberalization; privatization of public enterprises; removal of oil subsidies; and adoption of measures to stimulate production and broaden the supply base of the economy (Phillips 1987: 2; see also O. Olashore 1991: 70–87). Efforts at diversifying the productive base of the economy led to the development of several new government bodies, such as the Directorate of Food, Roads, and Rural Infrastructure, which was established to improve flows of resources to rural areas.

However, the greatest attention has been focused on the implementation of the first of the above list of policies: devaluation of the naira. It was widely (though not universally) agreed that the naira had been overvalued in the early 1980s, so devaluation was the first and fastest of the SAP policies to be implemented, with the institution first of what was called the Second-Tier Foreign Exchange Market. The exchange rate went from N1 = U.S.$1 in 1985 to N4 = U.S.$1 in 1987. By March 1992 the official exchange rate was N9 = U.S.$1; at that time, the government decided that the official exchange rate should be essentially equal to the black-market rate. This decision led rapidly to further devaluation, and by May–June 1992 the rate was about N20 = U.S.$1. The decline in the value of the naira continued; by December 1993 the parallel market rate was N40+ = U.S.$1.

Exchange rates may not seem to be central to an understanding of local economies or of the way in which economic activities in local communities are affected by global processes. However, in the case of Nigeria, exchange rates are fundamental to an understanding both of how people's livelihoods are being affected and to an understanding of how people perceive their economic situation. It is not just the newspaper columnists and professional business commentators who have been commenting on the rapid decline of the naira. Ordinary people—taxi drivers, market women, office workers—usually are familiar with the exchange rate, and even in small rural communities comments are often made to the effect that the decline in the value of the naira has affected the economic situation. It is not that these people are dealing in foreign exchange. Rather their comments reflect the situation that has developed during and since the oil boom—the importance of imported items and the fact that even those who work as farmers and traders buy goods that are either imported or made with imported raw materials.

Overall, the structural adjustment policies were implemented with great variability. For example, the degree to which public enterprises were privatized was variable. Although petroleum prices increased over the years, there has been a continuing debate on the complete removal of subsidies, and there was rioting in major cities when attempts were made to increase the price of fuel, for example, in fall 1993. Furthermore, all of the policies had political implications. As Julius Ihonvbere described the situation, "The gains [resulting from SAP policies] are constantly eroded by the inconsistency, insincerity, corruption and inefficiency of the government" (1993: 145). By 1993 discussions of Nigeria's economic problems pointed to massive corruption, high expenditures by the military, and a variety of "extrabudgetary" demands from all levels of government (Callaghy 1993). An official in Babangida's transitional government was quoted as having said that by mid-1993 the extrabudgetary requests that had not been honored exceeded N40 billion: "It appears that all units, ministries, departments, security agencies and the Presidency regard the approved official budget as a trivial and irrelevant document." He also pointed out the impossibility of "objectively determining" the actual revenue accruable to government (*The News*, October 11, 1993). As Thomas Callaghy makes clear, massive amounts of oil revenues had been siphoned off to private interests; in 1991, the *Financial Times* reported that about U.S.$3 billion of the oil windfall that Nigeria received as a result of the Gulf War was unaccounted for (Callaghy 1993: 493).

By 1993 it was clear that there were continuing major problems in the Nigerian economy. It is difficult to determine what exactly was the result of the Structural Adjustment Program, and what resulted from poor implementation, corruption, and other political factors. Some commentators argued that SAP itself was the cause of most of the problems; others argued that without SAP things would have been worse and that the economy would have improved had structural adjustment been more consistently implemented. The World Bank argues that there were improvements between 1985 and 1992 (1996a: 13–16; see also World Bank 1994). However, the common view among the Nigerian populace was expressed by newspaper and magazine headlines—such as "Nigerians became poorer and poorer amidst stupendous resources and wealth just because of incoherent economic policies and a badly managed structural adjustment programme" (*Tell,* April 13, 1992) and "the total effect of SAP was to shoot up the prices of food, housing and transportation. The army of unemployed persons expanded, and social services for the poor and the middle classes all but withered away" (*Citizen,* May 18, 1992).

The situation continued to worsen in the mid-1990s. In June 1993 the election for a civilian president was annulled (see Chapter 9), and in November 1993 General Sani Abacha took over the government. His first budget in early 1994 ostensibly ended many of the structural adjustment policies, such as the floating exchange rate; by 1995 the budget reinstated some of these policies (*Financial Times,* May 26, 1995). But the reality throughout this period was that the exchange rate continued to decline, reaching N100 = U.S.$1 at one point and then stabilizing at around N80 = U.S.$1. Consumer prices increased, and government services declined. There were also recurrent shortages of petrol, making transportation increasingly difficult and expensive. Newspapers and magazines again highlighted many of the problems. In December 1994 and January 1995, for example, pessimistic headlines appeared ("1994: A Year they wish to forget," *Sunday Tribune,* January 8, 1995; and "Consumers bid goodbye to 1994; confess it was rough," *Daily Times,* December 29, 1994). These articles emphasized the difficult conditions; the first quoted from individuals, such as a woman working as a secretary, who said, "The whole situation is hectic, especially with prices of food items. Poor people could not make ends meet" (*Sunday Tribune,* January 8, 1995, p. 9). Later in 1995, they focused on consumer prices, the exchange rate, and the increasing size of the Nigerian foreign debt. The story continued in 1996 and 1997. For example, in June 1997 a headline read, "Fuel scarcity triggers jump in food prices" (*The Guardian,* June 27, 1997).

Cartoons were especially effective at conveying the economic picture. One from December 1994 shows a person thinking about Christmas presents while studying his "retrenchment letter" (i.e., layoff notice; *Daily Times,* December 24, 1994). Another shows Nigerian citizens being attacked by animals and bees representing "hunger," "economic crunch," and "armed robbers" (*Daily Sketch,* June 8, 1995). A third shows a beggar sitting in front of a rich man with the caption "The poor has no food, the rich, no appetite, the middleclass wiped out! God bless Nigeria!" (*A.M. News,* June 29, 1995). And by June 1997 a cartoon captioned "The scarcity syndrome" shows a stripped Nigerian, with a tattered Nigerian flag, holding on to a suicide note; the many current scarcities are listed—"Scarcity of cash, scarcity of food, scarcity of shelter, scarcity of job, scarcity of vision, scarcity of truth, scarcity of leaders, scarcity of drugs, scarcity of conscience, scarcity of honour, scarcity of salary, scarcity of light, scarcity of fuel"—and the stripped man is saying, "What else but scarcity of life!" (*Post Express,* June 25, 1997).

Reports in the *Financial Times* and by the World Bank were less dramatic in their descriptions but nonetheless conveyed the continued deterioration of the Nigerian economy. The *Financial Times* summarized the situation in 1995: "After 25 years of oil exports worth more than $210bn, the country's per capita income of $320 is no higher than it was before the oil boom, and its external debt has reached $37bn, including arrears" (May 26, 1995, p. 1). It predicted that "Nigeria's drift and decline seems set to continue" (p. 8). The World Bank focused its analysis on poverty in Nigeria. It concluded that there were improvements in the 1980s but that these were followed by a rise in poverty and a deteriorating standard of living in the early 1990s. In addition, throughout the period from 1985 to 1992, the poorest households did not benefit from improvements that did occur. "Poverty ... worsened for the lowest income households, some 18 million people"; income distribution worsened, with "extreme" poverty increasing from 10 million to 14 million people (1996a: 62).

According to the World Bank, there was considerable variation in the extent of poverty in Nigeria by region, with regions in the north and southeast (especially the oil-producing areas) suffering the most (1996a: 42–44). The World Bank study also argues that there is concentration of poor individuals and households in poor communities and that there is greater poverty in rural than in urban areas. These conclusions, however, should not lead to a conclusion that people in regions with less than 25 percent of the population below the poverty line, as seems to be the case for Osun State in 1992–1993, were not affected by the economic crisis. In fact, it could be argued that areas that were less rural and less dependent on agriculture were affected more by the economic deterioration. Research on the effects of structural adjustment has examined the largely negative impact on industry (e.g., Ohiorhenuan 1987; Kayode 1987; Olukoshi 1991b); the mixed impact on agriculture (Usoro 1987; Titilola 1987; Guyer 1991); on workers (Amale 1991; Olukoshi 1989); and on those working in the informal sector, especially women (Dennis 1991; Trager 1989; Trager and Osinulu 1991). Abdul Mustapha (1991) argues that there has been an expansion in "multiple modes of livelihood" for all sectors and social groups, involving a variety of survival strategies. Urban workers and those in the informal sector added part-time farming to their repertoire, and middle-class and professional people have added informal-sector activities and farming to their income-earning strategies. Rural people have expanded their repertoire of nonfarm as well as farm-based activities. Not mentioned by Mustapha, but also important, are flows of income between households and communities; remittances and child fostering are ways in which households draw on resources generated by individuals and households elsewhere.[5]

Structural adjustment and the wider economic crisis have had complex and dynamic effects on the Nigerian population. Overall, it is clear that in the 1990s Nigeria was a society in severe economic crisis. An annual inflation rate estimated at 70–100 percent by June 1993 (*The Economist,* August 21, 1993) affected everyone, and overall living standards declined for the vast majority. In this context, how did people in Ijesaland perceive the situation, and what was their response?

Perceptions and Effects of SAP and the Economic Crisis at the Local Level

In late December 1994, one of the founding members of the Ijesa Solidarity Group stated that he didn't think the current situation in the country was a good one for investment, either by individuals or organizations. Two years later, in April 1996, the same individual said at an ISG meeting that "the situation in the country is so serious" it is even becoming difficult for people like himself to travel to Ilesa from Lagos for meetings. This man's view—of a situation so difficult and precarious that even those who had been involved in a variety of local development efforts no longer thought it worthwhile—reflects a common perception: that the continuing economic deterioration hindered a wide variety of activities. Nevertheless, as we shall see in Chapter 8, many local development efforts did continue, and some were successful. How did people in Ijesaland perceive the effects of SAP and the wider economic crisis on their livelihoods and other activities? And what were their attitudes about how they had been affected by the crisis?

Two surveys, one in May–June 1992 and the other in May–June 1996, provide insights on these questions.[6] The 1992 survey included three sets of questions about the effects of structural adjustment. One set focused on the overall effects; the second asked about the effects on travel; and the third asked about effects on contributions to the hometown.[7] On the question of whether SAP had affected their "overall way of life," 83 percent responded "yes" while 17 percent said it had not done so. When asked to explain more specifically how it had affected them, many, not surprisingly, gave explanations referring to some aspect of the high cost of living: 46 percent said that the cost of living is high or that the economic situation is difficult; another 22 percent referred to the cost of food, with some saying that they eat less or less regularly than before. Others referred to more specific effects: that their children contribute less; that farm expenses have increased; that they have less money than before. Several referred specifically to the devaluation of the naira, and others referred to problems with their business or job. A few also responded in terms of the social costs: that it is hard to entertain visitors or that they can't participate in town affairs as before.

There were also a few people, however, who said that they had not been affected by SAP. These included people who stated that they are not affected because their children or other relatives are supporting them; that they are not affected because they are not government employees; or because they are farmers. One person said that he didn't know what SAP is. Only two respondents said that they had been affected positively by SAP, stating that they are now making more profit in business than before structural adjustment.

There was a slight difference in the responses by sex: 88 percent of males and 78 percent of females said they had been affected by SAP. There was greater variation in terms of age, with 23 percent of those over 65 saying that they have not been affected by SAP, in contrast to only 10 percent of those between 36 and 50. This probably reflects the fact that older people are more likely to be either dependent on others such as children for support, or to not be working and therefore less likely to be affected by changes in jobs or incomes.

The second set of questions concerned whether SAP had affected the extent to which respondents traveled outside their town. Of those who responded to the question, 47 percent said that it had while 53 percent said it had not. The survey was taken during a period in 1992 when the first of what later became regular shortages of fuel occurred; the price of public transportation increased, and for a few weeks it was difficult for anyone to travel anywhere. It is therefore not surprising that many referred to the increasing cost of travel, saying that it had become too expensive to travel. Others indicated that they had reduced the number of times they travel. Others, however, said that they still had to travel for business so that there hadn't been any effect. Still others said that they don't travel anyway, so they had not been affected.

There are differences in the response to this question based on sex: 56 percent of males said that SAP had affected their travel, in contrast to only 40 percent of females, differences that may be due to the importance of regular travel for males and females. There were also age differences: 51 percent of those 65 and under say that the extent to which they travel has been affected, in comparison with 33 percent of those over 65.

The final set of questions dealt with the way in which SAP had affected respondents' involvement in activities in their hometown. Of those who responded, 36 percent said that it had while 64 percent said it had not. Some people would not be involved in hometown activities in any case, regardless of the economic situation, and 16 percent said that explicitly— that they are not affected because they don't participate. But others made clear that they can't participate, or that they participate less than before, because they have less money. Some said that they have to take care of their family before they contribute to the hometown, others that they are using their money on food that they would have used for contributions; still others referred to their inability to build or complete a house in their hometown. Overall, 65 respondents stated that they are less involved than before, that they have reduced their contribution, or that they couldn't participate in a specific activity at home. Only two people stated that contributions had increased.

Again, there are differences in terms of sex: 48 percent of males said that SAP had affected their involvement in the hometown, whereas only 27 percent of females were affected. Likewise, there is a difference by age, with 54 percent of those 65 and under stating that their involvement had been affected, as compared to 30 percent of those over 65. As we shall discuss further below, these negative impacts on involvement did not mean that people thought such participation unimportant, or that they no longer contributed at all. In fact, when we consider specific local development efforts, as well as individual engagement at home, such as building a house there, the majority still are involved in some way; this will be made clear in Chapter 8.

By 1996 Ijesas' views of the economic crisis and its impacts on their livelihoods and other activities had become even more negative. In the 1996 survey, 65 market traders, taxi drivers, and farmers in Ijebu-Jesa, Iwoye, and Iloko were asked about ways in which the economic situation had affected both their livelihoods and their participation in local activities. Essentially, 100 percent of those interviewed said that they had been affected by changes in the economy in the preceding year. Although a small number noted positive effects, a large majority recorded negative impacts.[8] Among market traders and farmers, 50 percent noted the increase in prices, saying that things had become "too expensive." Several farmers noted the increase in the cost of farm equipment, and 60 percent of the taxi drivers specifically referred to the increase in the cost of spare parts. Yet a few farmers said that the price at which they sell crops had increased. Both market traders and farmers had been forced to increase prices because of increased costs. Many traders said that their customers were no longer able to buy as much as before, saying that the customers had no money and therefore only buy when they must. Therefore, the traders said that they had made no profit. Farmers, and a few traders, in contrast, stated that since people still had to buy food they were still able to make sales. Although some taxi drivers stated that they had increased their prices, others indicated that they were unable to do so, since their customers complained. They noted that their costs were high, especially with the difficulty of obtaining spare parts and fuel, and yet they had fewer customers because the customers had no money. Overall, there is remarkably little variation in the responses. With the exception of those few farmers who saw improvements in their economic situation, the variation in all the responses mainly con-

sists of different estimates of the extent to which costs had increased, whether they have doubled, tripled, or quadrupled.

The respondents in the 1996 survey were also nearly unanimous in stating that the recent economic changes had affected their ability to travel, with 95 percent stating that travel outside the town had been affected in some way. Some said that they no longer travel at all, whereas others said that they had reduced the amount they travel. Many said that they have no money for travel and that transportation now costs too much. This affected their ability to travel to visit relatives elsewhere; 25 percent said that they had stopped visiting, and another 10 percent said that they visit less frequently than before. Similarly, 75 percent said that they send less to family members elsewhere than they did before, and 6 percent had stopped sending things at all. There was less sent to them by family members as well: 73 percent said that other family members now send less than before, and 5 percent said that they had stopped entirely. These results contrast with the 1992 survey results on the extent to which people regularly visit and send remittances to family elsewhere (see Chapter 4).

⚙︎   ⚙︎   ⚙︎

The responses given in the 1996 survey make it clear that most ordinary people in the Ijesa region were severely affected by the economic crisis in the country. Key aspects of their daily lives had been affected: the money they could make in their livelihoods; the money they had available for their own needs; their ability to travel and visit relatives; and their ability to help other family members with resources. At the same time, however, important efforts at local development were taking place in their communities, and many people were continuing to contribute to those efforts, at least in a small way. And with the government itself doing less and less to aid communities, there was more and more emphasis on the importance of self-help and development at the local level. A paradoxical situation resulted: most individuals and families had less money and resources to draw on while community demands for participation in local development efforts increased. Chapter 8 examines in more detail the ways in which Ijesas, both as individuals and in groups, sought to continue to carry out local development efforts despite the adverse economic circumstances.

Notes

1. Ido-Oko was not one of the towns originally selected for study. However, during the course of the research, I was told by several people about the *oba* and his development efforts and subsequently arranged an interview with him.

2. A partial analysis of this data appears in Trager (1998), referring to responses from only Osu and Ijebu-Jesa. The survey is described in Chapter 4.

3. Discussion of the period 1985–1993 is based in part on my chapter, "Structural Adjustment, Hometowns, and Local Development in Nigeria" (1997). The economic crisis and structural adjustment programs have received enormous amounts of attention, not only in the analysis of Nigeria but also elsewhere in Africa. My intention here is not to summarize the literature or debates but to provide an overview that helps to understand the local situation. For analysis of SAP in Nigeria, see, e.g., Phillips and Ndekwu (1987); Olukoshi (1991a); Ihonvbere (1993). For Africa, see Callaghy and Ravenhill (1993); Adepoju (1993); Gladwin (1991).

4. For discussion of the issues leading up to the debate and of the debate itself, see, e.g., articles in Olukoshi (1991a) and O. Olashore (1991).

5. Child fostering refers to sending a child to live in another household, where the child will be fed and (it is hoped) cared for, maybe even sent to school. In exchange usually the child provides services (e.g., housecleaning and childcare) for the family with which she is living. In other words, the child becomes someone else's foster child. Poor relatives may send a child to live with better-off relatives.

6. The 1992 survey has already been described (see Chapter 4). In May–June 1996 I took a smaller survey in Ijebu-Jesa, Iloko, and Iwoye, interviewing market traders, taxi drivers, and farmers. Sixty-five people were interviewed, including thirty-six women and twenty-nine men. The questions focused on their perceptions of changes in the economic situation and how their livelihoods had been affected, as well as on the extent of their involvement in hometown and local development activities. Although the questions were not the same as those used in 1992, they complement and extend the data available from that larger and more in-depth survey. My former student, Kim Boyajian, assisted me in coding and analyzing the 1996 data.

7. An earlier discussion of part of this data, from Osu and Ijebu-Jesa, appears in Trager (1997).

8. The questions asked specifically for effects of changes in the past year; respondents were asked, "In the past one year have you noticed changes in the economy that have affected you?" followed by specific questions such as whether prices at which goods are bought had changed (for market traders) and whether customers' ability to pay for services had changed (for taxi drivers). The survey also included questions about travel outside the town, as well as about participation in local organizations, activities, and projects.

8

Self-Help and the Practice of
Local Development in Ijesaland

*"By next year, we will have a marketplace there" [pointing to a large area
of cleared land].*
"Yes, in this town we have dreams."
"If you don't have dreams, then nothing happens."
—Conversation between two women involved
in development in Iloko, June 14, 1997

On Friday, June 16, 1995, I went with the manager of the Ijebu-Jesa
community bank to visit bank customers. Most of those we visited are
participating in the daily contribution scheme. We went first to a shop
that faces the marketplace, where there is a woman selling general merchandise—things such as toiletries, rubber soles for shoes, nails, and
buttons. As soon as I began asking about the bank, she brought out her
passbook—in fact she has two, one of which is already filled. It is a
very simple system, showing the date, amount of contribution, and
overall balance, so that there is a running total. Loans are also shown on
the same passbook. She began with the bank on September 15, 1994,
and has made 182 deposits. I looked quickly at the book and the
deposits seemed to be N20, N50, and sometimes N100. There seemed
to be a balance of about N5,000. She said that she has had two loans,
the first in November 1994 and the second in June 1995; the second
was for N5,000. The manager said that the second loan can be bigger
than the first, once they see that the person can pay back. She used the
loans to buy more merchandise. The second person we went to see is
selling soup ingredients—peppers and tomatoes—in the market. She,
too, said that she has had two loans and used them to buy more produce. She sells in the market and also from her house on other days.
Then we went to another shop that seemed to have just a little stock—
drinks, packaged soups, and macaroni. The woman there began with the
bank in July 1994; again she got out her passbook. Most of her deposits
are N20; sometimes she deposits N100. She has had two loans and has

used them to buy goods. I asked how the bank has made a difference. She said that in the past she got her capital from her children or other relatives—she wasn't banking with any bank. There's a big difference because now whenever she goes to the bank and says she needs money she can get it, whereas it is hard to go to someone to borrow, say, N50. She said that the bank has helped a lot. But she added that the problem is that the amount of money they're getting is very small compared to the rate of inflation. The bank manager commented that they can't give too much more than they are contributing, because they may not be able to pay it back. I asked her if there's been any problem in repaying, and she said there hasn't been, that it's been easy to repay.

Then we went to a tailor's shop that is upstairs in a building across the street from the market. A young man is the tailor there. He has a couple of small rooms with sewing machines; there were several other young men around. He said that he has five sewing machines and has been in this business for twelve years. He has sixteen apprentices. The manager told me that this man has a regular account in addition to par-ticipating in the daily contribution system; he showed me his passbook, and there were fewer entries in it than those of the others we visited. The manager indicated that this is a convenience for him to sometimes deposit money this way rather than in his regular account, so he can save small amounts when he has them. He started participating in the daily contribution system in March, so he has not yet taken a loan through it. When I asked what he would use a loan for, he said that he would use it to buy modern machines (the ones he has are old).

Then we went to the other side of the main road, across from the market. There is a large blue container there labeled "kerosene," and the manager wanted to introduce me to the woman who has that busi-ness. She is a young woman, a school teacher at the Muslim primary school in Ijebu-Jesa. She began this business—selling kerosene—with a loan; she hadn't been doing this before. She gets an overdraft of N20,000–N30,000 to enable her to buy kerosene, then she pays back within three months.

Then we went a little farther down the street to Jomo Variety Stores and talked with the man there. This is a much larger shop than any of the others, with a much wider variety of goods. He said that they have had two loans and that the loans have helped them enlarge the goods they are able to buy and thus enlarged their sales. He said that if they hadn't had help last time they would have had problems, since they had spent the money they had on some goods, which hadn't yet been sold, and they needed money to buy other goods—so the loan enabled them to buy the other goods. He has had the shop since 1987;

his wife has a shop in the market. They sell both wholesale and retail. They sell provisions and a variety of other things—luggage, drinks, watches, calculators, and small kerosene stoves. The man and his wife own the two shops together. They have apprentices as salesgirls, but he indicated that before, they have had paid employees. He buys the goods they sell in Lagos and Ibadan. He said that he doesn't like to have anyone come here to supply them because he doesn't want to be "gypped" (his term). He likes to go, see the goods, pay for them, and bring them back. According to the manager, this business is getting loans of N20,000 for purchasing goods.

We then went to see a woman in a house just a bit farther down the street from Jomo Variety Stores. There wasn't anything displayed outside, except some bread that someone was selling. The woman came out from inside the house, and the manager explained that she is buying farm produce and reselling; she buys kola nuts and palm oil from the farms, then resells them. She said that she sells the kola in the north. She gets loans for purchasing produce and then repays after she sells.

Finally, we went to a bakery, where we met the man who owns it. The man said that he is a farmer and that he had a business before in Ibadan. He started a bakery here in 1979 but closed it down in 1982. He was approached by one of the directors of the bank about starting it up again, and he did so in 1994. The bank paid N18,000 for the engine that runs the kneading machine and N25,000 for the metal for the loaf boxes. He is now baking bread four times a week and makes about 1,000 loaves of bread each time, from four bags of flour. He said that he makes N150 on each bag of flour, after all his expenses. He was basically indicating (and wanted to let the bank manager know) that he is short of capital—that although the bank gave capital for the equipment he doesn't have operating capital. He sells the bread here in Ijebu-Jesa and also in neighboring villages; he charters a taxi to take bread there. He sells on credit and people repay in forty-eight hours. A friend of the owner joined us. He told us that if the owner had more capital he could make the place neater and also have more money to transport the bread to sell it. The bank manager explained that the bank has about a 90 percent investment in the bakery. But the owner and his friend say that he doesn't have enough money to purchase ingredients. Later the manager explained to me that the bank had purchased the equipment for the bakery and so could not make any more loans at this time.

✿   ✿   ✿

In the deteriorating economic climate described in Chapter 7, how did individuals and groups in Ijesaland cope? What was their response, and how did they address the evident needs of their communities? One possible response would certainly have been to give up—to stop participating in and contributing to local development efforts. For the most part, however, this is not what happened, although individual members of the community may well have found it necessary to cut back on the level of their contribution. Instead, the more common response was to reemphasize the need for self-help, to develop new community projects, and to find ways to acquire the resources necessary to accomplish those projects. We have already seen how the community-day celebrations provided one means of obtaining resources. In this chapter, I will consider some of the actual projects attempted and carried out, as well as some of those that were discussed and debated but that did not lead to any results. I will also consider the extent of participation in these activities and how decisions were made about what to do.

In considering self-help and local development, it is useful to recognize that some development activities are undertaken by organizations and communities as a whole, whereas others are undertaken by individuals. To provide a sense of the entire array of efforts, from individual entrepreneurial ones to those involving entire communities, I will examine several examples. I begin by looking at some of the ways in which individuals have contributed to local development; then I move on to organizational and community-wide efforts.

Individuals and Local Development

There are basically three ways in which individuals see themselves as participating in local development. The first, and most common, is to contribute to organizational and community fund-raising for specific projects; this type of individual participation—in which all members of the community may be expected to take part—will be considered later in the chapter. The second way is for an individual to establish a presence of some sort in the community, typically by building a house there and, in some cases, by establishing some sort of economic enterprise. The third way is to engage in local philanthropy, for example, by donating something for the use of the entire community.

The building of houses and establishment of enterprises by individuals primarily benefit the individual and his or her family. However, these activities are also viewed as contributing to the development of the local community. As has already been discussed, the building of a house in one's hometown is seen as the first necessary step for anyone who has been successful outside the town. Among those interviewed in the survey taken in 1992, 46 percent of men and 14 percent of women had built a house at home. Only 27 percent of those 65 and under have built a house, as compared with 59 percent of those over 65. This is what would be expected: There are greater expectations for men to build in their hometown; and building a house at home is often something that people do over time, as they have money to put into it. Building a personal house is something an individual does, and the completion of a house often represents a significant measure of status and success. It is also seen as a measure of the community's development; if many successful community members build their houses at home (especially big, elaborate houses), this increases the status of the community as a whole.

Although many people try to build houses at home, a smaller number establish some type of economic base there. Those who move back home to live are more likely to do this. In Chapter 4, we saw examples of individuals who had moved back home and then established a small business, such as the woman who sells cooked food in Osu. Among wealthier Ijesas, some establish farms outside their hometown even when they themselves have not moved back home, and others have established small businesses. Some describe themselves as "gentlemen farmers" who have acquired land and developed a small farm, growing food crops such as yams and cassava and, in some cases, also putting in small fishponds. Some do this on their own, visiting the farm on a regular basis to take care of it; others employ workers to carry out the farming activities and to guard the fishpond. In either case, most of these farms are small, sideline activities, involving some degree of investment but earning relatively little income. For example, one individual told me that he had spent about N140,000 on building fishponds; he anticipated making some income from the ponds but said that he does not make any money from the crops that he plants.

Among those who have established small businesses, Chief A. O. Lamikanra is an example of someone who decided to leave Lagos while still relatively young and return to Ilesa. He decided to establish a bakery and, together with his wife, successfully set up a business with twenty-four employees, five vehicles to distribute the bread, and sales at schools and other institutions in the area. He was in the bakery business from 1981 to 1986 but found it difficult to continue once the government banned the importation of wheat in 1985; he eventually decided to go out of business, although he kept the equipment. Later, he began to raise chickens and produce eggs, and by the early 1990s he had also invested in beehives and was learning the art of beekeeping. However, this activity was on a much smaller scale than the bakery.

An exception to the "gentleman farmer" approach is the farm of a man in Ijebu-Jesa, G. O. Onibonoje. Having successfully established himself in

Farm and fishpond of a prominent Ijesa

the publishing business in Ibadan, he decided to build a house and establish a farm at home in Ijebu-Jesa. He began to set up his farm in 1978 while still based in Ibadan. By the end of 1981 he had built his house, located on the outskirts of the town overlooking the farm. He was able to acquire a substantial amount of land; by 1992 he had between 300 and 400 acres on a long-term lease from the government. He devotes a considerable amount of time to the farm, overseeing its operation with assistance from several of his grown children. He grows maize, yams, beans, and rice as food crops and produces palm oil as well. In addition, he has several fishponds in which he raises fish for sale.

Onibonoje described three reasons for establishing his farm. First, he wanted a challenge, something different from his publishing business. Second, his children were growing up outside Ijebu-Jesa, and he wanted them to identify with their home; he didn't "want them to be too urbanized." And third, he wanted to demonstrate to others in the town that he was doing something himself to help in the town's development. He had previously been involved in a variety of community activities, dating back to when he was a university student, including the reconstruction of the marketplace and the building of the town hall in Ijebu-Jesa. The town hall became a meeting point, and building it helped to mobilize the community: "The hall became the instrument for building the community into a cohesive body of people. It was a project that everyone liked, and therefore one could preach the gospel of unity and development." For Onibonoje, the most important aspect of such projects is the involvement of the people of the community, "to bring in various people from different stations of life, and let them know that they are the a-b-c of progress." In his view, the younger generation has to appreciate "that progress is recognizing people as agents of development; what's important is the philosophy that made the [town] hall happen, not the hall itself." Therefore, he now devotes himself to his farm, as his own contribution to local development, rather than to other community-wide projects. He believes that others are aware of what he is doing and see it as a contribution to the community.

Some individuals go beyond the building of their own house or establishment of a business or farm at home to make significant donations to the community as a whole or to members of it. These individuals may also donate to community-wide projects, as shall be discussed below. But they are people who have the resources to do something as individuals, and some prefer to act on an individual basis rather than as part of a larger group. Whether this is because they want to be recognized for their contribution, or because they believe that this is the one way that they can be sure that their money is used as they want it to be, such individuals are much like local philanthropists in other parts of the world. They see a problem and have the means to do something about it on their own. For example, in Ilesa, Lawrence Omole, whose eightieth birthday celebration was described in Chapter 6, is seen as someone who has contributed to a large number of projects and causes. He is best known for his individual philanthropy of paying for the education of many children from Ilesa over the years. In his autobiography, Omole describes how he began to provide funds to those who came to him requesting assistance and eventually established the Dr. Lawrence Omole Foundation to award scholarships to university students (1991: 123–136). Other examples are on a smaller scale but still very significant. In 1997 one individual in Iloko paid for a well and water-storage tank to be located in the center of the town, making water far more available to residents.

One of the most visible contributions to the Ijesa landscape in the 1990s was the establishment of Olashore International School, on the outskirts of Iloko. Several years before becoming *oba* of Iloko, Oladele Olashore decided to build a private secondary school there. Although he had previously made many contributions to local projects, such as the rebuilding of the palace when his father was *oba*, and had encouraged his friends to also donate to such projects, his own business and professional interests were focused in Lagos. Following a career at the upper levels of major government banks, he had established his own merchant bank in the late 1980s. (See Olashore 1998, his autobiography that details this and other aspects of his life.) In 1991 he began developing the plans for the school; construction began in 1992, and the doors opened to the first students in early 1994. As the school rose on a hill outside Iloko, many people commented that Oladele Olashore had "put Iloko on the map," both literally and figuratively.

The Olashore International School differs in several ways from the other individual contributions to local development discussed here. It is neither a community development project nor a for-profit enterprise; those who attend pay tuition, but the funds obtained are used for further development of the institution. It is on a much larger scale than most other efforts, having had a sizable investment of resources, especially in the first years. And those who attend are mainly not from the Ijesa area; the school attracts students from all over Nigeria, and they have relatively little to do with the local community. In other words, the institution's direct benefits primarily go to people from elsewhere, although there are a few students from Iloko who attend on scholarships.

Yet the school has had a substantial impact on the local community. It was the largest investment of any kind in the area during this period. The school has affected local employment in two ways. Some Iloko residents have obtained jobs or provided services to the school. And school employees from elsewhere have come to live in Iloko and have added to the local economy.[1] Since it is a boarding school, the students spend money in the community. Their parents come to Iloko to bring them to school and to attend visiting days, thereby making people elsewhere aware of the town. I met a woman in Lagos on one occasion who described her first visit to the school to explore whether it was suitable for her daughter. She said that as they drove along, with the road getting worse and worse, they were sure there was nothing there; seeing the school from a distance was "like a mirage rising on the landscape." They could not believe there would be something like the school there, with its substantial buildings, well-equipped classrooms, and comfortable dormitories. For the people of the town and region, the school became an important symbol of the success of one important member of the community and, by implication, of the community itself. They were proud that he had located the school in Iloko and not in Lagos or somewhere else. At the award ceremony in 1993 given by the Oriade LGA (described in Chapter 6), the school was described as a "multimillion-naira intellectual investment that will bring international fame." For Oladele Olashore himself, the school represents a contribution to education in Nigeria, as well as a contribution to the local community and its economy (see Olashore 1998: 155–162).

Organizational and Community Development Projects

There is no doubt that key individuals such as Oladele Olashore can have a considerable impact on the local community and its development. However, local development is not primarily an individual pursuit. Rather, it is something set as a goal by entire communities as well as by organizations within those communities. We have already discussed some of the major organizations in the communities studied. The question to be considered in the following discussion is what those organizations do. What are some examples of projects that have been undertaken and accomplished? Who participates in those projects? How are specific activities decided on and funded? And who benefits from them?

Building Projects: Town Halls, Palaces, and Infrastructure

As we have seen in Chapter 7, for many people development is equated with building something. In the past, the most common types of building projects were schools and hospitals. The Egbe Atunluse in Ilesa established the Ilesa Grammar School in the 1930s, and many similar projects were undertaken in other communities. In Iloko, the community contributed to the formation of the secondary school there, the Muslim Grammar School. People in Ijebu-Jesa undertook the construction of a hospital and usually refer to it as one of the major projects of the past. Infrastructure projects have also been significant. Both Iloko and Iwoye were able to put in electricity earlier than would have been possible had they waited for the government to do so.

During the research period, the only infrastructure project in the communities studied was an effort to improve the water supply in Iloko. Complaints were frequently voiced in Iloko about the poor water supply; although the town was supposed to be on a public water-supply line, it rarely, if ever, actually received water that way. Speeches at the first Iloko Day called for assistance from the government in reestablishing the water supply. Yet contributions made during that event were designated for the sinking of boreholes, with the idea that several boreholes in different locations around town would significantly improve the water supply. Unfortunately, most of the boreholes that were sunk were unsuccessful and did not provide any water. As a result, water remained a continuing problem in Iloko. As described above, one individual contributed a well and storage tank in the town center in 1997, making it possible for those living nearby to have much improved access to water.[2]

The most common type of building project in the 1990s was the construction of either a town hall or a palace or both. With the exception of

Ilesa, where the town hall was constructed in the 1930s, all of the smaller communities in the study were engaged in, or had recently built, either a town hall or a palace. Osu had recently built a town hall that faces the main road leading through town. Ijebu-Jesa had completed the construction of a large town hall and was in the process of rebuilding the *oba*'s palace. In Iwoye, the old "palace," or house for the leading chief of the town, was in complete ruins, and a major construction project was under way.[3] Land located behind the old palace had been cleared, and plans had been made to build not only a palace but also a health clinic.

The biggest construction project during this time was in Iloko. There, the palace had been rebuilt when Oladele Olashore's father was the *oba*. But there was no town hall. That became the major community development project of the period, with funds being collected, especially at the Second Iloko Day in 1993; construction began almost immediately. By the time of the Iloko Day celebration in 1995, it was possible for the event to take place inside the new community hall, even though funds were still being raised to complete it. From the first sign announcing the location of the "Ultra Modern Town Hall" in an uncleared field in 1993 to the holding of a major community event in the new building, only two years had elapsed. For the people of Iloko, this project was considered a major success and evidence of the ability of their town to mobilize resources for local development. This success is considered further below, in the discussion of funding and participation.

Community Banks

A completely new type of development effort occurred in the 1990s, representing an example of economic development rather than buildings or infrastructure. This was the establishment of community banks. A new government program, adopted under the Babangida administration, encouraged groups of people to establish a new type of bank—community banks.[4] In many instances, these banks were set up by wealthy people seeking new ways to earn money, with no interest in the community as such. But in the case of Ijebu-Jesa and Iwoye, members of the local community took the government program seriously and undertook the establishment of banks that were designed to improve access to banking facilities for local community members. Although the government provided the framework and set conditions for the establishment of community banks, groups could take varying approaches. In Ijebu-Jesa, the community bank was established by one hometown organization, whereas in Iwoye it was set up by an organization representing the entire community. The Ijebu-Jesa bank hired a professional manager, whereas that in Iwoye had a retired community member take on the job of manager. In both communities, the establishment of the community banks took place in the context of a variety of other community projects and development efforts.

The Ijebu-Jesa Community Bank. The community bank in Ijebu-Jesa opened in April 1993. It was established by the Ijebu-Jesa Group, a small organization of men from the town, most of whom are based in Ibadan. According to the first manager, there were ninety people who opened accounts when the bank opened. Most of these were savings accounts, which had a minimum deposit of only N50. By June 1993 the bank had more than 500 savings depositors. There were also a few current (checking) accounts with a minimum of N200. A few people had deposited larger amounts, which had to be left for three months in order to get higher interest rates. Most of the initial depositors were people residing in Ijebu-Jesa, but some were from neighboring towns; at the time, this was the only community bank in the area.[5] The bank was also trying to encourage wealthy people living outside Ijebu-Jesa to put some of their money into the bank. In the early months of the bank's existence, there were few loans made, as customers were required to have an account for several months before receiving any loans. There was also a requirement of two guarantors for a loan, as well as a written proposal describing the purpose of the loan.

By January 1995 the bank had hired a new manager, a young man who had previously worked at another community bank in Oshogbo. With a degree in banking and finance from the Polytechnic in Ibadan, and a certificate from the Institute of Chartered Bankers, he was anxious to demonstrate that a community bank could be managed well. He expressed commitment to the idea of a community bank as one that is set up and managed by people of the community. According to him, the community bank was "set up to help rural development, such as providing loans for cottage industry. It operates by first mobilizing funds from customers and then uses the money to give loans for productive activities."

The new manager introduced a daily contribution system, modeled on the traditional banking and credit systems of *esusu* and *ajo*. In this system, bank personnel went around to collect daily savings from customers, who can put in small amounts each day. These customers, unlike regular savings-account holders, do not earn interest on their accounts. But unlike the *ajo* system, they do not pay a service fee.[6] After contributing regularly for a period of time, such customers can receive loans, just as others can. "We go out to the people to mobilize funds; we don't just wait for people to come to us. We go to the market and other places to encourage people to establish accounts. Our staff is approachable, and the bank is more liberal in its loan policy [than a commercial bank]."

An individual must have an account for three months before receiving a loan. After that, bank personnel go out to ask if they need a loan for any-

Ijebu-Jesa Community Bank customer

thing. "We have canvassers, who go out to houses, shops, markets, to tell people about the community bank and what it can provide for them. The canvassers tell them about the daily contribution system and encourage people to sign up to participate in it." By January 1995 the bank had 200 people participating in the daily contribution system, with 2,000 customers overall. At that time, there was N500,000 in about forty outstanding loans. The smallest loan that had been made was for N1,200, which was given to a market trader. The maximum that had been given in a loan was N50,000.

For participants in the daily contribution system, after three months they can borrow double what they had in savings (e.g., if they had saved N100, then they could borrow N200). They start repaying the loans immediately. These loans are revolving; as soon as someone pays back the first loan, he or she can get another one. One woman was borrowing N20,000 every three months through this system, but most of the others, including those described in the introduction to this chapter, were getting smaller amounts. There had been no defaults. As the manager explained, "The staff study the customer and their business; they have seen that there are sales every day before giving out a loan."

Larger loans had also been made. The bank had targeted several types of activity for loans. These included transporters, as they wanted to improve transportation between the communities of the area and thought that they could assist people to go into local business. Six loans had been given, four for buses, two for taxis. By June 1995 four of the loans had been paid back. But the increasing price of fuel, due to the fuel shortages, had affected businesses in this sector, and the bank had stopped making loans for transportation. Another loan was for a bakery, described in the introduction of this chapter. The bank helped someone who had previously been in the bakery business to get new equipment, enabling him to restart the bakery. Short-term loans had also been given to produce buyers, enabling them to buy palm kernels and cocoa beans in the villages and then to sell them and repay the loans. A final area that had been targeted was farmers and livestock producers. About ten farmers had been given loans to provide them with funds for clearing, planting, and harvesting; when they sell the crop, they pay back the loan. Three people raising pigs and chickens had also been given loans, to be repaid when they sell the produce. This had the added benefit of helping provide lower-cost eggs to people in the Ijebu-Jesa area.

According to the bank manager, by 1995 the community bank in Ijebu-Jesa was considered by the customers to be "number one in Ijesaland; people prefer this bank to others in the area." This was because "we don't waste the customer's time, whatever the request is, whatever amount someone wants to withdraw, we never tell someone to come back, we always have funds available for withdrawal. Some community banks pay out funds in installments, and don't have the funds available at any one time to meet withdrawals. The Ijebu-Jesa bank doesn't do that."

By 1996 many community banks around the country had failed, but the one in Ijebu-Jesa was still in business. However, the manager reported that the overall economic conditions were affecting the bank's customers, and some people had not been able to repay their loans. The situation seemed to have deteriorated further by 1997, with one of the bank's board members reporting that most people were now unable to take loans because of the economic situation in the country, so the bank was not making money.

The Ijebu-Jesa Community Bank was not the first effort undertaken by the Ibadan-based Ijebu-Jesa Group. It is one of many activities in which the organization has been engaged over many years. According to Chief O. O. Fatodu, a member of the group who has moved back to Ijebu-Jesa to live, the organization has fifteen to twenty members, professionals and businesspeople who mainly live and work in Ibadan. Although they range in age from about fifty to seventy, they have all known each other for many years and have worked together for some time. According to Chief Fatodu, "The main purpose of the group is not for ourselves but for the development of the community. We see ourselves as a kind of pressure group that thinks out ways and means to bring the community up. It's a poor community, and we want to find ways to raise the standard of living." For example, in the mid-1970s, they used their influence to get the government to install water and electricity in the town sooner than might have happened otherwise. They also worked to get a post office in the town. Together with the community-wide organization, the Ijebu-Jesa Union Conference, the group assisted in the building of the town hall and in the ongoing efforts to rebuild the palace. In addition, the organization formed a business enterprise of its own, Egboro Nigeria Ltd. They began by selling soft drinks, beer, cement, and other products and by renting out chairs and canopies for parties. They employ a few people and have some women working as distributors. They intended to expand into productive activities as well but had not actually done so. The company "provides some means of livelihood" for those who work as distributors. "They can buy on credit and then resell, and also get a discount." And the business is "helping the community develop in this way, because it's possible to buy things locally, and people don't have to waste time traveling to Ilesa or Oshogbo for them."

According to Chief Fatodu, "The same frame of mind, of doing some-thing to help the community, led us to jump at Babangida's idea of commu-nity banks." They thought that if they could start one in Ijebu-Jesa it would help people; people wouldn't need collateral for loans. The commercial banks, like First Bank (which has a branch in Ijebu-Jesa), "only help the big-time farmers. If someone goes there to borrow N500 or N1,000 to buy goods, or for farming, they won't get a loan. We wanted to help the low people, the grassroots to develop. They need small amounts of capital for small enterprises."

According to the government policy under which the bank was formed, there must be a group that initiates a community bank. The Ijebu-Jesa Group became the initiator; they levied themselves and got as many people as possible to contribute N25,000. The minimum needed to start the bank, according to government policy, was N250,000. They began with N500,000. They sold shares at N1 per share, and buyers were allowed to own as little as 100 shares. Those who contributed large amounts included members of the organization and others. In an interview in 1995, Chief Fatodu, one of the bank's directors, listed the reasons why he thought the bank had been successful so far, in contrast to many in other communities. First, he said, they rented a building rather than spending their capital on constructing their own building. Second, the directors were not being remu-nerated in any way. Third, they only hired the staff necessary to handle the volume of work. Fourth, all the directors come home at least once a month to be at the bank and see what is going on. The directors are all prominent individuals, members of the Ijebu-Jesa Group. Chief Fatodu is the only one living in Ijebu-Jesa; he frequently visits the bank and is in regular contact with the staff. Finally, he said, their policy on giving loans has been selective and cautious, with a committee of staff and directors overseeing the decisions.

At the same time, the directors "don't allow themselves to be lured by the money there." The directors all have their own jobs and are not anxious to make money. "We see the bank as an investment and want to leave our money there, as a long-term investment." And since the community knows that the people in charge of the bank can be trusted, they "have confidence in the bank and that helps it to grow."

According to Chief Fatodu, the members of the organization "see what they are doing as a sort of experiment." He observed, "In other towns, you see a group starting something and then collapsing because of dishonesty within the group." Even at home, "there have been groups that have started something; it's been prosperous to begin with and later it collapsed because of distrust and dishonesty of some of the group. For example, members might ask for loans from the capital and not return it." In the case of the Ijebu-Jesa Group, the group has been together for a long time, he said, from school and university days. "We have tested one another. We're not a large group and we know each other well, we can trust ourselves." He continued: "And because of what we have been doing in the community, in the church, educational institutions, people have confidence in us. People feel that whatever we handle is likely to succeed. And we haven't abused that trust."

The community bank in Iwoye.   The community bank in Iwoye began several years later than that in Ijebu-Jesa, and it was organized differently. Although people in the community first began to talk about it in the early 1990s, the bank opened only in mid-1995. The intervening years were spent mobilizing the resources for the bank; constructing a new building for it; and getting government permission to open it. The Iwoye bank was viewed as a project of the community as a whole rather than an effort by a single hometown organization, as in Ijebu-Jesa. According to the manager, almost every individual from the town, "sons and daughters of the town, both men and women," bought shares in the bank. The minimum number of shares was 500 per shareholder, and one individual was not allowed to own more than 5 percent of the total shares. Although nearly everyone contributed, "the bulk of the capital came from those living in big towns; they purchased not less than 60 percent of the shares, while those living at home in Iwoye purchased about 40 percent."

There were three main sets of people involved in establishing the bank. The group that initiated the idea was the Iwoye-Ijesa Descendants Union, which represents everyone from Iwoye. The association purchased its own shares. Then other groups and hometown organizations bought shares—the Progressive Union, the Social Elites, a group called Club 79, and so on;

altogether, twenty-seven organizations participated. The third set of people was the individual shareholders; 250 individuals bought shares. As in Ijebu-Jesa, they were able to mobilize more than the government-required minimum of N250,000. In addition, those in Iwoye decided to build a new building for the bank, and they got contributions for the building as well as for equipment and supplies. Once the community had accomplished this, they still had to obtain government approval, following an inspection. This was delayed because of changes in the board overseeing the community banks nationwide.

The bank is managed by a board of directors appointed by the community as well as advisory committees, including a loan advisory committee so that the manager alone could not be pressured to make loans. Instead, the manager makes recommendations, and then the committee oversees the final decisions about loans.

I. A. Babatayo, a retired school administrator who is a native of Iwoye, was appointed the manager of the bank. Unlike Ijebu-Jesa, which hired a professional manager from outside the community, Iwoye chose Babatayo "because he is a native of the town who wants to stay in the town." He was interested in staying at home and contributing to the community's development. According to him, "I want to serve people; I want to leave behind a good name, not an edifice." The purpose of the bank "is to see that economic activities of the town and the area around it are improved. There's poverty here, and people don't have enough capital or assets to go to a commercial bank." He continued: "If we want people to grow, there should be a source for them to get capital. The bank will be for people like farmers and traders. We want to help reduce the poverty and disease among people in the town and help people plan for bigger businesses."

By June 1996, about one year after the bank opened, there were roughly 400 current (checking) accounts and 400 savings accounts. As in Ijebu-Jesa, the bank had begun a daily savings system, with a minimum of N5 per day; one contribution per month was paid as a fee for the service. The bank made loans for trading, manufacturing, and farming, but mainly for farming, providing short-term loans for those who plant food crops such as maize and vegetables. In the first year, all loans that had been given out had been repaid. Those who had opened accounts came not only from Iwoye but also from neighboring towns, including Ijebu-Jesa. The manager speculated that some people might prefer to have an account in a town different from the one they live in, so that their neighbors would not know about their finances.

As in Ijebu-Jesa, Iwoye's community bank was one among several community efforts at local development. In addition to the reconstruction of the *oba*'s palace, there were also plans to build a community health center. The palace, the health center, and the bank were all to be located in the town center, near the remains of the old palace and across from the small marketplace. Putting up a building for the bank led to delays in the construction of the palace, as the community diverted resources from one project to the other. By June 1996 the palace had not yet been completed, although a new *oba* had been installed. Completion of the palace became the main focus of later fund-raising activities. The foundation for the health center had also been laid. The center was a joint project of the town, the local government, and UNICEF, with the government providing materials, the community providing labor, and UNICEF providing equipment. Funds had been raised at Iwoye Day celebrations beginning in the early 1990s for these projects.

Similar methods were used to raise money for earlier projects. For example, beginning in the 1970s Iwoye had begun to raise money to install electricity in the town. However, before the project was completed, the government said they should wait for the government to put in electricity, so they put the project aside. They finally got electricity in the town in 1985. The money that had been raised was used instead for the grammar school. Community organizations had also discussed the establishment of a palm-wine factory, to be owned by the community. However, this project has not actually gotten under way.

In both Iwoye and Ijebu-Jesa, there seemed to be a genuine commitment to the idea of community banks. The successful establishment of community banks in these two communities seems quite different from the overall impression of community banks in the country as a whole, where both the community banks and the People's Bank, another Babangida effort to provide loans to low-income people,[7] were having many problems (*Third Eye*, June 19, 1995; *The Guardian*, April 15, 1996). A workshop on community banks nationwide examined the developments up to 1993 and even then highlighted some of the problems, demonstrating that even though "some banks were willing to support community members with loans ... many others merely took their funds and had them invested in income-generating assets in the cities" (Olowu and Oludimu 1993: 5–6; see also Mabogunje 1995).

Women's Income-Generating Projects: Owodunni Women's Group

In the 1980s and 1990s development efforts all over the world increasingly focused on women. One approach taken in many areas was to look for ways to improve women's capacity for earning income and improving women's livelihoods by helping them gain access to credit, resources, and skills (see Trager 1996a). Such projects were promoted mainly by international agencies and nongovernmental organizations. But agencies of that type were almost entirely absent in the Ijesa region before and during the period of research, although there were significant women's organizations in neighboring areas (see Trager and Osinulu 1991). There were also some government programs, begun during the Babangida regime. For the most part, however, people in Ijesaland were left to their own ideas and resources for local development, and most of the activities that were undertaken did not specifically focus either on women or on improving people's livelihoods. (The Community Banks did assist people with loans and credit, as we have seen, but did not specifically target women, although women did benefit from them.)

One exception to this general rule was a women's organization in Iloko, the Owodunni Women's Group. This organization first formed under the aegis of the Babangida government's Better Life for Rural Women program, but later adopted Owodunni for the name. In the mid-1990s it began to receive some assistance from a Nigerian NGO, the Association for Development Options in Nigeria (ADON), which itself had some funding from several external donors such as the U.S. Agency for International Development and the U.S. embassy in Lagos.

According to D. A. Adejola, a primary school teacher in Iloko and the president of the Owodunni Gari Processing Complex, when the group first formed in 1989 under the Better Life program it began a cooperative farm, growing maize, cassava, and soybeans. In 1996 it received assistance from ADON to begin a small *gari*-processing industry, located just off the road between Iloko and Ijeda. The group processes cassava from their farm into *gari* for sale, and individuals can also bring their own cassava there for processing. ADON provided the funds for equipment, the most important of which was a grinding machine. Members of the Iloko community provided money to construct sheds. In 1997 the site included a mud-brick shed housing the grinding machine, an open area with a roof for frying *gari,* and a well to provide water for soaking and fermenting the cassava. There was also an area where the cassava was left to ferment and for the water to be squeezed out of it before frying. The group has about twenty members, mostly women in their fifties and sixties who are farmers and traders. They work as a group every two weeks to grind cassava from their cooperative farm. Members, as well as others, can also pay to grind their own cassava at any time.

When they get together as a group, the women can carry out all of the stages of processing *gari* in one afternoon. They peel fresh cassava that has been brought from the farm and wash it with water from the well. Then they start up the grinding machine, with the assistance of a young boy, and feed the tubers one at a time into the machine; a relatively fine powder results, which is collected into basins. The freshly ground cassava is placed into bags and left to ferment for four days. In the meantime, cassava that has already been fermented is placed into a press to squeeze out the excess water. Then the fermented cassava is removed from the bag and placed through a sieve—a wooden box with a screen—so that lumps are removed. Finally, the *gari* is taken to the open stove, where it is "fried"—heated and stirred in a large metal pan so that all water and impurities are removed. The fried *gari* is then put into sacks for sale.

By carrying out the different stages of processing at the same time, the women in the Owodunni group are able to process a considerable amount of cassava in a relatively short period of time. This is possible only if there is sufficient cassava for there to be both fresh and fermented cassava available, and only if there are enough women working together to do all of the different activities involved (other than the grinding itself, *gari* processing remains a labor-intensive activity).[8]

In 1997 the members of the group were concerned that goats were able to get into the site easily; they wanted to build a fence. A year later, in June 1998, they had built a cement-brick wall around the whole area. They had done this by hiring bricklayers, but members of the group also assisted. They had also acquired an electric grinding machine to replace the diesel one they had been using and were planning to have electricity installed on the site.

Grace Faoye is the president of ADON, the NGO that assisted the Owodunni group. She formed ADON with several others, including people who are university professors in Ibadan and Ife. The organization was involved in several small projects in several communities. Faoye is herself from Iloko and based in Ibadan. She explained ADON's decision to assist the Owodunni group by saying that some years previous she had helped set up a weaving project in the neighboring town of Ijeda, her husband's hometown, and that people in Iloko had complained that she had done something for his hometown but not for her own. Then one of the external donor organizations that was funding some ADON activities asked whether ADON could do something like what she had done in Ijeda in another community. She thought Iloko would be a good place, "since people in the community are already involved in many community development activities. Just about all development that you see in Iloko was done by the people. I don't know of any other community where people have undertaken so much by themselves, and where there has essentially been no government involvement." ADON organized a meeting to find out what people in Iloko wanted. There was interest in establishing a *gari*-processing industry, so they decided to do so.

The Owodunni group did not limit itself to *gari* processing but had undertaken several other activities as well. The group has adult education classes, with a local primary school teacher teaching them to read and write in Yoruba. They have also begun several craft projects, such as learning to knit caps, with the intention of selling some of their products. There were some ideas for other activities, including agricultural processing, but by 1998 work had not yet begun on any other project.

The Owodunni group was not the only organization active in Iloko or the only organization focusing its efforts on women. Throughout this book, we have learned about some of the range of development activities in Iloko, from the community hall to boreholes for water, and in Chapter 5 we learned about some of the women's organizations in the town. By 1997–1998 another Nigerian NGO, the Center for Health Sciences Training, Research, and Development (CHESTRAD), had chosen Iloko and several neighboring communities in the LGA as a focus of its project activity. In fact, there was considerable evidence that the reputation that Iloko earned as a community that undertook its own "self-development" was encouraging even more activity. As the woman quoted at the beginning of this chapter said, "In this town we have dreams." Or as J. I. Omoniyi, chairman of the Iloko-Ijesa Development Committee, said, "Iloko-Ijesa has always depended on self-help for ... development." I will return to the extent of involvement in community development activities in Iloko and the other communities in the discussion of participation below.

Industrialization and Economic Development

The examples considered so far—in Iwoye, Ijebu-Jesa, and Iloko—suggest that it is possible for community organizations and entire communities to take on development projects that affect people's livelihoods and economic well-being. No longer are Ijesa communities simply building town halls and palaces, although they continue to do that as well. There is both a rhetoric and a reality that development should include improvement in local economic activities. However, none of the projects discussed so far involve any type of industrial development. Despite discussion of establishing cottage industries, no group has done so. As we have seen in Chapter 5, the Ijesa Solidarity Group debated ways of raising funds for industrialization. We have not yet considered what type of industrialization was being advocated either by ISG or by other organizations. In the discussion that follows, I will return to the ISG debate in order to consider what ideas were current regarding the possible types of industries. Despite the rhetoric and debate, no actual industrialization project was undertaken during the time of the study.

In 1991 and 1992, when the Ijesa Solidarity Group was still a new organization, there was great enthusiasm and optimism among its leaders about the possibility of establishing a local industry. For example, one of the founders of the organization said, "We want to industrialize Ijesaland, provide economic opportunities, and encourage people to stay or come back here by having jobs available." He went on to point out the impact of the brewery, saying that "I don't think there is a household that hasn't been affected in some way by the brewery, by someone having a job there, or through someone selling beer, or in some other way." According to him, about 1,000 people are employed at the brewery, and they are from all over Ijesaland. He continued,

> Ijesa Solidarity Group wants to encourage industry all over Ijesaland. At first our idea was that we would establish industries ourselves but now we have decided that it would be better to provide the infrastructure for industry, such as water and electricity. If government isn't doing this, then we have to do it ourselves, through self-help. We would like to set up an industrial park in a place like Ijebu-Jesa or Ibokun and encourage people to establish industries there.

Like this man, some thought that the best approach would be to acquire land in several of the Ijesa towns, then leave it to individuals to establish industry. Others thought they should do more to develop local infrastructure, for example, by exploring the possibility of using the waterfalls in Erin Ijesa, another small Ijesa town, as a source for water or hydroelectric power.

Still others argued that ISG should itself establish small industries. For example, in May 1992 the organization described an "investment corporation" that would "cause feasibility studies to be carried out and promote the establishment of several COTTAGE INDUSTRIES spread throughout Ijesaland. These Industries shall be jointly subscribed by the corporation and the local inhabitants who shall have substantial holdings in such industries" (Ijesa Solidarity Group, Minutes of Pro-Tem Council, May 9, 1992). Many people referred to the establishment of cottage industries, especially ones based on the processing of local agricultural products. One of the specific suggestions was that ISG should establish a rice mill for the processing of the rice grown in eastern Ijesaland, between Erin and Ikeji. As one of the leaders argued, there was no good facility for processing rice, and if there were then farmers would be encouraged to produce more; as a result, more rice would be processed. In discussing the importance of cottage industries, ISG leaders were especially concerned with setting up establishments in the smaller Ijesa towns rather than in Ilesa. They were well aware of the dominant role that Ilesa has had in both political and economic relationships in the region and wanted to de-emphasize Ilesa, even though most of them were themselves from Ilesa. Their long-term goals extended beyond Ijesaland, however; they believed that the economic efforts they pursued in Ijesaland could ultimately be extended to other parts of Osun State, even beyond to other parts of Nigeria.

In order to actually undertake a specific project such as a rice mill, the organization had to have agreement on how to go about doing that. As we have already seen in Chapter 5, there was considerable disagreement among ISG members over who should undertake industrial projects and over how to raise funds for such projects. Some simply wanted to acquire sites and encourage individual investment. Others thought that the organization should establish these industries, either by establishing a company to do so or by having the organization itself commit funds. One proposal for the rice mill, for example, was to first do a feasibility study, followed by the establishment of a company out of a development fund, and with additional shares being available both to ISG members and others. The suggestion was that perhaps 20 percent of the shares would be owned by ISG.

By 1994 there was considerably less enthusiasm for direct involvement of ISG in industrial projects. Some argued that the overall situation in the country was not good for investment of any type, whereas others believed that despite the political situation people must continue to invest and try to move ahead with the organization's goals. But as we have seen, there was little consensus about how this could be accomplished. Those with the greatest wealth, those who might be able to make the largest contribution to any industrial project, tended to be the most skeptical about the success of projects undertaken by organizations. In addition, some ISG members were concerned that those with the most money might dominate the organization. These concerns, combined with the deteriorating economic and political situation, meant that despite the good intentions and ambitious goals of ISG leaders the organization did not actually undertake any of the industrial efforts that had been discussed or follow any of the methods for raising funds that had been proposed.

The leadership was well aware of the situation. By May 1995 the president, E. A. Ifaturoti, was commenting that ISG had "succeeded in raising people's consciousness" but that they had not "succeeded in actually doing anything yet, we still haven't developed any industry or anything like that." He said, "What is needed is something at the grassroots; we need to find out what people want and what the problems are." According to him, at the ISG meeting that month there was criticism about the organization's lack of progress. Members agreed that "the goal of the organization is to bring progress all around for Ijesaland, for the farmers, for the common people, so SAP and the overall economic situation won't be so harsh on them." He said that one person spoke at the meeting, saying that they are not using the right vehicle for moving toward their goals—that it is as if they are driving a Jaguar in mountainous terrain; a Jaguar is a very good, powerful car but not good for that kind of terrain (a Land Rover would be better). So likewise ISG is not using the right vehicle. One of the problems was the organization's structure, with committee chairmen living in Lagos and members scattered all over; it was difficult to attend meetings. And when committee chairmen and others do meet, they do not come to any agreement. The debate and frustration about their lack of progress continued for several more years; the organization was also acquiring new leadership (see Chapter 5). And it also became increasingly concerned with other issues, such as local conflicts and Ijesa unity (see Chapter 9).

By 1998 ISG members, under new leadership, again met to discuss ways by which they could contribute to local economic development. In their meeting in June 1998, members had copies of a paper written by one member, an individual with many years of experience in local community development. He had prepared a proposal for the transformation of the Ijesa Solidarity Group into something resembling a nongovernmental development organization. As it turned out, the membership was not able to discuss the proposal at any length, and the individual who wrote the proposal was unable to attend the meeting. But several of the members voiced their support for his proposal, or at least for the fundamental goal that ISG continue to be concerned primarily about "the grassroots and ordinary people."

The Ijesa Solidarity Group was not the only organization discussing industrialization during this period. Several other organizations advocated industrial development in general, the establishment of cottage industries, and mining in the Ijesa region.[9] For example, in 1994 the Ilesa Chamber of Commerce published a brochure ("Ilesa: Yesterday, Today, Tomorrow") proposing a N100 million industrial development project. The brochure described the need for industrial development in general; one of the few specific projects mentioned was the mining of talc, which is locally available but of questionable quality. Similarly, as we have seen in Chapter 5, the Ijesa National Day celebration in 1993 had the goal of establishing a N50 million fund "for the industrialization of Ijesaland, that would maximize the utilization of raw materials of Ijesaland." The Council of Ijesa Societies was also discussing industrial projects during this period. According to their president, Chief A. O. Lamikanra, they had identified three levels: cottage industries, small-scale industries, and large-scale industries. The council did not want to establish industries itself but rather to promote their establishment, suggesting specific types of industry and then encouraging individuals to invest in them. They wanted these industries to be based on local raw materials and to expand employment in the area. At the Council of Ijesa Societies Award Ceremony in 1992, Chief Lamikanra said, "The special message for this year is industrialize; there are natural, mineral resources, agricultural, fertile soil, and there are accomplished people who can help Ijesa industrialization."

None of these discussions resulted in the initiation of any industrial projects. Most lacked specifics, and even where there were specific ideas, such as the proposal for a rice mill, the organizations were not able to mobilize the resources or to get agreement on how to go about such projects. In the *Ijesa Year Book* (1997), one of the authors comments, "Industrial activity, besides brewing and some steel works, is virtually nonexistent in Ijesaland" (Owosekun 1997: 40–50). This has continued to be the case despite considerable attention given to this issue by various groups. This is not surprising. To establish industry requires considerable resources. It also requires agreement on what industries will be viable, as well as a willingness on the part of those with resources to commit them to projects where others will oversee the expenditure of their money. This would be difficult in any economic environment, and that of Nigeria in the 1990s was hardly conducive to believing that such projects would be successful. Those with the money to spend were more likely to want to control their capital themselves than to provide it to an organization.

Efforts by organizations and communities to undertake local economic development in Ijesaland remain an unfinished story. The establishment of community banks and women's projects in Ijebu-Jesa, Iwoye, and Iloko indicates that it is possible for local organizations to undertake activities designed to improve economic conditions. Yet the lack of success in industrial projects illustrates the many difficulties. Particularly in the deteriorating economic context that everyone faced in the 1990s, even those individuals and organizations with wealth and resources could not be optimistic about prospects for local development. The political context exacerbated this situation. As we shall see in Chapter 9, the broader political situation as well as local conflicts made people even more pessimistic about the future. However, the overall picture is not completely negative; it is important to emphasize how much did take place and how much was accomplished, even in an increasingly pessimistic climate. The final section of this chapter therefore examines the extent to which people participated in the development activities described and the extent to which they viewed them as beneficial. It considers as well the issue of who sets the agenda for local development in the communities studied. Finally, I consider some of the differences among the communities studied.

Who Participates? Who Decides? Who Benefits?

Participation in local development is increasingly emphasized in the debate about how development takes place. Most of that debate focuses on situations where outside organizations—governments, NGOs, and others—come into a community with a development project. In communities such as those discussed here, where people are committed to self-help and to raising funds for their own development projects, participation by members of the community presumably is not a problem. However, just because a project is agreed to by a local development committee or by a local organization, it does not necessarily follow that all, or most, community members agree with the project or have been consulted about it. It is especially important to consider the issue of participation and involvement in decisionmaking when we recognize the key role played by community members residing outside the community, most of whom are wealthy and part of elite Nigerian society. Are they just another group of outsiders even though they are from the hometown community? How are their ideas and participation seen by those at home? Who makes decisions about the projects to be undertaken and about the money to be raised? And once the projects are undertaken and carried out, how are they viewed? Are they seen as beneficial to the local community and its members?

In the following discussion I consider several different types of data. First, in order to consider the issue of participation, I examine data from both the 1992 and 1996 surveys on respondents' involvement in their hometowns. Second, I consider information in the 1996 survey on participation in some of the specific projects discussed above as well as on respondents' perceptions of the benefits of those projects. Third, I will consider evidence of the decisionmaking and fund-raising processes. Finally, I will consider some of the differences among the towns. The data indicate that there is a great deal of agreement on the overall goals of local development efforts. At the same time, there is less direct involvement in decisionmaking among those who are living at home. The process of raising funds and setting goals seems to work better in the smaller communities, which is not surprising given the variety of organizations and viewpoints found in a city like Ilesa. And there is certainly the possibility of conflict, even in the smallest places, although that conflict may not be articulated directly.

Participation in hometown activities can be determined in several different ways. On the one hand, activities that are carried out essentially at individual and family levels constitute one type of participation. Such activities include building a house in one's hometown and sending money to family there (discussed above and in Chapter 4). On the other hand, activities involving community participation constitute another type of involvement. Such activities include membership in organizations and contributions to community-wide projects.[10]

Membership in hometown organizations reflects an interest in community activities. As we have seen, there are many such organizations in all communities, ranging from social clubs, to service and church organizations, to mutual assistance organizations. Of all the respondents, nearly half (48 percent) belong to at least one hometown organization, and several people belong to more than one. Both men and women belong to such organizations—52 percent of all men in the survey and 45 percent of women.

Likewise, people of all ages belong to these organizations (46 percent of those 65 and under, 56 percent of those over 65). Among the major activities of these organizations are assistance to members; assistance to others in town; and "contributing to the progress of the town." In other words, for a considerable number of people, membership in organizations is not only for one's own social benefit—although that is surely part of it—but also for the improvement of conditions in the community.

Even higher percentages of people interviewed in the 1996 survey in Iloko, Ijebu-Jesa, and Iwoye reported that they belong to an organization in their hometown: 66 percent of all respondents in that survey said they belonged to an organization. As in the earlier survey, the activities of these organizations ranged from assisting the members, to religious activities, to town development.

Interest in community affairs is shown not only through membership in organizations but also through contributions to local projects. In the 1992 survey, 34 percent of respondents said that they had contributed to at least one project. More men than women reported such contributions: 50 percent of males and 20 percent of females said that they had made contributions. There is not much difference by age, with 36 percent of those 65 and under and 29 percent of those over 65 reporting such contributions.

The types of projects and activities to which people contributed are revealing. Many reported contributions to the "development of the town" and to a "development fund" without specifying further the nature of the project. When contributions to specific projects were reported, the activities were for the most part construction projects: schools, hospitals, and town halls. Of those who reported contributions, 73 percent had made a contribution sometime in the past year. The most commonly reported way of contributing was to donate money: 88 percent of those who contributed gave money; 17 percent donated labor.

In the 1996 survey, a greater percentage of respondents (62 percent) reported that they had made contributions. Of those who did not contribute, several indicated that they didn't do so because they are not natives of the town. Of those who did contribute, they reported a range of projects to which they donated, from town halls and palaces, to community-day celebrations, to more general development funds and development levies. Like those in the 1992 survey, most of these respondents indicated that they had made contributions in the previous year, and nearly all their donations were monetary.

In an effort to explore further whether the recent economic crisis has affected people's contributions in their hometowns, respondents in 1992 were asked whether there had been any change in the way they contributed during the past five years and, if so, how. Of those who responded, nearly half (48.5 percent) said that there had been a change. Of these, more than half said that there was a change because the project was completed. However, others indicated a change in their economic situation as the reason: nine stated that they have less money to contribute because of SAP or the economic situation. Yet six people reported that they have increased their contribution. Likewise in the 1996 survey, 35 percent reported that there had been a change in their contributions in the previous year. Surprisingly, however, these respondents mainly reported increases in their contributions, with more than two-thirds of those who said there had been a change stating that their contributions had increased. I will return to this data below to suggest that the deteriorating economic situation by 1996 actually led to an expansion of efforts at local development and increased participation, at least in some communities.

The 1996 survey also inquired about contributions to specific projects in each community: the community hall and community-day celebrations in Iloko; the palace, community bank, and community day in Iwoye; and the palace and community bank in Ijebu-Jesa. Half of all respondents said they had contributed to at least one of these projects. In Iloko, 59 percent of the respondents had contributed to the town hall, the community day, or both; in Iwoye, 75 percent had contributed to at least one project; and in Ijebu-Jesa, 31 percent had contributed. Several people also reported other contributions—to the health center, to a general development levy, or to something else that was not specified.

In 1996 I also asked respondents whether they had benefited in any way from the local projects. A third of all respondents said that they had. Of these, most responded that they use one of the community banks; several others indicated that they had benefited from the community hall in Iloko. A few stated that they "benefit from everything."

In sum, an examination of the survey data on participation in community activities and contribution to community development indicates that a considerable number of people are involved in a variety of ways. Half of the respondents belong to organizations, and more than a third reported making contributions—primarily monetary—to community activities and projects. Many of the latter are specific projects, such as the building of a community facility, although more general contributions to community development funds are also reported. Despite the economic crisis, only a few respondents referred specifically to their economic difficulties in discussing their contributions and changes in them; others indicated that they had increased their contributions during this period. People in the communities surveyed in 1996 had both contributed to, and benefited from, the local projects in those communities.

But making a monetary contribution for a project is only one indication of participation. Beyond the contributions, it is important to consider who is making the decisions and the extent to which a range of community members are involved in those decisions. For projects such as those initiated by organizations like the Ijesa Solidarity Group, there is no intention of involving everyone in the community. Decisions are made by the organization, especially by its key members and leaders. Likewise, the Ijebu-Jesa Community Bank was, as we have seen, initiated by one organization. Although many in the community are both participating in the bank and benefiting from it, they were not involved in the decision to establish it. Yet the community bank in Iwoye was a project undertaken by an organization that is supposed to represent the entire community, just as the Iloko community has a community-wide organization that takes on the major projects there, such as the community hall. To what extent do people in these communities consider themselves involved in the decisions that were made, and to what extent do they participate in the fund-raising activities accompanying these projects?

I engaged in a conversation with two men—one old, one young—sitting outside a shop in the center of Iloko one afternoon in June 1995. The old man told a story to me and my research assistant:

> If I tell you that my daughter is getting married and I invite you to the wedding, and you come, and there's no one there, no daughter, no wedding. And then the next year I tell you that my daughter is getting married and invite you to the wedding. And you come and again there's no daughter and no wedding. Then what will you think the third time I invite you?

He told us this story to demonstrate why it was necessary for the third Iloko Day to focus on fund-raising within the community, since they had gotten donations from people outside on the first two Iloko Days, but the community hall was still not finished. He and the young man then explained to us how fund-raising takes place among members of the Iloko community. According to them, everyone who is from the town is expected to contribute something, as individuals, both males and females, with the exception of children and those who are students. "Everyone who is working is expected to pay. The amount is based on a person's economic power, and the committee decides the amount each person is to pay." For example, the young man explained that since he is a teacher, he is expected to pay a minimum of N500 every year. "The committee sends me a letter telling me how much I am expected to pay, and when I have the money I send it to the committee."

He gets a receipt, and every year the amounts that are collected and spent are recorded. "All indigenes, regardless of where they are living, are expected to pay." According to both men, people in Iloko like this system because with it "we have been achieving." The system of fund-raising has been in existence for a long time. People like this system, the young man said, because "as long as one is an indigene of this town, one has a link.

Wherever you live, people there meet regularly to discuss developments at home and the contributions people can make." The old man added that no one complains, that they all try to get the money to pay the amount they are asked to pay. I asked whether people outside ever stop paying. The young man said that before he returned to Iloko, he was teaching at Ibadan. Before the creation of Osun State he was in Ibadan, but after the new state was created he lost his job in Ibadan and had to come home; the creation of Osun State brought him home. He explained that when he was living in Ibadan he met with others from Iloko; they then contributed to development at home. "We were always informed of what was happening at home; you can't live in isolation."

The two men explained that the committee that requests the payments consists of Iloko people living in different towns, representing people residing in places such as Lagos, Ibadan, Kano, and so on. The committee, the young man said, consists of people who are "qualified, the right caliber." When I asked specifically whether everyone agrees with the project to raise funds for the town hall, or if there are some who would rather not pay, both men responded that everyone agrees, that there is no argument.

What was most striking about this conversation was that I had never met or spoken with either of the two men previously; neither had they known that I would be asking them any questions that afternoon. They had not, in fact, been selected or identified in any way, other than the fact that they happened to be sitting with some other men outside a building in the town center on that particular afternoon. Other random conversations with people in Iloko led to much the same type of response. Two other young men, a carpenter recently returned from Lagos and a man who had grown up in Iloko (although not originally from there), explained that everyone who is working is expected to contribute a minimum amount to the town hall project; men contributed N50 each and women N30. They said that they had each contributed four or five times. Those who live outside the town contribute more; for those inside the town, the elders decide how much each should contribute. When asked if there were any problems with paying, the two men explained that students and young people who are not working do not pay. And if a son is working and his parents are old, then the son is expected to pay his parents' contributions as well. The one who was not from Iloko explained that he, too, is expected to pay and does so, since he has lived there for many years and plans to stay.

In another conversation, a group of three women selling in the small Iloko marketplace told us that they contribute as individuals "for the development of the town." They said that they had contributed at Iloko Day for the town hall project. When I asked if there are other things they would like to see done in the town, they responded that "when the development committee sits with the chiefs and decides the next thing to do, then we will contribute the money." In their view, it is "the indigenes that live outside the town who are the ones who see things outside and know what to do. Once they tell us what is to be done, then we will contribute." They went on to explain that people residing in the town are involved in the decisions that are made. "The people outside come home and sit with some of those at home, and they decide. The committee and the chiefs sit together and discuss, and then they invite the whole town and give them their views and tell them what they are planning." A meeting on the previous Saturday was an example, they explained. These women, like the men, said that they support this way of doing things, "because everyone in the town, both men and women, is represented at the meeting."

Although the degree of consensus that exists in Iloko may be rather exaggerated by these men and women, the system they described for deciding about projects and for raising funds does reflect a community-wide process that has wide support. The meeting that the women referred to, for example, took place on a Saturday afternoon in June 1995 and was attended by about 200 people. A wide-ranging discussion of community problems occurred. Several of the chiefs and community leaders sat in front and ran the meeting; men and women, many of them elderly, sat in metal chairs facing the front. Unlike the first two Iloko Day celebrations, but like the third several months after this meeting, the entire discussion took place in Yoruba and Ijesa dialect; no English was used.

The first part of the discussion focused on fund-raising for the community hall. J. I. Omoniyi, the head of the Iloko Development Committee, said that the money that had been raised at the first two Iloko Days had been spent to get the hall to its current state; now they needed to raise money from community members in order to finish it. He also said that those who live at home had donated but that not everyone outside had contributed. He said that old people should talk to their children, tell them to "donate money and make sure they contribute to the development of the town." Later in the meeting, he announced that they had decided that May is not a good day for Iloko Day because farm produce is not yet ready; they would have the next Iloko Day in October. And it would take place in the new hall, "so everyone must pay so that the hall can be completed by then."

People spoke on other issues. One man raised the issue of the money that is spent on things such as funeral ceremonies, even when "people don't have money." He said that instead of spending money that way people should use it to send their children to school or for the development of the town. Others commented on this; for example, one of the senior chiefs pointed out that it is not required that people spend money when someone dies. "If someone has the money, that is fine, then spend it on the burial and the chiefs and other people will eat the food. But if they don't have money, they should just bury the body and not spend a lot of money, and they will still be respected in the town." He agreed that many people are not spending money on their children to send them to school. Others took up the theme of educating local children, saying that parents are sending their children to the farm or to work instead of to school. One man said that it used to be possible to count the number of Iloko children who were attending university and technical schools but that now students from Iloko don't have good enough grades to go to these institutions. Another said that "it is the duty of the parents to make sure that their children go to school and study. They can go to the farm to help after school hours."

Several leading individuals were introduced at the meeting, including a university professor from the town who was praised for his assistance to students in gaining school admission, and the head of the local government. Some comments were addressed to the local government administrator about some of the problems that needed to be corrected: paving local roads, providing drainage along the road near the community hall, and clearing the area near the maternity and health center. Some also raised problems regarding the local water supply. The local government chair responded by announcing that they would clear the bush; that they had paid to restore the water supply but that it was still not working; and that there were problems with the contractor responsible for paving one of the roads.

Finally, Omoniyi raised the issue of acquiring land for a community burial ground, and the chiefs announced that they had agreed on the land that would be given for this purpose.

This community meeting provided the opportunity for those residing in Iloko to raise and discuss issues with the development committee and the chiefs. Although several individuals spoke at the meeting, most of the comments came from community leaders: Omoniyi, the head of the development committee, the regent, other chiefs, and the local government chair. No women spoke, although many attended. In this respect, the meeting was quite different from those of the women's organizations described above and in Chapter 5.

The community meeting brought together the two major decisionmaking bodies in Iloko: the traditional chiefs and the Iloko Development Committee. At the time of the meeting, Chief Olusola Ogunsanya was one of the senior chiefs of Iloko as well as the *adele oba* (regent), a position he held from the time of the death of the late *oba*, Samuel Olashore, in 1989, until the installation of Oladele Olashore as *oba* in 1997. Although based in Lagos, where he is a businessman, Chief Ogunsanya came home to Iloko very frequently and oversaw activities there, in conjunction with the other chiefs, as well as with members of the development committee. As he explained it, these two sets of people—the chiefs and the development committee—work together. Chief Ogunsanya was himself a founding member of the development committee and considers himself to still be part of that group even though he is now a chief. According to him, the development committee takes care of all development projects while the traditional committee takes care of traditional duties. "The traditional committee is above the development committee, so the development committee comes to us with their plans." The chiefs implement the plans. "We control the people," he said. But, he said, the members of the development committee are "enlightened" and have the professional and educational backgrounds needed. "They are more superior than the traditional members" in that only a few of the chiefs are "enlightened and well-read."

The development committee has representatives of the various clubs and associations based in urban areas around the country. When a decision is made, these representatives report back to the members of their respective organizations. When they decide on a project, then they levy people for it. The amount levied depends on where one lives and the type of work one does. Those living at home are in two categories: those with low incomes, such as farmers, who pay minimal amounts, such as N50 or N100 (women pay less than men); and professionals and people in various businesses, who pay higher amounts. Then there are the people outside the town. According to Chief Ogunsanya, they have a list of all the sons and daughters who live outside, including their addresses. They "know how they are" and assess them one by one. For example, if they are salaried, then they know their grade (and hence their salaries); if they are in private business they can assess the business by such things as whether the person has a car, a house, and so on. Such people will be assessed a certain amount, such as N5,000 or N10,000. If a person can't make that amount, he'll pay less. Some who are underassessed will complain, because they'll be embarrassed that they haven't been asked to pay more, and so they will pay more than their assessment requires. The whole list is made public so everyone knows what others are being assessed. There is an element of competition, he said; if one person is assessed more than another, the second person will be embarrassed and will pay more. There are also some people that they do not levy at all—the wealthiest and most successful. Those individuals just pay an amount—they "know what to do"; that is, they know the amount to pay and can't be assessed. They are the ones "carrying the load."

Although a substantial amount of money had been raised at the first two Iloko Day celebrations, the development committee had decided by 1995 that they needed to be more successful in levying townspeople in order to finish the community hall. As we saw in Chapter 2, they had not had an Iloko Day in 1994 because, according to the regent, "the economic situation was too bad, people were disillusioned with the June 12 [political] palaver, and they felt people didn't have money and wouldn't come. Even the sons of the soil would have to spend a lot to come home." But the community hall still had to be finished, with flooring, electricity, windows, and landscaping remaining. So the committee decided to discuss why they had not gotten more funds in the previous levy and to find ways to get a better response, including the imposition of sanctions on those who did not contribute. Such sanctions included denying the use of facilities or not assisting when the individual had a family ceremony to carry out. The committee had a list of about 1,000 people residing outside Iloko, and it planned to reassess them, taking into account their current circumstances.

According to development committee head Omoniyi, everyone in the community is involved in decisions about projects that the committee undertakes. "We are very democratic, and before we begin any project we discuss the idea. We look at the options and the resources we have, and we agree on the project that has the most support." Sometimes they are unable to do as much as they would like; for example, although they give some support to the secondary school, they would like to do more but have not been able to. Overall, there is a cross-section of people involved in making decisions and supporting the projects undertaken by the community.

In Iwoye, as in Iloko, there also seemed to be considerable consensus about community involvement in decisionmaking and fund-raising. The two main organizations in Iwoye are the Iwoye-Ijesa Descendants Union (see Chapter 5) and the Iwoye-Ijesa Progressive Union (the IDU and the IPU respectively). The IDU had been established some thirty or forty years previously but went through a period of little activity. All townspeople are members of the IDU, whether educated or not, rich or poor, living inside the town or outside. The IPU, in contrast, is an "elite" organization, established in 1949 for educated people. It is open to anyone who has completed primary school. Initially mainly a social club, it became interested in development, especially in promoting education. It has set up scholarships to the local secondary school, as well as scholarships for universities and technical schools. It also tries to nurture the secondary school, so that "it is a pride to all of us," as the IPU general secretary put it. The IPU also tries to propose projects to the town as a whole. "We discuss what the town needs, formulate policy, and then send it to the IDU for them to take to the whole town. That way there is no conflict. It doesn't look like the educated people are trying to tell the others what to do."

According to some community members, those residing at home appreciate the educated community members residing outside for the part they play in planning activities and fund-raising. "People at home see that those outside bring good suggestions. People at home love them and take their advice. People know that those outside are trustworthy and that they will take good care of the things they are asked to do."

According to leading members of these two organizations, the chiefs are also included in the planning and decisionmaking. As one leader put it, "We carry them [the chiefs] along, and they carry us along with them." He said that the chiefs may suggest what they think is fit for the town. If the others think it is a good idea, and if the people at home support it, then they take the ideas to those outside. "We all work together." The chiefs attend the IDU meetings when they are held at home; when they are held outside Iwoye, one chief attends and reports to the others.

There are, however, differing views of how successful the community organizations in Iwoye have been at organizing development activities. Some community members expressed the view that the IDU and IPU had not been very successful in promoting local development. In one man's view, for example, the development efforts should support improved agriculture, since most local people are farmers. He argued that the organizations should help people see the importance of investing in agriculture. He felt that many in the town waste the money they get from the harvest "on burials, marriages, naming ceremonies" and so on rather than investing it in agriculture. According to him, Iwoye "has a lot of land, and we're also blessed with *ogogoro*, the local palm wine. But people don't use the land and agricultural resources well." He also did not see the community-day celebrations that had been held in the town as having been particularly successful in raising money for local projects.

Ijesa Communities and Community Development

One of the issues that arises in this discussion is the extent to which there are similarities or differences among the communities of Ijesaland in terms of their involvement in local development and in terms of their success at mobilizing resources and getting community involvement. As the discussion above indicates, not everyone in each community agrees with the projects undertaken. One would expect to find this; after all, every community everywhere is complex and has people with varying viewpoints. That is certainly the case in Yoruba communities, which are often split into factions.

Of the communities studied, the smallest, Iloko, had the most activity during the research period. Ijebu-Jesa, like Iloko, has a long history of local development efforts and, with the variety of organizations such as the Ijebu-Jesa Group, has been successful in carrying out significant projects such as the community bank. Iwoye, too, was successful in establishing its community bank, although other projects had not been completed. Since Ilesa is much larger, it is less likely to have community-wide projects. With many organizations, each group has undertaken its own projects. In addition, several Ilesa-based organizations have adopted ambitious goals for the entire Ijesa region. The Ijesa Solidarity Group and others, such as the Council for Ijesa Societies, were able to move forward on some of their goals but did not succeed in their community development efforts during this period. Osu had the least visible activity during this period, although there had been earlier efforts there, such as a town hall and palace.

Some of the differences among these communities result not from their size but from historical differences. As we have discussed in Chapter 3, communities in the northern part of Ijesaland have a history of independence from Ilesa; therefore people from those communities expect to participate in hometown affairs there rather than in Ilesa. Osu, in contrast, has historically close ties to Ilesa, and it is only recently that people from there have begun to emphasize it as an independent place and to focus on it, rather than on Ilesa, as the community to which they have strong ties.

There are other reasons for these differences among communities. For example, in Iloko, Chief Olusola Ogunsanya and J. I. Omoniyi believe that people there are more involved in local development than people in other communities. According to Chief Ogunsanya, "In Iloko we are like family, we band together." In addition, "People here aren't afraid to come home and show their money." More and more people are coming home, he said, and the town is expanding. For Omoniyi, one of the main reasons people are involved in self-help is that they feel that the local government hasn't done much for them; therefore they have to do things for themselves. "When the local government can come in and help, that is okay, but we don't want to wait for them." People are involved in Iloko, he said, because "first of all any Nigerian loves his hometown; wherever one goes, one likes to be linked with his hometown. Traditionally, whatever one becomes, if you neglect your hometown, then there is no respect from the people [at home]. The normal Nigerian must do something in his hometown." He went on to point out that the first thing a person must do is to build a house at home as soon as he can afford it. "The society expects you to build in your hometown. If you don't, the local society won't respect you as much. They'll believe that you're trying to not be part of them, that you are disassociating yourself from them. You are expected to have a residence in your hometown." He continued: "If you have a house or houses elsewhere and don't build at home, you will have no respect." Omoniyi also suggested that an individual should provide for his parents and build something for them at home. In addition, he said "a person should show an interest in the development of the town. If he doesn't, then he's not fulfilling the duties that are expected of him. One shouldn't just build a house at home but should also show interest in the town."

Of course, this does not explain why there should be more activity in Iloko than elsewhere. One difference that is usually not noted by those involved is the extent to which different communities have wealthy, successful members who are active at home. For a small community, Iloko may be exceptional in currently having several key individuals, both men and women, who are taking leading roles in local development. Even more important, Iloko has some individuals with considerable wealth who are able to also provide leadership in mobilizing the resources of others, both those within the community who are less well off, and those from elsewhere, including people who are not themselves members of the community. The success of the first two Iloko Day celebrations in raising funds was much greater than what most other communities were able to raise through such events.

Leaders in Iloko see the local development effort as a continual process, one that will lead to other projects in the future, and they point out that the projects in the 1990s followed earlier efforts. According to Chief Ogunsanya, even before the development committee was established the town had carried out several projects—the roads were built by manual labor, as was the first primary school in the town. The first project of the development committee was the construction of the maternity and health center in 1972. They collected money and also contributed labor; after it was completed, it was handed over to the local government, which provides the nurse. Later, they worked with the neighboring town of Ijeda to get electricity and streetlights. For this, members of the community were levied, and they also held a "launching" to collect donations from others. They collected N20,000, which at the time (1975–1976) was sufficient to complete the project. After that "we took a rest" until 1981, when the palace was built. This was the idea of Prince Oladele Olashore, who initiated the project and got contributions from friends. According to Chief Ogunsanya, only about 10 percent of the funds for the palace were contributed by the community. But "Prince Olashore went to the community to let us know about it, so that the community would be with him." The palace was completed by 1983 and was "the best of the best at that time."

After the palace, there was no major project until the development committee decided in 1990 that they should build a community center. They began the project, looked for and found a site, cleared it, and had plans drawn. Then they organized the first two Iloko Day celebrations to help raise funds for the center. Another recent project was the establishment of a day-care center, which was started by the community in the 1990s and then taken over by UNICEF and the local government. As Omoniyi pointed out, UNICEF was willing to get involved because "UNICEF likes to see that we have put our own money in first, so after we had done that, UNICEF was willing to get involved."

In the late 1990s new projects began in Iloko. After he became *oba*, Oladele Olashore discussed the idea of doing more for the women of the town and, along with other community leaders, wanted to establish a new marketplace. He also talked about trying to find other ways of assisting women to improve their livelihoods. In fact, by 1997–1998 two new efforts had begun in Iloko, both of which were likely to affect women in the community. The first was the building of the new marketplace. Whereas the old market consisted of a few sheds across the street from the palace, the new market was located on a large area of land that was cleared opposite the community hall. Cement stalls had been built by 1998, but no one was using the market yet at that time. The second effort was larger and more comprehensive and involved the Nigerian NGO CHESTRAD, which selected Iloko to be the focus of a project that became known as the Iloko-Oriade Community Development Initiative. This project took a participatory approach to local development and focused on health, literacy, employment, and microenterprise. Although it was designed to include neighboring communities, the project focused on Iloko specifically because of its past community development efforts as well as the interest of community leaders (*Beyond Science* n.d.; Dare n.d.; Lola Dare, personal communication).

CHESTRAD organized two community meetings, one in February 1997 and one in June 1997. These meetings were rather different from the one in 1995, described above, in that they were initiated by someone from outside the community, Lola Dare, the head of CHESTRAD, who is from Ilesa. They were well attended by community members, and at the February meeting many people—men and women, young and old—spoke up about what they felt were the needs of the community. The meeting in February was also unusual in that it was attended by Olikoye Ransome-Kuti, the former minister of health and at the time working at the World Bank's Better Health for Africa program. CHESTRAD concluded that they had "found at Iloko-Ijesha a good and perfect example of the practice of community participation and ... a most encouraging collaborative effort in the provision of health care as well as the provision of all the basic infrastructure that are so vital to development and the enhancement of their well-being" (*Beyond Science* n.d.: 44). However, the extent to which the CHESTRAD project affects local development, especially the extent to which it leads to a greater emphasis on efforts involving women, remains to be seen.

Iloko has also been successful in devising a means of levying community members that seems to be widely accepted. In a society where there is very little successful taxation (Guyer 1992), the ability of a community to essentially tax its members on a regular basis for a succession of projects is significant. When the new market was being built, some expressed concern that there were plans to once again raise the funds from community members, saying that it may get to a point where people feel unable to make further contributions. Although such feelings do not seem to be widespread, there is certainly the possibility that members of the Iloko community will see the levies as too frequent and too much and will therefore stop responding to requests. Yet the fact that some communities are successful in raising funds and completing projects suggests that others may be able to pursue similar goals.

⚶   ⚶   ⚶

Overall, in Iloko, as in Ijebu-Jesa, Iwoye, and, to a lesser extent, Ilesa and Osu, successful community development projects have taken place, initiated by leaders of the community themselves and with considerable involvement of community members. These activities have occurred in a context of severe economic difficulties and are significant for understanding the process of local development more generally. The Ijesa experience is placed in comparative perspective in Chapter 10.

Notes

1. When I was conducting informal interviews with people around Iloko, I met a man working as a guard at the school, who was renting a place to live in town. He commented on how welcoming the people of the town had been and indicated that he had become involved in some of the local development efforts. On another occasion, I met one of the teachers in the town center; he described some of the ways in which he was getting the students better acquainted with the town.

2. The Olashore International School, on the outskirts of town, had its own water supply, obtained by connecting to a line that supplies the brewery in Ilesa, directly from the main supply source for the region, located in Esa-Odo, beyond Ijebu-Jesa.

3. Iwoye, like many other smaller Ijesa towns, did not historically have its own *oba* but rather a *loja*, or leading chief, who was considered to be subordinate to the *owa* of Ilesa. In recent years, most of the Ijesa towns have begun to refer to the title of their leading chief as their *oba*, so that now smaller towns, especially in the northern part of the district, consider themselves to have *obas* in their own right, although the *owa* is still generally seen as the leading *oba* of the region. Historical and contemporary conflicts over chieftaincy titles and relationships between the towns and their chiefs are an important aspect of current discussions of unity and development in Ijesaland, as will be discussed in Chapter 9.

4. For more information on the community bank program in general, see Olowu and Oludimu (1993); Oludimu and Ayo (1995); Mabogunje (1995).

5. A community bank was apparently established in Ilesa around this same time, but like many others elsewhere in Nigeria, it did not ever seem to have any impact and did not stay open long.

6. *Esusu* is usually described as a "rotating savings association" where a group of people make regular contributions and then each member of the group is able to have access to the entire amount contributed, on a rotating basis; such associations have been described in many parts of the world. *Ajo* is a system in which an individual goes around, usually on a daily basis, and collects contributions from a set of regular customers who can then receive their contributions back at the end of

the month; usually one contribution of the month is paid as a service fee to the person running the collection system.

7. Both the People's Bank of Nigeria and the community banks were apparently modeled on examples from other parts of the world, such as Grameen Bank in Bangladesh, where there were successful systems of providing very small loans. Whereas the People's Bank was centralized, with branches around the country, the community banks were, as we have seen, organized to serve specific communities. Despite the rhetoric of providing funds to low-income people, there was considerable evidence that the People's Bank was overall a failure. Community banks, in contrast, were more variable, with some successes as well as many failures.

8. Women all over southwestern Nigeria process cassava for sale as *gari*, one of the staple foods of the region. Mostly *gari* processing is undertaken by individual women, but there have also been a number of development projects in communities throughout the region that have sought to assist women in their processing activities. Crucial variables in the success of these projects seem to be the size and expense of the equipment; whether it is easily maintained; the organization of the group; whether there is sufficient cassava available for processing to pay for the cost of the equipment; and whether sales are organized on a group or individual basis. I was not able to judge the "economic" success of the Owodunni *gari*-processing complex, but it seemed an organizational success, in that the women were involved not only in this activity but in others as well, as discussed below.

9. There is gold available on the outskirts of Ilesa, which has always been locally mined, but it is not clear if it is really suitable for large-scale exploitation; both government and local organizations frequently refer to the gold as an important resource.

10. Data from the two towns of Osu and Ijebu-Jesa were analyzed in Trager (1997).

9

The Elusive Goal of Unity:
Politics, Conflict, and Morality

The pronouncement that Government has proscribed certain associations because of their disruptive influence on the Transition Programme does not come as a surprise because of the manner in which the whole programme is being stage-managed.... It is a dangerous thing to enact laws which outlaw legitimate associations at grassroots.... Here in Ijesaland, there are many societies ... intent on doing something by way of self-help to improve living standards and the quality of life of the people. There are people from other parts of Nigeria living in Ijesaland. We give them hospitality and extend the warm hands of friendship to them. They themselves, although they appreciate the friendship and welcome..., feel more comfortable to form "Unions" based on their different ethnic groups so that they can together reach for benefits which as individuals they would have difficulty in attaining.... This is their birth-right. In a country in which Stateism has been allowed to supplant national citizenship, these Unions provide for the individual living far from home, the added security and defence of his basic rights. These Unions are not political organisations nor are they intended to exert undue influence on the political process. They represent the exercise by these various groups of their fundamental right of free association to ensure that none of their members suffers victimisation because he lives far away from home in his own country. Similarly, minority elements must be able to feel safe and have a sense of belonging as first class citizens in their country.... The signs are ominous that we have the ... potentials for disintegration and more requires to be done to promote national cohesion and national integration.... We do not achieve this by over-legislating. Our leaders must show themselves to be capable of putting into motion a system which ensures social justice and equal opportunity for all citizens. They must identify with the sufferings of the people.

—E. A. Ifaturoti, "Law and Tyranny,"
essay published in *Nigerian Tribune*, June 4, 1992

I most sincerely welcome you to this maiden meeting of our committee, which ... is charged with the responsibility of finding the "Ways and Means of forging permanent unity" among the "Warring" factions in Ijesaland and of stimulating our peoples socio-economic development.... As chairman of this Committee, I am hereby calling on all of us serving on

this Committee to take advantage of this golden opportunity to review our
traditional constitution in such a way as to achieve permanent peace,
unity and progress in Ijesaland.
    —Dr. Lawrence Omole, chairman, Ijesa Traditional Council Peace
                 Committee, Opening Speech, April 4, 1992

On Saturday, June 10, 1995, I attended a seventieth birthday celebration for a woman in Ijebu-Jesa. As soon as the church service ended, I
went to the grounds of the Ijebu-Jesa Grammar School, where a lecture
on Ijesa unity was to be given. When I got to the grammar school at
about 1:40 P.M. there were police outside and the gate was closed.
Several men were also standing around. We asked someone in another
car what was happening, and they said that the lecture had been can-
celed. Then one of the men came over and said he was the secretary of
the group holding the lecture. He said that they had applied to the
police and hadn't heard anything but that when they got there this
morning the police were there with a paper telling them that they
should reapply after June 12. So they had not been able to notify anyone in advance; they were very apologetic. I then joined others at the
reception for the birthday celebration, which had already begun.

✦   ✦   ✦

Just as the economic situation deteriorated in Nigeria in the 1990s, so, too,
did the political situation. Whereas the economic crisis developed over
many years, the political crisis had a dramatic turning point—the cancellation (annulment) of the results of the June 12, 1993, presidential election.
That event, and other events associated with it, affected local perceptions
and local activities in a variety of ways and for a considerable length of
time. At the same time, local politics continued within and among communities in Ijesaland. To many of those involved, these local issues are not
political at all because they do not directly involve government or seeking
power within government. But in a broader sense, the innumerable discussions of unity among Ijesas, the efforts to resolve conflicts among Ijesa
chiefs, and the lobbying efforts of hometown organizations are all examples of local political interaction. Neither do all conflicts and differences
get expressed in an overt political idiom. There are also moral and cultural
concerns that reflect differences and divisions among groups within contemporary Ijesa society.

    This chapter focuses on politics, conflict, and morality in order to con-
sider additional dimensions of hometown linkages. Whereas Chapters 7 and
8 consider the economic context for local development and how individuals
and organizations pursue development in that context, this chapter examines the political context. I begin with a discussion of the lengthy, failed

transition to civilian rule in the early 1990s and its impact on local activities. I then consider local relationships within and among Ijesa communities, where there is a great deal of rhetoric about unity but, in reality, many conflicts. The conflicts often appear in the form of chieftaincy disputes that reflect deeply rooted differences within the region. Finally, I consider less overt evidence of conflict, reflected in moral and cultural idioms about what people should do at home. Some of the moral conflicts that have appeared in other places (e.g., accusations of witchcraft) seem to show up rarely in Ijesa communities. But that does not mean that there are not underlying tensions and differences among groups and factions that surface in specific incidents and conflicts.

As people organize for their own development and seek the improvement of their own community and region, they may also seem to be emphasizing their own ethnic group over others. This leads to a key issue not only in Nigeria but also elsewhere: Are civil institutions, such as hometown organizations, really parochial institutions that exacerbate ethnic tensions in the society? Or are their benefits for local development sufficient to counteract those parochial qualities? Should they even be considered part of civil society? Ijesas themselves comment on the roles and importance of these institutions, as is clear from statements like that of E. A. Ifaturoti, quoted above; the issues of civil society and ethnicity are discussed further in Chapter 10.

The Opening and Closing of Political Space: Nigerian Politics and Local Organizations in the 1990s

When members of the Ijesa Solidarity Group commented on the deteriorating situation in the country in the mid-1990s, they were not merely noting the terrible economic conditions discussed in Chapter 7. They were also commenting on the political crisis that began in 1993. Although most of these individuals did not directly participate in politics in the sense of party politics and elections—in fact, they may not even have voted in the 1993 elections—they were deeply disappointed and depressed by the events of that year. What had earlier been viewed as a turning point away from military government toward civilian rule had become instead a transition from the existing military regime to a much worse one. Furthermore, ethnicity became a greater factor, with the first Yoruba to have been elected president ending up in prison, and there was open discussion of the likelihood of civil war and regional and ethnic conflict. The political events of the 1990s in the country as a whole affected people and organizations in the Ijesa area in a variety of ways. First, attitudes and perceptions shifted, from a degree of optimism about the future to great pessimism. Second, there were real political consequences of both the greater repression and the hardening of ethnic divisions. And third, efforts to garner resources for the area and its people, through lobbying and political pressure, continued regardless of the regime.

In the 1990s the Nigerian political system went from military rule through a very long, and ultimately unsuccessful, transition to civilian rule, to still more and worse military government, ending in June 1998 with the sudden death of the military leader, General Sani Abacha. The period began in 1985 with the coup led by General Ibrahim Babangida, who subsequently took the title of president. Early on, Babangida promised a return to civilian rule by 1990. The date for the transition kept changing in what newspapers and magazines came to call the "endless transition." Eventually, the transition date was set for August 1993, and elections took place for local and state officials during 1992. The presidential election, structured by the Babangida regime, was scheduled for June 12, 1993. Despite additional problems and a great deal of public skepticism about Babangida's true intentions, the election did take place, and initial results were reported, indicating that the candidate of the Social Democratic Party (SDP), Moshood K.O. Abiola, a wealthy Yoruba businessman, was winning. As it became apparent that Abiola would win the election, the announcement of results stopped. Then, on June 23, the military announced the decision to annul the election results, and on Saturday, June 26, Babangida gave a televised address claiming that electoral malpractice had led to the cancellation of the results.

In fact, however, local and international monitors of the election had judged it to be "free and fair." After two months of uncertainty about the next political steps for Nigeria, Babangida left office at the end of August 1993 and handed the reins of power to a civilian-led, but not elected, government led by businessman Ernest Shonekan. In November 1993, General Abacha, who had been in Babangida's government and stayed on in the Shonekan administration, took power. Although Abacha again promised that there would be elections and a transition to civilian rule, he quickly consolidated his power and personal rule and led an increasingly repressive government. Although an important prodemocracy movement developed in response to the cancellation of the 1993 elections and important opposition events occurred—most notably a strike by oil workers in 1994—Abacha's regime was successful in forcefully repressing much of the opposition and in buying off many former politicians. In June 1994, Moshood Abiola was arrested after he declared himself president; he was charged with treason and imprisoned. By 1997–1998 it was clear that the next so-called transition was likely to have Abacha himself as the only presidential candidate, and it was difficult to see any end to his rule. Suddenly, on June 8, 1998, news came that Abacha had died. His successor, General Abdulsalam

Abubakar, announced that a transition would take place in less than a year; this time elections did occur, in February 1999, with a retired general and former head of state, Olusegun Obasanjo, becoming Nigeria's first elected president since the early 1980s.[1]

Newspapers and magazines during these years emphasized the pessimism found throughout the country. As early as July 1995, *Tell* magazine ran a cover story ("No Handover Soon, Abacha Deceives the World") quoting General Abacha as saying "we cannot be rushed" in the handover to civilian rule and noting that this reinforced "the view that he intends to pursue his agenda of staying on til 1999" (*Tell*, July 10, 1995, p. 8). A month earlier, the same magazine began its lead story as follows: "There are two paramount fears in the lives of Nigerians today: the fear of government and the fear of the unknown" (*Tell*, June 12, 1995, p. 10).

In Ijesaland during this period, as in most of the country, people became increasingly disillusioned and pessimistic. Although most of those active in hometown organizations and projects were not directly involved in party politics, some were, including members of elected local government councils and others who may have become increasingly interested in their hometowns because of the political opportunities they foresaw. Whether or not they were directly involved in electoral politics, Ijesa people were well aware of and interested in political issues. Prior to the 1993 elections, they anticipated an improvement in the political system and expected greater room for their own local efforts. Following the cancellation of the elections, and especially after Abiola's imprisonment in 1994, there was an increasing sense of depression, a realization that there was little room for any type of politics; local efforts might well be meaningless in the overall political context of the period.

A useful way to think of the changes during this period is in terms of the opening and closing of political space, if *political space* is taken to mean the opportunity for a wide range of political and civic activities at all levels of society. When I began my research in late 1991, and during the period from 1991 through the first half of 1993, several political events were taking place. Elections for local and state officials took place. The new state, Osun State, was established, and groups lobbied for the location of the state capital (see below). Individuals discussed voting and their support for specific political parties, especially the SDP. Some of those I interviewed talked about spending more time at home, so that they could participate in politics and be considered viable candidates at the local level. One Lagos-based businessman was explicit in stating that one of the reasons for maintaining his connections at home was his interest in party politics. He explained that "in the past, people in the town would accept someone like me who was living outside as a leader, as someone who could do something for the town because he was outside and had contacts." But now, he said, "people think that someone in politics should have lived in Ilesa throughout. They won't accept someone who is outside or who has spent a substantial amount of time outside."[2]

Many emphasized the nonpartisan nature of their interests and activities. For example, one of the issues outlined for the Ijesa Solidarity Group meeting in June 1992 was "the need to establish a non-partisan political forum which will articulate our aspirations as a people, defend the values we treasure most, and constitute a permanent lobby for the protection of Ijesa rights." For those interested in party politics, as well as those who emphasized nonpartisan activities, the ongoing transition period of 1991–1993 represented a time when they could express those interests, organize groups, and act on their individual and organizational concerns.

By 1994, and during the following years, the perceptions of political space and related activities had changed dramatically. In December 1994, a little over a year after Abacha took power, I wrote in my notes: "[There is] a general sense of depression, discouragement, not knowing what can be done. [I] have heard comments like 'we're helpless' and several times have heard people discussing the impossibility of being able to plan anything." The local tone began to take on an air of desperation: "Many have also commented that they don't see how the country is going to get out of this situation."[3] People referred to the unpredictability of the situation. They also discussed what had happened to the press, saying that they no longer bought newspapers because there was nothing to read in them.

At the Ijesa Solidarity Group meeting in late December 1994, one person commented that the overall political situation had affected people's ability to be involved in groups like ISG. Another described the current government as an "evil government." Some wanted to spend more time discussing the political and economic situation, but others felt that was not appropriate, suggesting that such a discussion be saved for a later meeting. Most likely, they were concerned about any public discussion of current events. As one ISG member pointed out in an interview, people were not saying much in public, only in private conversations.

The situation continued to worsen, and people in Ijesaland continued to feel the impact. In 1996 one man commented that "it has never been so bad before" in Nigeria. Even in the 1960s, he said, you knew that if you were on the wrong side politically something might happen. "Now, it is a silent war." His implication was that the unpredictability and uncertainty were far worse; there was no specific pattern to the repression and no overt conflict taking place. This man went on to say that those in hometown organizations "can't do anything now. There is no money to travel home; the roundtrip from Lagos could cost at least N1,000, if there is petrol. People don't come to meetings, and if there is a meeting, nothing happens, you talk about the same thing each time." He continued: "The phones don't work so you can't communicate that way. So there is no way for people to communicate about things going on. So nothing is happening."

The feeling of depression and pessimism continued into June 1998, up until the time of Abacha's death. As one man in Ilesa commented shortly after Abacha died, "There has been both political and psychological depression, as well as economic depression." He went on, "It has never been as bad as it is now, certainly never as bad politically and psychologically. And the economic situation is also bad."

But the political situation in the 1990s not only affected people's perceptions and feelings; it also had real political consequences for local organizations and activities. There was real, although unpredictable, repression, which had direct impact on some individuals and events. And the hardening of ethnic divisions that occurred also affected local-level activities. The incidents and quotations at the beginning of this chapter indicate some of the ways in which local groups were affected by the increasing repression and ethnic divisions that accompanied the regime of General Abacha.

The most visible effect was when planned events did not take place. For example, Justice Kayode Eso planned to launch his new book in June 1996, but several friends were worried about his plans, as the book was critical of past and current governments. Eventually, the planned launching was postponed "because of concerns about what the government might do." In this case, unlike others around the same time, the government did not actually prevent the book-launching, but those involved postponed it in order to avoid a direct confrontation. And there were also incidents where specific events were prevented from occurring, as the description from my field notes of June 1995 at the beginning of this chapter indicates. On that occasion, a lecture was planned by an Ijesa organization to focus on Ijesa unity. The major problem for authorities was not the subject, the organization hosting the lecture, or the speaker himself, a university professor. Rather the problem was the date—June 10. It was two years since the June 12, 1993, election, and one year since Abiola had been imprisoned; military authorities were clearly nervous about the anniversary, which had become a focal point for discussion and activities by opposition groups. The authorities therefore wanted to prevent public gatherings that might have political overtones. So on the same day and in the same town, a birthday celebration took place that was attended by many prominent people, including former politicians and officials. No one tried to prevent that gathering. But the lecture, which would probably have been attended by a rather small audience (most who might have been interested were at the birthday celebration), was prohibited. It was eventually presented some months later, sponsored by a different organization.

In closing down certain events, the government instilled a caution and wariness among those who might be engaged in local community efforts. The repression was not general or all-encompassing. Rather, like much else during the period, it was unpredictable. People never knew which of a wide variety of events might capture the attention of authorities—a lecture, a book-launching, or something else. The result was that many activities did take place as planned, but a few did not, and probably a considerable number of others were never planned at all.

Another aspect of political repression was an attempt to ban certain types of organizations, ones that might be considered political and that might play a role in electoral politics. The article quoted at the beginning of the chapter, by E. A. Ifaturoti, was written as a response to the Babangida regime's ban on ethnically based organizations, which were seen as threats to "national unity" and to the then-ongoing transition. Although hometown organizations are for the most part ethnic associations, there was no evidence that any were actually banned. The government was primarily concerned with larger regional groups that could influence the elections, such as pan-Yoruba or Igbo associations. Nevertheless, the threat was clear and the implications evident, especially for an organization such as the Ijesa Solidarity Group, which encompassed more than one hometown and was functioning as a lobbying organization as well as a local development organization. From the point of view of its members, these organizations are not, as Ifaturoti wrote in his essay, "political organizations nor are they intended to exert undue influence on the political process." Rather, he argues that they are "legitimate associations at [the] grassroots [that are] doing something by way of self-help to improve living standards and the quality of life of the people" (Ifaturoti 1992b).

At the same time that ethnic groups were being discouraged from forming associations, there was an increasing sense of the importance of a base in one's home area, among one's own ethnic group. This was especially true after June 1993. Most Yoruba-speaking people believed that Abiola had been prevented from becoming president because he was Yoruba, and there was good evidence for this, such as statements by politicians from northern Nigeria to the effect that no one from the south should become president. The most vocal opposition to the military came from the south, and many leaders of the prodemocracy organizations were Yoruba. People were increasingly concerned about domination by the north. As one article described it, "The divide [between north and south] has been widened and differences sharpened as a lot of people are beginning to believe that the North is desirous of ruling those from the rest of the country perpetually. This is because with the last two years..., virtually all sectors of the country's life has been dominated by Northerners" (*The News*, April 8, 1996, p. 17).

There were open discussions and debates about the likelihood of another civil war, of the possibility for peaceful separation of the country into two sections (with Czechoslovakia as the model), and of the necessity for new political arrangements that would give more power to states. In the Ijesa area, most people were attempting to go about their daily lives and were not directly involved either in prodemocracy politics or in any of these debates. They were, however, very aware of the increasing ethnic tensions and of the possibility for these tensions to erupt into violence. Furthermore, a considerable number of Ijesas had lived in northern Nigeria for part of their lives or had relatives there; some had experienced the civil war of the late 1960s, and others had dealt with ethnic and religious tensions in the north in the 1980s. For all of these people, the hometown and home region were viewed as the only place in which they could really be secure.

Not only did regional ethnic divisions harden. Local subethnic differences also became more evident. Thus it was not just a question of south versus north, or of Yoruba versus Hausa. Rather, the many subgroups within regions and states also became more vocal about their interests—one Yoruba group against another, for example. Some of these conflicts resulted in local violence; one of the worst in the Yoruba area was the conflict between Ifes and Modakekes that periodically erupted into violence in the late 1990s (see Olaniyan 1992; Albert 1999). Decisions taken by the military government, such as the location of local government headquarters, exacerbated existing conflicts.

Among Ijesas, there were widespread feelings of discrimination within Osun State, a perception that Ijesa people were not getting adequate resources or benefits within the new state. This, like the broader ethnic tensions, helped to reinforce the conviction that people needed to identify and work with those from their own home area, that Ijesa people needed to work together. There were two types of results from these pressures. On the one hand, some organizations focused on lobbying efforts to secure resources for Ijesaland. On the other, there was great concern about the importance of Ijesa unity and the difficulty of achieving it.

Increasing ethnic division and tension became apparent in the many efforts throughout Nigeria to establish new states and LGAs, reflecting the interests of regional and ethnic pressure groups. As we have seen in earlier chapters, Osun State resulted from such pressures in 1991. Within Ijesaland, people worked not only for the formation of the new state but also for Ilesa to be named its capital. As we discussed in Chapter 5, the Ijesa Solidarity Group formed during this period, initially as a pressure group to work toward these goals. One of its first actions was to send a delegation to meet with an influential leader in northern Nigeria to seek his influence in having Ilesa selected as the state capital. In the view of those involved, it was important to name Ilesa as the capital because it would lead to a lot of development. Even when Ilesa did not become the capital, there was considerable optimism at first that the new state would benefit Ijesaland. For example, many of the civil service members working in Oyo State were said to be Ijesa (about 80 percent of the top ranks, according to one person), and the expectation was that they would be moved to the Osun State civil service. Since they were from Ijesaland, people thought they would live in Ilesa and commute to Oshogbo, only about fifteen miles away. However, the road between Ilesa and Oshogbo was in disrepair. The early assumption was that the road would be repaired so that people could travel between these two major cities in the new state; clearly this would benefit Ijesaland in other ways besides making it possible for civil servants to commute.

As time went on, however, Ijesas did not believe they were getting any benefits resulting from the new state. At the Ijesa Solidarity Group meeting in July 1992, only a year after the formation of Osun State, one of the founders commented that he didn't think people realized "how much they [Ijesas] were hated" in Oyo State until Osun State was created. He pointed out that Ijesas working in Oyo State were targeted and forced to move to Oshogbo and that "the instability in Osun State now reflects the fear and hostility of Ijesas." More specifically, another speaker, himself a civil servant, pointed out that the Ilesa-Oshogbo Road had still not been repaired. "When we were children in the 1940s," he said, "that road was already a showpiece in Nigeria. [Now] it is doing incalculable damage to the economy of Ilesa."

Within a few years, there were increasing complaints about the treatment of Ijesas within the state and new pressures to lobby for the formation of still another new state. Some of the complaints came from civil servants, who claimed that they were being treated badly in the Osun State government. They wanted organizations such as the Ijesa Solidarity Group to do something to help them. In 1996 a group of civil servants published an advertisement in a newspaper claiming discrimination in the state civil service. Although ISG members were sympathetic in general, they were reluctant to become too involved in this type of dispute, as they felt that would distract the organization from what had become its main goal: working on problems of community development. Some expressed the view that the civil servants should find their own solution to the difficulties they were having.

Nevertheless, in the mid-1990s the Ijesa Solidarity Group, as well as other organizations, once again became involved in lobbying for the new state of Oduduwa, which would encompass Ilesa and Ife. And, of course, they wanted Ilesa to become the state capital; they were very upset that some Ijesa chiefs supported the request of the Ooni of Ife that Ife become the capital. According to one of the ISG leaders, the strategy of supporting a new state was "to let people know about the situation of Ijesas in Osun State." He said that they recognized that it wasn't possible for every ethnic group in Nigeria to have its own state; neither should the Yoruba expect to have more states than they currently had. But there was a problem between "those who call themselves 'Osun proper' and the Ife and Ijesa peoples"; therefore they were supporting the request for a new Oduduwa State. At the ISG meeting in April 1996, one of the speakers stated that "the reason there is no development in Osun State is because Oshogbo is the capital." Further, he said that although Ife is important historically, Ilesa should be the capital of the new state.

Such views were not limited to members of the ISG, or even to Ijesas, but were widely shared by people from other Yoruba areas. For example, an academic who is Yoruba but not Ijesa commented to me that "Ijesas don't really fit into Osun State; in fact it's hard to fit them with any other group." Many people refer to "Osun proper," meaning Oshogbo and other towns to the north of Ilesa, seeing both Ijesaland and Ife as separate. But according to the same individual, Ife and Ilesa don't really fit together either, as "they are culturally and linguistically different."

In the end, the debate and controversy about a new Oduduwa State and its capital did not lead to any result; the military government did not create any more new states in the Yoruba-speaking area. That did not end the discussion of marginalization and discrimination, however. Rather, it intensified it. By the time of the June 1998 meeting of Ijesa Solidarity Group, much greater passion was generated by the problem of discrimination against Ijesas than by concerns about local development. One speaker argued that Ijesas had become so marginalized in Osun State that perhaps they should refuse to continue to be part of the state. Another speaker pointed to the poor state of infrastructure as evidence for discrimination against the area (repairs on the Ilesa-Oshogbo Road had still not been completed, for example). Members at the meeting agreed that the organization should play a larger role as a pressure group with regard to the situation of Ijesas within the state and the civil service. This was the same meeting where a proposal for transforming the organization into a nongovernmental development organization (see Chapter 8) was to be discussed. But there seemed to be greater concern for those of their own social and economic class working as civil servants than for the "common man at the grassroots" that the ISG founders had emphasized.

It is not clear whether a substantial shift in the goals of the organization was taking place, or whether this was simply a reemphasis of one of the original goals of the Ijesa Solidarity Group (see Chapter 5). In either case, it was clear that despite a military government that was disliked and feared, individuals and organizations continued to lobby for resources from that government. In the 1990s one major focus of the lobbying efforts was the formation of new states and local governments.[4]

Unity and Conflict: Local Politics in Ijesaland

When people in Ijesaland comment on discrimination and marginalization, they frequently connect these themes to the issue of unity. They argue that Ijesas need to unite because they are discriminated against. And they believe that they are discriminated against because they are not united. As we have seen in Chapter 2, a major theme in speeches, celebrations, and conversations is the need for unity among Ijesas. Here I want to examine in more detail what is meant by these calls for unity and to consider the sources of conflicts that stand in the way of unity. This, too, involves politics—not the politics of military government and transitions but the politics of local-level relationships among and within communities. Among Ijesas, much of the debate about local politics appears in the form of chieftaincy conflicts. As the statement by Lawrence Omole quoted at the beginning of this chapter indicates, chieftaincy conflicts are seen as standing in the way not only of unity but also of progress. These conflicts are, in other words, understood to be closely tied to prospects for local development.

Not all conflicts revolve around chieftaincy issues, however. There are other types of divisions, including that between the city of Ilesa and other towns, especially those in the northern part of Ijesaland. Although the town-district conflict is itself often reflected in chieftaincy disputes, it goes beyond that. There are also differences and conflicts that result from emerging social-class lines, between the elite and the ordinary, grassroots person, and between those abroad (who are usually members of the elite) and those at home who are primarily poorer and more rural. These differences are less overt than the chieftaincy and town-district conflicts and are usually expressed in more subtle and less direct ways. In addition to the lack of unity that results from differences among groups and categories of people, there is also the perception that lack of unity results from fundamental characteristics of Ijesa people—that Ijesas are too individualistic and therefore unable to work together to address issues of importance to them and their communities. As discussed in Chapter 4, some argue that the *osomaalo* tradition among Ijesas is the source of their individualism, leading each one to believe that he or she can succeed on his or her own.

This section begins with a discussion of events at which the need for unity is emphasized, followed by an analysis of comments about the reasons for the lack of unity. It then considers some of the ways in which chieftaincy issues have become sources of conflict, both within communities and among communities within the region. It also considers some of the ways in which chieftaincy disputes have become the idiom in which other disputes are expressed. The subsequent section considers some of the less overt forms of conflict and the way they are expressed in an idiom of morality rather than politics. This includes perceptions of the elite versus the grassroots, of those abroad and those at home, and of Ijesa individualism. The final section of the chapter focuses on specific efforts undertaken to resolve conflicts within and among Ijesa communities.

Ijesa Discussions of Unity

The problem of unity among Ijesas is a frequent refrain in conversations, interviews, and public events. Although occasionally there are celebratory references to unity, as at the Iloko Day celebration where Prince Olashore stated "you have seen what it is like to be united," much more commonly Ijesas lament the lack of unity within their communities and region. Major events are organized, focusing on the theme of unity. For example, in June 1992, as part of the seventieth-anniversary celebration of the Egbe Atunluse Ijesa, a symposium was organized ("The Unity of Ijesaland—the Concept: Is It Worth Working For? What Method to Achieve It?"). Several well-known Ijesa speakers addressed an audience made up largely of elderly individuals already committed to the importance of Ijesa unity. The speakers referred to most of the issues that recur in discussions of Ijesa unity.

The first speaker began by noting what happens when there is a lack of unity; according to him, qualified Ijesas do not receive government appointments because they do not lobby or help each other get such appointments. Furthermore, they do not work together to lobby for resources or to jointly organize economic endeavors. He then went on to comment on the forces that mitigate against unity, noting chieftaincy disputes and regional disputes between the northern Ijesa towns and the city of Ilesa. He argued that they need to work to achieve unity. First, "all chiefs and community leaders should push the need for unity." Second, "it's not just enough to preach unity, but they should show it by their actions." He asked why some people, from towns outside Ilesa, are referred to as *ara oko* ("bush person," or person from a rural place without a city connection—an insult to any Yoruba). He argued that when industries or banks are established the shares should be divided among Ijesa communities and that there needed to be greater investment to bring Ijesas back home. Finally, he said that now that Nigeria "is on the last stage of transition to civilian rule, Ijesas should unite" regardless of party affiliation; "they should get out for Ijesaland."

The second speaker, a chief known for his knowledge of local history, discussed Ijesa history and chieftaincy issues. His speech took on a historical perspective, arguing that Ijesas had been united in the past but that contemporary developments, such as the selling of land and disputes over land, had led to conflicts. Similarly, only when "what was never sold and never meant to be sold"—chieftaincy titles—was sold had disputes arisen over chieftaincies. He made several sophisticated points, saying that "what is tradition today is what our forefathers did. And what we do today will become tradition in thirty to forty years." Further, "our forefathers managed to run a viable society, without millions of naira" and were successful in prosecuting the Kiriji War of the mid-1880s because they were united. He said that traditions were never static, that there have always been ways and means of changing things. He went on to state that "what unity is is not conformity. People may disagree. But something is binding us together, and that is an idea, loyalty and patriotism, at the national level—the Ijesa national level." He went on to argue that loyalty to Ijesaland provided the base for loyalty to Nigeria as a whole: "Building loyalty to Ijesaland is building loyalty to the country." Like the previous speaker, this one referred to the use of derogatory terms, saying that they remind people of "when their great-grandfather carried yams like slaves to Ilesa." Finally, he said that there cannot be unity without a leader and that for the Ijesa "the unity of Ijesaland is predicated on one thing—the supremacy of the *owa*. Once that is challenged, and that challenge is allowed to go on, then that unity must disintegrate." With this statement, the chief referred to what many see as the crux of the Ijesa unity issue: the relationship between the Owa Obokun of Ijesaland and other chiefs in the region. I will return to this issue below.

The final speaker at the symposium, E. A. Ifaturoti, echoed much of what had been said by the others. He, too, referred to history, especially the Kiriji War period, noting that at that time "Ijesas regarded themselves as one family." Moving to the present, he noted that "Ijesas are very small, that the census figures show that Ijesas make up less than one-half million within Nigeria, and since they're very small, they can easily be forgotten and maltreated." Referring to the *owa* and the chiefs, he said, "Whatever the future political arrangements among chiefs, there is a need for those who call themselves Ijesa to defend their own rights. Unless we can secure and assure these, we haven't arrived." Thus "unity is necessary so that we can defend what we have an entitlement to, so we can defend our rights and prevent individuals from being denied things. Since we're small we can easily be mistreated."

A second major event focusing on unity occurred in 1995. This was a speech by professor Olu Odeyemi, entitled "Unity and Development of Ijesaland: The Way Forward." This speech was originally scheduled for June 10, 1995; as described above, the police did not allow the speech to take place at that time. It was finally given in December 1995 to a meeting of the Ijesa Solidarity Group. In this lengthy speech, Odeyemi not only referred to many of the same issues as the speakers at the Egbe Atunluse symposium but also argued that the lack of development in Ijesaland was due to the lack of unity. The speech concluded:

> The Ijesa have the potential to develop, but without unity there may be a standstill or degeneration of the existing development in the area. We are never known as failures in whatever we do. The Ijesa people have the essential personality traits for achieving rapid development of the area. They are generally hardworking, diligent, industrious, intelligent, consistent, persistent, persevering, steadfast, honest, forward-looking, enterprising, aggressive and resourceful. To translate all these good traits into development of Ijesaland, the people must first overcome their uncomplimentary attitudes of being uncooperative, unappreciative, disuniting, refractory, individualistic, excessively independent-minded and unbendable.
>
> There must be a drastic reorientation of our people to look at themselves as one, no matter to which town or village they belong.... It is high time we threw segregation, discrimination, hatred and dichotomy of town and village people into the dustbin of history. (O. Odeyemi 1995: 13)

Perhaps the most succinct and direct portrayal of the problem of Ijesa unity occurred in a third event, a speech by Bolanle Awe, a well-known academic who has strong ties to Ilesa through her mother's family. She was the reviewer of the autobiography of Lawrence Omole at the book-launching in 1993. In her speech she refers to the last chapter of the book, "which deals with [Omole's] visions as they affect Ijesaland. He hopes for a strong and united Ijesaland within a strong and united Nigeria, an Ijesaland where the component parts will keep alive their common history as 'children of Obokun, a proud people with a glorious past.'" She continues:

> This is probably the most important issue which this autobiography is raising for the Ijesa. My little experience of trying to mobilise the Ijesa for cultural development bears this out. The Ijesa are achievers, industrious, determined and ambitious. However, they have failed to make an impact on the national scene because they are too individualistic and have allowed centrifugal forces to be dominant in their interactions among themselves. Ijesa north sees itself as a separate entity from Ijesa south, and Ilesa town stands on its own! This spirit of non-cooperation, alas, is most pronounced among the elite; in spite of their exposure and high achievement, at both national and international levels, they still fail to see the wisdom of coming together! ...[I]t is apparent not only in politics but also in efforts to stimulate social and economic development. Every effort at development is met with cynicism and discouragement. No one expects success! No wonder Ijesa cities are in a state of decay and the roads in disrepair! No wonder the young never stay; they move out looking for greener pastures; they come home only for festive occasions when their associations talk of big projects which never get done! Yet it is clear that the Ijesa cannot wait for the benevolence of a government it cannot impress! (Awe 1993: 5–6).

These public statements, as well as many other statements about the problem of Ijesa unity, tend to combine several separate explanations for this problem. On the one hand, they refer to a problem of Ijesa "character"—the stereotype that the Ijesa people are hardworking, industrious, and so on but that they are also too "individualistic," too willing to think that each one can succeed on his or her own. On the other hand, they refer to structural and historical factors, including conflicts between the district and Ilesa, conflicts over chieftaincy titles, and conflicts over the interpretation of history. These latter explanations combine both past and current events; depending on the perspective and background of individuals, those events are interpreted in diverse ways.

History

Ijesas refer to history both as a source for information about their past and as a justification for the present. They are especially interested in the earliest periods of their history, the founding of Ijesa towns and formation of the kingdoms.[5] This is a period about which there is a degree of consensus as well as considerable contention. On the one hand, Ijesas agree that their ancestors came to the area from Ile-Ife. They also tend to agree that the Owa Obokun is not only the traditional ruler of Ilesa but also "the paramount ruler of Ijesaland" (Agbaje-Williams and Ogundiran 1992: 7). On the other hand, origin stories for some Ijesa towns indicate origins independent of Ilesa: either they were settled before Ilesa itself, or they can point to an independent ancestor who came from Ife and who was not connected to the ancestor responsible for founding Ilesa. Separate origins directly from Ife provide the basis for giving traditional rulers the right to wear a beaded crown, a major symbol for kingship. In other words, towns that claim an origin directly from Ife can also claim that their ruler is an *oba* in his own right. For example, a published history of the town of Ipetu-Ijesa, on the eastern edge of Ijesaland, begins, "It is evident that the Ipetu people are the direct descendants of Oduduwa at Ile-Ife" (Ogunjulugbe 1993: 1) and describes the relationship between Ipetu and Ilesa as one that evolved at a later time.

J.D.Y. Peel described the process of asserting independent origins in his 1983 book:

> When their relations with the centre [i.e., Ilesa] became so attenuated that they start to consider the village as their *ilu,* they start to develop institutions ... modelled on those of the centre. If the community prospered, they might eventually try to gain direct access to the regional system, demanding a beaded crown for their chief and asserting that his ancestor migrated from Ife. Communities, like individuals, did not believe that a lowly condition had to be permanent. (p. 75)

This process has continued into the present and in fact has intensified in recent years. Whereas most Ijesa historians agree that some towns did have separate or earlier origins, especially in northern Ijesaland, they do not agree on such origins for the majority of Ijesa towns. Yet increasingly, many of the smaller towns in the region are claiming that their traditional ruler is an *oba*, with the implication of his right to wear a beaded crown. This view contrasts with that expressed by most in Ilesa that the rulers of these towns should be called *loja* (or *oloja*), indicating a status subordinate to the Owa Obokun. The debates and disagreements about the interpretation of early Ijesa history continue to be the basis for differing understandings of the relationships between the city of Ilesa and the surrounding district, as well as for some of the disputes over chieftaincies (see below).

Many of the calls for unity try to draw on more recent history, especially the period of the Kiriji War in the late 1800s, when there was an alliance not only among the Ijesa but also between Ijesa and Ekiti people to the east; however, this period functions as a much less potent symbol than the origin stories. In recent years there have been several efforts to draw attention to the Kiriji period and the alliance known as the Ekitiparapo. A conference in 1986, on the centennial of the peace agreement between Ekitiparapo and Ibadan forces, brought together a large number of academics as well as Ijesa leaders to celebrate what is seen as a period of unity among Ijesa (see papers presented at the National Conference on the Centenary of the Kiriji/Ekitiparapo Peace Treaty, University of Ife, September 1986). Ceremonies also took place in several of the key Ijesa locations involved in the war. In 1993 there was a much smaller celebration of the final agreement between the warring parties that took place in 1893; as we have seen in Chapter 6, some proposed Kiriji as the central symbol for an Ijesa National Day, but this effort was unsuccessful. In fact, although the Kiriji War seems to be a period of Ijesa unity, this unity was short-lived; as Peel argues, the "end of the wars revived political disorder in Ijeshaland" (1983: 91).

Recent history, that is, from the 1940s through the 1960s, continues to demonstrate the problematic nature of Ijesa unity and is rarely referred to in the public statements advocating unity. Divisions between elite, educated Ijesas and the chiefs became increasingly important in the 1900s and were central to events in 1941. When party politics emerged, that became another line for division. This recent history is very much alive for many of the participants in today's events; in many cases, the fathers of those active today were among the key actors. As one person put it in an interview,

> The modern past is a catalyst to what is going on now. There were camps that formed during the [1941] riots, and [many of] the children continue to belong to those camps. The cleavages that resulted at that time continue to

be important today.... When politics came, the cleavage from the riots affected the alignments of groups. Some joined the Action Group, and those who were opposed to them joined NCNC [references to the two major national political parties of the 1960s]. Today, some people are trying to weld people together, but it is very difficult because of the feelings generated by past events. The sons have carried on the feelings from their fathers.[6]

Ilesa and the Region

The relationship between Ilesa and the other communities in Ijesaland reflects the varying interpretations of history described above, as well as the contemporary competition for resources. As has already been discussed, a key issue is whether local chiefs are *obas* in their own right or whether they are *loja* subordinate to the Owa Obokun of Ijesaland. Some examples of the implications of this division are considered in the discussion of chieftaincy conflicts in the next section. In addition, town-district relations revolve around the distinction between the *ilu* and the concept of *ara oko*. In his speech on Ijesa unity and development referred to earlier, Professor Odeyemi stated:

> We are all aware that over the years we have been dividing ourselves by our statements and actions. For example some look at themselves as more civilised than others whom they call "Ara Oko" (bushmen). It is not uncommon for those whose business had made them permanently resident in Ilesa township to see fellow brothers and sisters living in [smaller Ijesa towns] as "Ara Oko." ... What is the justification for Ilesa residents to call [residents of other places] bush people. What's the meaning of bush people? To my mind, bush people are the uneducated and uninformed people, a group to which about 70 percent of Nigerian belong. (O. Odeyemi 1995: 5)

Those from towns outside Ilesa argue that there has been discrimination against them both in the past and present. Not only are they referred to as *ara oko*; they also say there are actual differences in the treatment they receive. Historically, the outlying towns were dominated by Ilesa; after the Kiriji War, leaders from Ilesa were given land, and the smaller towns were expected to supply food to Ilesa. In the present, the argument continues, people in Ilesa continue to look down on the smaller towns. There is still a tendency for the best jobs and offices to be given to those from Ilesa. There is an "attitude that if something is going to go to one area of Ijesaland, people would rather see it go elsewhere, out of Ijesaland, than to another Ijesa town." As one person from Ilesa put it, "People outside Ilesa distrust Ilesa people, and they have reasons, very good reasons. People from Ilesa saw themselves as superior to those from other places in the region; and only those from Ilesa got jobs and positions." He went on, "They looked down on people from other Ijesa towns; so if someone applied for a job, he would be asked where he was from and if he said some place like Ijebu-Jesa, he wouldn't get the job. Similarly with school admission—all the secondary schools were in Ilesa, and it was harder for those from other towns to get into school." With this history, "those from other towns are now getting back at those from Ilesa. They won't help Ilesa; for example, those in government positions will see that Ilesa doesn't get anything."

At the same time, many of the same people, both from Ilesa and from the other Ijesa towns, agree that when they are dealing with people from outside the region they are all seen as Ijesa. "Nobody realizes whether you are an Ijesa of Oriade local government origin or Ijesa of Obokun local government origin, or indeed of Ilesa, or of Atakumosa local government origin—we are all referred to as Ijesas." Contradictions abound in these discussions. People argue for greater unity because "we are all Ijesa." At the same time, they decry past and current discrimination based on whether or not one is from Ilesa. And they also argue that, in the current competition for resources, they need to assert the independence of each community, because, as one prominent individual put it, "that is the manner in which benefits are dispersed, that is the only way to ensure benefits to one's own area." In fact, the present-day competition for resources underlies much of the significance placed on past relationships and prejudices. Each LGA, each small town with its traditional ruler, tries to garner resources through fund-raising, through prominent members, and through whatever benefits derive from government. In that context, arguments for Ijesa unity are not likely to lead very far, despite the recognition that they could achieve more in the competition for resources if they were more united.

Chieftaincy Disputes

Chieftaincy continues to be important to many Ijesas, despite the views of some that traditional rulers have no role in a modern nation. Chieftaincy positions represent important sources of status and influence and can provide access to resources. Chieftaincy politics and disputes revolve around several issues: disputes over succession to specific positions, especially the more important positions such as *oba* and high chiefs; disputes between chiefs within a specific town; and disputes between chiefs in different towns. Differing interpretations of history, as well as contemporary concerns, combine in these disputes.

Examples of each took place during the research period. Because of the system of succession that exists among the Yoruba, there is no automatic successor to a title. Rather, there is usually a system involving rotation among branches of a royal family (in the case of succession to the position of *oba*) or among differing branches of those families eligible for specific hereditary chieftaincy titles. The result is that when an *oba* or chief dies there may be several potential successors, and there is often considerable competition among them. *Obas* are selected by a set of chiefs known as the kingmakers, whereas other chieftaincy positions are filled by the *oba* from among those who are eligible. The process of filling a position may often go on for years, and even after a chief or *oba* is selected, there may be continued conflict, with some cases going to court. An example of such a situation occurred in Ijebu-Jesa following the death of the *oba* there in 1995. Two candidates contested for the title, and although one was selected fairly quickly, there was a continuing dispute, with the individual who was not selected taking the issue to court.

Disputes between chiefs reflect differing factions within a community. All Ijesa communities are complex; this complexity often appears in the holders of different titles within a town, who may have support from different groups and factions. Even when an *oba* has selected a particular person to fill a chieftaincy title, differences may emerge later on. The result can lead to serious disputes and conflicts, which, again, may lead to battles in court. Such a case occurred in Ilesa in the 1990s between the *owa* and one of his chiefs, the *risawe* (*Daily Sketch*, May 31, 1993). Other disputes can reflect issues of access to resources such as land.

Disputes between rulers and chiefs from different towns are particularly significant as a source of conflict that prevents Ijesa unity. We have already seen that there is increasing pressure from the smaller Ijesa towns to assert their own independence from Ilesa. This is especially true of towns in the northern part of Ijesaland, which have greater historical evidence of their independence, but it is also becoming more common among southern Ijesa towns. As we have already discussed, one approach is to assert that the traditional ruler is an *oba* in his own right. In some cases, this is accompanied by an effort to obtain a new title for the traditional ruler. This pattern was followed in both Ijebu-Jesa and Iloko; in Ijebu-Jesa, the new ruler sought approval for the title *egboro* instead of *ogboni*. He was not successful in this effort, however, as government approval is required for such a change in title, and he did not obtain this approval.

In Iloko-Ijesa, as we have seen in Chapter 6, Oba Olashore began to use both the title *aloko* as well as the title *ajagbusi-ekun*, claiming that the latter was in fact the original title used by his ancestors. But disputes between the traditional rulers of Ijesa towns are not limited to what title they use. These conflicts also involve real issues of access to power and resources. In the 1990s one of the major points of contention concerned the membership of the Council of Traditional Rulers. Many of the *obas* of towns in the district, especially in the north, felt that they were not adequately represented in an Ijesa council of chiefs headed by the *owa* and sought to establish their own council, which would bring together the traditional rulers of the LGAs in northern Ijesaland, Ibokun, and Oriade. This was a continuing source of conflict during the entire research period, between the *owa* and several other Ijesa *obas*, and it is likely to continue to be a major source of conflict among Ijesa chiefs and communities.

A great deal of energy and attention is devoted to chieftaincy conflicts. As is suggested in the following statement in the Ijesa Solidarity Group chairman's report, there is great concern that chieftaincy disputes will disrupt efforts to improve conditions in Ijesaland:

> The creation of Osun State came much as we had prayed and waited for it.... Soon after the creation of States the effervescent state of relationships between the Ijesa Chiefs and Obas boiled over leaving a legacy in which only our adversaries were net beneficiaries. The position remains very much the same now and is unlikely to change since what is at stake is the personal ego of the parties. They are all Ijesa and pay lip service to Ijesa Unity and it is difficult for any fair-minded Ijesa person to take sides. If all the parties to the various disputes understand that we the Ijesas are the only people to lose, it would be possible to resolve the disputes and to end the rancour. The position of the Group is that we should press forward for unity and the will to forge a common identity that transcends the trivial issues of precedence and ascendancy which is central to the disputes. If the Obas and Chiefs can withdraw from the State level at which they now ACT, and endeavour to resolve the matter as brothers, it will be the duty of the Group to ensure that our Obas and Chiefs receive equal recognition at State and National levels. This is a matter of great importance to our Group because any error in the attitude of our members could ruin the efforts we have put in thus far. (Ijesa Solidarity Group, Report of the Chairman, June 1992)

As a result of these concerns, many individuals and organizations engage in efforts to mediate and resolve chieftaincy conflicts. I will consider some of these efforts in the discussion of conflict resolution below.

Overall, chieftaincy remains an important force in Ijesaland and beyond, with many people competing for traditional titles and many others being given honorary titles in recognition of their wealth, power, and influence (Vaughan 1991: 319–322). As long as this continues to be the case, factional disputes within communities and disputes among communities over chieftaincy issues are not likely to end.

Morality, Culture, and Conflict

Conflict is not always overt or obvious. There may be far more subtle signs of conflict and tensions within and among communities. As rapid change takes place and as some people become visibly more wealthy than most others, the potential for increased tensions along lines of wealth and class clearly exists. In the Ijesa context, these tensions may be reflected in concerns about morality—about how one should behave and what one should do, especially with regard to the home community. There are two underlying potential fault lines: divisions based on wealth, and divisions based on whether one is "home" or "abroad." As we have seen, these divisions frequently are conflated in that those abroad are likely to be more wealthy than those at home; likewise, those who are wealthy—the "elite," as they are usually called by Ijesas themselves—are more likely to be living outside the hometown. We have already discussed the obligations and responsibilities that people express with regard to the hometown and have seen that there are expectations held by both those at home and those abroad that they should contribute to the development of the town. Yet even when people fulfill those expectations, there may still be conflict and tension. In some communities, it has become apparent that the idiom of witchcraft, or *juju*, has been used to express these tensions; in the Ijesa region, that idiom seems to be much less common.[7]

Early in my research, I had an informal conversation with some of the faculty in the sociology department at Obafemi Awolowo University. One commented that in choosing Ijesaland I had picked an excellent place to do my research, because "the Ijesas have the strongest links with their hometowns." She compared it to her own hometown in another part of Yorubaland and said that people don't go home there, because "they're afraid that something will happen to them if they do, they're afraid of *juju*." She went on to talk about all the rich Ijesas who have built big houses at home and given money. In other conversations with my research assistants and with others from other Yoruba areas, similar comments were made: in their region people are afraid to go home because they fear witchcraft but Ijesas do not have such fears. For example, my assistants said that many people from their area, in northern Yorubaland, are afraid to visit home because they fear that something bad will happen to them. "If you're successful, people at home may be jealous and carry out witchcraft against you." They gave the example of someone who began to build a house at home, then was in a bad car accident. So he stopped building and does not travel to his hometown anymore. This is why the area doesn't develop or progress: rich people are afraid to go back there, they said.

On another occasion, I was told a story about things happening in the same area in northern Yorubaland: A radio program reported that *juju* is being used by old men who are farmers; they kill young men and then have their spirits work on their farms. And that is how these men have bigger farms than others and are getting rich. One young man whose father was doing this saw that every day before they went to the farm his father washed his face with some water. One day he wasn't with his father, so he used the water to wash his own face. And then he could see the spirits; he saw the people who have died working in the fields.[8]

But one man from the same area who built a house in his hometown stated that there is nothing to fear. He said that people had told him something would happen if he went home because people would be jealous of his success. But he didn't believe that, and he went ahead and built his house and nothing happened to him. When I asked this man, and others, whether the same fears exist in the Ijesa area, most responded no, that Ijesa people have traveled more and are more educated. One man from Ilesa said that he didn't think one would find fears of witchcraft keeping people away because Ijesaland is a "liberated" place where people are more "civilized." "If someone tried to use evil power against someone else, they would be told by at least ten others not to do so, that they should find ways for their own children to benefit from the person who has money and resources, rather than using witchcraft against that person." Another prominent Ilesa man commented that the emphasis in Ilesa is "on showing off your success"; according to him, there is no fear that someone will try to use mystical powers to harm you. In fact, he said, it is the opposite: "You must show yourself. It is the culture. When your father dies, you must have a house of your own from which to bury your father and to entertain others who come for the burial. You shouldn't stay in the family house. If you don't have your own house, then you are an outcast."

When I asked whether there is resentment or jealousy at home of those who have been successful abroad, this man said, "No, on the contrary. People at home are proud that someone from their town is successful. They want people to display their success, to show off their success. And they hope to get there themselves someday [i.e., to be successful themselves]."

But he added that "people will expect you to help them and you will never be able to do all that they want. So then they [people at home] will talk about you."

This last comment suggests that there may indeed be occasions when underlying tensions and resentments erupt, if not in the form of witchcraft, then in some other way. And there are indications that beliefs about the potential for harm to be done through *juju* do exist in Ijesa towns. However, the one specific example that emerged during the research involved a situation where the threat was expressed at a community level, rather than at an individual level, and where the response, likewise, came from the community. At the community meeting that took place in Iloko in June 1995 (described in Chapter 8), the regent spoke at the end of the meeting about an unspecified threat to the town. He said that some people are trying to get evil powers from outside to disturb the progress of the town or to hurt some people in the town. He went on to say that anyone who is involved in this should desist and that the townspeople should respond, by Christians going to church and Muslims to the mosque, where they should all pray. He said that they would bring out the oracle at the junction in the town center to swear that anyone who is trying to betray the town will walk away from the town. Another man followed the regent's statement by repeating that anyone trying to harm the town will walk away from it.

A few days later the regent, Chief Ogunsanya, explained these comments in an interview. He began by saying that "everyone loves the town, but everyone doesn't love each other," and that there are some wicked people in every community. As the traditional head (this was before the coronation of Oba Olashore), he hears about things going on in the town, people come to him to report things, and he must decide whether to take some sort of action. He said that three people had come to tell him that they had had dreams or visions indicating that someone wanted to get power, to do something wicked, to do something that would throw the whole town into confusion. There is a deity for the town, *obalogun,* and the tradition is that if anyone plans evil against another in the community and there is a premonition that something evil is being planned, then they must perform the necessary ceremony. The ceremony takes place at the junction of the three roads in the town and involves asking that something will happen to the person who is planning evil. They do not know who is planning this—they just know that someone is and that this ceremony will prevent the person from carrying out his or her plan to acquire evil power.

Chief Ogunsanya explained that there had been some unhappiness about the land where the new town hall had been built, that some members of the family who had been farming there were unhappy that the land was taken away from them. But the land doesn't belong to them; it belongs to the community, and the community had decided to use the land for the town hall. When there were some problems, such as breakdowns in the tractor being used to clear the land, they decided to take action to prevent those involved from causing any more disruption through the use of mystical powers.

Their ritual actions were successful, thus demonstrating that the traditional ceremony works when used against someone who is planning evil. The regent said that in Iloko "we deal with any threat of anything wicked before it happens," so people aren't afraid to come home. He went on, "In other places, if something happens, even if it's natural, such as someone coming home and being in an accident, it may affect what people do for the next five years; they will be afraid to come home. But in Iloko, we take measures to prevent anything happening, so no one is afraid. People aren't afraid to come home and show their money." He continued: "In Iloko, we are like family, we band together. More and more people are coming home, and the town is expanding; it has doubled in size in the last few years."

When I asked the regent if there is jealousy of those who have done well, he said that jealousy still exists but less so than in the past. With education, people are less likely to be jealous. But if someone comes home and helps some family members and not others, then there may be resentment, and people may try to do something. They try to prevent this from occurring.

In this particular case, the community reacted to the threat by using a traditional response to the use of mystical power. By saying that the person would "walk away," they are utilizing a common response to those accused of being witches—to ostracize them from the community.

But the underlying moral issue of whether those who are away from home use their money and resources to benefit their kin and community can lead to tensions that are expressed in other forms.

One such incident occurred in another Ijesa town during the period of the research. Although it did not occur in one of the towns being studied, it drew in people from Ilesa in the effort to seek a resolution. The situation focused on a prominent businessman from Ikeji-Ile, a town on the eastern edge of the Ijesa region. The businessman, like other individuals discussed in this book, is based outside his hometown, in Ibadan, and had built a large house at home. He had also made several contributions to the town, having helped build the town hall, the palace, and the school. These contributions were recognized by those in the town, as well as other Ijesas; he was one of those whose activities were honored at several of the celebrations described in Chapter 6. But in the mid-1990s a group within the town began to turn against him and to make things difficult for him; by 1995, according to those who told me about this, he hardly went home anymore. But in turning against this man, the accusations were that he was from the wrong part of the town; all sides in the dispute turned to history and chieftaincy issues for support.

The historical situation was that there had been two groups of people who had originally settled the town, each coming from a different area. Later, a third group from Ilesa, sent by the *owa*, also settled there. The two original groups accepted the *owa*'s representative as the chief. Then in the early 1900s the town decided to move to a new location, closer to the road; this became a settlement called Ikeji Arakeji. But not everyone moved. About half of the *owa*'s group and one of the two first groups of settlers stayed. The man against whom the accusations were made is from the indigenous group that stayed. The *owa*'s group felt that this group, with this man as the leader, was trying to take over. The case, like many other chieftaincy disputes, went to court. In addition, the Ijesa Solidarity Group became involved in trying to resolve the dispute out of court (discussed in the next section).

In this case, unlike cases described in other parts of Africa, (e.g., Geschiere and Nyamnjoh 1998, an analysis of situations in Cameroon), the resentment and tensions underlying the position of a man who is far wealthier than others in his hometown are expressed not in the idiom of witchcraft accusations but rather in the familiar idiom of chieftaincy and historical disputes. Conflicts in Ijesaland seem most frequently to be couched in these terms, even when they may well originate in issues of morality (i.e., whether a wealthy person who is "abroad" is viewed as behaving appropriately with regard to his hometown). In effect, this dispute, like others, polarizes factions within the community and is expressed in political activity among those factions. The potential always exists for conflict and tension associated with differences of status and wealth.

The central issue in Ijesa communities is whether wealthy individuals are doing enough to benefit their kin and community. Who determines what is "enough" and how wealthy individuals decide how much to give, and to whom, are crucial. As several people pointed out to me, no one, no matter how wealthy, can give to every individual or cause that requests or expects something. Therefore, wealthy individuals must make decisions about how they will fulfill obligations and expectations. The fact that they share these expectations and understand the obligations does not make it any easier. Particularly in communities where there are only a few such individuals, the pressures and possibilities for dissatisfaction are considerable. Clearly, the potential for resentment and jealousy is considerable, especially given the extent to which wealthy people abroad make key decisions in setting the local agenda for development activities.

Conflict Resolution

There are many efforts to counterbalance the centrifugal tendencies in Ijesaland and many attempts to create unity. Many, but not all, of these efforts focus on chieftaincy disputes. Prominent individuals and organizations become involved in dispute resolution activities. Hometown organizations meet with participants in these disputes; they prepare recommendations for settling them; and they attempt to exert influence on their resolution. For example, the leader of one of the women's organizations in Lagos explained that the organization sends delegations home when there is "anything that needs attention, for example, issues between the chiefs, or between the chiefs and the *oba*." If there is a vacant chieftaincy position, "we can intervene to see that the right candidate is chosen, not necessarily those with lots of money." Similarly, when the Ilesa Frontliners met in May 1992, one of the major subjects of discussion was the position the organization was going to take in ongoing chieftaincy disputes. They noted two issues: the relationship between the Owa and the other chiefs, and the question of who is represented on the state Council of Chiefs.

When the dispute in Ikeji-Ile described above developed, several key individuals intervened in trying to resolve it; at a later stage, the Ijesa Solidarity Group became involved, as the focus of the conflict was a prominent member of that organization. ISG established a committee on peace and harmony to look into the things that cause conflict and prevent cooperation. As the ISG president stated, "With cooperation there is progress. When there was cooperation in Ikeji-Ile, they built a secondary school and a town hall. But now there is conflict, and everything is falling apart. The different groups can't come to any agreement. So getting cooperation is part of the route toward progress." The committee reported on its activities at the ISG meeting in April 1996. They had collected historical information and had talked with the *oba* and others in the town in order to determine the causes of the conflict and to try to find a resolution. They were in the process of writing a report on the situation. But in the meantime, the *oba* of the town had taken the case to court, and the ISG was trying to get them to settle out of court. Given the extent of interconnections, including intermarriage, among the factions, the ISG leadership was optimistic that a settlement could be reached. However, by mid-May 1996 a decision had been made to install a new chief, which meant that there would be two *obas*— one for each of the two different communities in the town.

At times the efforts to resolve conflicts move beyond Ijesa individuals and organizations. In 1992 the Osun State government established the Ijesa Traditional Council Peace Committee. The opening statement by the committee's chair, Lawrence Omole, is quoted at the beginning of this chapter. The deputy governor of Osun State, himself an Ijesa, set up the peace committee with the goal of achieving "permanent peace, unity and concord among the rank and file of all Ijesa sons and daughters" (Report of the Ijesa Traditional Council Peace Committee 1992). In addition to Lawrence Omole, the committee included two other prominent Ijesas (both members of the Ijesa Solidarity Group), four high chiefs from Ilesa, and four Ijesa *obas* from other towns. The peace committee's charge focused on the makeup of the traditional council of Ijesa chiefs; in addition, they also commented on Ijesa representation on the Osun State Council of Chiefs, where they believed Ijesa chiefs were underrepresented.

There were two very divergent starting points: The district chiefs argued that there should be a separate traditional council for each Ijesa LGA, as well as an overall coordinating council made up of representatives from each local traditional council; the Ilesa chiefs argued that "for the Ijesa Traditional Council to be really traditional" there should only be one council for the entire region of Ijesaland, and that separate councils would lead to fragmentation. Following several meetings, the peace committee came up with recommendations that seemed closer to the request from the district chiefs, proposing four local government councils and one overall group with representatives from each of the others. They also requested the state government to increase Ijesa representation on the state Council of Chiefs. The committee submitted its report to the deputy governor in July 1992 (*Daily Sketch*, July 8, 1992). However, no action was taken on the report at that time; given the political events of 1993, there was soon a situation where the deputy governor himself was no longer was in office. In later efforts to establish a separate council for northern Ijesaland, people referred to this committee's recommendations in support of their arguments.

Neither the formal conflict resolution efforts nor the informal ones have been particularly successful. Even when recommendations are made or decisions taken, the underlying disagreements continue. This is not surprising. Each Ijesa community is complex and has people and groups with varied interests. Within the region as a whole, there is even greater room for conflict. The debates about chieftaincy relationships and representation reflect the relationships among the towns, especially between the largest community of Ilesa and smaller communities, all of which are seeking to "develop" and "progress." Historically, Ilesa has been the dominant community in the region. Today, as individuals advance their own interests and contribute to the advancement of their communities, those from the smaller towns want to be sure that their own interests and concerns will be heard. The goal of unity, despite efforts at mediating and resolving conflict, is likely to continue to be elusive.

The Quest for Unity

Peel describes an incident in the 1860s when a prominent Ilesa chief, Odole Ariyasunle, in conflict with others, began to lose his following and influence and subsequently killed himself. Before he died, he is said to have cursed the Ijesa: "Casting aside the beads from his waist, he predicted that the Ijesha would never be united in one place until the beads were collected together; ... Ijesha would love each other abroad, but not at home" (1983: 79–80). Clearly, there are deep historical roots to the current complaints about the lack of unity among Ijesas. Despite the views of some today—that there was harmony in the past—the problem is not a new one. Yet the current context, both political and economic, has no doubt exacerbated existing divisions and tensions. The larger political system, which emphasizes the hometown and the need for identifying with one's place of origin, has exacerbated ethnic and subethnic tensions. This has been especially the case during the years of military rule. But the policies requiring a hometown base continue and are likely to be seen as even more important in an era of civilian government, of elections and party politics.

The local Ijesa interpretation of hometown affiliation complements and deepens these divisions. Despite the fact that they are all called "Ijesas," most people from the Ijesa region identify primarily in terms of their hometown, not their local government or the region as a whole. For the wealthy elite in particular, who want their contribution to local development to be known and acclaimed, it is important that their interest in the hometown be visible. For those remaining at home, especially those with little wealth or access to resources, their major route for both individual and community progress lies in the resources contributed by those who are residing outside. If someone builds a house in Ilesa rather than in his hometown (as a few individuals have done), it will be commented on by others at home. The individual's true commitment to his community will be questioned, unless he or she makes other contributions that demonstrate that commitment. There are, in other words, constant underlying tensions: between those at home and those away; between those with wealth and resources and those without; between smaller communities with fewer wealthy individuals and less resources and larger communities, especially Ilesa; and between and among different groups and factions both within communities and between communities. Chieftaincy disputes are the common idiom in which many of these tensions and divisions are played out.

At the same time, there is a constant effort to overcome these tensions and divisions, to create "unity" within specific communities and between communities. There is a recognition that lack of unity affects the ability to progress and develop. As a result, those living outside the hometown and region join together, as we have seen, in a wide variety of organizations through which they try to create unity. But as was the case in the past, it is still true that it is easier to "love ourselves abroad" than to do so at home.

Notes

1. My intention in this brief description of key political events is to simply provide the context for local attitudes and activities. For a detailed description of Nigerian politics and military regimes, including discussion of the Babangida regime and the failed 1993 election, as well as the first years of the Abacha regime, see Diamond (1995), especially pages 442–464. Also see the collection of articles "Transition in Nigeria?" in *Issue* (1999), on the 1999 elections.

2. As we have seen in Chapter 3, one of the pragmatic reasons for hometown involvement is the necessity of having a hometown base for specific activities, including politics.

3. I was in Nigeria during the June 1993 elections and intended to return during the summer of 1994, around the same time that the strike of petroleum workers began. After numerous telephone conversations with friends in the country, all of whom were unanimous in expressing the view that I should postpone my trip, I decided to do so. Therefore, when I spent a month in Nigeria in December

1994–January 1995 the differences in attitudes from my previous visit, in June 1993, were especially striking.

4. Other organizations also focused on new state formation. As early as May 1992, one of the Lagos-based hometown organizations discussed the idea of an Ijesa State, as well as a new LGA in the region. Even though no new state emerged, two new LGAs were established within the Ijesa region in the mid-1990s, as discussed in Chapter 3.

5. There are several published histories of Ijesaland, both in Yoruba and in English, that present origin stories for many of the towns in the region, provide lists of the kings of Ilesa, and provide versions of the historical relationships among the Ijesa communities (Abiola, Babafemi, and Ataiyero 1932; Oke 1969 [according to Peel much of this is plagiarism of Abiola]; and Oni n.d.). More recent and academic sources include Agbaje-Williams and Ogundiran, *Cultural Resources in Ijesaland* (1992). Many Ijesa towns have also printed their own histories, either as part of booklets prepared for celebrations or as books (e.g., J. O. Ogunjulugbe, *The History of Ipetu-Ijesa* [1993]).

6. See Peel (1983), Chapter 6, on political divisions both within Ilesa and between Ilesa and other communities in the late nineteenth to early twentieth centuries; see Peel's Chapters 9 and 11 on the 1941 riot and early party politics.

7. A number of recent publications focus on symbolic expressions of conflict through witchcraft in various parts of Africa. In particular, Geschiere (1997) and Geschiere and Nyamnjoh (1998) emphasize the "modernity of witchcraft" in contemporary political relations, noting the variation that exists within a common symbolic frame. Bastian (1993), a paper on witchcraft and Igbo rural-urban relations, which I saw in an unpublished version near the start of my research, was especially helpful in drawing my attention to this issue and led me to consider several new questions. The fact that I came across relatively little discussion among Ijesas of the fear of witchcraft leaves open the question of whether the fear is there but not expressed, or whether during this particular time period conflict and tension were expressed in other ways.

8. This story is an example of what Geschiere and Nyamnjoh call "zombie witchcraft," where witches "are reputed not to eat their victims as in older forms of witchcraft, but to transform them into zombies who can be put to work" (1998: 74). However, in contrast to the example they cite, where it is the new rich based in the city who are accused of being witches, in this story it is old men who are farmers who are accused of getting rich by killing their children and putting them to work.

10

Conclusion:
Communities and Development

What else is development other than helping your hometown?
—Niyi Akinnaso

This comment reflects and synthesizes the central issues of this book.[1] First, it raises the question of what a *community* is. Is it the place where one lives, or is it a place to which one has connections because it is the *hometown*? In the context of high mobility, how is a community formed, maintained, and understood? What are the implications for individual identity and for social action? Does everyone in the hometown understand their connections and obligations to it in the same way? If not, what are the divisions within such communities, and how do people shape their actions in terms of their own status and situation? Second, the statement raises the issue of what *development* is. Who defines *development*? What do they mean by the term? When people in Yoruba communities discuss their own commitment to *self-help,* does this mean something similar to the social scientist's concepts of indigenous development or "development from within"? How do people set out to achieve development, and what are the problems they encounter?

Beyond these two fundamental sets of questions, the quote also draws attention to broader issues. In the context of social, economic, and political change, it leads us to ask questions about an emphasis on "the home," on specific locales and attachments. What are the implications of such attachments to locale, to place, especially one that is usually defined by ethnicity? With the multitude of organizations associated with such places, what are the implications for civil society and for the idea of citizenship? Are hometown organizations a key locus for voluntary action and hence an important part of civil society? Or does their ethnic and regional base only reinforce societal divisions and mitigate against the formation of other sorts of attachments and linkages? How have economic and political crises helped to emphasize the importance of being connected to a local place, to a hometown? Conversely, what has been the impact of these crises on local communities?

Finally, how does the hometown become a locus not only of social action but also of cultural commitments? How do local morality and culture shape obligations and expectations with regard to the hometown? In what ways do ceremonial and symbolic activities help to bring people together while, simultaneously, social and cultural complexities result in continued conflict and tension within and among local communities?

This chapter examines these questions and issues not only for Ijesa communities but also in a broader comparative perspective, both within Africa and beyond the continent.

Community, Migration, and Hometown Linkages

It is evident that for the Ijesa Yoruba, *home* is a place of great importance, and the *hometown* is a locale with great significance and centrality in people's lives. Yet when we think of people with a great attachment to place, we usually think of people whose lives are spent in that place—a farming community, for example, where people are born, live, and die, leaving only occasionally to visit other places. In contrast, we have seen that in Ijesa communities the vast majority of people have been migrants for at least a part of their lives, and many have lived away from home for most or all of their lives. How, and why, do Ijesas continue to maintain such strong connections to places that they may have rarely visited or lived in, and how can we understand these connections and their implications for local society? Are the Ijesa unusual in this commitment, or do we find similar attachments in other contexts of high mobility? Indeed, as more and more people throughout the world are increasingly mobile, are such connections becoming more important elsewhere?

In considering the attachment to home, and the ways in which it is similar to, or different from, the attachments found in other regions of the world, it is helpful to examine these attachments from several perspectives: individuals involved in migration; the families, households, and kin networks of which they are a part; and the communities that claim them and that they claim.

Migration for individual Ijesas results in connections with people and institutions in more than one place. The concept of *multilocality* helps us to understand the connections that span more than one location: "We need to examine this population in terms of ... attachment to, and participation in, social and economic activities in a number of places" (Trager 1995b: 309).

Although I have emphasized the connections with the hometown here, the hometown is not the only locus of importance from the individual's point of view. Rather, an individual may be working in Lagos, participating in organizations and institutions there, while also traveling home regularly to participate in hometown activities. He or she may also be involved in activities in other towns and cities; someone from Osu or Ijebu-Jesa may also have connections in Ilesa, or in his or her spouse's hometown elsewhere. Not all such connections may be of equal strength or importance, but all have potential for the individual. At a given time, the ties in one locale may have greater claim, or may provide access to, resources (e.g., a job); at another time, claims and resources may be more important in a different locale.

Most who have analyzed the ties resulting from migration in Third World contexts have described them as "urban-rural linkages" and, in Africa especially, as connections to the "village." For example, Peter Geschiere and Josef Gugler point to the "special characteristic of urbanisation in Africa [of] the continuing commitment of many urbanites to 'the village'" (1998b: 309). I, too, have phrased these connections in terms of rural-urban linkages (see, e.g., Trager 1996b: 8–13). However, the conceptualization of these linkages as urban-rural or urban-village is limiting in two fundamental respects. On the one hand, it implies that there are only two places involved: the "rural" home and the "urban" place to which one migrates. But it is clear that for Ijesa migrants, at least, they are likely to have ties and activities in more than two places. Many have lived in several different places, and many more have family members in more than one locale. On the other hand, and even more problematic, is the assumption that the home place is "rural" or a "village" and the place to which one migrates is "urban." But when the home is a place like Ilesa, a Yoruba city with a population of more than 100,000, it is difficult to view it as a village.[2] Given the highly urban character of many Yoruba settlements, the emphasis on rural connections is particularly problematic.

Therefore, when considering the ways in which individuals function in a spatial context that includes several different locales, it is more useful to conceive of that space as "multilocal," the implication being that people participate in social activities and organizations in more than one place and move among these places. As migration becomes increasingly important for people in most regions of the world, and as contemporary communications and transportation make it possible for individuals to move and communicate over great distances, multilocality is likely to become the norm for increasing numbers of people. Recent studies of international migration have focused on "transnationalism," noting the ways in which connections are maintained by migrants between their country of origin and the country to which they migrate (e.g., Hsu 2000). In the transnational context, too, it is likely that these connections may increasingly span more than two places, as individuals and members of their families move between several locales while continuing to maintain ties at home.

Mobility and ties to multiple locales among individuals lead to social relationships that span place. Of particular importance for migrants are the relationships with families, households, and kin networks. In my study of migrants in the Philippines, I argued that "dispersed family networks" are formed, "which include interaction and ... support, among people who may be residing in two or more different places. These places may be the rural home and urban residence of the migrant, or they may include people in other cities, and even overseas" (1988b: 182). A similar situation exists among Ijesas, as we have seen in Chapter 4. Nearly everyone visits family and kin at home or in other places; many give gifts and remittances to close family members. Unlike the Philippines, where most ties are within nuclear-family or other close relationships, African kinship systems make possible connections with much wider sets of kin. As Geschiere and Gugler point out, the specific content of those connections may vary widely, not only depending on cultural context but also varying over time (1998b: 312). In some cases, nuclear families, including spouses, are separated by migration, and remittances and visits occur between them. For many others, the most important connections are between parents and children residing in different locations, or among siblings. However, there are many other possibilities. A child may be sent home to live with grandparents or other relatives, as we have seen in some of the life histories. Uncles, cousins, and other kin can play significant roles at key points, such as in gaining entry to a school or in finding a job. As Anthony O'Connor pointed out in his study of African cities, "More than in any other region [of the world] people belong to a combined rural-urban system of social and economic relationships. Many individuals have one foot in each world, and many families have at any given time some members in the city and some in the country" (1983: 272).

Studies in several African countries and among a variety of ethnic groups have demonstrated the importance of these social networks and the extensive interaction between those in the city and those in rural areas (Aronson 1971, 1978 for the Ijebu Yoruba of Nigeria; Gugler 1971, 1991; Gugler and Flanagan 1978 in southeastern Nigeria; Bartle 1981 in Ghana; Weisner 1976 and Ross and Weisner 1977 in Kenya). Others have focused on the flows of goods and money in the form of remittances between urban migrants and rural family members in an effort to examine the economic effects of these linkages (Adepoju 1974; Johnson and Whitelaw 1973/1974; Collier and Lal 1980). These studies, like those in other regions of the world that focus on rural-urban links in the migration process and the role of remittances (e.g., Stark 1980; Oberai and Singh 1980; Trager 1984,

1988b), emphasize the importance of social networks among family and kin, spanning multiple locales; they also note the reliance on such networks both for those at home and those who migrate.

Although links to family and kin networks play an important role in the migration process in many parts of the world, connections to the home community as a community are much more important in Africa than elsewhere. Dan Aronson, in his study of Ijebu Yoruba migrants in the city of Ibadan (1971, 1978), points out that "the various activities of migration, participation, and return [are] so normal that they can be encompassed by conceptualizing a single role system, continuous over time but slowly expanding over space to include migrant communities as extensions of those at home" (1971: 276). In his study of a Ghanaian community where migration was common, Philip Bartle suggests that an "extended community" was formed: "What I call the extended Obo community includes not only some people living in Obo ... but also a much larger number ... living in various places outside Obo. Since it includes people who identify or feel they belong to Obo, it includes many who were not born there, many who do not live there, many who have visited only a few times and even some who have not yet visited Obo" (1981: 126).

Recent studies have continued to confirm the centrality of connections to "home" in many regions of the continent (see, e.g., the papers in Trager 1996c and those in Geschiere and Gugler 1998a). As Geschiere and Gugler argue, the "urban-rural connection in Africa is not a matter of 'either ... or'; it is not a connection which is either maintained or broken.... It is clear that the connection is resilient, highly variable, with dynamics of its own and not just dependent on personal choice" (1998b: 315).

The multifaceted nature of the connections with the hometown among the Ijesa Yoruba is evident in the preceding chapters. The home community continues to be a source of identity, a place where one is known and where one's reputation is important. But it is not enough to say that one is from a particular place. Rather, a person is expected to act on the basis of that identity, to fulfill obligations to the hometown, to participate in organizations and activities with others from the community, both those who live at home and others living outside. In other words, it is not sufficient to claim a particular place, such as Ilesa or Iloko, as one's hometown; rather, the hometown also places claims on those who are its "sons and daughters." As we have seen, this is especially true for those who are successful, those who are identified as members of the elite. A man or woman who has achieved success in Lagos or elsewhere cannot claim to be truly successful unless he or she is recognized at home. Wealth and status achieved outside the community are significant, but only if one enhances that status by participating in hometown activities. Clearly, there are a variety of ways of doing this, including contributing to local development activities, participating in hometown organizations, taking chieftaincy titles, and organizing or participating in hometown celebrations. Some people do all of these things, whereas others may focus on a specific effort of interest to them.

But it is not just the desire to remain connected to community or to enhance one's status that leads to the continuing importance of hometown connections. Rather, structural features of Nigerian society also emphasize community of origin. As we have seen, access to key resources such as education may be affected by where one's hometown is. For those interested in participating in politics and government, connection with the home community is more important than ever. And many Ijesas feel that they are discriminated against in public arenas—by state government, for example—and that it is only in their home communities that they can have full access to resources. I will return to these issues below in the contexts of ethnicity and civil society.

Although the majority of Ijesas seek to keep ties with the home community, there are significant variations in the extent of those connections. Three sources of variation are gender, generation, and wealth. As we saw in Chapter 4, men as well as women retain ties to their hometowns. But there are differences in the ways in which men and women act on their connections. For men, building a house at home and belonging to a hometown organization are key ways in which they solidify their identity with the hometown. For women, building a house at home is much less common. In general, women's organizations also seem to be somewhat less active. Yet many women are active both in their own hometown and in that of their husband, thus multiplying the number of connections and organizations in which they participate. Some have argued that women migrants are less involved in their hometowns and have "weaker attachment to the rural area" (Gugler and Ludrun-Ene 1995: 264), and others have focused on women's hometown organizations that are "women's wings" of men's organizations, arguing that "by their very nature, women's wings constitute a subordinate body under the control of men's branches" (Denzer and Mbanefoh 1998: 132).

The Ijesa data do not support either of these perspectives. Women, like men, vary in the extent of their activity at home, with elite women, like elite men, being more involved. As the woman quoted at the beginning of Chapter 4 states, "We are just sojourners here, whereas our place of abode is at home; attachment to home is always there." For her, as for many other elite women, the attachment is not just an emotional one. They participate in hometown organizations, contribute to hometown development efforts, take chieftaincy titles, and in general act on their connections in substantial ways. In contrast, women with fewer financial resources are less likely to participate in hometown activities while they are living outside; when they do return home, they participate in more limited ways, having neither the financial resources nor the status of community leaders.

With regard to the organizations in which women participate, most of the Ijesa hometown organizations are, as we have seen in Chapter 5, segregated by gender, as well as by age; only a few of the women's organizations are women's wings of men's organizations. The others are separate associations, with their own leaders and their own agenda.[3] Although many of these organizations have not been particularly successful in carrying out their projects, that is also true of many of the men's organizations. Some, however, such as the women's group in Iloko that undertook the *gari*-processing project, have carried out some of the most successful development activities among those studied.

It is often assumed that with increasing migration and distance from the hometown, connections with home will become less important. Ijesas themselves often discuss their concern about whether their children will continue to identify with home, arguing that many of the children who grew up in Lagos or other cities no longer "know" their hometowns. At the same time, however, many of those who today are most active in maintaining connections with home are people whose own parents migrated out of Ijesaland. As we have seen, the *osomaalo* trading tradition meant that many Ijesas have migrated to other parts of Nigeria since the early 1900s. Thus, unlike many regions of Africa, where today's migrants are the first generation to have left the home community (Geschiere and Gugler 1998b: 312), many Ijesa migrants today are the children of those who left home to trade. Clearly, for most of them, connections with home continue to be important. As Gugler (1991) found in his restudy of Igbo migrants to Enugu, there continues to be an enduring commitment to the home community, as both structural constraints and cultural loyalties combine to continue to place emphasis on the hometown. Will this change in the future? Will the children of today's Ijesa migrants continue to come back to Ijesaland, to contribute money for the development of their communities as their fathers and mothers are doing now?

Given the evidence that is now available, it is likely that such ties will continue to be important for some time in the future, but with changes and variations as the situation changes. So long as the structural constraints—economic and political—continue, many will still feel that they need the security of a home base to which they can return. Cultural and symbolic events, such as community-day celebrations, are leading to a reemphasis on these connections. No doubt there will be some people in the future (just as there were in the past) who do not recognize their hometown or involve themselves in its activities. But for others, there is likely to be a cycle similar to that which their own parents followed: less involvement at home when they are in their twenties, thirties, and even forties, with a renewal of interest as they become older. As one woman told me about her seven-year-old daughter growing up in Ibadan, she thinks of Iloko as "home" even though she has hardly ever been there.

Hometowns and the Elite

Clearly, there is variation by wealth and status in the importance of hometown connections. If maintenance of hometown ties were simply a practical matter—of having a base to return to where one has land or access to other resources—then one would expect such connections to be most important for those with less wealth and fewer resources. Instead, it seems that extensive involvement at home is much more important for those who are well off and of high status. As such individuals explain, "If you are not recognized at home, you are nothing." For the elite, high status away from home must also be enhanced by maintenance of status at home. As we saw in Chapter 3, it is important for elite individuals to have recognition of their success, and that recognition needs to include recognition at home.

As I have argued elsewhere (see Trager 1998), elite individuals who are actively involved in furthering hometown interests and development can be seen as the contemporary equivalent of "big" men and women. Karin Barber has described "big men" of the past in Yoruba society:

> [Yoruba society was] animated by a dynamic, competitive struggle for self-aggrandisement which permeated the society from top to bottom. There was scope for people to create a place for themselves and expand it by their own efforts. Like the "Big Men" of New Guinea, they did it through the recruitment of supporters. A Yoruba proverb ... says "mo lowo, mo leniyan, ki lo tun ku ti mi o tii ni?" "I have money, I have people, what else is there that I have not got?" Money was one of the principal ways of gaining public acknowledgement as a big man; but "having people" constituted that acknowledgement itself. (1991: 183)

A key aspect of the notion of the *big man* is that it involves reciprocity; one can accumulate money and develop a network of supporters, but one also needs to work to retain them. There is great fluidity in such as system; money and supporters can be lost as well as gained. In Yoruba society, there are strong cultural expectations of generosity. Wealth earned elsewhere should not be used just for the benefit of the individual or for his family but for the larger community as well. The resources of elite individuals go beyond the money they themselves have to contribute. Perhaps even more important are their connections to others, as well as the influence that they have. As we have seen in the descriptions of community-day celebrations, influential community members are able to encourage contributions from their friends and acquaintances who are not from the community. The result is a network of elite individuals whose ties cut across their hometown bases and who assist one another in their local efforts. Implications of these elite connections are considered below, in the contexts of self-help and local development.

For individuals, then, there is a strong motivation to contribute and involve oneself in hometown activities. They are motivated by the belief that it is important to demonstrate and display one's success. Although this can be done by building a house at home, the involvement of elite Ijesas at home goes considerably beyond symbolic display. They are also motivated by a strong sense of obligation and commitment, of feeling that one must use one's own success to help promote the success of the community. The amount of time and energy, as well as money, devoted to hometown affairs is considerable. In other words, people are engaged in something that goes beyond self-aggrandizement or conspicuous consumption and display of wealth. For many, there is genuine concern with efforts to assist the local community, as we have seen in the discussions of organizations such as the Ijesa Solidarity Group and in the establishment of community banks, among other activities. These concerns and commitments are reinforced by community expectations; there are frequent exhortations for "sons and daughters abroad" to come back and develop the hometown. And for the most part, those who meet those obligations and expectations are praised and recognized as having made significant contributions.

Just because everyone, or nearly everyone, is involved in their hometown and committed to assisting it does not, of course, mean that there are no conflicts or tensions. Certainly for the elite, there must be limits and constraints on what one can do; no matter how wealthy or influential one is, one cannot fulfill all expectations or meet all demands. More generally, Ijesa communities are not homogeneous. Rather, they are complex, with varying groups and factions. Even the smallest of the communities studied has the potential for division along various structural lines—family and kinship networks, religious affiliations, occupations, and so forth. And in a city like Ilesa, the number of different groups and interests is vast. As we have seen in Chapter 9, two key potential sources of tension and conflict within communities are differences between those who are living at home and those who are away, and between the wealthy elite and the ordinary, "grassroots" community members. Conflict can result from perceptions that individuals are not fulfilling their obligations to the community. There is also the potential for conflict or disagreement over the setting of the agenda for development. This issue is discussed further below, in the context of how decisionmaking is carried out for local development.

The Idea of Community

Implicit in this discussion is the idea that the Ijesa hometown is a "community," not one bounded by geography but rather one whose members consider themselves attached to a particular geographical place. There is an actual geographic locus—the hometown—with recognized features; some are sizable cities such as Ilesa, others are small towns like Osu and Ijebu-Jesa, and still others are villages. Regardless of size, each of these places has recognizable features, including indigenous political institutions; economic activities including farming and trading; and physical structures such as schools and churches. Each of these places also has people who consider it to be their "home" because they are connected to it through recognized kinship networks; most frequently it is the home of their father and patrilineage, or, in the case of women, it is the home of their spouse through his patrilineage. But there is also a degree of choice and selection; many Ijesas can claim affiliation to more than one hometown, but most choose to associate themselves primarily with one place.

Although the community has a geographic locus, its membership is not limited to the people living within the boundaries of that space. Contrary to the notion that a community consists of the people living within a specific territory, the Ijesa hometown calls attention to the fact that a community can consist of people with shared identities and a shared focus of concern—the hometown—but whose residences span several locales. At any given time, a considerable percentage of Ijesa people are living outside their hometowns. Yet it is clear that regardless of where they are living, most consider the hometown to be "their" community, the one where they should build a house, assist kin, and help in development. In this, they are like other West Africans, such as the Ghanaians described by Bartle (1981) or the people in the Sahelian countries for whom Thomas Painter (1996) has coined the phrase *action space* to describe livelihood activities that span territory. Something similar may also be happening as a result of transnational migration, where transnational "communities" are forming that not only span space within a given country but also include people located in different countries and continents.

The implications of this notion of community as involving people whose residences and activities span several locales go beyond efforts to define *community*.[4] Recognition that community includes people in different places is important to understanding how development takes place; were it not for the contributions of those residing outside, much of what Ijesas consider to be development in their hometowns would not have occurred at all. Yet when development efforts are undertaken by external groups, this is often not recognized; a nongovernmental organization, for example, might decide to take a census in a location, focusing only on those residing there and ignoring the members of the community residing elsewhere.[5] The idea that community includes people living outside also affects political and economic behavior. For example, Ijesas (and others) may feel that they want to come home to vote, because that is where their major interests lie. The government, in contrast, has usually tried to prevent people from traveling home to vote in elections, arguing that they should vote where they live. The economic contributions that people make at home may also affect their ability and willingness to contribute in the place where they live and work. For example, if most who live in Lagos see themselves as only "sojourners" there, then they are not likely to feel any obligation to help improve the city or assist in its development.[6]

The result of the complex processes of identity with a hometown, and of cultural obligations and social action connected to that identity, is that there is a community that has a spatial locus but whose members are spread about. It is a real "community" nevertheless, in that its members interact with one another on a regular basis, know who the members are (though they certainly don't all know one another), and have ways of identifying one another. And like communities elsewhere, these communities have divisions and differences within them, as would be expected in any community.

Self-Help and Local Development

As we have seen throughout this book, the Ijesa have embraced the idea of development. Regardless of whether they are speaking in Yoruba or in English, or whether they are a highly educated professional person or a farmer or a trader with little formal education, nearly everyone uses the term *development* to refer to their goals and desires for their communities and region. Social scientists often assume that it is only outsiders—governments, international agencies such as the World Bank, academics—who want to see development of a region and who, as a result, undermine "traditional" ways of life.[7] When Ijesas state at public events and in private conversations that they want "development," what do they mean? Is their concept of self-help the same as the social scientist's concepts of local development and indigenous development? How do their efforts compare to activities in other parts of Nigeria and elsewhere?

As we have seen in Chapters 7 and 8, *development* has multiple meanings for Ijesas. For many, it refers to concrete physical evidence of progress and improvement—the construction of a town hall or palace, the building of a school, improvement in water supply or roads. Historically, the most noted efforts were those that involved building schools, of which the Ilesa Grammar School established by the Egbe Atunluse was the most prominent. In this, Ijesas resemble town improvement unions and hometown associations in other parts of Nigeria, where one of the early concerns was education (see, e.g., Bello-Imam 1995; Udoma 1987; and case studies in Honey and Okafor 1998). For some, "development is building: building things like town halls and houses ... roads and other infrastructure"; people want to be able to see "something visible" that their money was spent on. For others, development is not buildings, and especially not buildings like town halls and palaces. For them, it is contributions to improvement of the local economy, especially through establishment of industries but also through other efforts such as community banks. In recent years, economic development efforts have been the focus of much of the rhetoric about development among Ijesas, although in reality many of the local projects continue to be construction projects.

For Ijesas, self-help is the main strategy for achieving development, and their development efforts are focused on the local community or, in some cases, the region as a whole. Although there is some expectation that government will assist in the development process, that expectation is much less than it used to be. Ijesas have essentially accepted the idea that "government cannot do everything." Activity by external nongovernmental organizations in some of the communities is very recent and relatively unimportant; in fact, the evidence from Iloko suggests that the NGOs have followed self-help activities rather than the reverse. Given the attachment to the hometown discussed in the preceding section, it is not surprising that the dominant and most successful self-help efforts are those focused on specific communities. Fund-raising efforts for a specific local project, such as improvement of water supply or constructing a town hall, are much more likely to resonate with the population than requests for more general development funds, or requests for projects that will serve several communities or the whole region. Again, for the wealthy elite who contribute much of the funds for any project, most prefer to be able to see the results of their money. As a result, although there is a lot of discussion about industrial development, it is much harder to get donations for broad-based industrial projects. Community banks, in contrast, have been able to attract resources. The constraints and difficulties resulting from self-help as the main strategy for development are considered below.

Ijesas' focus on self-help in the local community is in many respects comparable to the contemporary emphasis in development debates on *indigenous development* and *participatory development*. For many years, the study and understanding of development emphasized processes that occur at the level of nations and regions, using measures such as GNP. More recently, there has been increasing recognition that actual economic change and development take place in specific communities and in specific sectors. There has also been increasing concern with the "human" side of development—not just macroeconomic indicators but quality-of-life issues such as health, education, and human rights. For example, Oxfam America (1991), a major international NGO, published a twelve-part definition of *genuine development:* among other things, it "enables people to meet their essential needs," "measures progress in human, not just monetary terms," and "respects local cultures." The organization also states that development "can only be carried out *by* people." In recent years, other major international organizations have likewise emphasized issues such as the empowerment of peoples, participation in the development process, and other ideas that respond in part to the criticism that development efforts have focused too much on economic growth and not enough on improving quality of life.

Most Ijesas, of course, are not engaged in, or even aware of, these international and academic debates.[8] Yet in many respects, their own approach to development coincides with the concerns articulated in these debates. In particular, the evidence discussed here exemplifies aspects of three current approaches in development debates: indigenous knowledge and institutions; the role of local organizations in development; and participatory development.

Indigenous Institutions and Local Organizations

In contrast to earlier ideas, which emphasized that "traditions"—such as indigenous beliefs and institutions like kinship—were obstacles in the development process, the indigenous-knowledge approach emphasizes the value of indigenous knowledge for development (see *Indigenous Knowledge and Development Monitor* 1999: 1). Much of the research has focused on "knowledge" such as the ideas and beliefs of farmers or traditional medical practitioners, but some has examined indigenous institutions. *Indigenous institutions* are defined as those that have arisen from endogenous, rather than exogenous, sources. Hometown associations would be considered endogenous, whereas an organization like Rotary would be considered exogenous (Blunt and Warren 1996: xiv). According to Peter Blunt and D. Michael Warren, indigenous institutions tend to be "invisible to the outsider" but are "most inclined to have and to use local knowledge, to respond quickly to changes, to handle conflict and to create climates of opinion influencing behavior" (1996: xiv). Rex Honey and Stanley Okafor suggest that hometown associations are "important institutional resources that are part of the indigenous knowledge system.... [They] bear eloquent testimony to the creativity, adaptability and responsiveness of indigenous knowledge systems" (1998: 2).

The evidence in this book likewise demonstrates that hometown organizations can be considered indigenous institutions that have been responsive to changing needs and demands. But hometown organizations represent just one of the ways in which people utilize and act on their hometown connections. Community-day celebrations can be seen as another example of an indigenous institution through which Ijesa people have drawn on traditional ideas in a creative way. As Chapters 2 and 5 demonstrate, Ijesas have used creative strategies for the mobilization of hometown linkages, including innovations in forming new organizations and in creating new "traditional" rituals (see also Trager 1993).

There is no clear-cut distinction between indigenous institutions and local organizations. Rather than distinguish between endogenous and exogenous institutions, Norman Uphoff suggests a continuum, ranging from "organizations that are clearly 'indigenous,' even primordial, with their origins going back indistinctly but certainly many generations, to organizations that are quite contemporary in their inspiration and modes of operation" (1996: vii). Uphoff suggests that the latter type blends into a wider category of "local organizations," which can include organizations that are locally based but not indigenous. This distinction, too, can be problematic, however.

Hometown organizations are clearly indigenous in the sense that they developed in Nigeria (and in other West African nations); no one from outside came along to help or encourage their formation. But they are not "primordial"; as we have seen, they initially arose in a specific historical context in the early twentieth century. If we were looking at them at that time period, we might well want to argue that they are "contemporary in ... inspiration and modes of operation." Yet local organizations can include ones whose origins and inspiration are quite clearly external but that have become part of the local landscape and an important set of institutions in which local people participate. Rotary clubs, for example, exist in every major town and city in Nigeria; many of the elite members of hometown organizations also belong to Rotary or other service organizations and are as active in contributing to Rotary projects as they are to hometown projects. Church-based organizations are another set of institutions with origins that are clearly external but that today may well be seen as local, with their own local organization and dynamics. Among Ijesas, most individuals would probably not make a distinction among church organizations, hometown organizations, and other organizations—occupational, service, and so on. They would not see some as indigenous and others as not; for them, these are all *local* organizations with important—and merely differing—roles.

Local organizations vary in both the ways in which they are organized and in the roles that they play in the development process. Research on peasant associations in francophone West Africa, for example, suggests some of the ways in which local organizations are influenced by both internal and external forces (Jacob and Delville 1994). Danielle Jonckers argues that in southern Mali there is an ideology, or "myth," of a tradition of communal and associational life that has helped to legitimize contemporary village associations. But, she suggests, there is actually a wide range of interests within these villages today; a process of social differentiation is taking place "under the mask of communal development" (my translation) (Jonckers 1994: 132–133). Similarly, Roch Mongbo's 1994 study of peasant associations in the Republic of Benin suggests that these organizations are places for a peasant elite to take advantage of external opportunities, which then aid their own individual strategies. In northern Ghana, "youth associations" have emerged, with "ascribed membership based on origin in a particular territory or ethnic affiliation" (Lentz 1995: 395). Like the Nigerian hometown organizations, they have developed in a context of mobility among an educated elite; like the peasant associations in francophone West Africa, they draw on a rhetoric of "common interests" with "the grassroots." Like Ijesa hometown organizations, these groups emphasize their "unity" and commitment to development; but in contrast to the organizations studied here, they have primarily focused on political or cultural projects, such as the creation of a separate district, or the organization of a cultural festival. Regardless of the terminology that is used either locally or by researchers— *local organization, peasant association, youth association, hometown organization*—it is clear that there is great complexity underlying what may seem to be village-based or communal-associational activity.

Likewise, local development efforts undertaken by such organizations are complex and varied, with varying degrees of success. Within Nigeria alone, a comparative study of local institutions throughout the country has demonstrated both the variety of local organizations and the range of development efforts in which they are engaged (Olowu, Ayo, and Akande 1991; Olowu and Erero 1996). As Dele Olowu and John Erero point out, their research

> underscores the variety of institutions existing in Nigeria. The distinction is not simply between formal [i.e., state] and informal [i.e., nonstate] structures or between exotic and indigenous structures. Rather, substantial overlap exists between these various categories. Depending on the history, circumstance, and personalities in each area, one indigenous institution may be relevant or irrelevant. (1996: 117)

By "relevant" or "irrelevant" they mean whether these institutions are contributing to local development, and whether they have meaning for the local population. By comparing several different types of local organizations, including formal local government as well as community development and other associations, the researchers were able to compare "successful" and "not-so-successful" cases, demonstrating that specific local dynamics contributed to the success of one type of institution in specific contexts (Olowu, Ayo, and Akande 1991: 121–128). A World Bank study of "community-based organizations" in Nigeria also demonstrated that they were "of diverse origins and forms, and were directed at a whole range of goals" (Francis 1996). Similarly, their successes at local development efforts also varied; "these organizations, viewed as agents of local development, face a number of common limitations [which arise] ... from the embeddedness of local associations in *particular* communities [and are] a corollary of their communitarian strengths" (Francis 1996: 30).

Studies of the role of local organizations in development have examined both their importance in the development process and their limitations (e.g., Esman and Uphoff 1984; March and Taqqu 1986). For example, in India, Yogesh Kumar has analyzed the strengths and weaknesses of Indian institutions with a long history—the village *panchayat*—in contributing to local development. He shows how these institutions have worked together with a new local institution, the *jal samati*, in water-supply programs in one region of India. In other words, local institutions are not necessarily based in years of history or tradition. Neither are organizations rooted in history and tradition necessarily the most successful in aiding local development.

The organizations described in Chapters 5 and 6 are in many respects good examples of the diversity, strengths, and weaknesses of local organizations. As we have seen, there are many different types of hometown organization, ranging from very small, gender- or age-based groups in specific communities to those that are organized on a community-wide or regional basis. Some are very active in local development efforts, whereas others are largely social clubs, existing for their own membership rather than for the community as a whole. Over time, some have been highly successful in organizing specific projects and then have weakened in their relevance to the local population, whereas others have gained strength and importance. Yet hometown organizations in Ijesaland, like hometown organizations throughout Nigeria and like some of the peasant and youth organizations elsewhere in West Africa, differ from many local organizations in other areas of the world. That difference is rooted in the dispersal of the community discussed above. These organizations focus on a particular locus—the hometown—but their membership is spatially dispersed. The resources they draw on are often externally generated, and without those external resources very little would actually occur in the way of "local" development. I will return to this issue below.

Participatory Development

Like indigenous knowledge and local organization, participatory development has emerged as a major approach in development research and practice. In simplest terms, *participatory development* describes methods to encourage the participation of ordinary people in the development process. Originally conceived as an alternative approach to development known as *participatory rural appraisal* and emphasizing concepts such as empowerment of rural peoples (see Chambers 1994, 1997), it has entered mainstream development organizations such as the World Bank (e.g., World Bank 1996b) and has generated considerable debate (e.g., Nelson and Wright 1995). Similar approaches using somewhat different conceptual frameworks include *development from within* (Taylor and Mackenzie 1992) and *people's self-development* (Rahman 1993). The term *self-reliant development* is also used in these and other discussions, a term that is certainly very similar to the term *self-help* used by the Ijesa and other Nigerians.

Key to all of these approaches is the idea that participation is essential to the development process. As D.R.F. Taylor describes it, "Participation is seen as both a goal and a means.... It is not induced from above but is generated from below by the populace itself [although] it can also be generated by the catalytic action of some external third agent" (1992: 236–237; see also Rahman 1993: 150). Participation is part of the entire process of development: "The local populace must enter the participation process at the first stage and be in control of all subsequent stages of action" (Taylor 1992: 240). For Taylor, participation operates at the level of the local community: "The definition of local scale will vary from place to place but it will usually be the smallest territory which is effective and efficient and which has meaning for the local people, who will define their own 'life space' in terms of their own values and realities" (p. 242).

The self-help development efforts undertaken by people in Ijesa communities would certainly seem to be good examples of participation in local development. Nearly all the efforts considered in this book are ones that have been initiated and organized by community members themselves, either as a whole community, such as the community-wide development councils; or by groups within the community, such as the various hometown organizations. Some have resulted from external policies, such as the government policy to encourage the establishment of community banks. Others have had some external support, such as the nongovernmental organization that supported the *gari*-processing project of the women's group in Iloko. But none of them were externally developed projects in the way that development projects most frequently occur, with representatives of outside agencies (governmental or nongovernmental, national or international) arriving in a community with a project that is supposed to help or develop the area, with locals having little input in the design and implementation of the project.

Despite the rhetoric about participation, it is still relatively unusual for development efforts to be initiated at the local level, with participation by local community members, and to utilize resources obtained either from the community itself or through networks of community members. This is not to say that the self-help approach taken by Ijesa communities resolves all problems or that there are no difficulties resulting from community self-reliance; some of these problems and difficulties are considered below.

One issue is whether there is an expectation that whole communities should participate in the decisionmaking and implementation of projects (Taylor 1992: 237). A related issue is whether there is recognition of internal differentiation within communities, as well as to what extent participation is encouraged that either accommodates or challenges local structures of power and authority. In the Ijesa communities, it is apparent that many of the most successful development efforts have been undertaken by relatively small groups within specific communities. The Ibadan-based hometown organization in Ijebu-Jesa that established the community bank there has a small, cohesive membership that was able to make decisions and mobilize its own resources effectively. In other cases, however, the organization undertaking development represents the entire community, as in the case of the Iwoye Community Bank. Whether in fact the *entire* Iwoye community was actually represented in the decisions is difficult to know, but in that case, at least, there is an organizational structure that encompasses much of the community, as well as an opportunity for all community members to participate by buying shares in the bank. Community-wide efforts seem to be most successful in the smaller communities, such as Iloko and Iwoye; we have seen the degree of participation by members of the Iloko community in a variety of activities, ranging from the community-day celebrations, to community meetings, to fund-raising for the community hall. In larger communities such as Ilesa, it is clearly much more difficult to expect or achieve participation by everyone, or even by a large portion of the population. By the same token, those efforts that go beyond the level of single communities, such as those advocated by the Ijesa Solidarity Group, present even greater difficulty.

This does not, however, mean that there is no differentiation or conflict, even in the smallest communities. In fact, as Taylor suggests, there may be both community cohesion and subcommunity tension at the same time; the forces for cohesion as well as the tensions and cleavages need to be taken into account. As he states, "Development from within must ... explicitly recognize and consider the realities of rural society as opposed to the mythology and must also accept that the community is a dynamic and changing entity" (1992: 245). In contrast to much of the rhetoric about participation in development, Taylor's approach does not make any assumptions about homogeneity or common interests among all community members. It also does not assume that "grassroots" people will challenge or confront those with greater power and resources.

In contrast, much of the literature on participatory development is concerned with the empowerment of people in rural communities, especially poor people. In his discussion of participatory approaches, Robert Chambers asserts that while differences within communities should be recognized, "the challenge is to ... recognize diversity, complexity and multiple realities *to empower those who are weaker and excluded*" (1997: 187; italics added). Elsewhere he argues that "whether empowerment is good depends on who are empowered, and how their new power is used. If those who gain are outsiders who exploit, or a local elite which dominates, the poor and disadvantaged may be worse off" (p. 217). His approach, in other words, contends that the local elite—those of higher status who are better off—as well as men are the ones who are likely to have power and decisionmaking authority; this implies that that power and authority should be challenged by others in the community—that the goal should be to empower those who are weaker.

However, the evidence in this book suggests that local realities are much more complex. Clearly, there are differences of power, wealth, and status in Ijesa communities. Among the most important distinctions is between those who reside in the hometown and those who are residing outside, especially those outside who are highly educated professionals, recognized as being members of the Nigerian elite. But it is exactly these same people who are looked to for expertise and resources in local development efforts. Certainly there are tensions, and the possibility exists for conflicts to emerge, as we have seen in Chapter 9. But at the same time, most Ijesas recognize these individuals as local leaders, as people who have been away from home and have ideas that they can bring back for local development, as people who have the personal resources and networks that can assist the community. To ignore such individuals in the local development process would be nearly impossible, as well as counterproductive.

Agendas, Interests, and Benefits:
The Role of Elites and External Resources

Regardless of the terminology used, the Ijesa approach of self-help has much value. It is clear that there have been many successes in accomplishing specific projects and in bringing together resources from community members to achieve local development goals. Yet questions can be raised about the role of self-reliant approaches in the overall development process. First, there are questions about the internal processes through which communities make decisions. Given the internal differentiation within any community, who is really involved in making decisions? Whose agenda is being followed? Who participates, and in what ways? How is participation encouraged? Who decides about fund-raising activities, and how successful are these? Second, questions need to be raised regarding the impact of self-help approaches in different communities. Do some communities have better access to resources than others, even within the same region? How do these differences among communities affect the regional development process? Third, in what ways do self-help approaches affect overall development? How do local development efforts connect with state and national efforts? If government cannot do everything alone, can communities do it all without government or other external assistance?

The first set of issues essentially revolves around questions like "Whose agenda?" and "What interests?" (see Trager 1998: 369). I have suggested above that it would be counterproductive to ignore the elite community members, as they are the ones most able to contribute to local projects in a variety of ways. However, it is also important to ask whether ordinary community members participate in meaningful ways, whether they have a "voice" with regard to decisions that are made (Taylor 1992: 249).[9]

It is evident from the examples of local development considered in Chapter 8 that elite community members, especially those residing outside, are central to the local development process. To a large extent, they are the ones who decide which projects to undertake. They are also the major source of resources, which include their own personal resources, as well as their external networks, which enable communities to draw on the resources of others. People look to the elite—those who are "enlightened"—for ideas and leadership. Yet "ordinary" members of the community, especially those residing at home, also play significant roles.

In communities like Iloko and Iwoye, there are several avenues through which those at home can voice opinions. First, the chiefs are seen as important local leaders who are included in decisionmaking councils. Second, there are community-wide organizations that meet, and in Iloko, at least, community meetings have taken place. At these meetings, however, not everyone speaks: older people, and men, are most visible in these public roles. Third, the numerous different organizations in all communities provide avenues for a variety of viewpoints and a variety of projects. Women's hometown organizations in Ilesa, for example, have undertaken some projects of particular interest to women, such as providing day care. And finally, fund-raising and levies provide a means through which the success of particular projects and their support from the population as a whole can be gauged.

Fund-raising for community projects is a form of informal taxation that in general has greater success than government taxation. As we have seen in Chapter 8, many people have willingly contributed money (or labor in some cases) to specific projects: the construction of town halls and *obas'* palaces; schools, hospitals, and electricity; and other projects seen as benefiting the entire community. Judging from the responses in interviews and conversations, there seems to be considerable agreement about the importance of contributing to local development. But this is a form of taxation that is voluntary, that is, there may be local sanctions against people who don't contribute, but it is clear that not everyone contributes to every project. Many people may want to contribute but don't have the ability. And others may not want to and can choose to avoid the levies. But if a lot of people choose not to contribute, then it is unlikely that a project can go ahead; even when most of the resources are provided by elite community members, it would be difficult to undertake major projects without considerable support throughout the community.[10]

A related question is the issue of who benefits from the projects undertaken. Is it the elite, residing outside, or those residing at home? In their study of the Fiditi Progressive Union (FPU), in another part of Yorubaland, Michael McNulty and Mark Lawrence find that "certain FPU projects have benefited certain executive members" (1996: 32); the leadership, as in Ijesa towns, consists mainly of elite men. In contrast, the projects discussed here have more widespread benefits. The community banks are probably the best examples of efforts with benefits extending to a considerable portion of the local population. Community members recognize those benefits and state that they are participating in the banks. Specific projects undertaken by specific groups, such as the women's organization in Iloko that has established the *gari*-processing project, are certainly seen by those involved as having benefits for them. The benefits of building projects are more difficult to gauge. Something like the new marketplace in Iloko will probably, in the long term, be significant for much of the population, especially for women. Town halls and palaces, in contrast, have more of a symbolic value, demonstrating that the community itself is successful and able to mobilize the resources for such a project. Most people living in the communities would argue that these buildings are meaningful and have value to them.

The most problematic types of development projects have been the efforts to establish industries. Despite the success of the brewery in Ilesa, other efforts have so far not materialized. Despite the widespread acceptance of a view that industrialization is important, and that industries based on local resources should be established, efforts by hometown organizations and larger groups, such as the Council of Ijesa Societies and the Ijesa Solidarity Group, have so far not been successful. These efforts, like the others discussed, are largely led by elite community members. The debate over whether industries can be established by communities or organizations, rather than by individual investors, is one that has not been resolved. Many of those with the largest access to resources for investment are unwilling to invest in something that would be controlled by others. It is likely that some of these individuals will eventually invest in economic enterprises, especially when the economic conditions in the country improve. Whether the establishment of industry will in fact benefit local populations living at home will depend a great deal on the type of industry, whether it is based on local resources, how many it employs, and so on.

The differentiation within hometowns along lines of gender, wealth, and residence at home or away means that there are many different interests and potential agendas within any given community. Just because everyone shares a hometown identity or, more broadly, an Ijesa identity does not mean that they see the local community and its needs in the same way. However, there is no simple equation between status and the type of development effort, that is, it is not possible to group all elite Ijesas together or to argue that they all support efforts that only benefit themselves. Neither is it possible to see women as a single group having similar interests; some elite women, like some elite men, are engaged in efforts to benefit members of the local community, whereas others are more focused on their own interests. Among those residing at home, likewise, there are different perspectives and concerns. With numerous different organizations in each community, it is possible for a wide variety of perspectives to be represented; some lead to successful projects, whereas others do not.

Differentiation Among Communities

Just as there are differences within each community, so, too, there are differences among communities in their success at undertaking projects and mobilizing resources. What are the implications of these differences for the region, as well as for relationships among communities? In an earlier publication, I commented:

> The recognition that "government cannot do everything alone" and the call for increased participation in local community development activities has broad implications for the way in which those activities are funded, structured, and carried out. In the context of structural adjustment and a broad economic crisis, there has been a dynamic response at the level of the community, with communities seeking to generate resources for a variety of perceived needs. However, the raising of money from individuals for community development leads to a new set of questions concerning how access to those resources is structured, and the differential implications for different communities in a region. (Trager 1997: 285)

There are two significant issues here. One is the way in which communities, like families and households, are engaged in *multiple modes* of income generation (Mustapha 1991). The other is that there is a kind of *privatization* of community development. In the context of structural adjustment and the economic crisis, it has become increasingly important for individuals and families to have survival strategies that draw on a variety of sources of income. It appears that communities are adopting similar strategies: they are looking not only to their own residents but also to wider networks of influential people for the material and social resources needed by the community. Although there has long been involvement of hometown organizations in mobilizing resources for specific projects, there was also an expectation of assistance from government as well. In recent years, the expectation that government will be involved in development at the local level has been reduced. Instead, communities are organizing activities (such as the community-day celebrations) in an effort to mobilize resources both from their own members and from others, especially from wealthy people who can be invited and honored at such events.

The result is that local efforts are dependent on private resources (regardless of how they were generated) of individuals, who, it is hoped, will "invest" in community development activities, not only in their own hometowns but also in the communities of their friends. These donations constitute a set of social investments, especially for those who are from the local area but who reside elsewhere, as well as for their friends and acquaintances who attend events, are given honorary chieftaincy titles, and so on. These people, in turn, will expect those who invited and honored them to reciprocate in the future; when a wealthy Ijesa invites a friend from another town to his hometown celebrations, he is well aware that he will be expected to attend future events and make donations in the other man's town.

As we have seen, the amount of money that can be raised for local development in this way is, in some cases, substantial and leads to significant community projects. However, not all communities are equally successful or have equal access to resources. Rather, this sort of privatization of community development can lead to significant differentiation among communities, even neighboring communities in the same region. If one small town has a wealthy individual interested in contributing to his hometown, someone who can draw not only on his own wealth but also on the resources of others in his personal network, and another nearby town does not have such a person, there may be significant differences in what the two communities are able to accomplish. Furthermore, if one place has not only wealthy individuals but also people who act as leaders in mobilizing others from the hometown and beyond and in helping to set the development agenda, then that place can see significant local development whereas another might not.

In Ijesaland, most people would point to Iloko and Ijebu-Jesa as places that have a history of community self-help, examples where community mobilization has resulted in the completion of specific projects. Other communities, including neighboring ones, have been less successful. That does not necessarily mean that they have not tried or that they don't have equally well-meaning and committed community members. It may simply mean that those communities with less success have fewer well-off members or less extensive personal networks on which to draw.

Similar processes are suggested by evidence from other regions of West Africa. For example, a study of the connections of elite urban residents of Abidjan, Côte d'Ivoire, with their hometown demonstrates that successful families used their position in Abidjan to benefit their place of origin. "The places of origin constitute privileged places to which are directed state and private resources. A new generation of elite has privileged the villages while investing financial and symbolic capital there" (my translation from Dubresson 1993: 283). At the same time, Alain Dubresson states, the villages receiving these resources have become better financed and have more "modern" facilities than other areas, including cities. David Pratten's study of migrant associations in Mali describes one association "sponsored by prominent commercial interests" including one important family; between 1981 and 1992 projects in the market center and surrounding villages represented by that association included "the construction of additional classrooms for five schools, a health center with dispensary, maternity ward and laboratory, an electrification program, a post office, four wells, two water towers, and two dams. Together, these projects represented a total investment of [U.S.$6.9 million]. Of this, 91 percent was generated by the migrant community" (1996a: 62–63). On the one hand, this type of development is impressive and highly significant. On the other hand, it is not likely that every community or region in Mali is benefiting in the same way. The result of such self-help development efforts is likely to be a highly uneven spread of the benefits of local development.

In Ijesaland, there have been some attempts to overcome the disparities among communities in the region. The Ijesa Solidarity Group devoted a great deal of its efforts to advocating regional development projects rather than projects that would benefit only the city of Ilesa or other specific communities. ISG's leaders recognized that many people from outside Ilesa felt that their communities had been discriminated against in the past and believed that locating specific projects in other places would help overcome some of the historical differences. Other than holding meetings outside of Ilesa, however, the ISG has not yet been successful in actually implementing any projects that would have regional benefits.

In many ways, Ijesa communities are engaged in exactly the kinds of efforts that have been advocated as being key to the development process: self-help, local development, and participation. The fact that such approaches to development can be beneficial is not questioned. As a study of self-reliant local development in South Africa points out, efforts of this type "reinforce the ... argument ... that there is scope for a new paradigm of development which draws upon local experience, and does not rely on imposed goals and practices. In order to succeed, such approaches need to be rooted in the culture, ideals and mindsets of the groups engaged in the development process" (Binns and Nel 1999: 406). In fact, one could argue that the ways in which Ijesas go about local hometown development efforts have lessons for people in other parts of the world, including the United States, where there is much less direct involvement of people in local community development.[11] At the same time, the question needs to be raised of how local self-help efforts affect overall development. What are the implications for large-scale development? Will many different communities working on their own community development efforts lead to changes in the region or nation? Or do these efforts become very localized and essentially parochial? In what ways do hometown development efforts connect with state and national efforts, and how do they relate to the government's role in development?[12]

One possible result would be for approaches and mechanisms at the local level to influence national government policies on development (Rahman 1993: 169). Ideally, this would probably mean cooperation and collaboration between government agencies and local groups. In some cases, local organizations, or groups of organizations, seem to be able to function effectively as intermediary organizations, working with the government or working within policy frameworks that encourage decentralization and local efforts (Bratton 1990; Pratten 1996a). But local initiatives can be co-opted and overwhelmed by government involvement; Taylor argues that in some cases local development efforts succeed because they remain "invisible" to those outside (1992: 250–251). When outside forces, both governmental and nongovernmental, become involved in local efforts, those in the local community may lose control of the decisionmaking process.

The problem in the long run, however, is that local communities are inevitably limited in the resources to which they have access. One of the people most involved in local development in Ijesaland brought this to my attention in one conversation. I was commenting on how much he and others in his community were doing with their own resources. He disagreed with my underlying premise—that such local initiatives were the best approach to development. He pointed out that there really are not many resources for development in Nigeria without the government. In other words, it may well be true that government cannot do everything alone. But the converse is also true: communities alone cannot carry out all the development that is needed. Ultimately there needs to be a balance between access to external resources, including those provided by government, and local initiative and direction. Ijesa leaders tend to be quite realistic about this, lobbying government officials for assistance in efforts such as road-building and water supply while simultaneously going forward with a variety of local projects. There continues to be pragmatism based on an expectation that government should in fact provide certain types of public goods but with the knowledge that frequently it does not.[13]

Civil Society and Ethnicity

As Chapters 7 and 9 demonstrate, the economic and political crises of the 1990s have helped to reemphasize the importance of local connections, and of maintaining one's base at home, for Ijesas and other Nigerians. As hometown organizations and development efforts continue to be crucial sites for local action, what are the implications for the larger society? Are these associations and activities indicative of the "vitality of civil society" (Agbaje 1990: 24)? Or do they represent an increase in the "ethnicization" of politics (Nyamnjoh and Rowlands 1998: 325) that in the long run is detrimental to social and political organization? Ijesas themselves have on occasion noted this problem, calling attention to the "tribalism" involved in locally based organization. Yet the hometown is, as we have seen, a place to which people have strong ties and where people feel that they are able to accomplish something. On the one hand, the rich associational activities found among the Ijesa suggest that there is indeed a vibrant civil society at the local level; on the other hand, the identities that help produce strong community involvement and participation also help to shape notions of the separation of those communities from others of differing ethnic identities.

Civil society became a sort of code phrase for a wide range of associational and citizen activity in the late 1980s and 1990s, not only in Africa but also elsewhere in the world. Political scientists analyzing political processes realized that much political activity occurred at levels other than the state, or formal government; activists in areas of the world ranging from Eastern Europe and the former Soviet Union to South Africa realized that a major aspect of democracy is the participation of citizens. The question of civil society was also associated with discussion of *civic engagement* not only in emerging democracies but also in countries such as the United States (e.g., Putnam 1993, 1995). The organization CIVICUS: World Alliance for Citizen Participation formed as a result of "the emergence of a global civil society and the opportunities this opens for the democratization of global economic mechanisms and political structures" (de Oliveira and Tandon 1994a: ix). From the point of view of those involved, "Citizen action is as multidimensional as the diversity of human endeavors. It may be local or global, small or massive, permanent or ephemeral, highly dramatic or almost invisible, confrontational or collaborative, spontaneous or organized, promoted by associations of like-minded individuals or by large civic movements" (de Oliveira and Tandon 1994b: 2).

Adigun Agbaje makes clear some of the impetus for the focus on civil society in Africa: against a background of poor performance by the state, there is a "(re)discovery of the vitality of civil society and the resourcefulness of non-state voluntary action and associational life on the continent" (1990: 24). As Michael Bratton has argued, "Associational life occurs in arenas beyond state control and influence ... and has an independent effect upon economy and society, as well as upon the formation, consolidation, and performance of the state itself" (1989: 426). A wide range of organizations and institutions are included in considerations of civil society. For example, CIVICUS (1994) summarizes activities from all areas of the world, ranging from organizations such as community-based groups and formal NGOs in Africa to the very broad set of organizations that receive tax-exempt status as philanthropic organizations in the United States. A publication bringing together brief descriptions of African civil-society organizations includes reports from trade unions, women's organizations, rural associations, and human rights organizations, among others (Sandbrook and Halfani 1993). In proposing a research agenda on civil society in Africa, Bratton likewise calls attention to the broad range of associations—from "ethnic development associations and old boys' networks," to "nongovernmental voluntary associations" including churches, to occupational and professional organizations including "not only industrial workers but market women, taxi drivers, and small farmers" (1989: 426).

Nevertheless, much of the subsequent analysis of civil-society organizations in Africa has focused on those that operate at national levels, including trade unions, journalists, human rights organizations, and formal NGOs. For example, Bratton focuses on what he terms "lead institutions" in civil society—Christian churches and labor unions—because of their "prominent size, density, and scope" (1994: 66–67). Others have argued that just because there are associations does not necessarily mean there is civil society (Harbeson 1994; Gyimah-Boadi 1994). As Victor Azarya has pointed out, there has been a tendency to exclude from civil society those associations with a "primordial" base, such as ethnic associations, "perhaps in order to keep kinship and primordial ties away from the civil space as much as possible." But as he suggests, many other organizations that are included, such as trade unions and professional organizations, "also defend very particular interests of specific sectors in society," raising the question of why some institutions are included and others are not (1994: 94–95).

In contrast, others have taken an approach to civil society that considers associations not in terms of whether they are small or large, formal or informal, but rather in terms of the ways in which people connect to them and their importance as a basis for social action. For example, Aili Tripp argues that women's organizations in Tanzania, many of which are small and informal, are creating "new arenas for political action" (1994: 166; see also Trager and Osinulu 1991; Soetan 1995). Likewise, research on hometown associations has demonstrated their importance as a basis for political action, both in cooperation with the state and as a form of activity replacing the state (Barkan, McNulty, and Ayeni 1991; see also Honey and Okafor 1998; Osaghae 1994).

If the concept of civil society is to be useful in understanding African society, this broader perspective must be used. The crucial question, in my view, is this: What are the organizations and activities in which people participate and through which they expect to be able to accomplish political and social objectives? As we have seen in this book, those organizations and activities associated with the hometown are among the ones having the greatest importance for Ijesas. Although hometown associations may be the most visible aspects of those connections, they are not by any means the only ones. Other activities, such as the organization of community-day celebrations, also represent important aspects of civil-society activity (Trager 1992). In what ways should these organizations and activities be considered part of civil society?

First, hometown-based activities and organizations have long been one way in which local people have sought to influence government in order to affect the distribution of public goods; in other words, they function as lobbies for local interests. They are intermediaries between local communities and all levels of government (Barkan, McNulty, and Ayeni 1991; McNulty and Lawrence 1996). We have observed numerous instances of such lobbying efforts: speeches at community-day celebrations requesting the government to improve the roads or water supply; delegations from the Ijesa Solidarity Group to advocate the formation of Osun State, with Ilesa as the new state capital; and meetings of hometown organizations that took positions on chieftaincy conflicts and sent delegations to state government leaders about those conflicts.[14] To some extent, the lobbying efforts may have been less visible during the research period, especially in the later years of the Abacha regime, as Ijesa leaders and organizations perceived that they were not likely to get many benefits from that government. Even then, however, some lobbying efforts continued.

Second, hometown-based activities also function to provide public goods for people and their communities—the self-help role that is considered at length above. As Eghosa Osaghae has argued in his analysis of large ethnically based unions of Igbo and Yoruba in the northern Nigerian city of Kano, these associations function as "providers of alternative public goods in situations where the state fails to provide them, or of complementary public goods where the state's provision is inadequate" (1998: 120). In recent years in Ijesa communities, the self-help efforts have had renewed emphasis as a result of the larger economic and political crises; as we have seen, many people felt that it was even more important during the period of structural adjustment (and lack of resources from the state) to contribute to hometown development efforts.

Third, these activities and organizations are ones in which local people have a voice. As Joel Barkan et al. (1991) pointed out, "Hometown associations have emerged as one of the few institutions at the community level which enjoy a high level of legitimacy in the eyes of the local populace" (p. 480). But it is not only the associations that have this legitimacy; so does the wide range of associated hometown-based activities, such as community-day celebrations and other ceremonies. This is not meant to romanticize the hometown, or to suggest that hometowns are homogenous organizations with no divisions or conflicts. That is clearly not the case, as is evident from the discussion in Chapter 9. Yet despite those divisions and conflicts, the hometown does represent for many—including those at home and those away—a place where their participation is both expected and welcomed. Hometown institutions are ones in which men and women, elders and younger people, educated and uneducated, can play a role and have some sort of say.

At the same time, they are also institutions and activities where elites—well-educated, relatively well-off, and usually residing outside the community—have played a particularly central role in articulating the needs of the community and setting the local development agenda. Dwayne Woods has argued in his analysis of hometown associations in Côte d'Ivoire that the urban elite has been instrumental in establishing these organizations and that the associations became vehicles for the reassertion of ethnicity in Ivoirian politics and that "they also served as a means for different social groups to have some impact on the distribution and redistribution of economic resources" (1994:471). In Côte d'Ivoire, as Woods shows, the political context is particularly important: The introduction of multiparty elections affected the roles played by associations, as they became the "locus of competition by urban elites in their struggle to gain a clientele base"; the result was increased competition within associations. Similarly, Francis Nyamnjoh and Michael Rowlands show how the changing political context in Cameroon has transformed the roles of regionally and ethnically based associations led by the elite. They argue that these associations were primarily directed toward cultural programs and self-help in the 1980s but that with "multi-partyism and the rise of oppositional politics" elite associations have tended "to reinvent or rework ethnic loyalties as part of the political mobilisation of regional support" (1998: 324).[15] Unlike Woods, however, they argue that in Cameroon the transformation associated with political change is helping to "subvert urban 'civil society' into familiar forms of ethnically defined patrimonialism" (1998: 334–335).

Clearly, the context in which hometown associations and other hometown-based activities takes place is important in affecting the ways in which elite leaders mobilize and work with those based at home (see also Barkan 1994). During the period in which the research in Ijesaland took place, leaders, under an increasingly repressive military government, emphasized the nonpartisan and nonpolitical character of their organizations and activities. But it was also clear during the brief period of elections in the early 1990s that organizations and hometowns sought the support of elected government officials, and no doubt some leaders would have used their support at home as a base for entering politics themselves. Many others, however, have become disillusioned with party politics in general. Even as party politics and elections reappear on the local scene, it is likely that many of those active in Ijesa hometowns will continue to avoid direct involvement in them.

It is also clear that hometown organizations and activities change over time in response to external forces as well as the interests of their members. In Ijesaland, the Ijesa Solidarity Group is a particularly good example of this. Clearly an elite organization with members both at home and away, it originally formed as a lobbying organization to work for the establishment of Osun State. A few years later it had been transformed into an organization with several goals, one of the most important being local development. Yet at the same time that the leaders emphasized their concern with Ijesaland, they also talked about the development of Osun State and even beyond. Such "local" and regional organizations, in other words, have the potential to become important in wider political and economic arenas, not simply as "ethnic" associations representing their own local interests.[16]

At the same time, the Ijesa Solidarity Group is also an example of an organization in which people come together because they see themselves as having a common identity, because they are all "Ijesa." Some have come to the group to complain about discrimination, especially within the new state government. This was increasingly a focus of discussion at ISG meetings in the late 1990s, whereas earlier it had not been. Likewise, nearly all the organizations and activities in specific communities are restricted to those people who claim the place as their hometown. There are a few exceptions to this: People in Iloko who are not from there state that they participate in community events; and members of the Egbe Atunluse point with pride to the fact that one of their leaders in the past was not Ijesa (Ifaturoti and Orolugbagbe 1992: 14). In many respects, then, the processes occurring in Ijesaland are similar to those elsewhere, which Geschiere and Gugler have described as the "politics of belonging" represented by "increasing obsession with 'autochthony' ... in which the village and the region assume new importance as a crucial source of power at the national level" (1998b: 310).

Studies in Cameroon demonstrate a variety of ways in which the "politics of belonging" is manifested in different regions and among different ethnic groups. Nyamnjoh and Rowlands argue that in the Grassfield chiefdoms of Cameroon "the overriding concern is with maintaining cultural integrity and identity in the belief that any weakening of identity would result in dissolution and absorption by powerful outside forces" (1998: 334). In the southwestern region of Cameroon, in contrast, the elites "espouse a more modernising discourse, pointing out that the people of the south-west have always been more developed economically, more receptive to change." They argue that "in their different ways both discourses sustain an idea of identity that resists incorporation into a larger totality whilst differing as regards the degree of exclusion or inclusion" (1998: 334). Cyprian Fisiy and Mitzi Goheen demonstrate the continuing emphasis on chiefship and titles in one chiefdom, Nso', where "identity and power have increasingly come to be centred on the Fon, the palace and 'traditional' institutions of government" (1998: 383). They describe the importance of "neotraditional" titles, which, like honorary chieftaincy titles among the Ijesa, are not hereditary titles but are given to the urban elite "in recognition of their contribution to the general welfare of their home area" (1998: 388). For the Nso', these titles have become a key symbol of their links with their home area. In each of these cases, the connections with home—the importance of maintaining a "traditional" ethnic identity—are shaped by larger social forces. As Fisiy and Goheen argue, "'Tribalism' can be thus seen not as an atavistic or irrational impulse but rather as a quest for meaning, power and security which is clearly rational in the current national political economy" (1998: 398).

The fact that this is the case elsewhere becomes evident when one considers how notions of common origin and identity form in relation to the larger context. In northern Ghana, for example, where "traditional" social organization is one of fuzzy boundaries, contemporary youth associations "appeal to a relatively vaguely defined common origin" (Lentz 1995: 407) in their efforts to mobilize as pressure groups for their own region and/or ethnic group. Beyond West Africa, Pratten shows how the "return to the roots" campaign of the government of Sudan has been "subject to local 'translations'" with migrant associations "adapting to the state's ideological, political and economic framework" (1996b: 27).

In each of these cases, the connections with home place, region, or ethnic group are traditional only in the sense that the place is one that can be claimed as a place of origin, a place recognized by both those at home and away, with recognized obligations and responsibilities. But the particular notion of "home" and of how to carry out those obligations and responsibilities varies with context. The home place may indeed be a specific village or town or city, as it seems to be for most Ijesas at present. But it can also be reshaped into a larger ethnic or regional identity, as seems to be occurring with both Yorubas and Igbos living in the northern Nigerian city of Kano. There, according to Osaghae, both groups have formed "centralized ethnic organizations ... that run along the lines of traditional 'empires', complete with kings and chiefs" (1998: 111; see also Osaghae 1994). This might seem to be a traditional form of organization for the Yoruba, who do have traditional kings and chiefs, but it is clearly not traditional for the Igbo; most Igbo communities in the past did not have kings or chiefs and are known for their relatively nonhierarchical structures. But in contemporary Nigeria, panethnic organizations, complete with kings and chiefs, have become a common feature of both political and ceremonial life. For example, in 1997 an Igbo Day celebration took place in Lagos, organized by the Igbo Council of Chiefs (*Post Express Wired*, September 25, 1997).

If ethnic and local institutions are placed in opposition to civil society, it becomes easy to argue that these are institutions to which people are connected because of their traditions and identities. From this, it is then easy to think of traditions and identities as immutable, as fixed in the minds and symbols of local people and cultures, forming the basis for their actions. In contrast, if ethnic and local institutions are seen as a part of a broader set of institutions and cultural constructs within which people act, then traditions and identities are seen as changing, both responding to broader social contexts and helping to shape those contexts. In some of the literature on civil society, ethnically based and local institutions are described as "primordial," implying a separation of these institutions from those of civil society and the state (Young 1994: 44–45; Azarya 1994: 92–95).[17] If *primordial* means something that is traditional, or "aboriginal," as in some dictionary definitions, it should be clear that contemporary associations and activities based on common home origin or ethnic identity are not primordial. True, they draw on symbols and ideas of tradition, whether the chieftaincy titles found in Nso', or the ideas of common origins found in Ghanaian associations, or the idea of a common ethnic identity among the Igbo in Kano.

In Ijesaland, aspects of all of these kinds of tradition are found. Chieftaincy titles are given to honor people, and these have meaning for some, although other Ijesas would argue that chieftaincy titles are no longer important. Most people identify with their hometown and act in terms of that identity, yet some people identify themselves as "Ijesa" rather than in terms of a specific hometown. Organizations like the Ijesa Solidarity Group also argue for Ijesa unity rather than a specific local identity. And in some circumstances, still other units form the basis for local identity: the LGA as well as the state (especially since the formation of Osun State). Clearly, these latter sources of local identity have no basis at all in "tradition," yet they operate in ways similar to the hometown and regional identities. Which particular unit and identity is selected in a particular instance depends a great deal on the changing contexts and contemporary structural realities in which people operate.

As Pratten has argued with regard to migrant associations in Sudan and

Mali, the combination of functions of these organizations—in which they both preserve traditions and promote modernity—enables them to "retain their legitimacy and dynamism, since they function as social, funeral and saving clubs and can in addition become job-finders, urban homes, substitute families, forums for discussion, springboards for political careers, and vanguards of rural development" (1996b: 74; see also Pratten n.d.). To argue that hometown-based organizations and activities are not part of civil society, or that because they are based in traditional and ethnic identities they are not key institutions for local people, would be to neglect a major dimension of political and social activity, one with great meaning for most involved. These activities are not separate from the broader social and political structures of Nigerian society but rather are interconnected with them.

Overall, the Ijesa situation is one where there are complex tensions and contradictions, where the links to home are a crucial basis for action and identity in contemporary society. But they are not the only sources of identity or the only bases for action. There are a variety of cross-cutting ties, both for the elites as well as for others. Most elite Ijesas are members of several organizations, ranging from church groups, to occupational and professional groups, to those based on school attendance. People move back and forth among these organizations, drawing on them for their identity and acting in concert with their fellow members, most of whom are *not* from the same hometown or region. As noted in Chapter 4, the calendar of any particular individual will include meetings and celebrations in connection with all of these identities, as well as with the hometown. And the varying sets of affiliation come together for significant occasions: when Oba Olashore was installed as *oba* of Iloko in 1997, one of the first groups to herald his achievement was the old-boy association of the secondary school that he had attended; that same afternoon, members of the association, few (if any) of whom are from Iloko, put up a plaque at the palace in Iloko in honor of Oba Olashore, their former president. As this example makes clear, it is not possible to speak of an individual Ijesa only in terms of his or her Ijesa identity or hometown identity. Much more significant are the range of affiliations on which people can draw and in which they participate. This is true of those residing at home as well, for whom trade and market associations, as well as religious organizations, are among the key sources of affiliation and identity.

In the long run, then, the importance of hometown and local affiliation for identity and action will depend to a large extent on the degree to which people can operate both locally and nationally. As Geschiere and Gugler suggest, the "connection [with home place] is resilient, highly variable, with dynamics of its own, and not just dependent on personal choice. On the contrary, there seem to be structural reasons why it remains crucial in the struggle over access to resources and, increasingly, over the definition of citizenship" (1998b: 315). To the degree that there is insecurity away from home and a sense that one's "citizenship" outside the home area is not assured, then local bases of identity and action will become increasingly important and may well result in the more negative aspects of ethnic identity—a renewed emphasis on one's own ethnic group, or local group, to the exclusion of others. But if people feel that they have access to resources, as well as the opportunity to pursue their own interests in wider arenas—living and working where they want, participating in local political processes, educating their children, and so on—then their local identities can continue to be the basis for many of the positive efforts that have been encouraged in hometown communities: a genuine concern for the development of the local community.

Yoruba Culture: "Our Tradition Is Very Modern"

Finally, we turn to the cultural context of hometown connections and local development. How do morality and culture shape obligations and expectations regarding hometown activities? How do ceremonial and symbolic activities provide meaningful arenas for Ijesa participation at home? To consider these questions, it is useful to examine some fundamental ideas about the continuity of Yoruba culture and its ability to incorporate new elements while maintaining core ideas.

Olabiyi Yai quotes Yoruba artists as saying "our tradition is very modern" and argues that this statement has meaning only in English, not in the Yoruba language, because "innovation is implied in the Yoruba idea of tradition" (1994: 113). Likewise, in a consideration of contemporary Yoruba divination practices, F. Niyi Akinnaso (1995) argues that the Yoruba successfully incorporate change and creativity while reaffirming "cultural certainties." Rather than place the notions of *continuity* and *change* or *traditional* and *modern* in opposition to one another, this perspective helps us to consider Yoruba culture in terms of change within continuity, of innovation and creativity as part of tradition. Examples of this pervade contemporary Yoruba society and culture, from religious practices (Barber 1991; Drewal 1992; Olupona 1991) to music (Waterman 1990) to textiles (Renne 1995). Whereas Aronson suggests that the acceptance of much that is new and "modern" could be understood as an example of *social* change combined with *cultural* continuity (1978: 187–189), others emphasize the incorporative features of both Yoruba culture and social practices. As Christopher Waterman puts it, "The incorporative nature of much Yoruba music is but one aspect of a more extensive culture pattern.... The Yoruba have in general been willing to adopt new ideas and practices, provided they prove efficacious" (1990: 15). Elisha Renne shows how the Bunu Yoruba, in the northern part of Yorubaland, accepted imported cloth (first brought to the area by Ijesa *osomaalo* traders in the 1930s): "By wearing clothing made of machine-woven cloth, Bunu villagers are showing *olaju*, sophisticated and 'civilized' behavior as Nigerians and as citizens of the world." But at the same time, they continue to use certain types of hand-woven cloth in specific contexts. For them, she argues, *olaju* means "enlightened progress," which must "include respect for traditions of the past" (1995: 188–189).

This perspective is equally useful in understanding the importance of hometown connections, the continuing obligations and expectations of maintaining ties with one's hometown, as well as the many innovations in the ways those ties are created and reinforced in contemporary Ijesa communities. The incorporation and integration of new features while maintaining traditions can be observed in a range of situations—from the actions of individuals, to the roles of traditional rulers, to ritual and ceremonial occasions. There is no aspect of Ijesa life that is not in some way "modern" and connected to the larger world beyond Ijesaland. At the same time, most Ijesas continue to see themselves as Ijesa, with connections to a particular hometown, and continue to try to fulfill cultural expectations and obligations with regard to that hometown.

At the individual level, migration out of Ijesaland is combined with maintenance of ties to family, kin networks, and community. The obligation to come home to bury one's father, and eventually to be buried oneself, has not changed; neither has the expectation that individuals will demonstrate their commitment to maintaining their "wealth in people" by being generous. Much like the Ijebu Yoruba described by Aronson in the 1970s, "the idiom of kinship and community remains a vital source of norms for aid and support...; high value still obtains to the proper expenditure of income upon children, friends, followers, and in general upon people ..." (1978: 188). This is true not only of the elite, or "big men," for whom efforts to maintain a network of supporters is particularly important. It is true to some degree for everyone, within limits. People recognize the differences between the ability of wealthy individuals to make contributions and that of an ordinary farmer or trader. But the expectation is there nonetheless—to do what is possible within one's capacity. We see this in the remittances that individuals provide to family and kin, with nearly everyone sending money or goods to kin at home. We also see this in the donations that nearly everyone makes through the organizations to which they belong for community development efforts.

At the same time, the specific content of these obligations and expectations has been modified as circumstances change. It is still highly valued to build a house at home, and well-off individuals generally do so. But it is also recognized that not everyone can do that, especially in today's economic conditions. More emphasis is now placed on contributions to community-wide development projects; small amounts donated for specific efforts are valued, encouraged, and expected even while it is recognized that only wealthy people can make the large contributions necessary to actually carry out a project. The types of projects undertaken are also changing. Town halls and *obas'* palaces remain a key focus, as they have been in other areas of Yorubaland (Berry 1985), but there has been an increasing emphasis on infrastructure (e.g., water) and economic development (e.g., community banks). For individual Ijesas, this range of activities is all part of the same underlying logic—that one has obligations to one's hometown that can be fulfilled in a variety of ways.

Acceptance of this underlying logic does not, of course, imply that there is consensus on how to fulfill obligations, or that everyone fulfills all the expectations, or even that it is possible to do so. On the contrary, there are often conflicts and differences of opinion over the goals of hometown organizations, as we have seen in the lengthy discussions within the Ijesa Solidarity Group about how to undertake economic development efforts. Individuals have limits on what they can provide, either to family or to the community; wealthy people, in particular, find that they have to strike a balance among the varying demands on their resources. Conflict can result when some in the community believe that others are not doing all they can or that they are favoring one faction over another. Nor do all projects that are undertaken succeed. Yet despite conflicts and problems in carrying out local efforts, there continues to be substantial agreement about the importance of helping the hometown. There are many calls for "sons and daughters abroad" to come home and help their community; even those who do not respond to these requests would never argue that these requests are wrong or culturally inappropriate.

The role of traditional rulers—chiefs and kings—is another area where innovation has become incorporated into tradition, although with considerable disagreement about the degree of innovation that is accepted. Traditional rulers continue to be important symbols of their communities, including cities like Ilesa as well as smaller towns and villages; they are also, in general, influential and powerful individuals. As elsewhere in West Africa, honorary chieftaincy titles (what Fisiy and Goheen [1998] call "neotraditional" titles) are given to key individuals to recognize their contributions. At the same time, there are differences of opinion about how much emphasis is, or should be, placed on traditional rulers in contemporary society, with a few people arguing that they shouldn't exist at all. But the vast majority continues to view chiefs and kings as having key roles to play. Most of the conflict and controversy is generated by disagreements over who should play these roles and how the roles should be enacted. There are constraints and boundaries; if a king or chief goes beyond these boundaries, then he is likely to be criticized and challenged. For example, an *oba* who is seen as acting only for his own personal interest and gain, and not for the good of the community, is criticized, as is one who makes too much of his power and influence in his personal relationships with others. But within those constraints and boundaries, there is considerable room for innovation. It has long been the case that those selected as chiefs and *obas* are people who are viewed as successful, usually those with education and wealth and, increasingly, people with extensive networks and resources outside the community.

The result is that the people selected for these positions are increasingly people who have been living outside the community and who may need to continue to spend considerable periods of time away in order to continue to be successful. Some communities have found ways to accommodate these needs. In Iwoye, for example, I was told that townspeople expected the new *oba* to continue his profession, which required him to spend time in Lagos. Innovations have also been made in the incorporation of religious beliefs and ritual so that it is now possible for Christians and Muslims to become *obas* and chiefs. Perhaps most important, the core idea that *obas* and chiefs represent and symbolize the community, and that they should act for the good of the community, has provided room for some to play significant roles in local community development. The *oba* of Ido-Oko (see Chapter 8) had initiated several projects in his small town. In Iloko, we have seen the extent to which Oba Olashore contributed to local development, both before and after becoming *oba*. Such traditional rulers fulfill the "traditional" demands of their positions by attempting to bring "modern" development to their communities.

Finally, celebrations and rituals provide room for considerable creativity while still reaffirming core ideas in Ijesa culture. Numerous ceremonies and celebrations take place to mark key events and successes in an individual's life: birthdays, funerals, award ceremonies, and so on. The success that is honored in these ceremonies is one that has taken place in the modern world. The birthday celebration for Lawrence Omole emphasized his success as a businessman; the award ceremonies described in Chapter 6 noted professional, educational, and national activities in honoring university professors, diplomats, and many others. But the key point in each of these ceremonies was that those who were honored had used their success not only for themselves but also for the good of the wider community, including not only Ijesaland but also Nigeria as a whole. Rituals, including the traditional (such as the installation of an *oba*) and the new (such as the community-day celebrations), incorporate key symbols that draw on Yoruba tradition as well as on new elements. In the events involved in the installation and coronation of Oba Olashore, for example, tradition was followed when the *oba*-elect stayed in the house of one of the other chiefs for a specified time period, although the length of time was modified from traditional practice. But accommodation to the *oba*'s Christian religion took place, and an entirely new ritual was incorporated when an "anointing ceremony" took place in a church shortly before the installation.

Community-day celebrations are a new tradition, or an "invented" ritual, in Ijesaland. But their success is determined in part by their ability to incorporate and integrate a range of symbols and elements. A brief recapitulation of the description of the second Iloko Day, in Chapter 2, helps to demonstrate how this has been carried out effectively:

> The narrow, partially paved road led out of Ijebu-Jesa toward Iloko, past the large cement-block building housing the headquarters of the Oriade local government offices. On the outskirts of Iloko, a large banner was strung over the road, announcing "Welcome to Iloko Day." At the crossroads in the center of the town, next to the palace, Mercedes and Peugeot 504 cars were turning to enter the grounds of the primary school. Talking drummers welcomed the visiting officials and other guests as they left their cars, while the local Boys Brigade band played on their trumpets and other instruments, creating a cacophony of disparate sounds. At one end of the primary school grounds, viewing stands were set up, with two rows of large upholstered chairs for the most important guests. The governor of Osun State, Alhaji Isiaka Adeleke, arrived in his car with sirens sounding, and stepped out, resplendent in a flowing turquoise *agbada*. Several ministers of the federal government followed, as well as the deputy governor of the state and the wives of both the governor and deputy governor. They were joined by *obas* from surrounding communities, all in white or brightly colored *agbadas* and with long necklaces of coral-colored beads and beaded walking sticks signifying their status as traditional rulers. All were seated on the upholstered chairs, under the brightly colored canopy....
>
> Groups of townspeople began arriving at the school grounds, taking their seats in metal chairs set up under canopies along the two sides of the field. Local chiefs—elderly men in dark *agbadas*—sat on one side. Banners announcing some of the local organizations—the Federation of Iloko-Ijesa Students Union, the Iloko Women Progressive Elites, and others—identified the location of members of those groups along the other side. Other visitors were seated on plastic chairs behind the government officials and traditional rulers....
>
> Meanwhile, the Boys Brigade band and a group from the Girl Guides continued to play. To the right of the master of ceremonies was displayed a large model of the community hall to be built with the funds that were to be raised as part of the day's activities.
>
> At 11:15 A.M., the national anthem was sung, signaling the official start of the festivities. Then the master of ceremonies announced that they would sing the Iloko anthem.

Here, we see the combination of the Boys Brigade band and the talking drummers; the governor and the local chiefs; the Iloko anthem and the Nigerian national anthem. Each of these elements is integrated with the others to create a festive celebration designed to celebrate the town, bring its members back home, and raise funds for community development. Furthermore, the successful "new tradition," like older traditions, was not static; in succeeding years, there were a variety of modifications, such as the decision to schedule the day at another time of year, to coincide with a traditional ritual from the past. Ijesas do not maintain primordial traditions at all cost. Neither do they give up all things Ijesa in order to be "modern." They remain Ijesa by becoming modern, drawing on a variety of symbols and practices from both their own society and culture and from others, and make them theirs.

Final Observations: An Ongoing Process

In Chapter 1 I suggested that the events and issues discussed in this book are part of an ongoing, unfinished process, one that I have been privileged to observe over many years. In 1999 and early 2000 I had two opportunities to return to Nigeria and to meet again with some of the key participants in these events and activities. This was a highly significant period in Nigeria. In May 1999 President Olusegun Obasanjo had taken office as the newly elected president of the country. In October, when I made my first visit after the elections, many Nigerians expressed renewed optimism about the future prospects of the country. A few months later, during my second visit, some of that optimism had already dissipated, particularly as incidents of local ethnic and religious conflict became more common in many regions of the country. It was also clear that wide-ranging economic problems had been left by the outgoing military regime and that it would take a long time and much effort to achieve significant economic improvement.

People in Ijesaland shared the sentiments of those throughout the country. They were pleased that the military rule had ended, but many years of disappointment had led them to be skeptical of any government. Most people continued to focus their involvement at the local level. In the Ijesa communities discussed here, the return to civilian government did not create any dramatic short-term changes. Rather, the activities, processes, and conflicts that were evident in the 1990s were still apparent. Hometown organizations continued to work on local development efforts in specific communities. The Ijesa Solidarity Group was going through its own process of transition, under new leadership and with younger members. Chieftaincy conflicts within the region continued to be a major concern, and with the formation of the new Ijesa North Traditional Council there seemed to be increased division between those in Ilesa and those in other towns, especially those in the north.

The central importance of hometown affiliation is not in question.

Recent observations suggest that the maintenance of hometown ties may be strengthening rather than weakening and spreading beyond the borders of Nigeria. During a conversation in March 2000, the Owa Obokun of Ilesa told me that he had recently paid a visit to Ijesas living in the United States and that he hoped to follow up with U.S.-based groups interested in the development of Ijesaland. It is likely that in the future we will see transnational as well as internal linkages of Ijesas with their home communities, indicating that both internal and international migration can result in similar patterns of ties linking people across spatial boundaries. There is also evidence that members of younger generations of Ijesas share the interests of their parents in maintaining connections with home. Those who are now in their thirties and forties are beginning to be concerned about their hometowns, to come home for major social events and participate in local organizations and activities. The wedding ceremony of the son and daughter of prominent Ijesas brought many young Ijesa elites home for a weekend in early 2000. Whether their ties will be as intense as those of their fathers' generations will likely depend not only on their own preferences but also on what happens in Nigeria during the next few years.

Whether the self-help efforts of Ijesa organizations and communities will lead to development in the region is also open to question. Have recent events led away from local and regional development? One senior Ijesa man suggested during an interview in October 1999 that recent events in the region meant that Ijesaland was on a downward trajectory, away from development. Perhaps the situation is best illustrated by the Yoruba term quoted in Chapter 7—*itesiwaju*. As described there, *itesiwaju* means to inch forward, moving slowly toward attaining one's goal. If we approach the question from this perspective, then we can argue that each new effort may represent a small step, which may or may not be successful in the long term. But overall, some of these efforts—a water tank in one community, a women's project, a community bank—are leading to improvement in the lives of the people of Ijesaland.

Notes

1. This statement has now been quoted in a number of contexts: in my own article (Trager 1998); by Aidan Southall (1988) on the basis of my relating it to him; and in Osaghae's study of Igbo organizations in Kano (1994: 15). Perhaps it has now been overused, but I would suggest rather that the statement strikes a chord with those doing research on rural-urban linkages and hometown organizations, as it reflects the central concern of those whose activities we are studying. Therefore, with thanks to Dr. Akinnaso, who is both an anthropologist and an individual with ties to his own hometown, Idanre in Ondo State, I once again draw on this quote.

2. It is true that many Ijesas would characterize all Ijesa towns, including

Ilesa, as "villages" in the sense that they are places without many modern ameni-ties. I would argue, however, that it is useful to keep the indigenous concept of city in mind, as well as to note the important urban changes that have occurred in medium-sized Yoruba cities such as Ilesa (see Trager 1985a).

3. Some of the difference between my perspective and that of Denzer and Mbanefoh is based on the definitions of *hometown association*; in the volume to which Denzer and Mbanefoh contributed, the only hometown associations studied are those that are considered "apex" or "umbrella" organizations, which bring together a number of organizations into one community-wide association (see Okafor and Honey 1998: 10). In fact, Mbanefoh's own case study in the same vol-ume contradicts this perspective by including other women's associations beyond the "apex" organization (1998). These differing perspectives of the types and roles of hometown organizations are considered further in the discussion of civil society and ethnicity below.

4. The definition of community has long been problematic, with a long histo-ry of discussion and debate in the social sciences. Among the seminal contributions in recent years has been that of Benedict Anderson's concept of "imagined commu-nities" (1983). Although his focus is on the nation and nationalism, he remarks that "all communities larger than primordial villages of face-to-face contact (and per-haps even these) are imagined" (1983: 15). He goes on to point out that one can dis-tinguish among communities not by whether they are false or genuine but "by the style in which they are imagined. Javanese villagers have always known that they are connected to people they have never seen, but these ties were imagined particu-laristically—as indefinitely stretchable nets of kinship and clientship" (1983: 15–16). The Ijesa communities are similar, in that the bases for connections are largely determined by kinship. However, my emphasis here is on the actual place—the hometown—on which community is focused.

5. See Painter (1996) for examples of development problems resulting from not taking into account the movements and multiple residences of people in the Sahelian region of West Africa.

6. A few years ago, I was describing my research to a university professor and his wife in Port Harcourt. They pointed out this concern to me, noting that while it may be beneficial to villages and small towns to have the involvement of people in their hometowns, it was likely to have detrimental effects on the large cities, since people who consider their community to be their hometown would not be likely to contribute to the development of those cities, even though they actually spend most of their lives there.

7. Clearly, there are many highly sophisticated analyses of the development process, and not everyone makes these assumptions. Yet I have been struck by the extent to which assumptions are made that "development" is always something brought or imposed from outside.

8. Still, some Ijesas are so engaged. One of the most fascinating aspects of contemporary local development efforts not only in Ijesaland but also elsewhere in Nigeria is the participation of Nigerian social scientists in local community devel-opment efforts; the best known are those involved in Awe, in Oyo State (see Egbe Omo Ibile Awe 1982; Lawrence and Titilola 1998), but there are also an increasing number of Ijesas active in their hometowns who have spent many years of work on development issues elsewhere.

9. Taylor, drawing on Bratton (1990), uses the notion of *voice* to consider local organizations vis-à-vis the state; I think it is equally useful in considering the issue of the nature of participation at the community level.

10. McNulty and Lawrence (1996) provide an example in another part of Yorubaland of a situation where there was disagreement over redirection of funds from a town hall project to restoring electricity in the town; one group based outside the town refused to provide additional funds until the town hall project began again (p. 32).

11. For example, two U.S. communities to which I have personal ties of my own—Racine, Wisconsin, where I live, and Cape Cod, Massachusetts, where I spend summers—have recently begun so-called sustainable community efforts, which, among other things, are supposed to involve local community members in setting community goals for sustainable development. At a recent meeting on education as part of the Sustainable Racine effort, only eight to ten people showed up; there would almost certainly be more people in attendance at a meeting on education or other community needs in an Ijesa community.

12. In some cases, the privatization of public resources is taken to the extreme, as in the building of new capitals in the hometowns of the presidents of Côte d'Ivoire: not only did President Houphuet-Boigny make Yamassoukro, his hometown, the capital, but his successor attempted to do the same in his own hometown (see *New York Times*, January 7, 2000). Some of those interviewed by the *New York Times* reporter believe that this is the way "development" takes place and that eventually communities throughout the country will get the same benefits when they have political leaders; others recognized that in an age of multiparty politics the precedent set by Houphuet-Boigny cannot be followed. In Nigeria, former President Babangida did not make Minna, his hometown, the capital, but he did make sure that a lot of resources went there.

13. Unfortunately, even those activities of government that may seem most obviously to be public goods may cause harm to local communities. For example, most would agree that roads are something that should be provided by the government. In Nigerian communities, as elsewhere in the world, people lobby their government to provide roads to their towns. Sometimes communities engage in self-help to begin building a road, but inevitably they ask help from the government when it comes to getting the road paved. Ijesa communities have done this successfully over the years, resulting in roads that have improved access, aiding not only travel but also trade. Elsewhere in Nigeria, communities have engaged in similar efforts. Just as I was writing this, in late December 1999, I learned of the debacle that resulted in part from road construction in one community in southeastern Nigeria, Odi in Bayelsa State, in the Niger Delta. Some years earlier, I had visited Odi; the unpaved road had been built by community members and was passable by vehicles only in the dry season. For years, the village had lobbied to have the road paved. This finally occurred in 1999, linking the village to the "new Nigeria"; in November 1999 this road provided access to Nigerian military personnel who burned and razed the village, thus destroying nearly all of the individual and community self-help efforts that had taken place over many years (Miriam Isoun, personal communication; see also Africa Policy Information Center, December 23, 1999).

14. Chieftaincy positions are not formally part of the three-tiered government structure—local, state, and federal government—but since they are recognized and installed by the government, government does play a role in chieftaincy institutions, including the resolution of conflicts.

15. In passing, Nyamnjoh and Rowlands (1998: 324) call attention to the overseas networks of Cameroonian elite organizations; theirs is one of the few discussions of the increasing role of diaspora networks and the Internet in the activities of locally based associations in West Africa.

16. Lachenmann (1994) argues in a related vein in an analysis of peasant associations in Senegal, i.e., that they should be seen in the framework of "social movements" operating not only at the grassroots level but also having the potential to influence other spheres of action in the society and therefore with the potential to influence the development of civil society.

17. Both Young (1994) and Azarya (1994) refer to an earlier discussion by Ekeh (1975), in which he contrasts two publics of African politics, a "primordial public" that is "*moral and operates on the same moral imperatives as the private realm*" and a "civic public" that is "*amoral and lacks the generalized moral imperatives operative in the private realm and in the primordial public*" (Ekeh 1975: 92; italics in original). Although Ekeh recognizes that the "primordial public," including ethnic voluntary associations, is something that emerged in the context of colonialism and later postindependence politics, the term *primordial* is in itself misleading.

References

Abiola, J.D.E., J. A. Babafemi, and S.O.S. Ataiyero. 1932. *Itan Ilesa* [History of Ilesa]. Ilesa.

Adepoju, Aderanti. 1974. "Migration and Socio-Economic Links between Urban Migrants and Their Home Communities in Nigeria." *Africa* 44: 383–395.

Adepoju, Aderanti, ed. 1993. *The Impact of Structural Adjustment on the Population of Africa: The Implications for Education, Health, and Employment.* London: United Nations Population Fund in association with James Currey and Heinemann.

Africa Policy Information Center. "Nigeria: Odi Massacre Statements." December 23, 1999. An e-mail posted by Africa Policy Information Center. <www.africapolicy.org>.

Agbaje, Adigun. 1990. "In Search of Building Blocks: The State, Civil Society, Voluntary Action, and Grassroot Development in Africa." *Africa Quarterly* 30, 3/4: 24–40.

Agbaje-Williams, Babatunde, and Akinwumi Ogundiran. 1992. *Cultural Resources in Ijesaland.* Ilesa: Ijesa Cultural Foundation.

Ajifolokun II, Kabiyesi Ajayi Palmer, Oba of Ijebu-Jesa. 1991. "Address on the Occasion of the First Ijebu-Jesa Day." Program of Events of the First Ijebu-Jesa Day Celebrations, November 2, 1991.

Akinnaso, F. Niyi. 1994. "Linguistic Unification and Language Rights." *Applied Linguistics* 15, 2: 139–168.

Akinnaso, F. Niyi. 1995. "Bourdieu and the Diviner: Knowledge and Symbolic Power in Yoruba Divination." In *The Pursuit of Certainty: Religious and Cultural Formations*, ed. Wendy James. London: Routledge, pp. 234–257.

Albert, Isaac Olawale. 1999. "Ife-Modakeke Crisis." In *Community Conflicts in Nigeria: Management, Resolution, and Transformation*, ed. Onigu Otite and Isaac Olawale Albert. Ibadan: Spectrum, for Academic Associates Peaceworks, pp. 142–175.

Aluko, J. O. 1993. *Osomalo: The Early Exploits of the Ijesa Entrepreneur.* Ibadan: African Book Builders.

Amale, Steve. 1991. "The Impact of the Structural Adjustment Programme on Nigerian Workers." In *Crisis and Adjustment in the Nigerian Economy*, ed. Adebayo Olukoshi. Lagos: JAD, pp. 123–136.

Amasa, Deacon (Dr.) Dele. 1993. "A Clarion Call on Ijesa People." In the First Ijesa National Day brochure.

Anderson, Benedict. 1983. *Imagined Communities: Reflections on the Origin and Spread of Nationalism*. London: Verso.

Aronson, Dan R. 1971. "Ijebu Yoruba Urban-Rural Relationships and Class Formation." *Canadian Journal of African Studies* 5, 3: 263–279.

Aronson, Dan R. 1978. *The City Is Our Farm: Seven Migrant Ijebu Families*. Cambridge, MA: Schenkman.

Awe, Bolanle. 1993. "My Life and Times: Reflections by Dr. Lawrence Omole: A Review" (MS). Presented at the launching of the book in the Nigerian Institute of International Affairs, March 18, 1993.

Awe, Bolanle. 1995–1996. "The Importance of Historical Research for the Ijesa." In Ijesa Solidarity Group, *Launching of Ijesa Historical Research Fund, Commemorative Brochure, 1995–1996*.

Awe, Bolanle, and B. Agbaje-Williams. 1997. "Cultural Evolution and Resources in Ijesaland." In *Ijesa Year Book*. Lagos: MIJ.

Azarya, Victor. 1994. "Civil Society and Disengagement in Africa." In *Civil Society and the State in Africa*, ed. John W. Harbeson, Donald Rothchild, and Naomi Chazan. Boulder: Lynne Rienner, pp. 83–100.

Barber, Karin. 1991. *I Could Speak until Tomorrow: Oriki, Women, and the Past in a Yoruba Town*. Washington, DC: Smithsonian Institution.

Barber, Karin. 1994. "The Secretion of Oriki in the Material World." *Passages* 7: 10–13.

Barkan, Joel D. 1994. "Restructuring Modernization Theory and the Emergence of Civil Society in Kenya and Nigeria." In *Political Development and the New Realism in Sub-Saharan Africa*, ed. David E. Apter and Carl G. Rosberg. Charlottesville: University Press of Virginia, pp. 87–116.

Barkan, Joel D., Michael L. McNulty, and M.A.O. Ayeni. 1991. "'Hometown' Voluntary Associations, Local Development, and the Emergence of Civil Society in Western Nigeria." *Journal of Modern African Studies* 29, 3: 457–480.

Bartle, Philip F.W. 1981. "Cyclical Migration and the Extended Community: A West African Example." In *Frontiers in Migration Analysis*, ed. R. B. Mandal. New Delhi: Concept, pp. 105–139.

Bascom, William R. 1955. "Urbanization among the Yoruba." *American Journal of Sociology* 60: 446–454.

Bascom, William R. 1959. "Urbanism as a Traditional African Pattern." *Sociological Review* 7: 29–43.

Bastian, Misty L. 1993. "'Bloodhounds Who Have No Friends': Witchcraft and Locality in the Nigerian Popular Press." In *Modernity and Its Malcontents*, ed. Jean Comaroff and John Comaroff. Chicago: University of Chicago Press, pp. 129–166.

Bello-Imam, I. B. 1995. *An Ethnographic Survey of South Ibie Clan of Etsako West Local Government, Edo State, Nigeria*. Ibadan: Vantage.

Berry, Sara S. 1985. *Fathers Work for Their Sons: Accumulation, Mobility, and Class Formation in an Extended Yoruba Community*. Berkeley: University of California Press.

Beyond Science, n.d., volume 1 no. 1, published by CHESTRAD (the Center for Health Sciences Training, Research, and Development).

Binns, Tony, and Etienne Nel. 1999. "Beyond the Development Impasse: The Role of Local Economic Development and Community Self-Reliance in Rural South Africa." *Journal of Modern African Studies* 37, 3: 389–408.

Blunt, Peter, and D. Michael Warren. 1996. "Introduction." In *Indigenous*

Organizations and Development, ed. Peter Blunt and D. Michael Warren. London: Intermediate Technology Publications, pp. xiii–xv.

Bratton, Michael. 1989. "Beyond the State: Civil Society and Associational Life in Africa." *World Politics* 41, 3: 407–430.

Bratton, Michael. 1990. "The Politics of Government-NGO Relations in Africa." *World Development* 17, 4: 569–587.

Bratton, Michael. 1994. "Civil Society and Political Transitions in Africa." In *Civil Society and the State in Africa*, ed. John W. Harbeson, Donald Rothchild, and Naomi Chazan. Boulder: Lynne Rienner, pp. 51–81.

Callaghy, Thomas M. 1993. "Political Passions and Economic Interests: Economic Reform and Political Structure in Africa." In *Hemmed In: Responses to Africa's Economic Decline*, ed. Thomas M. Callaghy and John Ravenhill. New York: Columbia University Press, pp. 463–519.

Callaghy, Thomas M., and John Ravenhill, eds. 1993. *Hemmed In: Responses to Africa's Economic Decline*. New York: Columbia University Press.

Chambers, Robert. 1994. "The Origins and Practice of Participatory Rural Appraisal." *World Development* 22, 7: 953–969.

Chambers, Robert. 1997. *Whose Reality Counts? Putting the First Last*. London: Intermediate Technology Publications.

CIVICUS: The World Alliance for Citizen Participation. 1994. *Citizens: Strengthening Global Civil Society*. Coordinated by Miquel Darcy de Oliveira and Rajesh Tandon. Washington, DC: Civicus.

Clarke, William H. 1972. *Travels and Explorations in Yorubaland (1854–1858)*, ed. J. A. Atanda. Ibadan: Ibadan University Press.

Collier, Paul, and Deepak Lal. 1980. *Poverty and Growth in Kenya*. World Bank Staff Working Paper no. 389. Washington, DC: World Bank.

Commemorative Brochure and Program. 1992. First Iloko Day Celebrations, May 2, 1992.

Constitution of the Ijesa Ladies Improvement Society–Ilesa. 1987.

Constitution of the Ijesha Young Women Progressive Society. 1970, revised 1986.

Coronation Program, Coronation, and Official Presentation of Instrument and Staff of Office, Ajagbusi-Ekun of Iloko-Ijesa, April 5, 1997.

Dare, O. O. N.d. "Linking Health and Development in Nigeria: The Oriade Initiative" (draft ms).

Dennis, Carolyne. 1991. "Constructing a 'Career' under Conditions of Economic Crisis and Structural Adjustment: The Survival Strategies of Nigerian Women." In *Women, Development, and Survival in the Third World*, ed. H. Afshar. London: Longman.

Denzer, LaRay, and Nkechi Mbanefoh. 1998. "Women's Participation in Hometown Associations." In *Hometown Associations: Indigenous Knowledge and Development in Nigeria*, ed. Rex Honey and Stanley Okafor. London: Intermediate Technology Publications, pp. 123–134.

de Oliveira, Miguel Darcy, and Rajesh Tandon. 1994a. "Foreword." In *Citizens: Strengthening Global Civil Society*, by CIVICUS, coordinated by Miquel Darcy de Oliveira and Rajesh Tandon. Washington, DC: Civicus, pp. vii–x.

de Oliveira, Miguel Darcy, and Rajesh Tandon. 1994b. "An Emerging Global Civil Society." In *Citizens: Strengthening Global Civil Society*, by CIVICUS, coordinated by Miquel Darcy de Oliveira and Rajesh Tandon. Washington, DC: Civicus, pp. 1–17.

Diamond, Larry. 1995. "Nigeria: The Uncivic Society and the Descent into Praetorianism." In *Politics in Developing Countries: Comparing Experiences* with *Democracy*, 2nd ed., ed. Larry Diamond, Juan J. Linz, and Seymour Martin Lipset. Boulder: Lynne Rienner, pp. 417–491.

Drewal, Margaret Thompson. 1992. *Yoruba Ritual: Performers, Play, Agency.* Bloomington: Indiana University Press.

Dubresson, Alain. 1993. "Urbanistes de l'interieur: les cadres de la prefecture de Toumodi (Cote d'Ivoire)" In *Pouvoirs et Cites d'Afrique Noire: Decentralisations en questions*, ed. Sylvy Jaglin and Alain Dubresson. Paris: Karthala, pp. 259–284.

Egbe Omo Ibile Awe. 1982. *Awe Development Plan (An Opticom Approach).* Central Planning Committee of the Egbe Omo Ibile Awe.

Ekeh, Peter P. 1975. "Colonialism and the Two Publics in Africa: A Theoretical Statement." *Comparative Studies in Society and History* 17, 1: 91–112.

Esman, Milton J., and Norman Uphoff. 1984. *Local Organizations: Intermediaries in Rural Development.* Ithaca: Cornell University Press.

Eso, Kayode. 1996. *The Mystery Gunman.* Ibadan: Spectrum.

"Exclusive Interview with the Orisa and Former Regent of Iloko Ijesa, Chief 'Sola Ogunsanya." N.d. *Iloko Chronicle*, a magazine published by the Federation of Iloko Ijesa Students' Union, pp. 18–24.

Fadipe, N. A. 1970 (1939). *The Sociology of the Yoruba.* Ibadan: Ibadan University Press.

Federal Republic of Nigeria. 1989. *Report of the Survey of Internal Migration, December 1986.* Lagos: Federal Office of Statistics.

Federal Republic of Nigeria. 1992. *Official Gazette* 79, No. 56, 1991, Population Census (Provisional Results), November 30, 1992.

Fisiy, Cyprian, and Mitzi Goheen. 1998. "Power and the Quest for Recognition: Neo-traditional Titles among the New Elite in Nso', Cameroon." *Africa* 68, 3: 383–402.

Francis, Paul. 1996. *State, Community, and Local Development in Nigeria.* World Bank Technical Paper No. 336.

Geschiere, Peter. 1997. *The Modernity of Witchcraft: Politics and the Occult in Postcolonial Africa.* Charlottesville: University Press of Virginia.

Geschiere, Peter, and Josef Gugler. 1998b. "Introduction: The Urban-Rural Connection—Changing Issues of Belonging and Identification." *Africa* 68, 3: 309–319.

Geschiere, Peter, and Josef Gugler, eds. 1998a. "The Politics of Primary Patriotism." *Africa* 68, 3.

Geschiere, Peter, and Francis Nyamnjoh. 1998. "Witchcraft as an Issue in the 'Politics of Belonging': Democratization and Urban Migrants' Involvement with the Home Village." *African Studies Review* 41, 3: 69–91.

Gladwin, Christina H. 1991. *Structural Adjustment and African Women Farmers.* Gainesville: University of Florida Press.

Gugler, Josef. 1971. "Life in a Dual System: Eastern Nigerians in Town, 1961." *Cahiers d'Etudes Africaines* 11: 400–421.

Gugler, Josef. 1991. "Life in a Dual System Revisited: Urban-Rural Ties in Enugu, Nigeria, 1961–1987." *World Development* 19: 399–409. Published in revised form in Josef Gugler, ed. 1997. *Cities in the Developing World: Issues, Theory, and Policy.* New York: Oxford University Press.

Gugler, Josef, and William G. Flanagan. 1978. "Urban-Rural Ties in West Africa." *African Perspectives* 1: 67–78.

Gugler, Josef, and Gudrun Ludwar-Ene. 1995. "Gender and Migration in Africa South of the Sahara." In *The Migration Experience in Africa*, ed. Jonathan

Baker and Take Akin Aina. Uppsala: Nordiska Afrikainstitutet, pp. 257–268.

Guyer, Jane. 1992. "Representation without Taxation: An Essay on Democracy in Rural Nigeria." *African Studies Review* 35, 1: 41–79.

Guyer, Jane I., with Olukemi Idowu. 1991. "Women's Agricultural Work in a Multimodal Rural Economy: Ibarapa District, Oyo State, Nigeria." In *Structural Adjustment and African Women Farmers*, ed. Christina H. Gladwin. Gainesville: University of Florida Press, pp. 257–280.

Gyimah-Boadi, E. 1994. "Associational Life, Civil Society, and Democratization in Ghana." In *Civil Society and the State in Africa*, ed. John W. Harbeson, Donald Rothchild, and Naomi Chazan. Boulder: Lynne Rienner, pp. 125–148.

Harbeson, John. 1994. "Civil Society and the Study of African Politics: A Preliminary Assessment." In *Civil Society and the State in Africa*, ed. John W. Harbeson, Donald Rothchild, and Naomi Chazan. Boulder: Lynne Rienner, pp. 285–300.

Hobsbawm, Eric. 1983. "Introduction: Inventing Traditions." In *The Invention of Tradition*, ed. Eric Hobsbawm and Terence Ranger. Cambridge: Cambridge University Press, pp. 1–14.

Hobsbawm, Eric, and Terence Ranger, eds. 1983. *The Invention of Tradition*. Cambridge: Cambridge University Press.

Honey, Rex, and Stanley Okafor, eds. 1998. *Hometown Associations: Indigenous Knowledge and Development in Nigeria*. London: Intermediate Technology Publications.

Hsu, Madeline Y. 2000. "Migration and Native Place: *Quiaokan* and the Imagined Community of Taishan County, Guangdong, 1892–1993." *The Journal of Asian Studies* 59, 2: 307–331.

Ifaturoti, E. A. 1992a. "An Address on the Occasion of the Council of Ijesa Societies First Merit Awards Day." In Council of Ijesa Societies Ilesa, First Merit Awards Day for Distinguished Sons/Daughters and Corporate Bodies brochure, April 18, 1992, p. 64.

Ifaturoti, E. A. 1992b. "Law and Tyranny." *Nigerian Tribune*, June 4, 1992.

Ifaturoti, Loja M.A., and O.I.A. Orolugbagbe. 1992. *The History of Egbe Atunluse Ile Ijesa: The Flagbearers of Ijesa Enlightenment in the Twentieth Century*. (No publ. info.).

Ihonvbere, Julius O. 1993. "Economic Crisis, Structural Adjustment, and Social Crisis in Nigeria." *World Development* 21, 1: 141–153.

Ijesa Solidarity Group. 1992. Report of the Chairman, June.

Ijesa Solidarity Group Constitution. N.d.

Ijesa Solidarity Group Minutes of Pro-tem Council, May 9, 1992.

Ijesa Solidarity Group Newsletter, December 1991.

Ijesa Year Book. 1997. Lagos: MIJ.

Indigenous Knowledge and Development Monitor. 1999. "Editorial" 7, 3: 1.

"Interview with the Saba of Iloko Ijesa Chief Ajewole Ifaloye on the Selection of the New Aloko of Iloko-Ijesa." N.d. *Iloko Chronicle*, a magazine published by the Federation of Iloko Ijesa Students' Union, pp. 37–38.

Issue. 1999. "Transition in Nigeria?" *Issue: A Journal of Opinion* 27, 1.

Jacob, J.-P., and Ph. Lavigne Delville, eds. 1994. *Les Associations paysannes en Afrique: Organisation et Dynamiques*. Paris: Karthala.

Johnson, G. E., and W. E. Whitelaw. 1973/1974. "Urban-Rural Income Transfers in Kenya: An Estimated Remittances Function." *Economic Development and Cultural Change* 22: 473–479.

Jonckers, Danielle. 1994. "Le mythe d'une tradition communautaire villageiose dans la region Mali-Sud." In *Les Associations paysannes en Afrique: Organisation et Dynamiques*, ed. J.-P. Jacob and Ph. Lavigne Delville. Paris: Karthala, pp. 121–134.

Kayode, M. O. 1987. "The Structural Adjustment Programme (SAP) and the Industrial Sector." In *Structural Adjustment Programme in a Developing Economy: The Case of Nigeria*, ed. Adedotun O. Phillips and Eddy C. Ndekwu. Ibadan: Nigerian Institute of Social and Economic Research, pp. 145–155.

Krapf-Askari, E. 1969. *Yoruba Towns and Cities*. Oxford: Clarendon.

Kumar, Yogesh. 1996. "Building on the *Panchayat:* Using *Jal Samitis* in Uttar Pradesh." In *Indigenous Organizations and Development*, ed. Peter Blunt and D. Michael Warren. London: Intermediate Technology Publications, pp. 123–131.

Lachenmann, Gudrun. 1994. "Civil Society and Social Movements in Africa." In *Les Associations Paysannes en Afrique: Organisation et dynamiques*, ed. J.-P. Jacob and Ph. Lavigne Delville. Paris: Karthala, pp. 61–95.

Laitin, David D. 1986. *Hegemony and Culture: Politics and Religious Change among the Yoruba*. Chicago: University of Chicago Press.

Lamikanra, Chief A. 1992. "Address by the President, Council of Ijesa Societies." In Council of Ijesa Societies Ilesa, First Merit Awards Day for Distinguished Sons/Daughters and Corporate Bodies brochure, April 18, 1992, p. 33.

Lamikanra, Chief A. 1993. "Address by the Chairman Ijesa National Day Planning Committee." In First Ijesa National Day brochure.

Lawrence, Mark F., and S. Tunji Titilola. 1998. "Hometown Associations as Development Catalysts: The Case of the Egbe Ibile Omo Awe." In *Hometown Associations: Indigenous Knowledge and Development in Nigeria*, ed. Rex Honey and Stanley Okafor. London: Intermediate Technology Publications, pp. 36–44.

Lentz, Carola. 1995. "'Unity for Development': Youth Associations in Northwestern Ghana." *Africa* 65, 3: 395–429.

Mabogunje, A. L. 1995. "The Capitalisation of Money and Credit in the Development Process: The Case of Community Banking in Nigeria." *African Journal of Institutions and Development* 1, 2: 1–14.

March, Kathryn, and Rachel Taqqu. 1986. *Women's Informal Associations in Developing Countries: Catalysts for Change?* Boulder: Westview.

Mbanefoh, Nkechi. 1998. "Women's Participation in Hometown Associations." In *Hometown Associations: Indigenous Knowledge and Development in Nigeria*, ed. Rex Honey and Stanley Okafor. London: Intermediate Technology Publications, pp. 123–134.

McNulty, Michael L., and Mark F. Lawrence. 1996. "Hometown Associations: Balancing Local and Extralocal Interests in Nigerian Communities." In *Indigenous Organizations and Development*, ed. Peter Blunt and D. Michael Warren. London: Intermediate Technology Publications.

Mongbo, Roch. 1994. "La Dynamique des organisations paysannes et la negociation quotidienne du 'developpement rural' a la base. Une etude de cas au Benin." In *Les associations paysannes en Afrique: Organisation et dynamiques*, ed. J.-P. Jacob and Ph. Lavigne Delville. Paris: Karthala, pp. 135–154.

Mustapha, Abdul Raufu. 1991. *Structural Adjustment and Multiple Modes of Social Livelihood in Nigeria*. United Nations Research Institute for Social Development, Discussion Paper 26.

National Conference on the Centenary of the 1886 Kiriji/Ekitiparapo Peace Treaty. 1986. "War and Peace in Yorubaland." University of Ife, September 1986.

Nelson, Nici, and Susan Wright, eds. 1995. *Power and Participatory Development: Theory and Practice*. London: Intermediate Technology Publications.

Nigeria. 1964. *Population Census of Nigeria, 1963*. Lagos: Federal Census Office.

Nigerian Institute of Social and Economic Research. 1997. *Nigeria Migration and Urbanization Survey, 1993*. Ibadan: Nigerian Institute of Social and Economic Research (NISER).

NTA Ibadan Presents. 1997. "The Portrait of an Altruist: A Documentary on the Installation and Coronation of Oba Oladele Olashore Ajagbusi-Ekun." Iloko-Ijesa (video).

Nyamnjoh, Francis, and Michael Rowlands. 1998. "Elite Associations and the Politics of Belonging in Cameroon." *Africa* 68, 3: 320–337.

O'Connor, Anthony. 1983. *The African City*. New York: Africana.

Oberai, A. S., and H. K. Manmohan Singh. 1980. "Migration, Remittances, and Rural Development: Findings of a Case Study in the Indian Punjab." *International Labor Review* 119: 229–241.

Odeyemi, Olu. 1995. "Unity and Development of Ijesaland: The Way Forward." Talk presented at a seminar organized by the Ijesa Solidarity Group at Ijebu-Jesa Town Hall, December 9, 1995.

Odeyemi, Yetunde Abosede. 1999. "Land Use Inventory and Change Detection in the Urban-Rural Fringes of Ilesa Area." M.S. thesis, Department of Geography, Obafemi Awolowo University, Ile-Ife, Nigeria.

Ogunjulugbe, J. O. 1993. *The History of Ipetu-Ijesa*. Ibadan: University Press.

Ohiorhenuan, John F.E. 1987. "Re-Colonising Nigerian Industry: The First Year of the Structural Adjustment Programme." In *Structural Adjustment Programme in a Developing Economy: The Case of Nigeria*, ed. Adedotun O. Phillips and Eddy C. Ndekwu. Ibadan: Nigerian Institute of Social and Economic Research, pp. 133–143.

Okafor, Stanley, and Rex Honey. 1998. "The Nature of Hometown Voluntary Associations in Nigeria." In *Hometown Associations: Indigenous Knowledge and Development in Nigeria*, ed. Rex Honey and Stanley Okafor. London: Intermediate Technology Publications, pp. 9–16.

Oke, M. O. 1969. *Itan Ile Ijesa* [History of Ijesaland]. Ibadan: Ogun.

Olaniyan, Richard. 1992. "The Modakeke Question in Ife Politics and Diplomacy." In *The Cradle of a Race (Ife from the Beginning to 1980)*, ed. I. A. Akinjogbin. Port Harcourt, Nigeria: Sunray, pp. 266–286.

Olaniyan, Richard. 1997. "Installation of Yoruba Obas and Chiefs" (draft ms).

Olashore, Oba Oladele. 1998. *Joy of Service: An Autobiography*. Lagos: CSS.

Olashore, Oladele. 1991. *The Challenges of Nigeria's Economic Reform*. Ibadan: Fountain Publications.

Olashore, 'Tunde. 1991. "Welcome Address Delivered by Prince 'Tunde Olashore, Chairman Ijebu-Jesa Day Celebration Committee, on the Occasion of the Celebration of the First Ijebu-Jesa Day." November 2, 1991.

Olowu, C.A.B., and O. L. Oludimu. 1993. "Impact of Community Banking on Investment Patterns in Nigeria: An Overview." Paper presented at the National Workshop on Impact of Community Banking on Investment Patterns at the Local Level, Makurdi, July 14–16, 1993.

Olowu, Dele, S. Bamidele Ayo, and Bola Akande. 1991. *Local Institutions and National Development in Nigeria*. Ile-Ife, Nigeria: Research Group in Local Institutions in collaboration with Obafemi Awolowo University Press.

Olowu, Dele, and John Erero. 1996. "Governance of Nigeria's Villages and Cities through Indigenous Institutions." *African Rural and Urban Studies* 3, 1: 99–121.

Oludimu, Olufemi, and Bamidele Ayo. 1995. "Democratisation and Local Participation in Governance: The Case of Community Banks in Southern Nigeria." In *Governance and Democratisation in Nigeria*, ed. Dele Olowu, Kayode Soremekun, and Adebayo Williams. Ibadan: Spectrum, pp. 131–146.

Olukoshi, Adebayo. 1989. "Impact of IMF–World Bank Programmes on Nigeria." In *The IMF, The World Bank, and the African Debt: Volume 1—The Economic Impact*, ed. Bade Onimode. Institute for African Alternatives. London: Zed, pp. 219–234.

Olukoshi, Adebayo. 1991b. "Prevalent Misconceptions of the Nigerian Adjustment Programme." In *Crisis and Adjustment in the Nigerian Economy*, ed. Adebayo Olukoshi. Lagos: JAD, pp. 76–87.

Olukoshi, Adebayo, ed. 1991a. *Crisis and Adjustment in the Nigerian Economy.* Lagos: JAD.

Olupona, J. K. 1991. *Kingship, Religion, and Rituals in a Nigerian Community: A Phenomenological Study of Ondo Yoruba Festivals*. Stockholm Studies in Comparative Religion 28. Stockholm: Almqvist and Wiksell International.

Omole, Lawrence. 1991. *My Life and Times: Reflections—an Autobiography.* Lagos: MIJ.

Omole, Lawrence. 1992. "Opening Speech." In *Report of the Ijesa Traditional Council Peace Committee*, appendix A, April 4, 1992.

Omoni, Michael Oluwole. 1984. *The Development of Town Unions in Ife and Ijesaland, 1930–1960.* M.A. thesis, Department of History, University of Ife, Ile-Ife, Nigeria.

Oni, J. O. n.d. *A History of Ijeshaland*. Ile-Ife, Nigeria: Fadehan.

Orolugbagbe, I. O. Adedeji. 1997. "Educational Development in Ijesaland." *Ijesa Year Book*. Lagos: MIJ.

Osaghae, Eghosa E. 1994. *Trends in Migrant Political Organizations in Nigeria: The Igbo in Kano*. Ibadan: IFRA (French Institute for Research in Africa).

Osaghae, Eghosa E. 1998. "Hometown Associations as Shadow States: The Case of Igbos and Yorubas in Kano." In *Hometown Associations: Indigenous Knowledge and Development in Nigeria*, ed. Rex Honey and Stanley Okafor. London: Intermediate Technology Publications, pp. 111–121.

Owomoyela, Oyekan. 1988. *A Ki i: Yoruba Proscriptive and Prescriptive Proverbs.* Lanham, MD: University Press of America.

Owosekun, Akinola A. 1997. "The Ijesa Economy." *Ijesa Year Book*. Lagos: MIJ, pp. 40–54.

Oxfam America. 1991. "What Is Development?" *Oxfam America News*, winter issue.

Painter, Thomas M. 1996. "Space, Time, and Rural-Urban Linkages in Africa: Notes for a Geography of Livelihoods." *African Rural and Urban Studies* 3, 1: 79–98.

Peel, J.D.Y. 1978. "Olaju: A Yoruba Concept of Development." *Journal of Development Studies* 14, 2: 139–165.

Peel, J.D.Y. 1980. "Inequality and Action: The Forms of Ijesha Social Conflict." *Canadian Journal of African Studies* 14, 3: 473–502.

Peel, J.D.Y. 1983. *Ijeshas and Nigerians: The Incorporation of a Yoruba Kingdom, 1890s–1970s*. Cambridge: Cambridge University Press.

Phillips, Adedotun O. 1987. "A General Overview of SAP." In *Structural*

Adjustment Programme in a Developing Economy: The Case of Nigeria, ed. Adedotun O. Phillips and Eddy C. Ndekwu. Ibadan: Nigerian Institute of Social and Economic Research, pp. 1–12.

Phillips, Adedotun O., and Eddy C. Ndekwu, eds. 1987. *Structural Adjustment Programme in a Developing Economy: The Case of Nigeria*. Ibadan: Nigerian Institute of Social and Economic Research.

Post Express Wired. September 25, 1997. "New Yam Festival, Igbo Day Holds Oct 4." <www. postexpresswired.com>.

Pratten, David T. 1996a. "Reconstructing Community: The Intermediary Role of Sahelian Associations in Processes of Migration and Rural Development." *African Rural and Urban Studies* 3, 1: 49–78.

Pratten, David T. 1996b. *"'Returning to the Roots': Migration, Local Institutions, and Development in Sudan*. London: SOS Sahel.

Pratten, David T. n.d. *Bamako Bound: The Social Organisation of Migration in Mali*. London: SOS Sahel.

Putnam, Robert D. 1993. *Making Democracy Work: Civic Traditions in Modern Italy*. Princeton: Princeton University Press.

Putnam, Robert D. 1995. "Bowling Alone: America's Declining Social Capital." *Journal of Democracy* 6, 1: 65–78.

Rahman, Md. Anisur. 1993. *People's Self-Development: Perspectives on Participatory Action Research, A Journey through Experience*. London: Zed; and Dhaka: University Press Limited.

Ranger, Terence. 1993. "The Invention of Tradition Revisited: The Case of Colonial Africa." In *Legitimacy and the State in Twentieth-Century Africa: Essays in Honour of A.H.M. Kirk-Greene*, ed. Terence Ranger and Olufemi Vaughan. London: MacMillan, pp. 62–111.

Rempel, Henry, and Richard A. Lobdell. 1978. "The Role of Urban-to-Rural Remittances in Rural Development." *Journal of Development Studies* 14: 324–341.

Renne, Elisha P. 1995. *Cloth that Does Not Die: The Meaning of Cloth in Bunu Social Life*. Seattle: University of Washington Press.

Ross, Marc Howard, and Thomas S. Weisner. 1977. "The Rural-Urban Migrant Network in Kenya: Some General Implications." *American Ethnologist* 4, 2: 359–375.

Sandbrook, Richard, and Mohamed Halfani. 1993. *Empowering People: Building Community, Civil Associations, and Legality in Africa*. Toronto: University of Toronto, Center for Urban and Community Studies.

Shonekan, Ernest A.O. 1985. *Economic Outlook—1985 vs. 1983: Nigeria's Economic Recovery*. New York: African American Institute.

Soetan, Funmi. 1995. "Democratisation and the Empowerment of Women: The Role of Traditional and Modern Women's Associations in Nigeria." In *Governance and Democratisation in Nigeria*, ed. Dele Olowu, Kayode Soremekun, and Adebayo Williams. Ibadan: Spectrum, pp. 79–95.

Southall, Aidan. 1988. "Small Towns in Africa Revisited." *African Studies Review* 31, 3.

Stark, Oded. 1980. "On the Role of Urban-to-Rural Remittances." *Journal of Development Studies* 16, 3: 369–374.

Taylor, D.R.F. 1992. "Development from Within and Survival in Rural Africa: A Synthesis of Theory and Practice." In *Development from Within: Survival in Rural Africa*, ed. D.R.F. Taylor and Fiona Mackenzie. London: Routledge, pp. 214–258.

Taylor, D.R.F., and Fiona Mackenzie, eds. 1992. *Development from Within: Survival in Rural Africa.* London: Routledge.

Titilola, S. O. 1987. "The Impact of the Structural Adjustment Programme (SAP) on the Agriculture and Rural Economy of Nigeria." In *Structural Adjustment Programme in a Developing Economy: The Case of Nigeria*, ed. Adedotun O. Phillips and Eddy C. Ndekwu. Ibadan: Nigerian Institute of Social and Economic Research, pp. 177–184.

Tomori, Siyanbola. 1995. "Entrepreneurship within the Nigerian Economy: Past, Present, and Future—a General Survey." Keynote address at Conference on Entrepreneurship within the Nigerian Economy: Past, Present, and Future, in honor of Dr. Lawrence Omole, Ile-Ife, Nigeria, October 11, 1995.

Trager, Lillian. 1976. "Yoruba Markets and Trade: Analysis of Spatial Structure and Social Organization in the Ijesaland Marketing System." Ph.D. dissertation, University of Washington.

Trager, Lillian. 1976/77. "Market Women in the Urban Economy: The Role of Yoruba Intermediaries in a Medium-Sized City." *African Urban Notes* 2, pt. 2: 1–9.

Trager, Lillian. 1979. "Market Centers as Small Urban Places in Western Nigeria." In *Small Urban Centers in Rural Development in Africa*, ed. A. Southall. Madison: University of Wisconsin, African Studies Program, pp. 138–157.

Trager, Lillian. 1981. "Customers and Creditors: Variations in Economic Personalism in a Nigerian Marketing System." *Ethnology* 20: 133–146.

Trager, Lillian. 1984. "Migration and Remittances: Urban Income and Rural Households in the Philippines." *Journal of Developing Areas* 18, 3: 317–340.

Trager, Lillian. 1985a. "Contemporary Processes of Change in Yoruba Cities." In *City and Society: Studies in Urban Ethnicity, Life-Style, and Class*, ed. A. Southall, P. J. Nas, and Ghaus Ansari. Leiden: Leiden Development Studies No. 7, pp. 127–151.

Trager, Lillian. 1985b. "From Yams to Beer in a Nigerian City: Expansion and Change in Informal Sector Trade Activity." In *Markets and Marketing*, ed. Stuart Plattner. Lanham, MD: University Press of America. Monographs in Economic Anthropology No. 4, pp. 259–285.

Trager, Lillian. 1987. "A Re-examination of the Urban Informal Sector in West Africa." *Canadian Journal of African Studies* 2: 238–255.

Trager, Lillian. 1988a. "Rural-Urban Linkages: The Role of Small Urban Centers in Nigeria." *African Studies Review* 31, 3: 29–38.

Trager, Lillian. 1988b. *The City Connection: Migration and Family Interdependence in the Philippines.* Ann Arbor: University of Michigan Press.

Trager, Lillian. 1989. "Generating Income and Employment in Rural and Urban Areas of Sub-Saharan Africa." Paper presented at Senior Policy Seminar on Poverty and Adjustment in Sub-Saharan Africa, Abidjan, October 23–27, 1989.

Trager, Lillian. 1992. "The Hometown and Local Development: Creativity in the Use of Hometown Linkages in Contemporary Nigeria." *Journal of Nigerian Public Administration and Management* 1, 2: 21–32.

Trager, Lillian. 1993. "New Wine in Old Bottles: Community Day Celebrations and the Hometown." *Passages*, issue No. 6, Northwestern University Program of African Studies.

Trager, Lillian. 1995a. "Women Migrants and Rural-Urban Linkages in Southwestern Nigeria." In *The Migration Experience in Africa*, ed. Jonathan Baker and Tade Akin Aina. Uppsala: Nordiska Afrikainstitutet, pp. 269–288.

Trager, Lillian. 1995b. "Women Migrants and Hometown Linkages in Nigeria:

Status, Economic Roles, and Contributions to Community Development." In *Women and Demographic Change in Sub-Saharan Africa*, ed. P. K. Makinwa-Adebusoye and An-Magritt Jensen. Liege: Ordina Editions for International Union for the Scientific Study of Population, pp. 291–311.

Trager, Lillian. 1996a. "Women, Income, and Employment in Rural and Urban Areas of Sub-Saharan Africa." *Gender and Development in Africa: Journal of the Centre for Gender and Social Policy Studies, Obafemi Awolowo University, Ile-Ife* 1, 1: 17–73.

Trager, Lillian. 1996b. "Introduction—Mobility, Linkages, and 'Local' Institutions in African Development." *African Rural and Urban Studies* 3, 1: 7–23.

Trager, Lillian, ed. 1996c. Special issue on rural-urban linkages, *African Rural and Urban Studies* 3, 1 (ca. 1998).

Trager, Lillian. 1997. "Structural Adjustment, Hometowns, and Local Development in Nigeria." In *Economic Analysis Beyond the Local System*, ed. Richard Blanton, Peter Peregrine, Deborah Winslow, and Thomas D. Hall. University Press of America, for the Society for Economic Anthropology, pp. 255–290.

Trager, Lillian. 1998. "Hometown Linkages and Local Development in Southwestern Nigeria: Whose Agenda? What Impact?" *Africa* 68, 3: 360–382.

Trager, Lillian, and Clara Osinulu. 1991. "New Women's Organizations in Nigeria: One Response to Structural Adjustment." In *Structural Adjustment and African Women Farmers*, ed. Christina H. Gladwin. Gainesville: University of Florida Press, pp. 339–358.

Tripp, Aili Mari. 1994. "Rethinking Civil Society: Gender Implications in Contemporary Tanzania." In *Civil Society and the State in Africa*, ed. John W. Harbeson, Donald Rothchild, and Naomi Chazan. Boulder: Lynne Rienner, pp. 149–168.

Udoma, Udo Sir. 1987. *The Story of the Ibibio Union—Its Background, Emergence, Aims, Objectives, and Achievements.* Ibadan: Spectrum.

Uphoff, Norman. 1996. "Preface." In *Indigenous Organizations and Development*, ed. Peter Blunt and D. Michael Warren. London: Intermediate Technology Publications, pp. vii–xi.

Usoro, Eno J. 1987. "Development of the Nigerian Agricultural Sector within the Framework of the Structural Adjustment Programme." In *Structural Adjustment Programme in a Developing Economy: The Case of Nigeria*, ed. Adedotun O. Phillips and Eddy C. Ndekwu. Ibadan: Nigerian Institute of Social and Economic Research, pp. 167–176.

Vaughan, Olufemi. 1991. "Chieftaincy Politics and Social Relations in Nigeria." *Journal of Commonwealth and Comparative Politics* 29, 3: 308–326.

Warren, D. Michael, Remi Adedokun, and Akintola Omolaoye. 1996. "Indigenous Organizations and Development: The Case of Ara, Nigeria." In *Indigenous Organizations and Development*, ed. Peter Blunt and D. Michael Warren. London: Intermediate Technology Publications, pp. 43–49.

Waterman, Christopher Alan. 1990. *Juju: A Social History and Ethnography of an African Popular Music.* Chicago: University of Chicago Press.

Weisner, Thomas S. 1976. "The Structure of Sociability: Urban Migration and Urban-Rural Ties in Kenya." *Urban Anthropology* 5: 199–223.

Woods, Dwayne. 1994. "Elites, Ethnicity, and 'Hometown' Associations in the Côte d'Ivoire: An Historical Analysis of State-Society Links." *Africa* 64, 4: 465–483.

World Bank. 1993. *World Development Report, 1993.* New York: Oxford University Press.

World Bank. 1994. *Adjustment in Africa: Reforms, Results, and the Road Ahead.* New York: Oxford University Press.

World Bank. 1996a. *Nigeria: Poverty in the Midst of Plenty—the Challenge of Growth with Inclusion, a World Bank Poverty Assessment.* World Bank, Population and Human Resources Division, Africa Region, Report No. 14733-UNI.

World Bank. 1996b. *The World Bank Participation Sourcebook.* Washington, DC: World Bank.

World Bank. 1998. "African Development Indicators 1997." *Findings*, May issue.

"Write Up on the First Ijesa National Day and Launching of a N50 million Industrial Development Fund." 1993. First Ijesa National Day brochure.

Yai, Olabiyi Babalola. 1994. "In Praise of Metonymy: The Concepts of 'Tradition' and 'Creativity' in the Transmission of Yoruba Artistry over Time and Space." In *The Yoruba Artist*, ed. Rowland Abiodun, Henry J. Drewal, and John Pemberton III. Washington, DC: Smithsonian Institution, pp. 107–115.

Young, Crawford. 1994. "In Search of Civil Society." In *Civil Society and the State in Africa*, ed. John W. Harbeson, Donald Rothchild, and Naomi Chazan. Boulder: Lynne Rienner, pp. 33–50.

Index

Adagunado, Chief Alex O., 95–96
Adejola, D. A., 182
Adeleke, Alhaji Isiaka, 18–19, 27, 148
Adeniyi, Abdulraman Abidoye, 80–81
Adewale-Adediran, Prince Michael, 122
Adeyeye, Oba J. A. II, 151–152
ADON. *See* Association for
 Development Options in Nigeria
Agbaje, Adigun, 261
Agbaje-Williams, B., 61
Agbeja, J. O., 79–80
age group, 95, 96–97
agriculture. *See* hometown, farming in
Aiku, Chief Bamidele, 125
Ajifolokun, Kabiyesi Ajayi Palmer II,
 34
ajo (savings group), 175, 202n6
Akinmokun, Chief I. O., 122, 124
Akinnaso, F. Niyi, 5, 56, 235, 268
Alegebeleye, Chief Florence, 92
Aronson, Dan, 51, 239, 268, 269
Association for Development Options in
 Nigeria (ADON), 182, 183
associations: 4, 90, 91, 92; Benin,
 Republic of, 249; Cameroon, 263;
 church, 79, 92, 248; civil society,
 261–263, 265–266; community-
 based, 250; Côte d'Ivoire, 263; eth-
 nic, 205, 212–213; francophone
 West Africa, 248–249; functions,
 266–267; Ghana, 249, 265; Igbo,

262, 265–266; Mali, 258, 266–267;
 Nigeria, 249–250; participation in,
 92–94; Sudan, 265–267; types, 91,
 93. *See also egbe;* hometown organizations; nongovernmental organizations
Awe, Bolanle, 8, 61, 116, 122, 124, 219

Babatayo, I. A., 180
banks. *See* community banks
Barber, Karin, 52, 242
Barkan, Joel, 263
Bartle, Philip, 239
Benin, Republic of, associations, 249
Binns, Tony, 259
Blunt, Peter, 247
Bratton, Michael, 261
buildings: houses, 51, 59–60, 77, 79,
 168–169, 199; public, 173–174

Callaghy, Thomas, 157
Cameroon: associations, 263; chieftaincy titles, 265; ethnicity, 264–265
celebration. *See* ceremony
Center for Health Sciences Training,
 Research, and Development
 (CHESTRAD), 184, 201
ceremony: award, 102, 119–127; birthday, 128–129; communal, 129–134;
 coronation of *oba,* 134–142,
 271–272; Kiriji War centenary,

131–132; life cycle, 127–128. *See also* Community Day; National Day; ritual

Chambers, Robert, 253

CHESTRAD. *See* Center for Health Sciences Training, Research, and Development

child fostering, 164n5

children: hometown connections, 54, 241–242, 274; of migrants, 75, 76, 79

cities as migrant destination, 66

CIVICUS: World Alliance for Citizen Participation, 260, 261

civil society, 5, 260; Africa, 261–262; ethnic associations, 263, 265–266; hometown organizations, 260, 262–268; primordialism, 266, 277n17

Clarke, William H., 61–62

community concepts of, 3, 244–245, 275n4; decisions and elite, 189, 191–192, 194, 197, 254; migration, 244–245; transnational, 3, 244, 276n15. *See also* hometown

community banks, 174, 181, 203n7; Ijebu-Jesa, 165–167, 175–179; Iwoye, 179–181

Community Day, 11, 130; hometown connections, 31–33; Ijebu-Jesa, 6, 22–23, 26, 28, 32–34; Ijebu Yoruba, 30; Ijesaland, 22–26; Ilesa, 131; as indigenous institution, 248; as invented tradition, 30–31, 33–34, 272–273; language at, 25, 32; objectives, 28–29; organization, 22–23; success of, 31–34; themes, 11, 26–28; variation, 24–25. *See also* Ijesa National Day; Iloko Day

conflict, chieftaincy, 223–225, 230–232; and the elite, 225–227, 229; ethnic, 213–214; Ijesa, 216, 222–225; intra-community, 224, 226–230; morality, 226–230; resolution, 230–232

contributions to hometown, 190–194; changes in, 191

cooperation. *See* unity, Ijesa

Côte d'Ivoire: associations, 263; hometown connections, 258; local development, 276n12

Council of Ijesa Societies–Ilesa: award ceremony, 101–102, 119–123; industrialization efforts, 187

Council of Iloko Women, 100

Denzer, LaRay, 240

development: benefits from, 191, 255; community banks, 174–181; concepts of, 5, 147–151, 245–246; Côte d'Ivoire, 258; debate about, 145–146; decisions about, 254–255; economic, 149–150; elite and, 196, 200, 253–256; empowerment, 253; government, 276n13; hometown organizations, 103–107, 110–111, 113–114, 117, 177–178, 195–198, 249–250; Ijesa region, 12, 151–152; indigenous institutions, 247–248; individual contributions, 168–172; industrial, 184–187; infrastructure, 173; limitation of, 259–260; local, 5–6, 151–153, 168, 248–250; Mali, 258; *osomaalo* tradition, 150–151; participation, 188, 190–194, 197; participatory, 250–253; privatization of, 256–257, 276n12; problems, perceived, 152–153; public buildings, 173–174; South Africa, 258–259; traditional rulers, 140–142, 195, 197–198; United States, 259, 276n11; variation among communities, 198–200; women's projects, 181–184. *See also* fund-raising for local development; self-help

disputes. *See* conflict

Dubresson, Alain, 258

economic crisis, 158–159; effects in Ijesa region, 160–163; Nigeria, 153–160; regional variation in, 159

education: hometown organizations, 104; local development, 195

egbe (associations, clubs), 4, 90, 91, 92.

See also associations; hometown organizations

Egbe Atunluse Ile Ijesa (Egbe Atunluse; Ijesa Improvement Society), 98, 99, 103–105; history of, 103–104

Egbe Cooperative Ajajeseku (Osu town), 72–73, 92–93

Ekeh, Peter, 277n17

Ekitiparapo Alliance, 61. *See also* Kiriji War

elite: association membership, 91, 93, 197; and conflict, 225–227, 229; decisionmaking, community, 189, 191–192, 194, 197, 254; hometown connections, 242–243; hometown development, 196, 230, 240, 253–255; hometown identity, 4

Erero, John, 249

Eso, Kayode, 4, 55, 107, 110, 122, 124, 126, 129, 211

esusu (savings and credit organizations), 72–73, 92, 93, 202n6; community banks, 175

ethnicity, and civil society, 5, 260, 263–266; and politics, 212–213, 263–264; "politics of belonging," 264–265; primordialism, 266, 277n17; and state formation, 213–216; subethnic conflict, 213–214

ethnographic research, long-term, 8–9

exchange rate, 34n3, 155; and structural adjustment, 156–158

Fadipe, N. A., 90

Fafowora, O. O., 124

Falobi, Janet, 74–75

Falobi, S. O., 73–74

family, visits to, 83–84. *See also* migrants; migration; remittances

Famurewa, Janet, 72–73, 92

Faoye, Grace, 183

Fatodu, Chief O. O., 177–179

Fisiy, Cyprian, 265

Francis, Paul, 250

Friendly Mothers Society (Ijebu-Jesa town), 99

fund-raising for local development, 181, 192–194, 196–197, 200–202, 254–255

gari processing, 203n8; as women's project, 182–183

Geschiere, Peter, 237, 238, 239, 241, 264, 267–268

Ghana: associations, 249, 265; migration, 239

gifts. *See* remittances

Goheen, Mitzi, 265

Gugler, Josef, 237–241, 264, 267–268

Guyer, Jane, 201

Hobsbawn, Eric, 30, 34

hometown: and age, 51; and birthplace, 50; business in, 169; and change, 269–270; children and, 54, 241–242, 274; and Community Day, 31–33; conflict, 232–233; connections with, 51–52, 236–237, 239–242, 273–274; contributions to, 168–172, 190–191, 193–194, 196; Côte d'Ivoire, 258; definition, 2, 3, 37, 49–50; development, 152–153, 173–181, 191, 197–198; differentiation within, 254, 256; elite and, 4, 196, 230, 240, 242–243, 253–255; farming in, 73, 74, 169–171; houses in, 51, 59–60, 77, 79, 168–169, 199; identity, 3, 37, 38, 52–57, 267–268; and innovation, 269–270; Mali, 258; participation, 189–190, 192–197; philanthropy, 171–172; as political base, 209–210, 233n2; proverbs about, 37, 57–58; retirement to, 54; return to, by migrants, 68–69; women and, 51, 78–79, 82, 240–241; and Yoruba culture, 269–270. *See also* community; hometown organizations; life histories of migrants; urban-rural linkages

hometown organizations: activities, 95–99, 101–102, 190; age and, 95–97; change in, 264; characteristics, 94; and civil society, 260,

262–268; and community banks,
175, 178–180; community-wide,
100–102; definitions, 118n1, 275n3;
and development, 103–107,
110–111, 113–114, 117, 177–178,
195–198, 249–250; and ethnicity,
264–266; functions of, 262–263;
gender and, 95; history of, 103–104,
106, 107; in Ijesaland, 12, 91;
indigenous institutions, 247–249;
membership in, 189–190; northern
Nigeria, 102; participation in, 72, 74,
78, 92–94; and politics, 209–210,
264; regional, 102–103; and state
formation, 213–216; and women,
97–99, 100, 182–184, 240, 241,
275n3; Yoruba, 255. *See also* associations; *egbe;* hometown
Honey, Rex, 247
houses. *See* hometown, houses in

IBL. *See* International Breweries
Limited
Ido-Oko (town), development in,
151–152
Ifaloye, Chief Ajewole, 141
Ifaturoti, E. A., 5, 9, 108, 114, 119–120,
131, 186, 205, 212, 218
Ifaturoti, Loja M. A., 104
Igbo: associations, 262, 265–266;
migrants, 241
Ihonvbere, Julius, 157
Ijebu-Jesa (town): community bank,
165–167, 175–179; Community Day,
22–23, 26, 28, 32–33, 101; descrip-
tion, 48; identity with, 53–54; organ-
izations, 101, 177. *See also* Friendly
Mothers Society; Ijebu-Jesa Group;
Ijebu-Jesa Union's Conference;
Ladies Friendly Society
Ijebu-Jesa Group, 177–179
Ijebu-Jesa Union's Conference, 101
Ijesa (region and people): chieftaincy
disputes, 223–225, 231–232; culture
and innovation, 269–273; description, 8, 38, 41–43; development, par-

ticipatory, 251–253; development in,
153, 254–256; and economic crisis,
162–163; economy, 41, 61–62; history, 38, 41, 43, 47–49, 61–63, 116,
199, 202n3, 217–218, 220–222,
234n5; hometown organizations,
92–103; identity, 54–56; individualism, 27, 62, 80; language, 41; local
government areas in, 41, 58; migration, 41, 61–65; population, 43;
structural adjustment, perception of,
160–163; town-district relations,
222–223; United States, Ijesas in,
274; unity, 27, 42, 105, 121, 126,
216, 222–225, 232; variation among
communities, 256–258; warfare,
nineteenth-century, 61. *See also* Ijesa
Council of Traditional Rulers; Ijesa
Cultural Foundation; Ijesa National
Day; Ijesa Society–Lagos; Ijesa
Solidarity Group; Ijesa Traditional
Council Peace Committee; *specific
towns*
Ijesa Council of Traditional Rulers,
224–225, 231–232, 273
Ijesa Cultural Foundation, 102–103
Ijesa Improvement Society. *See* Egbe
Atunluse Ile Ijesa
Ijesa Ladies Improvement Society,
98–99
Ijesaland. *See* Ijesa (region and
people)
Ijesa National Day, 23, 27, 102,
130–134
Ijesa Planning Council, 105
Ijesa Society–Lagos, award ceremony,
124
Ijesa Solidarity Group (ISG), 102;
change in, 264; and conflict resolution, 231; and development,
110–111, 113–114, 117, 145–146,
187, 258; goals, 108–109, 112, 115;
history, 107, 111; and Ijesa unity,
116–117; and industrialization,
184–186; leadership, 114–115;
membership, 111; and politics, 212;

and state formation, 108, 115, 118, 213–216

Ijesa Traditional Council Peace Committee, 231–232

Ijesa United Trading and Transport Company (IUTTC), 103, 106

Ijesa Women's Association, 78–79

Ijesa Young Women Progressive Society, 97–98

Ikeji-Ile (town), dispute in, 229–231

Ilesa (city): commercial center, 44, 46–47; Community Day, 131; description, 43–44, 46; education in, 46; history, 46, 61; life histories, 76–80; organizations, 101–102; Owa Obokun, king of, 21, 38–39, 274; population, 47; as Yoruba city, 46. *See also* Council of Ijesa Societies–Ilesa; Egbe Atunluse Ile Ijesa; Egbe Omo Ibile Ijesa; Ijesa Ladies Improvement Society; Ijesa Planning Council; Ijesa United Trading and Transport Company; International Breweries Limited

Ilesa Chamber of Commerce, 187

Ilesa Frontliners, 96–97

Ilesa Grammar School, 104

Ilesanmi, Chief Moses, 76–78

Ilesanmi, T. M., 58

Ilesa Social Elite, 89, 95–96

Iloko. *See* Iloko-Ijesa (town)

Iloko Day, 1; description, 15–21, 25–26; donations at, 20, 21; second Iloko Day (1993), 15–21, 28; third Iloko Day (1995), 25–26, 32; variations, 25, 28–29. *See also* Community Day

Iloko-Ijesa (town): anthem, 16–17, 34; chiefs, 195–196; community meetings, 194–195, 201; coronation of *oba,* 134–142; description, 49; fundraising in, 192–194, 196–197, 200–202; identity with, 53; intracommunity tension, 227–229; life histories, 75–76, 80–81; local development, 171, 182–184, 192–197, 199–200; migration, 65; organiza-

tions, 89–90, 100–101; women's projects, 182–184. *See also* Council of Iloko Women; Iloko Day; Olashore International School; Owodunni Women's Group

Iloko-Ijesa Development Committee, 100–101, 195–197, 200

Iloko-Oriade Community Development Initiative, 201

Iloko Progressive Ladies–Lagos, 99

Iloko Women's Forum, 89–90

ilu. See hometown

India, local institutions, 250

industrialization: as economic development, 149–150, 255–256; and hometown organizations, 101–102, 121, 187; and Ijesa National Day, 133; and Ijesa Solidarity Group, 113–114, 184–186; industry, cottage, 113, 185

innovation: and hometown connections, 269–270; and ritual, 271–273; and traditional rulers, 270–271; in Yoruba culture, 268–269

International Breweries Limited (IBL; Ilesa), 44–45, 103, 106–107

Iragbeji, Osun State (town), 80

ISG. *See* Ijesa Solidarity Group

itesiwaju (progress), 148, 274

IUTTC. *See* Ijesa United Trading and Transport Company

Iwara (town), 54

Iwoye-Ijesa (town): change in, 75; chiefs, 197–198; community bank, 179–181; description, 48–49; life histories, 73–75; local development, 180–181, 197–198; migration, 68; organizations, 100, 179, 197, 198

Iwoye-Ijesa Descendants Union, 74, 100, 179, 197, 198

Iwoye-Ijesa Progressive Union, 74, 197, 198

Jonckers, Danielle, 248–249

juju. See witchcraft

June 12, 1993 crisis, 206, 208–211. *See also* politics

Kiriji War: centenary, 131–132, 143n4;
and unity, 221. *See also* Ekitiparapo
Alliance

Ladies Friendly Society (Ijebu-Jesa), 99
Lamikanra, Chief A. O., 3, 27–28, 101,
120–121, 131, 169, 187
Lawrence, Mark, 255
Lentz, Carola, 249, 265
LGA. *See* local government area
life histories of migrants, 72–81
livelihood strategies, 159, 256
local government area (LGA): identity
with, 55–56; Ijesa, 41. *See also*
Oriade Local Government
Ludrun-Ene, Gudrun, 240

Mali: associations, 249; hometown
links, 258
Mbanefoh, Nkechi, 240
McNulty, Michael, 255
migrants: characteristics, 64–65; children of, 75, 76, 79, 241–242; destinations, 66, 68; and family, 70–72,
81–84; and hometown, 68–69,
72–75, 78, 82; houses of, 59; Igbo,
241; in Lagos, 76–80; life histories,
72–81; in northern Nigeria, 73–77;
and remittances, 84–86, 88; women,
51, 72–75, 78–79, 82; and work,
72–83. *See also* migration; *osomaalo*
migration: and age, 65, 68; and community, 244–245; and development,
275n5, 276n6; and education, 65;
and gender, 64–65, 67–69; Ghana,
239; and length of stay, 67; links
with family, 238–239; links with
hometown, 11, 236–237; in Nigeria,
60, 86n1; patterns, of Ijesa, 11,
61–65, 81–82; reasons for, 66–67,
69–70, 81–82; and remittances,
84–86, 87n12, 88n14, 238–239;
transnational, 237–238; urban-rural
links, 238–239; and visiting family,
83–84; Yoruba, 60. *See also*
migrants; remittances

mobility. *See* migrants; migration
Mongbo, Roch, 249
multilocality, 3, 60, 236–238

Naira (Nigerian currency), exchange
rate, 34n3, 155–158
Nel, Etienne, 259
NGOs. *See* nongovernmental organizations
Nigeria: currency, exchange rate, 34n3,
155–158; economic conditions,
153–159; political change, 273;
political crisis, 207–213; poverty in,
159
nongovernmental organizations
(NGOs), 183, 184, 201; and civil
society, 261
Nyamnjoh, Francis, 263–265

oba. See traditional ruler
occupations of migrants, 72–83. *See
also osomaalo*
O'Connor, Anthony, 238
Odeyemi, Olu, 125, 218–219, 222
Odi, Bayelsa State, 276n13
Oduduwa State, 115, 118n3, 214, 215
Ogunsanya, Chief Olusola, 195–196,
199, 200, 228–229
Okafor, Stanley, 247
Oke Bode (town), 61–62
olaju (enlightenment), 148, 150, 269
Olashore, Oba Oladele, 15, 24, 25,
35n9, 53, 122, 124, 125, 126, 155,
267; coronation of, 134–142
Olashore, P. A., 75–76, 87n11
Olashore, 'Tunde, 22–23, 26, 28, 53–54
Olashore International School,
171–172, 202n2
Olowu, C. A. B., 181
Olowu, Dele, 249
Oludimu, O. L., 181
Olukoshi, Adebayo, 156
Omole, Lawrence, 105, 106, 108, 122,
124, 126, 206, 231; birthday celebra-
tion, 128–129; philanthropy, 171
Omoniyi, Funke, 93, 100

Omoniyi, J. I., 17–18, 25, 100–101, 194–195, 197, 199
Onasanya, Oluremi, 78–79
Onibonoje, G. O., 169–171
Oriade Local Government: award ceremony, 124–125; community development initiative, 201
oriki (praise poems), 52
Orolugbagbe, O. I. A., 104
Osaghae, Eghosa, 262, 265–266
Osinulu, Clara, 182
osomaalo (Ijesa traders), 59, 60, 62–63, 67–68, 103, 241; definition, 86n3; and development, 150–151; influence of, 80
Osu (town): change in, 73; description, 47; development in, 199; life histories, 72–73. *See also* Egbe Cooperative Ajajeseku
Osun State, 41; discrimination in, 214, 215; formation, 108, 213; and Ijesa Solidarity Group, 108, 115, 118, 213–216
Owa Obokun (king of Ijesa), 21, 38–39, 274
Owodunni Women's Group (Iloko), 182–184, 203n8
Owomoyela, Oyekan, 37
Oxfam America, 247

participation in hometown development, 188–195, 197–198
Peel, J. D. Y., 50, 62, 147–148, 220, 232
Philippines, migration and family, 238
politics: change in political space, 209–211; chieftaincy, 224–225; and ethnicity, 212–213; and Ijesa unity, 221–222; June 12, 1993 crisis, 206, 208–211; and repression, 211–212
"politics of belonging," 264–265. *See also* ethnicity
Pratten, David, 258, 265–267
proverbs about hometown, 37, 57–58

Ranger, Terence, 30
religion and *oba*'s coronation, 135–136

remittances, 84–86, 87n12, 88n14
Renne, Elisha, 269
ritual: incorporation of symbols, 271–272; and innovation, 271–273; and invented tradition, 30–31, 33–34, 271–273. *See also* ceremony; Community Day
Rotary Club, 248
Rowlands, Michael, 263–265

SAP. *See* Structural Adjustment Program
second generation. *See* children
self-help, 26–27; in Iloko, 184, 199–200; and participatory development, 251–253; as strategy, 246; variation among communities, 198–200. *See also* development
Shonekan, Ernest, 154
South Africa local development, 258–259
state formation in Nigeria, 108, 115, 118, 213–216, 234n4. *See also* Oduduwa State; Osun State
Structural Adjustment Program (SAP): effects of, 157–159; effects on contributions, 191; and livelihood strategies, 159; in Nigeria, 155–157; perceptions of, in Ijesa region, 160–163

Takuro, Dorcas, 128
Tanzania civil society, 261–262
taxation. *See* fund-raising for local development
Taylor, D. R. F., 251, 252, 254
Thomas, Irene, 82, 122–123, 126
Thompson, Chief Samuel Olatunde, 128
tradition, invented, 30–31, 33–34, 272–273
traditional ruler *(oba):* characteristics of, 136–137, 141; coronation of, 134–142; and development, 140–142, 271; and innovation, 271; roles of, 270–271
Trager, Lillian, 30, 50, 181, 182, 238, 256

transnational connections, 3, 274, 276n15
Tripp, Aili, 261–262

United States: Ijesas in, 274; local development, 259, 276n11
unity, Ijesa, 27, 42, 105, 121, 126; and conflict resolution, 231–232; and conflicts among Ijesa, 216, 222–225, 232; and history, 218, 220–222; and hometown identity, 232–233; importance of, 217, 219; and politics, 221–222
Uphoff, Norman, 248
urban-rural linkages, 3, 237, 239; of women, 240–241. *See also* hometown; hometown organizations; multilocality

visits to family, 83–84

Warren, D. Michael, 247
Waterman, Christopher, 268
witchcraft: and beliefs about coming home, 226–228, 234n7; and local conflict, 226–228, 234n8
women: and association membership, 92–95; and civil society, 261–262; *gari* processing, 182–183; and hometown connections, 51, 78–79, 82, 240–241; and hometown organizations, 240–241; and local development, 181–184, 190; returned migrants, 72–75
Woods, Dwayne, 263
World Bank, 154–157, 159

Yai, Olabiyi, 268
Yoruba: "big men," 242; Bunu, 269; cities, 237, 274–275n2; concepts of development, 147–148, 245–246; culture and innovation, 268–269; Ijebu, 51, 239; migration, 60; in northern Nigeria, 265–266; organizations, 90–91, 102; proverbs, 37; spelling, 10; sub-ethnic conflict, 213–215. *See also* Ijesa

About the Book

The pattern of migrants maintaining strong ties with their home communities is particularly common in sub-Saharan Africa, where it has important social, cultural, political, and economic implications. This book explores the significance of hometown connections for civil society and local development in Nigeria. Rich ethnographic description and case studies illustrate the links that the Ijesa Yoruba maintain with their communities of origin—links that both help to shape social identity and contribute to local development.

Trager also examines indigenous concepts of "development," demonstrating how the Ijesa Yoruba bring their understandings of development to efforts in their own communities. Placing her work in the context of national political and economic change, she raises questions about the motivations, implications, and consequences of local development efforts, not only for the communities and their members but also for the larger polity.

Lillian Trager is professor of anthropology at the University of Wisconsin–Parkside. She is author of *The City Connection: Migration and Family Interdependence in the Philippines* and has published widely on development in Nigeria.